SALLUST

II

LCL 522

SALLUST

FRAGMENTS OF THE HISTORIES

LETTERS TO CAESAR

EDITED AND TRANSLATED BY

JOHN T. RAMSEY

HARVARD UNIVERSITY PRESS
CAMBRIDGE, MASSACHUSETTS
LONDON, ENGLAND
2015

Library of Congress Control Number 2014951391
CIP data available from the Library of Congress

ISBN 978-0-674-99686-1

Composed in ZephGreek and ZephText by
Technologies 'N Typography, Merrimac, Massachusetts.
Printed on acid-free paper and bound by
The Maple-Vail Book Manufacturing Group

CONTENTS

CONTENTS

For Sarah
my loving wife

PREFACE

No lengthy justification need be offered for including Sallust's *Historiae* in the Loeb Classical Library. Although fragmentary, the *Historiae* is arguably *the* most important source for Roman history in the post-Sullan age for the years 78–67 BC, at the terminus of which the speeches and letters of Cicero begin to shine a bright light on events in the last decades of the Republic. For the decade of the 70s, however, our sources are woefully sparse, and therefore the remains of Sallust' great history are all the more welcome for the contribution they make to our knowledge. John Rolfe, whose Loeb volume of Sallust appeared in 1921, remarked in the preface to the first impression (p. viii) that "a complete translation of Sallust was submitted, including all the fragments on the basis of Maurenbrecher's edition of the *Histories*," but the general editors decided to include in the Loeb only the orations and letters excerpted from the *Historiae.* Nearly a century later, the Loeb has now been expanded to include all surviving fragments of the *Historiae,* not simply according to Maurenbrecher's 1893 edition, but edited afresh, incorporating many advances in scholarship as well as fragments not known to Maurenbrecher. Text and translation of the orations and letters, together with the two pseudo-Sallustian *Letters to Caesar*, are based on Rolfe's earlier Loeb, thoroughly revised and now equipped with notes. All else, the bulk of this volume, is entirely new, and the translations are my own. The two *Invectives,* previously included in the Loeb volume of Sallust, may now be consulted in Shackleton Bailey's edition of Cicero's *Letters to Quintus and Brutus* (LCL 462).

I have consulted with profit two translations, one in Italian, by Paolo Frassinetti (1963), and one in English, by Patrick McGushin (1992–1994). In the later 1991 edition of Frassinetti (with Lucia di Salvo), the translation underwent minor revisions, especially in the accompanying notes, and the Latin text of Maurenbrecher, with minor divergences, was added on facing pages. Maurenbrecher's numbering of the fragments was adhered to in both the 1963 and 1991 editions, with notations of possible improvements to the scheme offered here and there.

McGushin's translation, by contrast, does not print the Latin text, which is a decided drawback, but it is less dependent on Maurenbrecher. McGushin's ordering of the fragments is significantly different from Maurenbrecher's, and his translation takes into account notable improvements to the Latin text, although textual matters are not so easily presented in the context of only an English translation. McGushin translates several fragments whose texts have been somewhat or, in one instance, significantly amplified since Maurenbrecher's day, thanks to the discovery of tattered remains on papyrus or on parchment (e.g., in this edition, frr. 1.97, 98; 2.8, and fr. inc. 2). In addition, McGushin translates thirty-one fragments of doubtful authenticity found in Perotti's *Cornucopiae* and not known to Maurenbrecher (frr. dub. 25–55 in this edition), and two others omitted by Maurenbrecher (fr. inc. 38 and

fr. dub. 16 in this edition). Lastly, of particular usefulness is McGushin's commentary, which synthesizes and
makes readily accessible a rich body of scholarship. For
the convenience of readers who want to consult that commentary, each fragment in this Loeb edition is accompanied by a notation of the equivalent number in McGushin
(Mc).

A third recent edition of tremendous value is that
of Rodolfo Funari (1996), which offers in two volumes
Latin text and commentary in Italian. Funari confines
himself to the fragments transmitted by quoting sources,
excluding the considerable body of material preserved in
codex or on papyrus, the latter of which he treated in a
separate 2008 publication. His 1996 edition strictly ad-
heres to the numbering and ordering of the fragments by
Maurenbrecher. Where his contribution is greatest—and
I readily confess that his edition was of tremendous help
to me—is in faithfully reproducing the text of each and
every quoting source, no matter how small a portion of a
fragment it preserves; and he equips these quoting sources
with textual notes. His commentary covers both linguistic
and historical matters, and he takes into account views
expressed by McGushin in his commentary. Funari does
not, however, try to present a consolidated Latin text of
each fragment when there are multiple quoting sources,
nor does he seek to print Sallust's *ipsissima verba*, as opposed to providing, instead, a faithful report of the paradosis of the quoting source(s). Moreover, in the case of
Servius, by failing to avail himself of the Harvard edition
for *Aeneid* 1–5, which makes it apparent which fragments,
or parts of fragments, are quoted by Servius, which by
Servius *auctus,* and which by both, Funari fails to give an

accurate account of the testimonia in more than fifty instances. The most serious drawback to Funari's 1996 edition, however, is that, through no fault of the author, the work is simply not as accessible to the scholarly world as it deserves to be. Few copies were acquired by libraries in North America and abroad, as demonstrated by the existence of only twenty-three records in WorldCat, and my attempt in 2012 to purchase a copy by writing to the publisher and by scouring booksellers in this country and abroad met with no success. I am indebted to my friend Andrea Balbo of the University of Turin for putting a copy at my disposal until such time as Dr. Funari himself was so kind as to present me with an inscribed copy, for which I thank him most sincerely.

Presently, Dr. Funari is collaborating with Antonio La Penna on the production of a new edition of the *Historiae,* which will be accompanied by an Italian translation and a philological, linguistic, and historical commentary. Funari is taking responsibility for fragments preserved in codex and on papyrus, while La Penna is editing fragments transmitted by quoting authors. De Gruyter has announced March 2015 as the publication date for volume one, containing the fragments of Book 1, and the plan is to release the remaining books either individually or in groups, by installments.

Now at the conclusion of slightly more than two years of labor, it is my pleasure to express sincere gratitude to many friends and colleagues who assisted me with this project. I begin by going back nearly fifty years and thanking my former teacher and mentor at Harvard, Glen Bowersock, for introducing me to the speeches and letters from Sallust's *Histories* as part of an undergraduate, semester-long tutorial. And I credit a course of lectures given in 1968 by another former teacher, the late Robert Ogilvie, with enhancing my appreciation for the writings of Sallust, when I was reading *literae humaniores* at Balliol. In connection with the present Loeb volume, earlier drafts were read and commented on by the following scholars: Book 1 (Gesine Manuwald and Andrew Dyck), Book 2 (Anthony Woodman), Book 3 (Robert Kaster), Book 4 (John Briscoe), Book 5 (Dominic Berry), Fragmenta incertae sedis and Fragmenta dubia (Andrew Dyck and Dominic Berry). As mentioned in the Preface to volume 1, Robert Kaster kindly read and critiqued my text and translation of the two pseudo-Sallustian *Letters to Caesar,* whose publication was reserved for the present volume. None of these generous readers is to be held responsible for imperfections that remain, and all are to be thanked for countless brilliant proposals and suggestions, the majority of which have made their way into these pages under a cloak of anonymity. To have acknowledged each and every contribution by naming the originator was simply not feasible in the Loeb format. I also wish to thank the following scholars who kindly advised me from time to time on sundry points: Michael Alexander, Jerzy Linderski, Michael Reeve, Chris Pelling, John Vaio, Michael Winterbottom, and John Yardley. John Briscoe, who, as noted above, read and commented on a draft of Book 4, deserves to be singled out for special mention. John has been a generous and patient consultant on a wide-ranging set of issues, and I owe him a huge debt of gratitude. His experience as editor and commentator on Livy, and more recently as a contributor to the monumental *Fragments of the Roman Historians,* made him the ideal sounding board whenever a problem or question arose regarding how best to edit or translate one of the fragments of Sallust.

Lastly, it remains to repeat from the Preface to volume 1 an expression of sincere appreciation to the series editor, Jeffrey Henderson, and to Richard Thomas, executive trustee, who have offered support and encouragement at every step of the way. To them I owe the invitation to produce this new Loeb edition of Sallust's *opera omnia.* I appreciate the generosity of my friend and former roommate at Harvard, John Denis of Lexington, Massachusetts, who read and assisted with correcting of proof, and I acknowledge with gratitude all of the professional help afforded me by Michael Sullivan and other members of the production staff, including especially Cheryl Lincoln, managing editor at Technologies 'N Typography. The open-source software Antiquity À-la-carte, an interactive, online atlas compiled by the Ancient World Mapping Center of the University of North Carolina at Chapel Hill, was employed to collect and organize material for the maps in this volume, which were drawn by Phil Schwartzberg of Meridian Mapping.

J. T. Ramsey
University of Illinois at Chicago
August 22, 2014

GENERAL INTRODUCTION

Information concerning Sallust's life and career, his writings, and the manuscript tradition of his *opera omnia*, including *spuria*, will be found in the introduction to volume 1. The ordering of the fragments of S.'s *Historiae* in this volume is governed by well-accepted principles adopted by recent editors (Maurenbrecher and McGushin), without necessarily arriving at the same results in every instance. It is taken for granted that events were arranged by S. annalistically and divided into clusters organized around domestic and political affairs, interspersed with events abroad in separate theaters of war, treated year by year. The clearest proof that this was the system adhered to by S. is provided by the chance survival of three bifolia (double leaves) that once belonged to a fifth-century codex written at Fleury (the *Codex Floriacensis*) that most probably contained a complete text of the *Historiae*. From two of those bifolia (preserved on folios 15 through 18 of a palimpsest at Orléans, the *Codex Aurelianensis 192*), it is possible to reconstruct approximately one-third to one-half of one whole gathering that happens to preserve text that was found close to the end of Book 2 (fr. 2.86) and two fragments from early in Book 3 (frr. 3.6–7).[1] From this evidence, we can tell that S. divided his account of the Sertorian War for the year 75 BC into a minimum of two separate parts of Book 2. This fact emerges from observing that the text found on what would have been the third folium in the gathering (or fourth if a quinio), frr. 2.79–80, describes operations against Sertorius in the autumn of 75, whereas a scant one or two pages earlier, on the first folium, which preserves fr. 2.74 on its recto and verso, we find an account of operations conducted by P. Servilius Vatia (cos. 79) against the Isaurians in Anatolia. Hence, since there is clearly not enough space in this quire between pages 1 and 3 (or 1 and 4, if a quinio) to accommodate an account of fighting against Sertorius by Pompey and Metellus during the height of the campaign season in 75, S. must have treated those operations earlier,[2] in a separate section of Book 2, re-

---

[1] See Bloch, *Didascaliae,* 61–76, and Perl, "Codex der Historiae Sallusts," 29–38, esp. 33–35, who modifies slightly Bloch's reconstruction by arguing for a gathering of five instead of four bifolia, a quinio as opposed to a quaternio. If Perl's conclusions are accepted, then the gaps between fr. 2.74 and fr. 2.79 and between fr. 2.86 and fr. 3.6 must be doubled in size—from circa 40 lines to circa 80 lines of an OCT text—by allowing for the loss of one additional double-sided page.

[2] As explained below, this edition assigns the battles of Valentia, Sucro, and Segontia to their traditional date in 75, not a year earlier as argued by Konrad (see n. 5), which accounts for the placement of frr. 45–56 in Book 2. But even if we accept Konrad's revised chronology, surely S. covered other operations of the Sertorian War in the year 75 before he devoted a separate section to the minor skirmishes covered on the surviving sheets of parchment near the end of Book 2.

serving for later in the same book events belonging to the autumn/winter.[3] We also discover from this extant portion of the codex that political events in Rome in 74 BC were treated at the end of Book 2 (fr. 2.86D on the verso of fol. 6, or 7 if a quinio), while Book 3 introduced a new topic belonging to that same year, namely the command against the pirates that was entrusted to the praetor M. Antonius (3.6–7 on the recto and verso of fol. 8 or 10). This means that S. allowed the narrative of a year to be divided between books, a feature observable also in the case of Books 1 and 2 (sharing parts of the year 77 BC), and perhaps in the case of Books 3 and 4 (for the year 72) and Books 4 and 5 (for the year 68).

A third partially preserved bifolium that once belonged to the *Floriacensis* (pieced together from fol. 20 of the

---

[3] It may be going too far to accept the view of Perl, "Kompositionsprinzip der Historiae des Sallust," 317–37, who argues that S. systematically divided each year into a summer section and a winter section, after the fashion of Thucydides, whom S. emulated in many other respects (see vol. 1, pp. xliii–xlvi). Rich, "Structuring Roman History," 27, categorically rejects Perl's theory. We can, however, see that from time to time S. inserted into his narrative helpful chronological markers. For instance, fr. 2.66 continues the narrative of the year 75 by noting that "in the same year" (*eodem anno*) Curio, the governor of Macedonia, began a military operation in "early spring" (*principio veris*). In addition, fr. inc. 65 informs us that S. was in the habit of subdividing the four seasons of the year into three parts corresponding to early, middle, and late (*novum, adultum, praeceps*). This claim suggests that S. found such precise terminology useful in parceling out narratives spanning one or more years, breaking them into discrete parts according to different seasons of the year.

Aurelianensis and *Berolinensis lat. 4° 364*) likewise provides several valuable clues for discerning S.'s method of organizing his material. The first of the four fragments that we owe to that scrap of a bifolium (fr. 2.38, = eleven lines forming column 1 of the recto) happens to record the transition from 76 to 75 BC by announcing the entry into office of the consuls of 75, L. Octavius and C. Cotta. The third and fourth fragments (frr. 2.41 and 43, = eleven lines forming columns 1 and 2 of the verso) demonstrate that S. moved quite rapidly in his narrative of urban affairs from January to the midpoint of the year 75. This conclusion follows from the fact that no more than two-and-a-half columns of text in the codex (= ca. fifteen lines in an OCT) separated fr. 38 (announcing the opening of the year 75) from the speech of the consul C. Cotta (fr. 2.43) found on the verso of the same folium, a speech that we can tell from fr. 41 must have been delivered circa June of 75.

From the collective evidence of the three bifolia discussed above, we can discern that S. grouped events by category, since the fragments mentioned in the previous paragraph (frr. 2.38–39, 41, and 43) comprise a section in Book 2 where S. covered urban and political affairs of 75 BC, after which, toward the end of Book 2, he treated seriatim two wars abroad. This latter fact emerges from the contents of the two bifolia preserved from the end of Book 2 and the opening of Book 3, the ones discussed earlier that preserve fr. 2.74, describing Servilius' operations in Cilicia (at the eastern end of the Roman empire), followed, after a short gap of one or two pages, by an account in frr. 2.79–80 of operations by Pompey late in 75 in the Sertorian War (at the western end of the Roman world).

The vast majority of the fragments of S.'s *Historiae* are preserved, however, not on the parchment of codices or on papyri but transmitted to us by quoting sources comprising grammarians, rhetoricians, commentators, and others, who took an interest in S.'s language or style or cited him as the authority for some factual information. As an aid to an editor in deciding where to place a fragment, these quoting sources, in addition to often signifying the book of the *Historiae* from which a fragment is taken,[4] will sometimes provide useful clues that reveal the context of S.'s words. For instance, Servius (ad *G.* 4.218) states that according to S. the Celtiberians "consecrate themselves to their kings and refuse to outlive them" (fr. 1.110), and Plutarch (*Sert.* 14.5) describes how it was the custom in Spain for the bodyguard of a commander to refuse to outlive him if the commander was killed in battle, calling this practice a "consecration" (κατάσπεισις). Plutarch then goes on to illustrate this custom by describing a scene in which Sertorius' devoted native followers rescued him from a city, after a defeat, by hoisting him up onto their shoulders and over the city walls, a scene that is strikingly reminiscent of fr. 1.111 (twice quoted by the fourth-century writer Nonius Marcellus). Traces of that stirring

---

[4] An asterisk (*) is placed after the number of a fragment for which no book number is supplied by the quoting source(s). The symbol † is used to signify that a reported book number is not accepted by this edition (frr. 1.23, 88; 2.23; 3.3, 14, 19, 30, 66; 4.3, 6, 48); †† to indicate that the book number is variously given by quoting sources (frr. 2.55; 3.10); and ††† to indicate that the text is assigned by the quoting source to a work other than the *Historiae* (frr. 1.87; 4.62; fr. inc. 63; fr. dub. 18).

rescue may be found in another passage of Servius (ad *Aen.* 9.555), where the commentator gives a précis, rather than quoting S.'s exact words. Given all of these separate but converging pieces of information—the assignment to Book 1 by Nonius and Plutarch's account of the event early in the Sertorian War—we can plausibly assign fr. 1.111 to the first year or two of Metellus Pius' conduct of the war in 79–78 BC.

To take another example, the fourth-century grammarian and commentator Aelius Donatus (ad Ter. *Ad.* 310) remarks in the case of a partial quotation from fr. 1.98 that S.'s words concerned fear experienced by one Septimius. We are fortunate to be able to flesh out the small portion of the fragment preserved by Donatus with a bit more of the text that has survived on a scrap of a fourth-century parchment codex (*P. Vindob. L 117*). The expanded context makes it possible to identify Septimius as a subordinate military commander under M. Domitius Calvinus, the governor of Nearer Spain, who was defeated by Sertorius in 80 BC. Lastly, to give one final example of a different sort, sometimes, as in the case of fr. 1.43, where we find a close verbal echo in an author who is known to have drawn upon S., it is possible not only to work out the probable context of a fragment but also to offer an attractive emendation of the text, which is likely to have suffered corruption in transmission.

In constructing this edition, I have adopted the traditional chronology for the Sertorian War, placing Pompey's arrival in Spain and the Battle of Lauro in the spring of 76 and assigning the battles of Valentia, Sucro, and Segontia to 75. If on the contrary, Konrad is correct in placing the Battle of Lauro one year earlier, in 77, and the other three battles in 76, rather than 75,[5] then the fragments assigned in this collection to the spring and summer of 75 (frr. 2.45–56) will have to be placed earlier in Book 2, prior to the cluster of fragments reporting urban events in the first half of the year 75 (frr. 2.38–44). Likewise, the fragments relevant to the Battle of Lauro and other military action assigned to 76 (frr. 2.25–33) will have to be moved one year earlier, to precede frr. 2.22–24 (domestic affairs in 76). In arranging the fragments spread over the course of the Third Mithridatic War, which broke out in 74 BC, I have adopted the chronological framework adhered to in *CAH* 9[2] (pp. 231–44), placing the siege of Cyzicus in the winter of 73–72, not 74–73; the Battle of Cabira in the summer of 71; the Battle of Tigranocerta on October 6, 69; Lucullus' crossing of the Euphrates in the summer of 68; the siege of Nisibis in the winter of 68–67; and the Battle of Zela in the summer of 67.

Outlines at the beginning of each book and headings and notations within the text and translation provide chronological signposts to help the reader keep track of the course of events in the revolt of Lepidus (78–77 BC), the Sertorian War (80–71 BC), the Mithridatic War (74–67 BC), and the revolt of Spartacus (73–71 BC), the four major, multiyear conflicts that are distributed across two or more books of S.'s *Historiae*. Fragments known to belong to a given book but which cannot be assigned to a reasonably secure context are placed at the end of each of

[5] "New Chronology," 157–87. Modern scholars remain divided over whether to accept the traditional or the revised chronology, with Seager, *Pompey*, 33, choosing the former, and *FRHist* 3.531, the latter.

the five books. These fragments are generally grouped in clusters, by topic (battles, other operations in war, miscellany). I have relegated to the "unassigned" category more fragments than some previous editors have chosen to do, while on occasion I have ventured to place some fragments in a specific context while acknowledging that rival possibilities are worth considering (e.g., frr. 1.44; 2.16; 3.34). If one were to insist on absolute certainty in assigning a fragment to a specific context, many more fragments would have to be relegated to the "unassigned" category. Some sixty-nine fragments that are above suspicion but cannot be assigned to a specific book, "frr. inc." (= *fragmenta incertae sedis,* fragments of uncertain placement), including a good number (thirty-two) that Maurenbrecher distributed in Books 1–5, are presented immediately after the fragments comprising Book 5. They are arranged topically, and within topics, in the order of earliest quoting source first. Finally, a further fifty-five fragments that may or may not be genuine S. but that have been included in previous collections, "frr. dub." (*fragmenta dubia et spuria* = doubtful and spurious fragments), are presented in one final section. To have omitted some or all of the fragments that cannot confidently be credited to S. or to the *Historiae,* even if in some cases we can be reasonably certain that they are not genuine S., would have invited the surmise that they were somehow overlooked. Better to err on the side of inclusiveness than the reverse.

One of the foremost aims of this edition has been to make the text and the translation of the fragments as accessible and as authoritative as possible within the limits prescribed by the Loeb Classical Library, which does not permit space for lengthy commentary or detailed textual notes. Next to each fragment is placed the corresponding number assigned to it in the editions of Maurenbrecher (M), McGushin (Mc), Dietsch (D) and Kritz (K). This will make it possible to find each fragment in any one of those other four editions without having to consult a table. At the same time, it will reveal at a glance how the placement of any given fragment agrees with, or differs from, the scheme adopted by prior editors. An effort is made to give a comprehensive report of quoting sources, placing first the one or more sources that preserve the whole or the bulk of a fragment. Secondary sources that transmit only a portion of a fragment or contribute a paraphrase or précis are set apart by being enclosed within braces, thus { }. For fragments whose book number is attested, if the text is quoted by more than one source, a notation is added to indicate the source(s) to which we owe the book number. Italic type is employed to present fragments that are not the *ipsissima verba* of S. but a précis of his account, and within italics, boldface is used to call attention to individual words or phrases (including the Greek equivalents in Greek sources) that may have been drawn directly from S.

Textual notes are kept to a bare minimum, the apparatus being shaped by an eclectic approach: positive when it seems helpful to provide supporting evidence for the reading(s) adopted; at other times, negative, when it seems useful to report conjectures or evidence in the manuscripts that may be worth considering for the purposes of arriving at a different text. For each quoting source, it is briefly stated why the words of S. were cited, whether the aim of the quoting author was to use S. to exemplify the meaning of a word, to illustrate a point of grammar or morphology, to elucidate a historical fact, or to provide some piece of geographical or cultural information. Next, since the fragments on their own, taken one at a time, are often very brief and resemble snatches of an overheard conversation, it is desirable to orient the reader by giving a sense of the probable context. With this goal in view, the translation of most fragments is preceded by brief introductory remarks set in italics, together with the mention of relevant ancient sources.

In marked departure from all past editions of the *Historiae,* this one employs lowercase, not upper, for the initial letter of the opening word of quotations that do not form a complete sentence, except when the opening word permits us to surmise that we are dealing with the beginning of a new sentence (such as, for instance, *Nam, Namque, Igitur,* or the like). Similarly, a full stop is not placed at the end of incomplete sentences, and fragments lacking sentence structure are indented slightly to set them apart from text that will stand on its own. In adhering to the principles of orthography outlined in volume 1 (pp. lxi–lxii), the text in this edition differs from that of Maurenbrecher, in that it employs throughout spellings that we can be confident were favored by S. rather than aiming to reproduce, as Maurenbrecher does, the orthography of the later quoting sources. The editions of Kritz and Dietsch, and more recently the Teubner and Oxford editions of Kurfess and Reynolds, which include the speeches and letters from the *Historiae* and a selection of fragments, provide good precedents for employing the orthography adopted in this Loeb. All of these past editors recognized the validity of printing the remains of the *Historiae* in conformity with the orthography typically adopted in editing the text of the *Catiline* and *Jugurtha*. When the text printed in this Loeb differs from the paradosis in orthography only (e.g., *quom* substituted for *cum*), no note of this is made in the apparatus, except in the case of the *Floriacensis*.[6] Divergences from the text of Maurenbrecher are listed on pp. 529–36, followed by two concordances showing the order of fragments in other editions (pp. 537–78). The work is rounded out with an Index Fontium (pp. 579–90), an Index Nominum (pp. 591–611), and four maps (pp. 614–18).

[6] Reynolds in his OCT (p. xxv n.2), by contrast, elected to reproduce the orthography of the *Floriacensis* as an exception to his practice elsewhere, but since even that manuscript occasionally preserves traces of what must have been the original Sallustian orthography (e.g., *quom*, fr. 3.44.5), it seems appropriate to restore these spellings throughout.

REFERENCES

Works by Sallust are referred to by title only, except in instances where confusion might arise. All dates are BC, unless indicated to the contrary. Sigla for the manuscripts of authors who preserve the fragments may be found in the editions of ancient works listed below. Names of ancient authors and titles of their works are abbreviated as in *OCD*[4]. Citations from Plutarch's *Lives* are according to the edition of Ziegler.

The following are abbreviations of frequently cited works:

CAH	*Cambridge Ancient History.* 2nd ed. Cambridge, 1982–2000.
CSEL	*Corpus Scriptorum Ecclesiasticorum Latinorum.* Vienna, 1866–.
FRHist	*The Fragments of the Roman Historians,* vols. 1–3, ed. T. Cornell. Oxford, 2013.
GL	*Grammatici Latini,* vols. 1–7, ed. H. Keil et al. Leipzig, 1855–1880. Supplement (vol. 8), ed. H. Hagen. Leipzig, 1870.
ILS	*Inscriptiones Latinae Selectae,* ed. H. Dessau. Berlin, 1892–1916.

K-S	Kühner, R., and Stegmann, C. *Ausführliche grammatik der lateinischen Sprache: Satzlehre.* 2 vols. 2nd ed. Hannover, 1914. Corr. repr. 1976.
LSJ	Liddell and Scott, *Greek-English Lexicon.* 9th ed. rev. H. Stuart Jones. Oxford, 1940.
MRR	*The Magistrates of the Roman Republic.* 3 vols. T. R. S. Broughton. Atlanta, 1951–1952, 1986.
OLD	*Oxford Latin Dictionary,* ed. P. G. W. Glare. Oxford, 1968–1982.
TLL	*Thesaurus Linguae Latinae.* Leipzig, 1900–.

CONSPECTUS OF EDITIONS OF ANCIENT AUTHORS CITED

Adnot. super Luc.	*Adnotationes super Lucanum,* ed. I. Endt. Leipzig, 1909.
Ambr.	Ambrosius, *De fuga saeculi,* ed. C. Schenkl, CSEL vol. 32.2.
Ampel.	L. Ampelius, *Liber memorialis,* ed. E. Assmann. Leipzig, 1935.
Anon. *brev. expos. Verg. G.*	Anonymi *brevis expositio Verg. Georgicorum,* ed. H. Hagen, *Appendix Serviana,* vol. 3.2 Servius. Leipzig, 1902. 193–320.
Ars anon. Bern.	*Ars anonyma Bernensis,* ed. H. Hagen, *GL Supplementum.* vol. 8.62–142.
Arus.	Arusianus Messius, *Exempla elocutionum,* ed. H. Keil. *GL* 7. 449–514. Cited by page number of Keil and A. Della Casa's edition (Milan, 1977).

Ascon.	Q. Pedius Asconius, *Orationum Ciceronis quinque enarratio*, ed. A. Clark. Oxford, 1907.
Audax	Audax, *De Scauri et Palladii libris excerpta*, ed. H. Keil. *GL* 7.320–62.
Aug. *Civ.*	Aurelius Augustine, *De civitate Dei*, ed. B. Dombart et A. Kalb. Leipzig, 1981⁵.
—— *Reg.*	*Ars breviata eiusdem regulae*, ed. H. Keil. *GL* 5.496–524.
Bede	Bede, *Liber de orthographia*, ed. H. Keil. *GL* 7.261–94.
Charis.	Charisius, *Ars grammatica*, ed. H. Keil. *GL* 1.1–296. Cited by page number of Keil and C. Barwick's edition (Leipzig, 1925, corr. repr. 1964).
Cledon.	Cledonius, *Ars grammatica*, ed. H. Keil. *GL* 5.1–79.
Comm. Bern. ad Luc.	*M. Annaei Lucani Commenta Bernensia*, ed. H. Usener. Leipzig, 1869.
Consent.	Consentius, *Ars de nomine et verbo*, ed. H. Keil. *GL* 5.338–85.
Corn.	*Cornucopiae seu Latinae linguae commentarii.* Niccolò Perotti. Basil, 1526: citations reported by R. Oliver, *TAPA* 1947. 413–17.
Diom.	Diomedes, *Ars grammatica*, ed. H. Keil. *GL* 1.299–529.
Donat. ad Ter.	Aelius Donatus, *Commentum Terenti*, ed. P. Wessner, 2 vols. Leipzig, 1902–5.

Donat. ad Verg.   Ti. Claudius Donatus, *Interpreta-tiones Vergilianae,* ed. H. Georgii, 2 vols. Leipzig, 1905–6.

Donat. *Ars*   Aelius Donatus, *Ars grammatica,* ed. H. Keil. GL 4.355–402.

Dosith.   Dositheus, *Ars grammatica,* ed. H. Keil, *GL* 7.363–436.

Dub. nom.   *de dubiis nominibus,* ed. H. Keil, *GL* 5.567–94.

Eutych.   Eutyches, *Ars de verbo,* ed. H. Keil, *GL* 5.442–89.

Exc. Andecav.   *Excerpta Andecavensia,* ed. M. De Nonno. *RFIC* 121 (1993).

Exc. Bob.   *Excerpta Bobensia ex Charisii arte grammatica,* ed. H. Keil, *GL* 1.531–65.

Exsuper.   Julius Ex(s)uperantius, *Opusculum,* ed. N. Zorzetti. Leipzig, 1982.

Festus   Festus, *De verborum significatu,* ed. W. M. Lindsay. Leipzig, 1913. Cited by page number of L. Müller's edi-tion (Leipzig, 1839) and Lindsay's.

Fr. Bob.   *Fragmentum Bobiense de nomine et pronomine,* ed. H. Keil, *GL* 5.555–66.

Fronto   Fronto, *Epistulae,* ed. M. P. J. van den Hout 2nd ed. Leipzig, 1988.

Gell.   Aulus Gellius, *Noctes Atticae,* ed. P. K. Marshall. Oxford, 1968.

Gloss. 5   *Excerpta ex libro glossarum.* In *Cor-pus glossariorum Latinorum,* ed. G. Goetz. Vol 5. Leipzig, 1894.161–255.

REFERENCES

Gloss. Vatic.	*Glossarium Vaticanum*, ed. A. Mai, *Classicorum auctorum e Vaticanis codicibus editorum*, vol 8. Rome, 1836.
Gloss. Verg.	Scriptoris incerti *Glossarium Vergilianum*, ed. H. Hagen, *Appendix Serviana*, vol. 3.2 Servius. Leipzig, 1902.527–29.
Gran. Lic.	Granius Licianus, *Quae supersunt*, ed. M. Flemisch. Leipzig, 1904.
Hieron. *Ep.*	Jerome, *Epistulae*, ed. I. Hilberg, *CSEL* vols. 54–58.
———. in *Dan.*	Jerome, *commentarii in Danielem prophetam*, ed. F. Glorie. *S. Hieronymi presbyteri opera*. 1.5. Turnhout, 1964.
———. in *Hab.*	Jerome, *commentarii in Habacuc prophetam*, ed. M. Adriaen, *S. Hieronymi Presbyteri Opera*. 1.6. Turnhout, 1970.
———. *Sit. et nom.*	Jerome, *De situ et nominibus locorum Hebraicorum, Onomastica sacra*, ed. P. de Lagarde, 2nd ed. Göttingen, 1887.118–90.
Isid. *Etym.*	Isidore of Seville, *Etymologiarum siue Originum libri XX*, ed. W. M. Lindsay. Oxford, 1911.
Macrob. *Exc. Bob.*	*Excerpta Bobiensia de libro Macrobii de differentiis et societatibus Graeci Latinique verbi*, ed. H. Keil. *GL* 5. 631–55.

———. *Exc. Paris.*   *Excerpta Parisina ex libro Macrobii de differentiis et societatibus Graeci Latinique verbi,* ed. H. Keil. *GL* 5. 599–630.

———. *Sat.*   Macrobius, *Saturnalia,* ed. R. Kaster. Oxford, 2011.

Mar. Victor. *Rhet.*   Marius Victorinus, *Explanationes in rhetoricam Ciceronis,* ed. C. Halm, *Rhetores Latini minores.* Leipzig, 1863.153–304.

Mart. Cap.   Martianus Capella, *De nuptiis Philologiae et Mercurii,* ed. J. A. Willis. Leipzig, 1983.

Non.   Nonius Marcellus, *De compendiosa doctrina,* ed. W. M. Lindsay. Leipzig, 1903. Cited by page number of J. Mercier's 2nd edition (Paris, 1614) and Lindsay's.

Phoc.   Phocas, *Ars de nomine et verbo,* ed. H. Keil. *GL* 5.405–39.

Placid. *Gloss.*   Lutatius Placidus, *Glossae,* In *Corpus glossariorum Latinorum,* ed. G. Goetz. Vol. 5. Leipzig, 1894.3–104.

Pomp.   Pompeius, *Commentum artis Donati,* ed. H. Keil. *GL* 5.81–312.

Porph.   Pomponius Porphyrio, *Commentum in Horatium Flaccum,* ed. A. Holder. Innsbruck, 1894.

Prisc.   Priscianus, *Institutiones grammaticae,* ed. M. Hertz. *GL* 2 and 3.1–384.

Prob.

Probus, *Catholica nominum et verborum,* ed. H. Keil. *GL* 4.3–43; *Instituta artium,* ed. H. Keil. *GL* 4.45–192.

Ps.-Acro

Pseudacro, *Scholia in Horatium vetustiora,* ed. O. Keller. Leipzig, 1902–1904.

Ps.-Apul.

L. Caecilius Minutianus Apuleius, *De orthographia,* ed. M. Cipriani PhD diss. (Università degli studi Roma Tre, 2009), available online.

Ps.-Ascon.

Pseudasconius, ed. T. Stangl, *Ciceronis orationum scholiastae.* Vienna, 1912.181–264.

Quint.

Quintilian, *Institutio oratoria,* ed. M. Winterbottom. Oxford, 1970.

Rufin.

Rufinus, *De metris oratorum,* ed. H. Keil. *GL* 6.565–78.

[Rufin.] *Schem. dian.*

Ps. Iulius Rufinianus, *De schematis dianoeas,* ed. C. Halm, *Rhetores Latini minores.* Leipzig, 1863.59–62.

———. *Schem. lex.*

Ps. Iulius Rufinianus, *De schematis lexeos,* ed. C. Halm, *Rhetores Latini minores.* Leipzig, 1863.48–58.

Sacerd.

Marius Plotius Sacerdos, *Artes grammaticae,* ed. H. Keil. *GL* 6.414–546.

Sacerd. fr.

cited from De Nonno, *RFIC* 111 (1983): 401–9.

Schol. Bemb.

The Scholia Bembina, ed. J. F. Mountford. Liverpool, 1934.

Schol. Bern.   *Scholia Bernensia ad* Vergili Bucolica et Georgica, ed. H. Hagen. Leipzig, 1867.

Schol. Bob.   *Scholia Bobiensia,* ed. T. Stangl, *Ciceronis orationum scholiastae.* Vienna, 1912.75–179.

Schol. Γ ad Hor.   *Scholia Horatiana quae in V et codicibus ad recensionem G vel G¹ pertinentibus continentur.* in *Pseudoacronis Scholia in Horatium vetustiora,* ed. O. Keller, 2 vols. Leipzig, 1902–1904.

Schol. Gronov.   *Scholia Gronoviana,* ed. T. Stangl, *Ciceronis orationum scholiastae.* Vienna, 1912.279–351.

Schol. in Iuv.   *Scholia in Iuvenalem vetustiora,* ed. P. Wessner. Leipzig, 1931.

Schol. Luc.   *Scholia ad Lucanum,* vol. 3 of Lucan, *Pharsalia,* ed. K. Webe. Leipzig 1831.

Schol. Stat.   *Lactanti Placidi qui dicitur commentarii in Statii Thebaida et commentarius in Achilleida,* ed. R Jahnke. Leipzig, 1898.

Schol. Vatic.   *Scholia non Serviana ad Georgica e codice Vaticano 3317* (10th c.) in Servius, vol. 3.1, ed. G. Thilo. Leipzig, 1887.

Schol. Veron.   *Scholiorum Veronensium in Vergilii Bucolica, Georgica, Aeneidem Fragmenta,* ed. H. Hagen, *Appendix Serviana,* vol. 3.2 Servius. Leipzig, 1902.393–450.

Serg. *Explan.* Sergius, *Explanationes in artem Donati,* ed. H. Keil. *GL* 4.486–565.

Serv. (Serv. auct.) Servius (Servius *auctus*/Danielis), *In Vergilium commentarii* ad *Aen.* 1–5, Harvard ed. Cambridge, Mass., 1946–65; for the remainder, ed. G. Thilo and H. Hagen. Leipzig, 1881–1902.

———. *Comm. in Don.* Servius, *Commentarius in artem Donati,* ed. H. Keil. *GL* 4.405–48.

Solinus C. Iulius Solinus, *Collectanea rerum memorabilium,* ed. Th. Mommsen. 2nd ed. Berlin, 1895.

Steph. Byz. Stephanus of Byzantium, *Ethnicorum quae supersunt,* ed. A. Meineke. Berlin, 1849.

GENERAL BIBLIOGRAPHY

EDITIONS OF SALLUST'S *HISTORIAE* IN WHOLE OR IN PART INCLUDING TRANSLATIONS AND COMMENTARIES

Batstone, W. W., trans. Sallust, *Catiline's Conspiracy, The Jugurthine War, Histories* (speeches, letters, and select frr.). Oxford World's Classics. Oxford, 2010.

Brosses, C. de. *Histoire de la République Romaine dans le cours du VIIe siècle, par Sallust.* Dijon, 1777.

Dietsch, R., ed. Gai Sallusti Crispi *Opera quae supersunt.* Vol. 2, *Historiarum reliquiae.* Leipzig, 1859.

Ernout, A., ed. with French translation. Salluste, *Catilina, Jugurtha, Fragments des Histoires* (speeches and letters only). 13th rev. and corr. printing by J. Hellegouarc'h. Paris, 1989.

Frassinetti, P., ed. *Opere e frammenti di Caio Sallustio Crispo.* Turin, 1963. Rev. ed. with L. Di Salvo, adding Latin text to Italian translation. Turin, 1991.

Funari, R., ed. C. Sallusti Crispi *Historiarum fragmenta.* 2 vols. Amsterdam, 1996.

Funari, R., and A. La Penna, eds. C. Sallustius Crispus, *Historiarum Fragmenta,* Vol. 1, *Historiarum fragmenta lib. 1 Orationes, Epistulae.* Berlin/New York, 2015.

Gerlach, F. D., ed. C. Sallusti Crispi *Catilina, Jugurtha, Historiarum reliquae.* ed. maior, 3 vols, Basel, 1823–1831; ed. minor, Basel, 1832 (= the two editions cited by Kritz)—ed. Leipzig, 1856 (= the edition cited by Dietsch and Maurenbr.).

Jacobs, R., H. Wirz, and A. Kurfess, eds. C. Sallusti Crispi *De coniuratione Catilinae liber: orationes et epistulae ex historiis excerptae.* 11th ed. Berlin, 1922.

Jordan, H., ed. C. Sallusti Crispi *Catilina, Jugurtha, Historiarum reliquae codicibus servatae.* Berlin, 1887.

Kritz, F., ed. Gai Sallusti Crispi *Opera quae supersunt.* Vol. 3, *Historiarum fragmenta.* Leipzig, 1853.

Kurfess, A., ed. C. Sallusti Crispi *Catilina, Jugurtha, Historiarum fragmenta ampliora.* 3rd ed. Leipzig, 1957.

Maurenbrecher, B., ed. Gai Sallusti Crispi *Historiarum reliquiae.* Fasc. 1, Prolegomena ; fasc. 2, Text. Leipzig, 1891–1893.

McGushin, P., trans. Sallust, *The Histories.* 2 vols. Oxford, 1992, 1994.

Reynolds, L., ed. C. Sallusti Crispi *Catilina, Jugurtha, Historiarum fragmenta selecta.* Oxford, 1991.

Watson, J. S., trans. Sallust (*Catiline, Jugurtha,* speeches, letters, and select frr. of *Historiae,* two *Epistles to Caesar*), Florus, Velleius Paterculus. Bohn's Classical Library. London, 1872.

Woodman, A. J., trans. Sallust, *Catiline's War, The Jugurthine War, Histories* (speeches, letters, and select frr.). Penguin Classics. London, 2007.

GENERAL BIBLIOGRAPHY

EDITIONS OF PSEUDO-SALLUST AND COMMENTARIES

Cugusi, P. Sallust, *Epistulae ad Caesarem.* introd., testo crit. e comm. Caliari, 1968.

Ernout, A. Pseudo-Salluste, *Lettres a César, Invectives.* Budé edition. Paris, 1962.

Kurfess, A. *Appendix Sallustiana.* Fasc. 1, *Epistulae ad Caesarem.* Teubner ed. Lepizig, 1970.

Paladini, V. C. Sallustius Crispus, *Epistulae ad Caesarem.* testo crit., trad. e comm. filol. 2nd ed. Bologna, 1968.

Vretska, K. C. Sallustius Crispus, *Invektive und Episteln.* Vol. 1, Text und Übersetzung; Vol. 2, Kommentar, Wortindex zur Invektive. Heidelberg, 1961.

GENERAL

Bennett A. W. *Index verborum Sallustianus.* New York, 1970.

Bischoff B., and H. Bloch. "Das Wiener Fragment der Historiae des Sallust" (P. Vindob. L 117). *Wiener Studien* 13 n.s. (1979): 116–29.

Bloch, H. "The Structure of Sallust's *Historiae:* The Evidence of the Fleury Manuscript." In *Didascaliae: Studies in honor of Anselm Albareda,* edited by S. Prete, 61–76, and two figures. New York, 1961.

Brunt, P. *Italian Manpower, 225 BC–AD 14.* Oxford, 1971.

Buffa, M. F. "Sallustio, Hist. III 58 e IV 12* M." *Civ. class. e crist.* 1 (1980): 195–206.

Caviglia, F. "Note su alcuni frammenti delle Historiae di Sallustio (Bellum Sertorianum)." *Maia* 18 (1966): 156–61.

Clausen, W. "Notes on Sallust's *Historiae.*" *AJPh* 68 (1947): 293–301.

De Nonno, M. "Frammenti misconosciuti di Plozio Sacerdote." *Riv. di Filol. e Istr. Class.* 111 (1983): 385–421.

———. "Nuovi apporti alla tradizione indiretta di Sallustio, Lucilio, Pacuvio e Ennio." *Riv. di Filol. e Istr. Class.* 121 (1993): 5–23.

Ernout A. "Salluste, *Histoires* IV 40." *Rev. Philol.* (1925): 57–59.

Funari, R., ed. *Corpus dei papiri storici greci e latini.* Parte B, Storici Latini. 1, Autori noti. vol. 2, Caius Sallustius Crispus. Pisa, 2008.

Hauler, E. "Zur Sallustkritik." *Wiener Studien* 17 (1895): 122–51.

Hellegouarc'h, J. *Le Vocabulaire latin des relations et des partis politiques sous la République.* 2nd ed. Paris, 1972.

Jürges, P. *De Sallustii Historiarum reliquiis, capita selecta.* Einbeck, 1892.

Katz, B. R. "Sallust and Varro." *Maia* 23 (1981): 111–23.

———. "Two fragments of Sallust." *RhM* 124 (1981): 332–40.

Keyser, Paul T. "Geography and Ethnography in Sallust." PhD diss., Univ. of Colorado at Boulder, 1991.

———. "From Myth to Map: The Blessed Isles in the First Century B.C." *AncW* 24 (1993): 149–68.

———. "Sallust's *Historiae,* Dioskorides and the sites of the Korykos captured by P. Servilius Vatia." *Historia* 46 (1997): 64–79.

Konrad, C. "Why Not Sallust on the Eighties?" *AHB* 2 (1988): 12–15.

———. *Plutarch's Sertorius: A Historical Commentary.* Chapel Hill, 1994.

———. "A New Chronology of the Sertorian War." *Athenaeum* 83 (1995): 157–87.

La Penna, A. "Le Historiae di Sallustio e l'interpretazione della crisi repubblicana." *Athenaeum* 41 (1963): 201–74.

———. "Per la ricostruzione delle Historiae di Sallustio." *Stud. Ital. Filol. Class.* 35 (1963): 5–68.

———. "Sallustio, *Hist.* II,83 M." *Riv. di Filol. e Istr. Class.* 99 (1971): 61–62.

Lindsay, W. *Nonius Marcellus' Dictionary of Republican Latin.* Oxford, 1901.

Meyer, Elizabeth A. "Allusion and Contrast in the Letters of Nicias (Thuc. 7.11–15) and Pompey (Sall. *Hist.* 2.98M)." In *Ancient Historiography and Its Contexts: Studies in Honour of A. J. Woodman,* edited by C. Kraus, J. Marincola, and C. B. R. Pelling, 97–117. Oxford, 2010.

Oliver, R. "New Fragments of Latin Authors in Perotti's *Cornucopiae.*" *TAPA* 78 (1947): 376–424.

Otto, A. *Die Sprichwörter der Römer.* Leipzig, 1890; repr. 1971.

Pelling, C. B. R. See Plutarch.

Perl G. "Der alte Codex der Historiae Sallusts." *Bull. d'Inf. de l'Inst. de Recherche et d'Hist. des Textes* 15 (1967–1968): 29–38.

———. "Das Kompositionsprinzip der Historiae des Sallust (zu Hist. fr. 2,42)." *Actes XIIe Conf. Eirene.* Amsterdam, 1975: 317–37.

Plutarch, *Rome in Crisis: Nine Lives.* Translated by Ian Scott-Kilvert and Christopher Pelling. London, 2010.

Putschen, H. *Grammaticae latinae auctores antiqui.* Hanau, 1605.

Rapsch J., and N. Dietmar. *Concordantia in corpus Sallustianum.* 2 vols. Hildesheim, 1991.

Rich, J. "Structuring Roman History: the Consular Year and the Roman Historical Tradition." *Histos* 5 (2011): 1–43.

Rosenblitt, J. Alison. "The '*deuotio*' of Sallust's Cotta." *AJPh* 132 (2011): 397–427.

Sapere, A. "Problemas textuales en Salustio, *Historiae* II 43: la anexión de Cirene como provincia romana." *Argos* 32 (2008–2009): 191–202.

Scanlon, Thomas F. "Reflexivity and Irony in the Proem of Sallust's *Historiae.*" In *Studies in Latin Literature and Roman History* 9 (Collection Latomus 244), edited by Carl Deroux, 186–224. Brussels, 1998.

Schulten, A. "Eine unbekannte Topographie von Emporion." *Hermes* 60 (1925): 66–73.

Seager, Robin. *Pompey the Great: A Political Biography.* 2nd ed. Oxford, 2002.

Shackleton Bailey, D. R. "Sallustiana." *Mnemosyne* 34 (1981): 351–56.

Syme, R. "A Fragment of Sallust?" *Eranos* 55 (1957): 171–74.

———. *Tacitus.* 2 vols. Oxford, 1963 corr. repr.

———. *Sallust.* Berkeley, 1964.

Trovato, S. "Sallust's *Historiae* in Eumenius' *Pro instaurandis scholis.* A New Source for Fragment I.11 Maurenbrecher." *Rev. d'Hist. des Textes* n. s. 5 (2010): 281–90.

Ward, A. *Marcus Crassus and the Late Roman Republic.* Columbia, 1977.

SIGLA

V	Vaticanus lat. 3864 (9th c.)
	frr. 1.49 (*oratio Lepidi*), 1.67 (*oratio Philippi*), 2.43 (*oratio Cottae*), 2.86 (*epistula Pompei*), 3.15 (*oratio Macri*), 4.60 (*epistula Mithridatis*)
Floriacensis	5th-c. parchment codex, rustic capitals, double columns
	Parts of eight leaves that once comprised four bifolia (preserving frr. 2.38, 39, 41, 43.1a–1, 74, 79, 80, 86A–D; 3.6, 7, 42, 44), reconstructed from the following:
A	Aurelianensis 192, ff. 15–18, 20 (a palimpsest containing Jerome's *Commentary on Isaiah*)
B	Berolinensis lat. 4° 364
R	Vaticanus Reginensis lat. 1283B
P. Vindobonae L 117	4th-c. parchment codex, rustic capitals, double columns
	Part of a bifolium, preserving frr. 1.97, 98
Pap Ryl III 473	Manchester, The John Rylands Library, Papyrus 473

Pap. Oxyrh. 68
6B.20/L (10–13)a

Fragments from a papyrus roll, written in rustic capitals in the 2nd/3rd c. (?) and recovered from Oxyrhynchus, preserving fr. inc. 2 Oxford, Sackler Library (Papyrology Rooms), 68 6B.20/L (10–13)a

Fragments from the same roll as *Pap Ryl III 473,* preserving fr. 2.8

To the right of the number of each fragment are given the numbers assigned in the editions of Maurenbrecher (M), McGushin (Mc), Dietsch (D), and Kritz (K).

Notations placed after the number of some fragments:

*   fragment cited without an indication of the book number.
†   fragment assigned to a different book by citing source(s).
††   two or more book numbers given by citing sources.
†††   fragment assigned to a work other than the *Historiae* by the quoting source(s).

Italics signifies that a fragment is not a direct quotation. Boldface within italics identifies words possibly used by S., including their Greek equivalents in Greek sources.

{ }   enclose secondary sources
[ ]   enclose explanatory material within translations
⟨ ⟩   enclose supplements within translations
[[ ]]   enclose words in a translation rendering suspect Latin words
* * *   signify in a translation that one or more Latin words are corrupt

THE HISTORIES

BOOK 1

OUTLINE

LIBER I

PREFACE, FRR. 1–16

Programmatic Statement, frr. 1–7

1 1M, Mc, D, K

Res populi Romani M. Lepido Q. Catulo consulibus ac
deinde militiae et domi[1] gestas conposui.[2]

Rufin. *GL* 6.575.18–22 analyzes the meter of each word and
phrase comprising this fragment. Prisc. *GL* 3.73.10–13: to illustrate locative in *–ae.*

{Prisc. *GL* 3.64.18–19 (*ac . . . composui* [sic]): loc. in –ae; Donat.
ad Verg., *Aen.* 1.1 (p. 7G.17–24) likens the placement of *rem* [sic]
ahead of *populi Romani* in S. to Virgil's placement of *arma* ahead
of *virum* in the opening line of the *Aeneid.*}

[1] militiae et domi] domi et militiae *Prisc. GL* 3.73.   [2] *om.*
Prisc. 3.73

2 8M, 2Mc, 6D, 7K

Nam[1] a primordio[2] urbis ad bellum Persi Macedonicum

Prisc. *GL* 3.188.15–16; Serv. & Serv. auct. ad *Aen.* 1.30: to illustrate gen. *Persi,* as opposed to *Persis.*

{*ad bellum . . . Macedonicum* (Serv. ad *Aen.* 8.383 [*om.* Persi];
Prob. *GL* 4.24.28, 4.28.18; Sacerd. *GL* 6.479.9–10; Charis. *GL*

BOOK 1

PREFACE, FRR. 1–16

Programmatic Statement, frr. 1–7

1 1M, Mc, D, K

Announcement of theme and starting point of the narrative (78 BC).

I have compiled the military and civil deeds of the Roman people for the consular year of Marcus Lepidus and Quintus Catulus, and for the years thereafter.[1]

[1] Concluding in 67 BC, a span of twelve years (*bis senos . . . annos,* Auson. *Ep.* 22.63)

2 8M, 2Mc, 6D, 7K

Possibly this fr. formed part of S.'s discussion of his predecessors in the field of Roman history.

For from the very beginning of the City[1] down to the Macedonian War against Perseus[2]

[1] Traditionally 753 BC.   [2] In 171–168.

---

[1] *om. Serv.*   [2] *Prisc. 3.188 (cf. Liv. praef. 1)*: principio *Serv. (cf. Tac. Ann. 1.1.1)*

1.68.20–21 = p. 86B.16 [*om.* ad]); *Persi* (*Exc. Bob. GL* 1.541.39): all to illustrate gen.; (Prisc. *GL* 3.30.20–21) to illustrate *ad* + acc. with reference to time.}

3 4M, 3Mc, 2D, 2K

Sallustius . . . in libro primo Historiarum dat Catoni bre-vitatem—**Romani generis disertissumus** ⟨**multa**⟩[1] **paucis absolvit**—**Fannio** vero **veritatem**.

Mar. Victor. *Rhet.* p. 203H.26–28.

{"*Romani generis disertissimus*" (Serv. & Serv. auct. ad *Aen.* 1.96 and Pomp. *GL* 5.158.23–24: to illustrate the superlative with the gen. sing. of a collective noun); (Ampel. 19.8: Cato the Censor was so described by S.); cf. Hieron. *Ep.* 61.3.3, crediting Cato with being "*R. gen. disertissimus*," without attribution to S.; Cato praised by S. for his brevity (Porph. ad Hor. *Sat.* 1.10.9; Ps.-Acro ibid.: *quod multa paucis absolverit*).}

   [1] *Ps.-Acro:* summa *suppl. Mähly*

4 2M, 4Mc, 4D, 4K

   recens scrip⟨sit⟩[1]

Charis. *GL* 1.216.29 = p. 280B.13: reporting that in his commentary on Book 1 of S.'s *Histories,* the second-century AD commentator Aemilius Asper stated that *recens* is sometimes an adv., sometimes an adj. ("recent[ly]").

   [1] *Kritz:* scrip. *N:* scripsi *Cuyck:* scrip⟨tum⟩ *Keil*

3 4M, 3Mc, 2D, 2K

Praise for two previous writers of history: M. Porcius Cato, the Elder Cato (cos. 195, cens. 184), author of the Origines, *one of the earliest prose histories of Rome to be written in Latin (FRHist no. 5); and C. Fannius, an anti-Gracchan historian of the latter half of the 2nd cent. BC (FRHist no. 12).*

Sallust . . . in Book 1 of his Histories *ascribes brevity to Cato*—**the most eloquent of the Roman race**[1] **relates ‹many things› briefly**—but **truthfulness to Fannius**.

[1] Cf. Catullus' description of Cic.: "most eloquent of Romulus' descendants" (49.1, *disertissime Romuli nepotum*).

4 2M, 4Mc, 4D, 4K

Possibly a reference to Sisenna, if recens *is an adj. (as it appears to be from the context of the quotation in Charisius) and refers to recent, i.e., contemporary history relative to the writer (cf.* Jug. *95.2). If* recens *is an adv. (describing an immediate predecessor of S.), two possible candidates are Sisenna (d. 67 BC) and Licinius Macer (d. 65 BC).*

he wrote[1] recent [history]

[1] Or if *scripsi* is the correct reading: "I wrote," referring, perhaps, to the *Bellum Catilinae*.

5* 3M, 5Mc, inc. 1D, 1.5K

nos in tanta doctissumorum hominum copia

Serv. auct. ad *Aen.* 2.89: to illustrate the pl. *nos* standing for the sing.; Serv. and Serv. auct. ad *Aen.* 4.213 to illustrate *nostra* standing for *mea.*

6* 6M, 7Mc, 5D, 6K

neque me divorsa pars in civilibus armis movit a vero

Arus. *GL* 7.494.5 = p. 205DC: to illustrate *moveo* + *a/ab* + abl. of place. Book number has dropped out of Arusianus' text; ‹I› is Mai's suppl.

7 10M, 6Mc, deest in D et K

QUOD **CATO**: . . . *Meminit huius Sallustius in principio libri primi Historiae.*

Adnot. super Luc. 3.164

Civil Discord, frr. 8–16

8 7M, 8Mc, 7D, 8K

Nobis primae dissensiones vitio humani ingeni evenere, quod inquies atque indomitum semper in certamine[1] libertatis aut gloriae aut dominationis agit.

Prisc. *GL* 2.157.14: to illustrate adjs. of third decl. in *–es,* like *inquies,* common to all three genders.

{Serv. auct. ad *Aen.* 4.245 (*inter certamina* [sic] *dominationis aut libertatis agit*): to illustrate the verb *ago = in actu est* [be engaged in].}

5* 3M, 5Mc, inc. 1D, 1.5K

The challenge of being measured against one's predecessors.

we, amid such a vast abundance of very learned men

6* 6M, 7Mc, 5D, 6K

Pledge to be objective and impartial, despite being a partisan of Caesar in the recent civil war.

nor did my allegiance to a different side in the civil conflict divert me from the truth

7 10M, 6Mc, not included in D and K

M. Cato Uticensis (d. 46) was mentioned in the preface, doubtless because he was a leading political figure in the faction opposed to Caesar, whose cause Sallust espoused in the civil war (cf. previous fragment).

"Which Cato [conveyed from Cyprus upon the far-off seas.]": . . . Sallust mentions this **Cato** in the preface to the first book of his Histories.

Civil Discord, frr. 8–16

8 7M, 8Mc, 7D, 8K

The seeds of dissention sprout from a flaw in human nature.

The earliest conflicts arose among us as a result of a defect of human nature, which restlessly and without restraint always engages in a struggle for freedom or glory or power.

---

[1] in certamine] inter certamine *(FG) vel* inter certamina *(PT) codd. Serv.*

9 11aM, 9Mc, 8D, 9K

1 Res Romana plurumum imperio valuit Ser. Sulpicio et M.
Marcello consulibus, omni Gallia cis Rhenum atque inter
mare nostrum et Oceanum, nisi qua paludibus invia fuit,
2 perdomita. Optumis autem moribus et maxuma concordia
egit inter secundum atque postremum[1] bellum Carthaginiense.[2]

Mar. Victor. *Rhet.* p. 158H.17: war is a necessary prelude to *pax*
(peace), a word derived from *pactum* (that which is agreed to
[after a conflict]).

{*Pan. Lat.* 9.19.4 (*Romana res plurimum terra et mari valuit*)
an apparent allusion to S. (*ut legimus*) but not by name; Non.
p. 92M = 131L.6 (§1 *cis Rhenum . . . perdomita*); cf. Amm. Marc.
15.12.6 (*omnes Galliae nisi . . . inviae fuere* [sic]); Serv. ad *Aen.*
6.540; Aug. *Civ.* 2.18.4 and 3.21.1 paraphrase §2.}

[1] ultimum *Serv.*   [2] post Carthaginiense ‹causaque ***
non amor iustitiae, sed stante Carthagine metus pacis infidae
fuit.› *suppl. Maurenbr., exempli gratia, ex Aug. Civ. 2.18.4.*

10 11bM, 10Mc, 9D, 10K

1 At discordia et avaritia atque ambitio et cetera secundis
rebus oriri sueta mala post Carthaginis excidium maxume
2 aucta sunt. Nam iniuriae validiorum et ob eas discessio
plebis a patribus aliaeque dissensiones domi fuere iam
inde a principio, neque amplius quam regibus exactis,
dum metus a Tarquinio et bellum grave cum Etruria posi-

[1] See *Cat.* 33.3n. and n. 3 below.

9 11aM, 9Mc, 8D, 9K

Augustine (Civ. 2.18.4) paraphrases the last sentence of this frag-ment, stating that it was found in the exordium of Book 1 of S.'s Histories *and that fr. 10 came "immediately" (*continuo) *after-ward.*

The Roman state enjoyed the greatest extent of its do-minion in the consulship of Servius Sulpicius and Marcus Marcellus [51 BC], when all Gaul lying to the west of the Rhine and between the Mediterranean and the Atlantic had been subdued,[1] apart from where it was inaccessible owing to marshes. On the other hand, it functioned with the best morals and the greatest degree of harmony be-tween the second and the final war with Carthage.[2]

[1] By Julius Caesar as proconsul of the two Gauls and Illyricum in 58–50. [2] Between the years 201 and 149.

10 11bM, 10Mc, 9D, 10K

The destruction of Carthage (in 146) ushered in moral decline. Immediately after the remarks in fr. 9 (see introd. note, above), S. treated civil disharmony, which spanned the period extending from the date of the expulsion of Rome's last king, Tarquinius Superbus, (traditionally in 510) until the Second Punic War (218–201).

But disharmony and greed, as well as ambition and other evils typically arising from success increased very greatly after the destruction of Carthage. Indeed, abuses on the part of the stronger and, as a consequence, secessions of the plebeians from the patricians[1] and other internal dis-putes existed right from the beginning. And the fair and moderate exercise of power after the expulsion of the kings did not last any longer than it took to put aside apprehen-sion caused by Tarquin and a serious war with the Etrus-

11

SALLUST

3   tum est, aequo et modesto iure agitatum. Dein servili
    imperio patres plebem exercere, de vita atque tergo regio
    more consulere, agro pellere et, ceteris expertibus, soli in
4   imperio agere. Quibus saevitiis et maxume fenore op-
    pressa plebes, quom adsiduis bellis tributum et militiam
    simul toleraret, armata montem Sacrum atque Aventinum
    insedit, tumque tribunos plebis et alia sibi iura paravit.
5   Discordiarum et certaminis utrimque finis fuit secundum
    bellum Punicum.

Aug. *Civ.* 2.18.5–7: assigns a paraphrase of the last sentence of fr.
9 and the present fragment to the *exordium* of Book 1.

{Aug. *Civ.* 3.16.1 (§2 *aequo et modesto iure agitatum, dum metus
. . . positum est* [sic]); Arus. *GL* 7.502.2 = p. 237DC (§2 *nam iniuriae validiorum*); *Schol. Vatic.* ad *G.* 4.238 (§2 *iniuria* [sic] *validiorum*); Aug. *Civ.* 3.17.1–2 (§3 *Deinde* [sic] *servili imperio . . .
Punicum*); Donat. ad Ter. *An.* 36 (§3 *dein servili imperio patres
p. e.*); §4 *armata . . . insedit* (Arus. *GL* 7.480.13 = p. 156DC; Serv.
auct. ad *Aen.* 8.479 om. *armata*; Diom. *GL* 1.444.1 om. *armata*);
cf. Aug. *Civ.* 5.12.14 (a paraphrase of §§2–5).}

11 15M, 11Mc, 112D, 106K

quietam a bellis civitatem

Arus. *GL* 7.504.21 = p. 246DC: to illustrate *quietus* + *a/ab* + abl.

12 12M, 12Mc, 10D, 11K

Postquam remoto metu Punico simultates exercere va-
cuom fuit, plurumae turbae, seditiones et ad postremum
bella civilia orta sunt, dum pauci potentes, quorum in gra-

cans.[2] Afterward, the patricians lorded it over the plebeians as if the latter were slaves, regulated their lives and persons in kingly fashion, drove them from their land, and leaving everyone else without a share, wielded power all by themselves. Oppressed by such savageries, and especially by interest on debt (since as a result of continual wars they were being subjected simultaneously to taxation and military service), the plebeians took up arms and occupied the Sacred Mount and the Aventine.[3] And at that time, they brought into being for themselves the tribunes of the plebs and other rights. The Second Punic War marked an end of disharmonies and struggle on both sides.

[2] According to tradition, the Etruscan king Lars Porsenna waged war against Rome in a vain attempt to restore the expelled king Tarquinius.   [3] Sallust combines two rival traditions, one associating the first secession in 494 with the Sacred Mount, a hill ca. three miles northeast of Rome, the other linking it with the Aventine, the southernmost of the seven hills of Rome, next to the Tiber.

11 15M, 11Mc, 112D, 106K

Rome enjoyed a period of tranquility in the first half of the second century.

the community at peace from wars

12 12M, 12Mc, 10D, 11K

Civil discord and moral decline arose after the threat posed by Carthage was removed by its destruction in 146.

After the fear of Carthage had been removed and the way was clear for pursuing rivalries, there arose a great many riots, insurrections, and in the end, civil wars, while a

13

tiam plerique concesserant, sub honesto patrum aut plebis nomine dominationes adfectabant; bonique et mali cives adpellati non ob merita in rem publicam—omnibus pariter conruptis—sed uti quisque locupletissimus et iniuria validior, quia praesentia defendebat, pro bono ducebatur.

Gell. 9.12.15 (*postquam . . . vacuum fuit*): as part of a discussion of *metus* with an objective gen. ("fear of X") and subjective gen., ("X's fear") + Aug. *Civ.* 3.17.5 (*plurimae . . . ducebatur*).

{Arus. *GL* 7.462.2–3 = p. 462DC (*quorum in gratiam plerique concesserant*): to illustrate *concedo in gratiam*.}

13* 16M, 13Mc, 12D, K

Ex quo tempore maiorum mores non paulatim, ut antea, sed torrentis modo praecipitati; adeo iuventus luxu atque avaritia conrupta, ut merito dicatur genitos esse, qui neque ipsi habere possent res familiaris neque alios pati.

Aug. *Civ.* 2.18.10: cited to illustrate the corruption of Roman morals.

{Aug. *Civ.* 2.19.1 (*maiorum mores . . . corrupta est*).}

14 13M, 14Mc, 13D, K

omniumque partium decus in mercedem conruptum erat

Arus. *GL* 7.484.18 = p. 171DC, quoting this fragment and fr. 60: to illustrate (erroneously) *in* + acc. = *causa* + gen.

powerful few, to whose influence the majority had succumbed, aspired to despotism while purporting to act in the honorable name of the senate or commons.[1] It was not on account of their services to the nation that citizens were given the name "good" or "bad," since all were equally corrupt. Rather, each person in proportion to his enormous wealth and superior strength resulting from injustice, was regarded as "good" because he was maintaining the status quo.

[1] Cf. *Cat.* 38.3.

13* 16M, 13Mc, 12D, K

After the destruction of Carthage in 146, or upon the victory of Sulla in the civil war in 82 (cf. Cat. 11.1–5)—it is impossible to say to which S. refers here—an increase in luxury accelerated moral decline.

And from that time, the manners of our ancestors were discarded not gradually, as previously, but after the fashion of a torrent; to such an extent was our youth corrupted by luxury and greed that it may rightly be stated that men were born who could neither maintain possession of their own property nor permit others to do so.

14 13M, 14Mc, 13D, K

Same context as fr. 13. Greed dominates Roman politics.

and the respectability of all factions had degenerated into a quest for gain

15* 17M, 15Mc, 11D, 14K

Eo quippe tempore disputatur quo iam unus Gracchorum occisus fuit, a quo scribit **seditiones graves coepisse** *Sallustius.*

Aug. *Civ.* 2.21.2.

16 18M, 43Mc, 33D, 38K

Et relatus inconditae olim vitae mos, ut omne ius in viribus esset.[1]

Adnot. super Luc. 1.175 to illustrate the statement that "might (*vis*) became the standard (*mensura*) of right (*ius*)."

{Fronto p. 157.14–15, *omne ius in validioribus esse* is most likely a paraphrase (see fr. dub. 3).}

[1] in validioribus esse *Fronto*

HISTORICAL BACKGROUND, FRR. 17–47

The Social War (91–87 BC), frr. 17–21

17* 19M, 16Mc, 14D, 15K

Tantum antiquitatis curaeque maioribus[1] pro Italica gente fuit.

Serv. ad *G.* 2.209: to support the view that *antiquus* approaches the meaning of *carus* (dear); Fronto p. 159.18, commenting on a meaning of *antiquitas* (*OLD* 5) coined by S.

{*Gloss. Verg.* p. 528H.11–12, paraphrases S. thus: *antiquior cura quae maioribus . . . fuit.*}

15* 17M, 15Mc, 11D, 14K

The murder of the tribune of the plebs Ti. Gracchus in 133 marked the inception of strife (cf. Vell. 2.3.3, quoted below, fr. 16).

Indeed the discussion[1] *takes place at the time when one of the Gracchi was already slain, from which point, as Sallust writes,* **serious insurrections began**.

[1] In Cicero's *De Re Publica,* a dialogue set in 129.

16 18M, 43Mc, 33D, 38K

Possibly the same context as fr. 15, since Vell. 2.3.3 states that after the murder of Ti. Gracchus "right was overwhelmed by might" (inde ius vi obrutum).

And there was a reversion to the former custom of living an uncivilized life, such that all right was based on might.

HISTORICAL BACKGROUND, FRR. 17–47

The Social War (91–87 BC), frr. 17–21

17* 19M, 16Mc, 14D, 15K

Early history of Rome's dealings with the peoples of Italy during the period of conquest.

Such regard and concern did our ancestors have for the people of Italy.

---

[1] *post* pro Italica gente *Fronto*

18* 20M, 17Mc, 15D, 3.81K

Citra Padum omnibus lex Licinia[1] fraudi[2] fuit.

Cledon. *GL* 5.76.24–25: to illustrate *citra* + acc.

[1] *Casselius*: Lucania *cod.*   [2] *Casselius*: fratra *cod.*: ingrata *Maurenbr.*: parata *Landgraf*

19* 21M, 18Mc, inc. 2D, 1.16K

atque omnis Italia animis discessit

Adnot. super Luc. 3.632 and 6.347: to illustrate *discedo = dividi* (3.632) or *separari* (6.347), "to be split apart" or "to be separated [from]."

20* 22M, 19Mc, 17D, K

post defectionem sociorum et Latii

Donat. ad Ter. *Ad.* 458: to illustrate *deficere* (*defectio*) applied to desertion on the part of a *socius* (ally).

21* 23M, 20Mc, 36D, 19K

Quippe vasta Italia rapinis, fuga, caedibus

Serv. auct. ad *Aen.* 8.8: to illustrate the adj. *vastus = desertus.*

18* 20M, 17Mc, 15D, 3.81K

A contributing cause (maxima causa, *Ascon., p. 68C.5) of the revolt of Rome's Italian allies in 91 was the consular Lex Licinia Mucia of 95, which purged from the citizen rolls the names of persons who falsely laid claim to Roman citizenship despite being natives of allied communities in Italy south of the Po River.*

The the Licinian law was injurious to all people on this side of the Po.

19* 21M, 18Mc, inc. 2D, 1.16K

The revolt of Rome's Italian allies in the Social War of 91–87.

and all Italy broke away with fervor

20* 22M, 19Mc, 17D, K

Same context as fr. 19.

after the revolt of the allies and Latins[1]

[1] I.e., those possessing Latin rights (see *Jug.* 39.2n.). For this sense of *Latium,* see *Jug.* 69.4n.

21* 23M, 20Mc, 36D, 19K

Devastation of Italy caused by the Social War (91–87).

Indeed Italy, desolate as a result of plundering, flight, massacres,

The Civil War (88–82 BC), frr. 22–35

22 24M, 21Mc, 19D, 21K

postremo ipsos colonos per miserias et incerta humani generis orare

Serv. auct. ad *Aen.* 10.45: to illustrate the meaning of *per miserias* with *orare,* meaning "to be petitioned by one who has suffered woes" (*rogari ab eo qui miserias pertulit*).

23† 25M, 22Mc, 2.66D, 2.75K

[primo][1] incidit[2] forte per noctem in lenunculum[3] piscantis[4]

Non. p. 534M = 857L.30 (assigned to "*Hist. lib II*"): to illustrate the word *lenunculus* meaning a "small fishing vessel." The apparent intrusion of *primo* into the text possibly arose from a scribal notation that "lib. II," which immediately precedes *primo,* should be corrected to "lib. I" (so Jürges 7).

[1] *Müller*   [2] *Mercier*: indicit *codd.*   [3] *Quicherat*: lenunculo *codd.*   [4] *ed. 1476 (cf. Amm. Marc. 16.10.3,* lenunculo . . . piscantis*)*: piscandis (piscandi *D*[A]) *codd.*

24 144M, 25Mc, 21D, 23K

nexuit catenae modo

Prisc. *GL* 2.536.10: to illustrate the pf. of *necto.*

The Civil War (88–82 BC), frr. 22–35

22 24M, 21Mc, 19D, 21K

When Gaius Marius fled for his life from his enemy, the consul L. Sulla, he tried to reach Africa by sea in the spring of 88, but stormy weather forced him to land on the coast of Latium south of Rome, near Circeii. There he sought help from some herdsmen (Plut. Mar. 36.5).

finally, he appealed to the farmers themselves, pleading his wretchedness and the vagaries of the human condition

23† 25M, 22Mc, 2.66D, 2.75K

After being captured and released subsequent to the episode reported in fr. 22 (cf. Plut. Mar. 38.2–39), Marius seized a small fishing vessel, by means of which he made his way to an island off the coast; there he secured passage on a ship to complete his interrupted flight to Africa (App. B Civ. 1.62).

during the course of the night, he happened by chance upon a fisherman's skiff[1]

[1] Or "happened by chance upon men fishing from a skiff," if *lenunculo* of the codd. is retained and *piscantis* is construed as acc. pl. D. O. of *incidit,* as Müller interprets it.

24 144M, 25Mc, 21D, 23K

Possibly describing the barrier erected by Marius across the Tiber to prevent supplies from reaching Rome during the siege in the summer of 87 (App. B Civ. 1.67, 69).

he joined together [boats, timbers?] in the manner of a chain

25* 28M, 23Mc, inc. 4D, 1.25K

bellum quibus posset condicionibus desineret

Serv. auct. ad *Ecl.* 5.19: to illustrate *desino = omitto.*

26 26M, 24Mc, 20D, 22K

nihil esse de re publica neque libertate populi Romani pactum

Arus. *GL* 7.498.8 = p. 221DC: to illustrate *paciscor* with *de* + abl. of thing.

27 29M, 26Mc, 115D, 114K

libertatis insueti

Arus. *GL* 7.486.16 = p. 177DC: to illustrate the adj. *insuetus* + gen.

25* 28M, 23Mc, inc. 4D, 1.25K

In the late spring or summer of 87, Metellus Pius (pr. 89) and his army were summoned from Samnium, where he was battling Italians still in revolt, to defend Rome against Cinna and Marius (Dio fr. 102.7; App. B Civ. 1.68).

[the senate/consuls? ordered Metellus] to break off the war on whatever terms he could [work out with the Samnites]

26 26M, 24Mc, 20D, 22K

Possibly a denial on the part of Cinna and Marius that they were bound by a prior agreement to refrain from doing as they pleased when Rome surrendered to them in late 87. Kritz, followed by Maurenbr., less plausibly connected these words with a denial by the consul Cinna in 87 that he was bound by his oath to uphold Sulla's legislation of 88 (Plut. Sull. 10.6–7).

that no commitment had been made concerning the government and the freedom of the Roman people

27 29M, 26Mc, 115D, 114K

Possibly describing the slaves who joined the side of Marius and Cinna in 87 in response to an offer of freedom (App. B Civ. 1.69). In particular, perhaps describing the slaves known as "Bardyaei," who formed Marius' personal bodyguard and ran amuck after Rome fell to Marius and Cinna in late 87 (Plut. Mar. 43.4–5). Alternatively, the reference may be to people encountered abroad by Sertorius (in Mauretania) or by the governors of Cilicia or Macedonia.

unaccustomed to freedom

28 42M, 34Mc, 27D, 33K

ut Sullani fugam [innocentem][1] in noctem conpo-
nerent

Arus. *GL* 7.484.13 = p. 170DC: to illustrate the phrase *in noctem*
meaning "into the night."

[1] *del. Hoeven ut dittographiam*

29 32M, 27Mc, 18D, 20K

quis rebus Sulla suspectis[1] maxumeque ferocia regis
Mithridatis in tempore bellaturi[2]

Arus. *GL* 7.487.1 = p. 178DC; Donat. ad Ter. *Phorm.* 464: to
illustrate *in tempore* = *opportune.*

[1] quis . . . suspectis: *om. Donat.*   [2] ‹re›bellaturi *Pecere
(cf. Tac. Ann. 12.50.4; Frontin.* Str. *1.1.1.)*

30 33M, 28Mc., 85D, K

Maturaverunt exercitum Dyrrachium[1] cogere.

Arus. *GL* 7.459.13–14 = p. 83DC: to illustrate *cogo* + D.O. acc.
and acc. of place to which.

[1] *Keil*: brachium *N1*: Durachium *corr. Parrhasius.*

28 42M, 34Mc, 27D, 33K

After Rome fell to Cinna and Marius in late 87, many who be-
longed to the opposing faction fled to join Sulla in the East, so as
to escape reprisal (Liv. Per. 84; Plut. Sull. 22.1). Maurenbr. and
McGushin prefer the less probable context of the Battle of the
Colline Gate (Nov. 82), in which Sulla's left wing suffered a crush-
ing defeat, leading to despair that lasted well into the night (App.
B Civ. 1.93; Plut. Sull. 29.9).

so that the partisans of Sulla were arranging their
flight for after dark

29 32M, 27Mc, 18D, 20K

Possibly forming part of the description of Sulla's decision to re-
turn quickly to Italy to face his enemies and how this influenced
him to conclude a peace agreement with Mithridates in 85 that
was not destined to last.

and Sulla, mistrusting these circumstances [promises of
reconciliation made by the Cinnan regime?] and especially the savagery of king Mithridates, who would make
war[1] at an opportune time

[1] Or "revolt," if ‹*re*›*bellaturi* is accepted into the text.

30 33M, 28Mc., 85D, K

In the spring of 83, Sulla mustered his army at Dyrrachium, on
the Adriatic coast, preparatory to invading Italy (Plut. Sull. 27.1).

They hastened to muster the army at Dyrrachium.

31* 34M, 29Mc, 23D, 27K

Inde ortus sermo, percontantibus utrimque: satin salve, quam grati ducibus suis, quantis familiaribus copiis agerent.

Donat. ad Ter. *Eun.* 978: to illustrate the adv. *salve* meaning *integre, recte, commode.*

32* 35M, 30Mc, 24D, 29K

*Hic est **Marius**, qui **invita matre Iulia adeptus est consulatum**, de quo Sallustius meminit.*

Adnot. super Luc. 2.134: a detail included in a note on the battle near the town of Sacriportus, where in the spring of 82 Sulla defeated the younger Marius and caused him to flee to Praeneste in Latium.

33* 36M, 31Mc, 26D, 31K

et Marius victus duplicaverat bellum

Serv. ad *Ecl.* 2.67: to illustrate *duplico* meaning *augeo.*

31* 34M, 29Mc, 23D, 27K

Description of events leading up to the desertion of the army of the consul Scipio to Sulla during negotiations in 83 (Cic. Phil. 12.27; Liv. Per. 85; App. B Civ. 1.85). Cf. fr. 79.

Then conversation arose [between the soldiers in the two opposing armies], questions being put from both sides whether they were faring reasonably well, how much favor they enjoyed with their respective commanders, and how great were their personal resources.

32* 35M, 30Mc, 24D, 29K

In 83, the son of the late C. Marius (VII cos. 86) was chosen consul for 82, despite being only twenty-six (Vell. 2.26.1) or twenty-seven years old (App. B Civ. 1.87). [Aur. Vic.] De vir. ill. 68.1 is the only other source to attest the distress of Marius' mother, Iulia, the aunt of the future dictator Julius Caesar.

This is the **Marius** who **obtained the consulship against the wishes of his mother Julia**, about which Sallust makes mention.

33* 36M, 31Mc, 26D, 31K

Sulla's siege of the town of Praeneste, where the younger Marius and his shattered army sought refuge after being defeated by Sulla at the Battle of Sacriportus in the spring of 82 (App. B Civ. 1.87), caused Sulla's enemies to send a series of relief expeditions in a vain attempt to rescue Marius.

and the defeat of Marius had intensified the war

34 37M, 32Mc, 25D, 30K

apud Praeneste locatus

Prisc. *GL* 3.67.1: to illustrate the use of a prep. with the name of a town.

35* 38M, 33Mc, 28D, 32K

Carbo turpi formidine Italiam atque exercitum[1] deseruit.

Serv. & Serv. auct. ad *Aen.* 2.400: to illustrate *turpis* as an epithet of "fear"; *Adnot. super Luc.* 2.548: added to an explanation of how Carbo came to "lie in a Sicilian grave" (cf. fr. 45).

[1] exercitum atque Italiam *Adn. Luc.*

The Tyranny of Sulla (82–80 BC), frr. 36–47

36 44M, 36Mc, 30D, 35K

ut in M.[1] Mario, quoi[2] fracta prius crura bracchiaque, et oculi effossi, scilicet ut per singulos artus exspiraret

Adnot. super Luc. 2.174: in a note explicating the role of Catulus in bringing about this execution.

{*Comm. Bern. ad Luc.* 2.173 (*qui* [sic] *per singulos artus exspiraret*): similar to note by *Adnot.* scholiast; [Rufin.]. *Schem. dian.* p. 62H.14–15 (*ut in M. Mario, cui fracta prius crura * * * artus expiraret*): to illustrate the rhetorical device of *exacerbatio*, the stirring of indignation at horrendous deeds.}

[1] *Rufinianus*: Gaio *WC Adn. Luc.*   [2] qui *Comm. Bern.*

34 37M, 32Mc, 25D, 30K

Same context as fr. 33; Sulla put Q. Lucretius Afella in charge of the siege of Praeneste (Liv. Per. 88; Plut. Sull. 29.15).

stationed at Praeneste

35* 38M, 33Mc, 28D, 32K

Flight of Cn. Carbo (III cos. 82) from Italy, abandoning an army of ca. fifty thousand men (App. B Civ. 1.92; cf. Plut. Sull. 28.17).

Out of base fear, Carbo abandoned Italy and his army as well.

The Tyranny of Sulla (82–80 BC), frr. 36–47

36 44M, 36Mc, 30D, 35K

Shortly after Sulla's final victory in the civil war in November 82, M. Marius Gratidianus (II pr. 84?), the son of C. Marius' sister and a leader in the Cinnan regime, was put to death. His cruel execution took place at the instigation of Q. Catulus (cos. 78) and was carried out at the tomb of Catulus' father (cos. 102), across the Tiber, in retribution for Gratidianus' role in driving the elder Catulus to suicide soon after Gaius Marius and Cinna took possession of Rome in late 87.

as in the case of Marcus Marius, whose legs and arms were first broken and his eyes gouged out, undoubtedly so that he might die limb by limb

37 45M, 37Mc, 94D, 96K

et liberis eius avunculus erat

Donat. ad *Ter. Hec.* 258 and *Phorm.* 872 (om. *et*): to illustrate
dat. + *esse* to express a familial relationship.

38 47M, 38Mc, 22D, 26K

quom arae et alia dis sacrata supplicum sanguine
foedarentur

Serv. auct. ad *Aen.* 2.502: to illustrate *foedare* meaning *cruentare*
(to stain with blood).

39* 48M, 39Mc, deest in D et K

⟨οἱ δὲ⟩[1] *νωμενκλάτορες*, ὥς φησιν ὁ Αἰμίλιος ἐν τῷ
ὑ⟨πομνή⟩ματι[2] τῶν Σαλλουστίου Ἱστοριῶν, ὀνομασταὶ
καὶ ἀνα⟨φω⟩νῆται[3] τῶν τογάτων . . . εἰσίν.

Lydus, *Mag.* 3.8.

1–3 *suppl. Fussius*

40 49M, 40Mc, 31D, 36K

Igitur venditis proscriptorum bonis aut dilargitis

Prisc. *GL* 2.392.21: to illustrate the depon. verb *(di)largior* used
in a passive sense.

{Gell. 15.13.8 (*dilargitis proscriptorum bonis* [sic]).}

37 45M, 37Mc, 94D, 96K

Catiline, the husband of Gratidianus' sister (Comm. Bern. ad
Luc. 2.173), *carried out the execution described in fr. 36 (cf. Plut.
Sull. 32.4; Ascon. pp. 84, 87C).*

and he was an uncle to his children

38 47M, 38Mc, 22D, 26K

*During the Sullan proscriptions (November 82–June 1, 81), the
victims were hunted down without mercy.*

when altars and other objects sacred to the gods
were sullied with the blood of suppliants

39* 48M, 39Mc, not included in D and K

*S. may have referred to nomenclators (slaves whose function it
was to supply their masters with the names of persons they wished
to greet in a familiar fashion) in connection with the hunting
down of persons who were not public figures but included on
Sulla's proscription lists simply because of their wealth (Val. Max.
9.2.1).*

Nomenclators, *as Aemilius states in his commentary on
Sallust's Histories, are those who identify citizens by saying their names out loud.*

40 49M, 40Mc, 31D, 36K

*Sulla and his supporters profited from the confiscated property of
the proscribed.*

And so, after the goods of the proscribed had been sold or
given away as gifts

41 50M, 41Mc, 32D, 37K

nihil ob tantam mercedem sibi abnuituros

Arus. *GL* 7.450.16 = p. 47DC: to illustrate *abnuo* + dat. of person and acc. of thing.

42 51M, 42Mc, 35D, 39K

quo patefactum est rem publicam praedae, non libertati repetitam

Arus. *GL* 7.506.31 = p. 253DC: to illustrate *praedae* (dat.) = *ad praedam.*

43* 31M, 35Mc, deest in D et K

ut [Sullae][1] dominatio, quam ultum ierat, desidera-
retur

Adnot. super Luc. 2.139: to illustrate Lucan's description of L. Sulla as *"ultor."*

[1] *del. Figari (cf. Exsuper. 5 [32Z]* ut Cinnana ac Mariana quam ultum ierat dominatio quaereretur).

41 50M, 41Mc, 32D, 37K

Sulla's distribution of land to his veterans as a reward for their service ensured their loyalty to him. Land had to be found in Italy for 23 demobilized legions (App. B Civ. 1.100), some 120,000 men (ibid. 1.104)—the actual number being, perhaps, closer to 80,000 (Brunt, Italian Manpower, 305).

< Sulla was confident? > that on account of such great recompense they would refuse him nothing

42 51M, 42Mc, 35D, 39K

The reign of terror after Sulla's victory exposed the pretense that the civil war had been fought to rescue the Republic from tyranny (Exsuper. 5 [32Z]).

by which it was revealed that the republic had been recovered for the sake of plunder, not freedom

43* 31M, 35Mc, not included in D and K

Same context as fr. 42. The fact that the scholiast quoted S. to illustrate Lucan's description of Sulla as "avenger" (ultor), taken with the close verbal resemblance of this fragment to a statement in Exsuperantius, who drew heavily upon S.—"people desired the tyranny of Marius and Cinna on which Sulla had proceeded to exact vengeance"—makes it seem probable that S. was commenting on the excesses of Sulla after his capture of Rome.

so that people longed for the tyranny [[of Sulla]] on which he had proceeded to exact vengeance

44 57M, 49Mc, inc. 82D, inc. 48–49K

Nam Sullae dominationem queri non[1] audebat . . . qua offensus[2]

Arus. *GL* 7.504.11 = p. 244DC: to illustrate *queror* + acc.; Donat. ad Ter. *Phorm.* 371: to illustrate a relative pron. (here *qua*) referring back to a noun (here *dominationem*) that is separated from it by an unspecified number of intervening words.

[1] queri non] *om. Donat.*   [2] qua offensus] *Keil in app.*: neque (est *V:* fuit *Maurenbr.*) offensus *RCO Donat.*: *om. Arus.*

45* 52M, 44Mc, 38D, 42K

simulans sibi alvom purgari

Serv. & Serv. auct. ad *Aen.* 2.20; Isid. *Etym.* 11.1.133; *Gloss. Vatic.* p. 34M; *Gloss. Verg.* p. 528H.24–25: to illustrate the meaning of the word *alvus* (bowel).

46 53M, 45Mc, 39D, 44K

Id bellum excitabat metus Pompei victoris Hiempsalem in regnum restituentis.

Gell. 9.12.14 {Non. p. 140M = 205L.30 (*id . . . victoris*)}: to illustrate objective gen. with *metus.*

44 57M, 49Mc, inc. 82D, inc. 48–49K

Possibly describing Pompey (so de Brosses and Kritz) or the future dictator Julius Caesar (so Maurenbr.), an object of suspicion in Sulla's eyes, because Caesar was married to Cinna's daughter and was linked to Marius through his aunt Julia, Marius' widow. S. may refer to Caesar's decision to go abroad in 81 to put distance between himself and Sulla (Plut. Caes. 1.7).

For he did not dare to complain about Sulla's tyranny . . . offended by which

45* 52M, 44Mc, 38D, 42K

In 82, Pompey was sent to Sicily by Sulla (Plut. Pomp. 10.2), with imperium *granted by the senate (Liv. Per. 89), to crush the "Marian" forces. At Lilybaeum, Pompey executed Cn. Carbo (III cos. 82), who first requested a delay to relieve his bowels (Plut. Pomp. 10.6; Val. Max. 9.13.2). The appointment of the interrex L. Flaccus in November (MRR 2.68) indicates that both consuls were dead by that date.*

pretending that he was having a bowel movement

46 53M, 45Mc, 39D, 44K

In 81, after Pompey crushed the "Marian" forces under Cn. Domitius (son-in-law of Cinna, cos. 87–84) in Africa, he invaded Numidia, captured Domitius' ally King Iarbas, and installed Hiempsal as monarch (Plut. Pomp. 12.6–7; App. B Civ. 1.80).

That war [with with the Numidians] was stirred up by the fear of the victorious Pompey, who was restoring Hiempsal to his kingdom.

47 46M, 46Mc, 84D, K

Magnis operibus[1] perfectis, obsidium coepit[2] per L. Catilinam legatum.

Festus p. 193M = 210L.9–11: to illustrate the existence of the second decl. form *obsidium,* likening it to the nouns *subsidium* and *praesidium;* elsewhere (p. 198M = 218L.2–3), Festus expresses preference for the third decl. form *obsidio.*

[1] *edd.*: opibus *X*   [2] cepit *ed. Ald. 1513*

DOMESTIC AFFAIRS AND REVOLT OF LEPIDUS (78–77 BC), FRR. 48–72

48 54M, 47Mc, 40D, 90K

De praefecto urbis, quasi possessione[1] rei publicae, magna utrimque vi contendebatur.

Arus. *GL* 7.499.1–2 = p. 224DC: to illustrate *praefectus* + gen.

[1] *Keil*: possessio *N1*: possessore *Lindemann*

49 55M, 48Mc, 41D, 45K

47 46M, 46Mc, 84D, K

The future conspirator Catiline, as a legate of Sulla(?), oversaw a siege perhaps in 82–80 (MRR 3.192).

After the completion of great siege works, he began the blockade through his deputy commander Lucius Catiline.

DOMESTIC AFFAIRS AND REVOLT OF LEPIDUS (78–77 BC), FRR. 48–72

48 54M, 47Mc, 40D, 90K

In 78, the consuls M. Lepidus and Q. Catulus quarreled over the selection of the City Prefect, an official deputized to serve in an honorary capacity as a substitute for the consuls when they went in the spring to the Alban Mt. (ca. thirteen miles southeast of Rome) to celebrate the Latin Festival (Feriae Latinae).

On both sides there was violent contention over the City Prefecture, as if over the control of the nation.

49 55M, 48Mc, 41D, 45K

As a prelude to launching a revolution toward the end of his consulship in 78, M. Lepidus (father of the future Triumvir) criticizes the tyrannical power and radical legislative reforms of the dictator L. Sulla. Since Sulla is portrayed as being still alive (§§1, 5, 16), this speech belongs to the opening months of 78, before Sulla's death and public funeral in the early part of that year (frr. 50–53). Anachronistically, too, Sulla is described as still ruling with an iron fist (§§7–8, 24), although in the previous year he had retired into private life.

37

Oratio Lepidi Consulis Ad Populum Romanum[1]

1 "Clementia et probitas vostra, Quirites, quibus per ceteras gentis maxumi et clari estis, plurumum timoris mihi faciunt advorsum tyrannidem L. Sullae, ne, quae ipsi nefanda aestumatis, ea parum credundo de aliis circumveniamini—praesertim quom illi spes omnis in scelere atque perfidia sit, neque se aliter tutum putet quam si peior atque intestabilior metu vostro fuerit, quo captis libertatis curam miseria eximat—aut, si provideritis, in tutandis[2] periculis magis quam ulciscundo teneamini.

2 "Satellites quidem eius, homines maxumi nominis, optumis maiorum exemplis, nequeo satis mirari, qui dominationis in vos servitium suom mercedem dant et utrumque per iniuriam malunt quam optumo iure liberi 3 agere: praeclara Brutorum atque Aemiliorum et Lutatiorum proles, geniti ad ea quae maiores virtute peperere 4 subvortunda. Nam quid a Pyrrho, Hannibale, Philippoque et Antiocho[3] defensum est aliud quam libertas et suae

---

[1] The title and text of this speech are transmitted by **V** (Vat. lat. 3864, ff. 119v–20v). Citations from §§11, 19, and 23, as noted below, are assigned to Book 1 by Arusianus and Diomedes.

[2] vitandis *Asulanus, sed cf. OLD s.v. tutor 3*

[3] nam quid . . . Philippo et Antiocho] nam quid a Pyrrho, Hannibale, aequor‹e› et terra *[sic] Donat. ad Ter. Phorm. 243 (cf. fr. dub. 6)*

---

[1] Lepidus' opening remarks recall the exordium of the speech of the Corinthians to the Spartans in Thucydides 1.68.1. [2] I.e., their tyranny over the Roman people and their own enslavement to Sulla. [3] E.g., D. Junius Brutus and Mam. Aemilius Lepidus, the future consuls of 77, and Q. Lutatius Catulus, consul with Lepidus in 78.

The Consul Lepidus' Speech to the Roman People [fr. 49]

"Your mercy and integrity, Citizens, which make you supreme and renowned throughout other nations, cause me the greatest apprehension in the face of the tyranny of Lucius Sulla, apprehension that you may be duped as a result of failing to believe others capable of acts which you yourselves regard as abominable[1]—especially since Sulla's hope for success depends entirely upon crime and treachery, and since he thinks that he cannot be safe, unless he is even worse and more detestable than your dread of him so that under the spell of this fear you may allow your wretchedness to take away your concern for freedom. Alternatively, I fear that if you are on your guard, you may be more occupied in guarding against dangers than in taking vengeance.

"I cannot wonder enough at Sulla's minions, men bearing very distinguished names and having the excellent models of their ancestors, who submit to their own enslavement as the price of their dominion over you and prefer this double iniquity[2] to living as free men on the securest legal footing: for instance, the glorious descendants of the Bruti, Aemilii, and Lutatii,[3] born to overthrow what their ancestors produced by their prowess! For what was kept safe from Pyrrhus, Hannibal, from Philip and Antiochus,[4] if not liberty and each man's abode and our

[4] Pyrrhus, king of Epirus; Philip V, king of Macedon; and Antiochus III, king of the Seleucid empire in the Middle East, contended with Rome in major wars fought in 280–275, 200–197, and 192–190, respectively. The Carthaginian general Hannibal ravaged Italy from 218 to 203 during the Second Punic War.

5 quoique sedes, neu quoi nisi legibus pareremus? Quae
   cuncta scaevos[4] iste Romulus quasi ab externis rapta tenet,
   non tot exercituum clade neque consulum et aliorum prin-
   cipum quos fortuna belli consumpserat, satiatus, sed tum
   crudelior, quom plerosque secundae res in miserationem
6 ex ira vortunt. Quin solus omnium post memoriam humani
   ⟨generis⟩[5] supplicia in post futuros conposuit, quis prius
   iniuria quam vita certa esset, pravissumeque[6] per sceleris
   inmanitatem adhuc tutus fuit, dum vos metu gravioris serviti a repetunda libertate terremini.

7   "Agundum atque obviam eundum est,[7] Quirites, ne
   spolia vostra penes illos[8] sint ; non prolatandum, neque
   votis paranda auxilia. Nisi forte speratis taedium iam aut
   pudorem tyrannidis Sullae esse et eum per scelus occu-
8 pata periculosius dimissurum. At ille eo processit ut nihil
   gloriosum nisi tutum et omnia retinendae dominationis
9 honesta aestumet. Itaque illa quies et otium cum libertate,

   [4] saevus iste Romulus] *Serv. ad* Ecl. 3.13

   [5] *Orelli*

   [6] *Manutius (ed. Ald. 1509):* parvissimeque V *(cf. fr. 67.1 for*
   the same error)

   [7] Agundum . . . eundum est] *Donat. ad Ter. An. 254*

   [8] illum *ed. Brix. 1495, fort. recte*

   ───────────────

   [5] Lit., "left-handed," a derogatory description of Sulla, whose
   radical reorganization of the Roman state caused him to resemble
   Romulus as a second founder of the nation.

   [6] C. Norbanus (cos. 83) and C. Marius (cos. 82) committed
   suicide to avoid capture; Cn. Carbo (III, cos. 82) was executed by
   Pompey (fr. 47), and L. Scipio (cos. 83) fled to Massilia to escape
   being killed in the proscriptions.

privilege of being subject to nothing except the laws? And [fr. 49] all these things this perverse[5] Romulus holds in his possession, as if they had been seized from foreigners. He is not sated with the destruction of so many armies and consuls[6] and other leading men, whom the fortune of war had devoured, but is more cruel at a time when success turns most men from wrath to pity. As a matter of fact, he alone of all men within human memory has devised punishments against later generations, so that they might be assured of injury before being born.[7] Shockingly, he has been protected up to now by the enormity of his crimes, while the fear of a still more cruel slavery deters you from reclaiming your liberty.

"Action must be taken, Citizens, and resistance must be made so that *your* spoils may not be in the hands of those men;[8] there must be no delay, nor is help to be procured by means of vows to the gods. Unless, perhaps, you hope that Sulla now experiences weariness or shame at his tyranny and that he will with greater peril relinquish objects criminally seized.[9] On the contrary, he has reached the point that he thinks nothing glorious unless it is safe, and regards all that contributes to the retention of his tyranny as honorable. Hence, that state of repose and tranquility combined with freedom, which many upright men

[7] By depriving the children and grandchildren of the proscribed of the right to hold public office (Plut. *Sull.* 31.8); cf. *Cat.* 37.9.

[8] I.e., Sulla and his followers, those called "minions" (*satellites*) in §§2, 12.

[9] Cf. Thuc. 2.63.2, regarding the danger that is inherent in voluntarily relinquishing tyranny.

quae multi probi potius quam laborem cum honoribus
10 capessebant, nulla sunt; hac tempestate serviundum aut
imperitandum; habendus metus est aut faciundus, Qui-
11 rites. Nam quid ultra? Quaeve humana superant, aut
divina inpolluta sunt? Populus Romanus, paulo ante gentium moderator, exutus imperio, gloria, iure, agitandi
inops[9] despectusque, ne servilia quidem alimenta relicua
12 habet. Sociorum et Lati magna vis civitate pro multis et
egregiis factis a vobis data per unum prohibentur et plebis
innoxiae patrias sedes occupavere pauci satellites merce-
13 dem scelerum. Leges, iudicia, aerarium, provinciae, reges
14 penes unum, denique necis civium et vitae licentia. Simul
humanas hostias vidistis et sepulcra infecta sanguine civili.
15 Estne viris relicui aliud quam solvere iniuriam aut mori
per virtutem, quoniam quidem unum omnibus finem natura vel ferro saeptis statuit, neque quisquam extremam
necessitatem nihil ausus nisi muliebri ingenio exspectat?

---

[9] agitandi inops] *Arus. GL* 7.480.3 = *p. 272DC*

---

[10] The option of living honorably, without taking any part in
public affairs, no longer exists because one must either assert
one's rights as a citizen or submit to being a slave to Sulla and his
minions.   [11] Sulla abolished the distribution of a monthly
ration of grain to Roman citizens at a fixed price, a privilege that
had existed since the tribunate of C. Gracchus in 123.   [12] See
fr. 20n.   [13] Italian communities that had supported Sulla's
opponents in the civil war were stripped of their Roman citizenship (Cic. *Dom.* 79) and land was confiscated from them
to provide colonies for Sulla's discharged veterans (see fr.
43).   [14] Sulla's appointment as dictator "for the purpose of
restoring the nation" (*rei publicae constituendae*) in late 82, an
office he did not relinquish until 80 at the earliest, or possibly 79,

used to pursue zealously in preference to toil combined [fr. 49]
with political office,[10] are no more. In this era, one must
be a slave or a commander; one must feel fear, Citizens,
or inspire it. For what other choice is there? Or what human principles remain, or what divine principles are un-
sullied? The Roman people, a short while ago the control-
ler of the nations, has been stripped of power, glory and
rights; without the means to live and an object of contempt, it does not have left even the rations of slaves.[11]
Through the act of one man, a large throng of our Italian
allies and of those belonging to communities classified as
Latin[12] are deprived of the citizenship[13] granted by you in
return for their many distinguished services. The ancestral abodes of the guiltless commons have been seized by
a few of his minions as the wages for their crimes. In the
power of one man are the laws, the courts, the treasury,
the provinces, kings, in short, control over the life and
death of citizens.[14] You have beheld at the same time human sacrifices and tombs stained with the blood of citizens.[15] Is anything left for true men except to put an end
to injustice, or to die valiantly, inasmuch as Nature has
appointed one and the same end for all, even for those
encased in iron,[16] and no one awaits the final inevitability,
daring nothing, unless he is of a womanish temperament?

gave him carte blanche to institute radical reforms, the chief aim
of which was to strengthen the power of the senate, to which he
transferred jury duty from the equestrian class.

[15] For the execution of Marius Gratidianus beside the tomb
of the Lutatian gens (see frr. 36–37).

[16] Similar to Demosthenes' observation (18.97) that death
cannot be escaped by barricading oneself in a room.

16   "Verum ego seditiosus, uti Sulla ait, qui praemia turba-
17 rum queror, et bellum cupiens, qui iura pacis repeto. Scilicet, quia non aliter salvi satisque tuti in imperio eritis,
nisi Vettius Picens et scriba Cornelius aliena bene parta[10]
prodegerint, nisi adprobaritis omnes proscriptionem in-
noxiorum ob divitias, cruciatus virorum illustrium, vastam
urbem fuga et caedibus, bona civium miserorum quasi
18 Cimbricam praedam venum aut dono datam. At obiectat
mihi possessiones ex bonis proscriptorum; quod quidem
scelerum illius vel maxumum est, non me neque quemquam omnium satis tutum fuisse, si recte faceremus. Atque illa, quae tum formidine mercatus sum, pretio soluto
iure dominis tamen restituo, neque pati consilium est ul-
19 lam ex civibus praedam esse. Satis illa fuerint, quae rabie
contracta toleravimus, manus conserentis inter se Romanos exercitus et arma ab externis in nosmet vorsa. Scelerum et contumeliarum omnium finis sit; quorum adeo

---

[10] *Orelli*: parata V

---

[17] L. Vettius was an *eques,* who had served under Pompey's
father in 89 (ILS 8888) and later played a role as informer in 62
at the time of the Catilinarian conspiracy and in 59 during Caesar's consulship. He sold to Cicero a villa that had once belonged
to Catulus (Cic. *Att.* 4.5.2).

[18] Doubtless one of the thousands of Cornelii who were ex-
slaves of the proscribed to whom Sulla gave freedom and Roman
citizenship (App. *B Civ.* 1.100, 104). This clerk in Sulla's dictator-
ship was later urban quaestor under Caesar (Cic. *Off.* 2.29), possibly in 45 or 44 (*MRR* 3.62).

[19] See *Jug.* 114.1n.

"But according to Sulla, I who criticize the rewards of [fr. 49] civil commotion am rebellious; I who reclaim the rights of peace am craving war. Evidently because you, the Roman people, will not otherwise be safe and sufficiently secure in your dominion, unless Vettius[17] of Picenum and the clerk Cornelius[18] squander assets belonging to others and acquired by honest means, unless all of you approve the proscription of innocent men on account of their wealth, the torture of distinguished citizens, the desolation of the City as a result of banishments and assassinations, the putting up for sale or the giving away of the goods of wretched citizens, as if those goods were the spoils of the Cimbri.[19] But Sulla criticizes me for having possessions derived from the goods of the proscribed. And this indeed is the very greatest of his crimes, the fact that neither I nor anyone at all was really safe if we did what was right.[20] Moreover, that property which at that time I bought through fear, even though I paid the asking price, I nevertheless restore now to its rightful owners, and it is not my intention to allow there to be any booty derived from citizens. Let those sufferings be enough which we have endured as the product of frenzy: Roman armies fighting hand to hand against each other, and our arms turned away from outsiders against our very selves. Let there be an end of all crimes and outrages which fail to cause Sulla any feeling of regret, so much so that he counts them as deeds

[20] By refusing to share in Sulla's guilt through profiting from the proscriptions. Even the innocent act of showing horror at the gruesome death of one of Sulla's victims was punished on one occasion by the immediate execution of the sympathizer (Val. Max. 9.2.1).

45

Sullam non paenitet ut et facta in gloria numeret et, si liceat, avidius fecerit.[11]

20   "Neque iam quid existumetis de illo, sed quantum audeatis vereor, ne alius alium principem expectantes ante capiamini, non opibus eius, quae futiles et corruptae sunt, sed vostra socordia, qua raptum ire[12] licet et quam au-
21 deas,[13] tam videri felicem. Nam praeter satellites conmaculatos quis eadem volt aut quis non omnia mutata praeter victoriam?[14] Scilicet milites, quorum sanguine Tarulae Scirtoque, pessumis servorum, divitiae partae sunt? An quibus praelatus in magistratibus capiundis Fufidius, an-
22 cilla turpis, honorum omnium dehonestamentum? Itaque maxumam mihi fiduciam parit victor exercitus, quoi per tot volnera et labores nihil praeter tyrannum quaesitum
23 est. Nisi forte tribuniciam potestatem evorsum profecti sunt, per arma conditam a maioribus suis, utique iura et iudicia sibimet extorquerent, egregia scilicet mercede,

---

[11] ut et facta . . . fecerit] *Diom. GL 1.412.20; Dosith. GL 7.415.20–21 (om.* ut)

[12] qua raptum ire] *Madvig:* quam raptum iri V
[13] audeat *Laetus*   [14] victorem *Kritz*

---

[21] Cf. Thuc. 1.69.2, concerning the need to have regard for not the extent of wrongs suffered but rather how to defend against them.

[22] "Fortunate" (*felicem*) alludes to Sulla's agnomen Felix (see *Jug.* 95.4n.).

[23] The indefinite "you" singular (*audeas*), in contrast with the plural *audeatis* above ("how much daring you have"), turns the remark into a generalization about "one's daring." Or, adopting the emendation *audeat,* "in proportion to what *he* (Sulla) dares."

[24] Both are otherwise unknown.

[25] Governor of Farther Spain in 80 (after holding a praetor-

done in glory, and, were it permitted, he would do them   [fr. 49]
again more eagerly.

"But I now no longer worry about what you think of
that man but about how much daring you have,[21] for fear
that while you are waiting, each for someone else to assume the lead, you may be taken prisoner beforehand, not
by his forces (which are insignificant and degenerate) but
as a result of your own lack of resolve, thanks to which
permission is being granted to go on a plundering spree
and to seem fortunate[22] in proportion to one's daring.[23]
For who shares his aims, apart from his crime-stained
minions, or who does not desire a complete change, except
for the victory? Is it, do you suppose, the soldiers, at the
price of whose blood riches have been produced for the
vilest of slaves such as Tarula and Scirtus?[24] Or is it those
who in pursuing a political career were treated as less
worthy than Fufidius,[25] a vile, womanish servant, a blot
upon all public offices? Hence I derive my greatest confidence from the victorious army, which has gained nothing
through so many wounds and hardships except a tyrant.
Unless perhaps they set out to overthrow the power of the
tribunes, which their forefathers had established by arms,
and to rob themselves of their rights and the courts,[26] in
exchange, no doubt, for exceptional wages, when, ban-

ship in 81?), where he was defeated by Sertorius (frr. 95–96).
Possibly he is to be identified with the ex-centurion—variously
called Aufidius (Plut. *Sull.* 31.4), Fursidius (Oros. 5.21.3), or
Furfidius (Flor. 29.25)—who persuaded Sulla to draw up an official list of proscribed victims, instead of carrying out indiscrimi-
nate slaughter.

[26] By allowing the courts to be placed exclusively under the
control of small panels comprising senatorial jurors (cf. §13n.).

quom relegati in paludes[15] et silvas contumeliam atque invidiam suam, praemia penes paucos intellegerent.[16]

24 "Quare igitur tanto agmine atque animis incedit? Quia secundae res mire sunt vitiis obtentui[17]—quibus labefactis, quam formidatus est, tam contemnetur—nisi forte specie concordiae et pacis, quae sceleri et parricidio suo nomina indidit. Neque aliter rem publicam et belli finem ait, nisi maneat expulsa agris plebes, praeda civilis acerbissuma, ius iudiciumque omnium rerum penes se, quod 25 populi Romani fuit. Quae si vobis pax et conposita intelleguntur, maxuma turbamenta rei publicae atque exitia probate, adnuite legibus inpositis, accipite otium cum servitio et tradite exemplum posteris ad rem publicam suimet sanguinis mercede circumveniundam!

26 "Mihi quamquam per hoc summum imperium satis quaesitum erat nomini maiorum, dignitati atque etiam praesidio, tamen non fuit consilium privatas opes facere, 27 potiorque visa est periculosa libertas quieto servitio. Quae si probatis, adeste, Quirites, et bene iuvantibus divis M. Aemilium consulem ducem et auctorem sequimini ad recipiundam libertatem!"

---

[15] relegati in paludes] *Arus. GL 7.505.9 = p. 248DC*
[16] intellegerint *Orelli*
[17] Quia secundae . . . optentui] *Porph. ad Hor. Epist. 1.18.29; Sen. Controv. 9.1.13 (om.* quia: res secundae [sic])

---

[27] Cicero (*Agr.* 2.71) similarly characterizes in a negative fashion the land intended for settlements under Rullus' agrarian bill in 63. [28] Seneca (*Controv.* 9.1.13) informs us that the rhetorician Aurellius Fuscus once commented on how this aphorism of S. surpassed the brevity of a similar observation in Greek by Thucydides (*sic:* the quotation coming, in fact, from pseudo-Demosthenes [*Ep. Phil.* 13, modeled on Dem. *Ol.* 2.20]).

ished to swamps and woods,[27] they realize that insult and [fr. 49] resentment are their portion, while true rewards are in the hands of just a few men!

"Why, then, does the tyrant go about with such a great following and assurance? Because success serves as a wonderful screen for vices[28]—if a reverse occurs, he will be despised as much as he is now feared—unless, perhaps, it is out of a pretense of harmony and peace, which are the names he has conferred on his criminal treason. And he asserts that in no other way can the nation and an end of war exist, unless the commons remain driven from their lands (the cruelest plunder of citizens) and the control and jurisdiction over all matters, which once belonged to the Roman people, remain in his own hands. If this is what you recognize as 'peace' and 'order,' give your approval to the utter disruption and destruction of the nation; bow assent to the laws which have been imposed upon you; accept a tranquility combined with slavery, and hand down to future generations a model for defrauding the nation at the price of their own blood.

"For my own part, although through this supreme power[29] enough had been gained as measured by the glorious name of my ancestors, my status and even my protection, nevertheless it was not my plan to amass personal wealth, and it seemed to me that freedom accompanied by danger is preferable to servile tranquility. If you endorse this view, Citizens, let your presence be felt, and with the kindly aid of the gods, follow Marcus Aemilius, your consul, as your leader and advocate for the recovery of freedom!"

[29] The consulship.

49

Public Funeral of Sulla, frr. 50–53

50* 58M, 50Mc, 29D, 34K

Mox tanta flagitia in tali viro pudet dicere.

Schol. Gronov. ad Cic. *Rosc. Am.* 90 (p. 312St.4–5): commentating that as a youth Sulla indulged in many vices (cf. fr. 53).

51 59M, 51Mc, 90D, 92K

ut in ore gentibus agens

Arus. *GL* 7.488.10–11 = p. 183DC: to illustrate *in ore* + dat. meaning *in conspectu* + gen.; Donat. ad Ter. *Ad.* 93 (om. *ut*): to illustrate *in ore* + dat.

52 60M, 52Mc, 37D, 40K

insanum aliter sua sententia atque aliorum[1] mulierum ‹lubidine›[2]

Charis. *GL* 1.194.23–24 = p. 253B.3: to illustrate S.'s use of *aliter* = *alias* (cf. fr. 108).

[1] *Maurenbr.*: aliarum *codd.*   [2] *scripsi*

53* 61M, 53Mc, deest in D et K

ὁ δ οὔτε νέος ὢν περὶ τὰς ἐπιθυμίας ἐμετρίαζε διὰ τὴν πενίαν, οὔτε γηράσας διὰ τὴν ἡλικίαν, ἀλλὰ τοὺς περὶ

Public Funeral of Sulla, frr. 50–53

50* 58M, 50Mc, 29D, 34K

The scholiast who preserves this fragment identifies Sulla as the person being spoken of. The context may have been S.'s description of Sulla's public funeral in the spring of 78 (Plut. Sull. 38), in connection with which S. passed judgment on Sulla's character and moral depravity.

I soon blush at mentioning such monstrous vices in a man of such standing.

51 59M, 51Mc, 90D, 92K

Perhaps the same context as the preceding fr., commenting on the public scrutiny to which Sulla's unabashed shamelessness was exposed.

that he living in the sight of the whole world

52 60M, 52Mc, 37D, 40K

Perhaps the same context as frr. 50–51, commenting on Sulla's love affairs with married women (cf. fr. 53).

by his own admission, frenzied in other respects and from his ‹lust›[1] for others' wives

[1] Text uncertain.

53* 61M, 53Mc, not included in D and K

Perhaps the same context as frr. 50–52, commenting on Sulla's hypocrisy in violating his own laws aimed at curbing immorality.

Sulla did not let the poverty of his youth or his time of life as an old man set limits to his desires; but, as Sallust says,

γάμων καὶ σωφροσύνης εἰσηγεῖτο νόμους τοῖς πολί-
ταις, αὐτὸς ἐρῶν καὶ μοιχεύων, ὥς φησι Σαλούστιος.

Plut. *comp. Lys. et Sull.* 3 (41).3

54   62M, 54Mc, 53D, 89K

Idem fecere ‹M.›[1] Octavius et Q. Caepio sine gravi
quoiusquam expectatione neque[2] sane ambiti publice.

Serv. auct. ad *Aen.* 4.283: to illustrate *ambio* + acc. = *rogo* + acc.

[1] *scripsi*   [2] expectione neque] *Daniel:* exspectat iuno-
nique *F*

55   63M, 55Mc, 43D, 46K

Quin lenones et vinarii laniique ‹et›[1] quorum praeterea
volgus in dies usum habet, pretio conpositi

Non. p. 257M = 392L.47–48: to illustrate *conponere* = *redimere*
(to buy up).

{Charis. *GL* 1.75.20 = p. 96B.2 (*quin vinarii ‹laniique›*): to illustrate the noun *lanius*.}

[1] *Müller*

he imposed upon his fellow citizens laws to regulate marriage and chastity, while at the same time he himself was carrying on love affairs and committing adultery.

54 62M, 54Mc, 53D, 89K

Possibly as historical background to M. Lepidus' proposed grain law (Gran. Lic. p. 34F; cf. speech of Philippus, fr. 67.6), S. referred to M. Octavius (tribune of the plebs 99–87), who abrogated C. Gracchus' grain law and substituted a more modest bill (Cic. Brut. 222; Off. 2.72) and to Caepio, who as quaestor in 100, opposed passage of the grain law proposed by the populist tribune L. Saturninus (Rhet. Her. 1.21).

Marcus Octavius and Quintus Caepio did the same [tried to curb the largess of distributing grain to the populace] without anyone really expecting this and assuredly without having been asked publicly.

55 63M, 55Mc, 43D, 46K

Lowly, urban supporters won over by Lepidus with largess.

In fact, pimps and wine makers and butchers and those besides with whom the common throng has daily dealings, collected together for a price[1]

[1] Exsuper. 6 [37Z] attests Lepidus' popularity with the commons as a result of "numerous instances of public and private largess" *(multis muneribus publice privatimque largitis).*

56* 64M, 56Mc, 42D, inc. 52K

tyrannumque et Cinnam maxuma voce adpellans

Serv. auct. ad *Aen.* 4.214: to illustrate the use of a proper name
as a term of abuse.

{*tyrannumque et Cinnam appellantes* (Mar. Victor. *Rhet.*
p. 215H.17; Serv. auct. ad *Aen.* 1.5, om. *appellantes,* to illustrate
–*que* + *et*).}

57* 65M, 57Mc, 46D, 49K

Magna vis hominum convenerat agris pulsa aut civitate
eiecta.

Serv. auct. ad *Aen.* 1.270: to illustrate *vis* = *copia.*

58 66M, 58Mc, 44D, 47K

uti Lepidus et Catulus decretis exercitibus maturrume proficiscerentur

Charis. *GL* 1.205.21–22 = p. 266B.29–30: to illustrate the superl.
adv. *maturrime.*

59 67M, 59Mc, 16D, 18K

Tunc vero Etrusci[1] cum ceteri‹s›[2] eiusdem causae ducem
se nanctos[3] rati maxumo gaudio bellum inritare.

Non. p. 31M = 46L.23: to illustrate *inritare* = *provocare.*

{Arus. *GL* 7.486.10 = p. 176DC (*maximo . . . inritare*): to illustrate *inritare bellum.*}

[1] *Mercier:* et posci *codd.*   [2] *Mercier*   [3] *Mercier:*
nactus *codd.*

56* 64M, 56Mc, 42D, inc. 52K

The consul M. Lepidus was accused by his enemies of reinstituting the tyranny of Cinna (cf. speech of Philippus, fr. 67.19).

with a very loud voice calling him a tyrant like Cinna[1]

[1] Lit., "both a tyrant and a Cinna."

57* 65M, 57Mc, 46D, 49K

Dispossessed landowners in the vicinity of Faesulae attacked Sulla's veterans, who had been given land confiscated in that region of Etruria (Gran. Lic. p. 34F).

A large body of men had assembled, driven from their lands or expelled from their community.

58 66M, 58Mc, 44D, 47K

Same context as fr. 57: consuls were sent to Etruria to quell uprising (Gran. Lic. p. 35F).

⟨the senate voted?⟩ that Lepidus and Catulus set out very quickly with their authorized armies

59 67M, 59Mc, 16D, 18K

M. Lepidus made common cause with the Etruscan rebels, whom he had been sent to suppress (Gran. Lic. p. 35F).

But then the Etruscans, together with the rest belonging to the same cause, thinking that they had acquired a leader, fomented war with the greatest delight.

60* 69M, 64Mc, 45D, 48K

Etruria omnis cum Lepido suspecta in tumultum erat.

Arus. *GL* 7.484.20 = p. 171DC, quoting fr. 14 and this fragment: to illustrate (erroneously) *in* + acc. = *causa* + gen.

61 71M, 60Mc, 91D, 93K

    prudens omnium quae senatus censuerat

Arus. *GL* 7.503.7 = p. 241DC: to illustrate *prudens* + gen. of thing.

62* 72M, 61Mc, inc. 93D, inc. 62K

Igitur senati decreto serviundumne sit?

Donat. Ter. *An.* 365 {*Schol. Bemb.* ad Ter. *Eun.* 237 (*igitur senati decreto*)}: to illustrate the archaic spelling of the gen. sing. of *ornatus* and *senatus* in *–i.*

63 73M, 62Mc, deest in D et K

    plebei tribuniciam potestatem

Prisc. *GL* 2.243.11: to illustrate the gen. sing. *plebei* of *plebes* (as opposed to *plebis,* gen. of *plebs*).

64 68M, 63Mc, 49D, 53K

    Lepidum poenitentem consili[1]

Charis. *GL* 1.253.11 = p. 331B.14; Dosith. *GL* 7.408.18: to illustrate the pres. principle of the impers. verb *paenitet.*

    [1] *om. Dosith.*

60* 69M, 64Mc, 45D, 48K

Same context as fr. 59.

All Etruria was suspected of being inclined to an uprising with Lepidus.

61 71M, 60Mc, 91D, 93K

M. Lepidus realized that the senate's true motive for summoning him back to Rome from Etruria in order to hold the elections for 77 was really to deprive him of his army (App. B Civ. 1.107).

aware of all that the senate had decided

62* 72M, 61Mc, inc. 93D, inc. 62K

Same context as fr. 61. Lepidus ponders his options.

Therefore, is it the case that one must be subservient to the senate's decree?

63 73M, 62Mc, not included in D and K

Early in his consulship, M. Lepidus had rejected a call for the restoration of the powers of the tribunate (Gran. Lic. p. 34F) but later made that very demand (see fr. 67.14).

the tribunician power of the plebs

64 68M, 63Mc, 49D, 53K

It is impossible to say what "decision" Lepidus regretted, whether to negotiate with the senate for a peaceful settlement in 78 (Maurenbr.) or to adopt the strategy of attacking Rome and leaving his province of Cisalpine Gaul in the hands of his legate Brutus (Kritz).

Lepidus, regretting his decision

65* 74M, 65Mc, 89D, 57K

Nam talia incepta, ni in consultorem vertissent,[1] rei publicae pestem factura

Donat. ad Verg., *Aen.* 1.37 (p. 18G.12–14) and *Aen.* 4.316 (p. 399G.9–10): to illustrate *incepta* meaning "intentions."

[1] in consultorem vertissent] inconsulto revertissent *p. 399G*

66* 75M, 66Mc, 47D, 50K

qui aetate et consilio ceteros anteibat

Serv. ad *Aen.* 9.244 quotes S.'s description of Philippus to explicate the meaning of Virgil's *"annis gravis atque animi maturus."*

67 77M, 67Mc, 48D, 51K

Oratio Philippi in Senatu[1]

1 "Maxume vellem, patres conscripti, rem publicam quietam esse aut in periculis a promptissumo quoque defendi, denique prava[2] incepta consultoribus noxae esse. Sed con-

[1] The title and text of this speech are transmitted by **V** (Vat. lat. 3864, ff. 120v–22r). Citations from §§5 and 19, as noted below, are assigned to Book 1 by Arusianus and Nonius.
[2] *corr. Manutius (ed. Ald. 1509):* parva V *(error idem, fr. 49.6)*

[1] The first words uttered by Philippus recall the opening words of Dem. *orat. exord.* 33.1: Μάλιστα μέν, ὦ ἄνδρες Ἀθηναῖοι, βουλοίμην ἄν ("most of all, men of Athens, I might wish").

65* 74M, 65Mc, 89D, 57K

Criticism of the revolutionary designs of Lepidus similar to that voiced by Philippus (fr. 67.1 and n. ad loc.).

For such undertakings [he asserted?], unless they recoiled on their proponent, would produce havoc for the nation

66* 75M, 66Mc, 47D, 50K

S.'s description of the senior consular L. Marcius Philippus (cos. 91, cens. 86).

who surpassed the rest in seniority and judgment

67 77M, 67Mc, 48D, 51K

When the year 77 opened with an interregnum in the absence of consuls to assume office (§22), and M. Lepidus (cos. 78) was threatening Rome with an army (§§10, 22) to press his demand for a second consulship and the reversal of Sulla's reforms, including the restoration of the powers of the tribunes (§14), the senior consular L. Marcius Philippus (cos. 91; cens. 86 under the Cinnan regime) argued for the passage of a senatus consultum ultimum (§22) to crush Lepidus' revolt. Although this speech gives the impression of being paired as a counterpoint to Lepidus's speech (fr. 49), after the fashion of the speeches assigned to Caesar and Cato in the Bellum Catilinae *(§§51–52), the two speeches in Book 1 of the* Historiae *were delivered approximately one year apart and would have stood at some distance from each other in the complete text of the* Historiae.

Philippus' Speech in the Senate

"I might wish most of all, Members of the Senate,[1] for our nation to be tranquil or for it to be defended amid dangers by its most enterprising citizens, or finally for evil under-

tra seditionibus omnia turbata sunt, et ab eis quos prohibere magis decebat; postremo, quae pessumi et stultissumi decrevere, ea bonis et sapientibus faciunda sunt.

2 Nam bellum atque arma, quamquam vobis invisa, tamen quia Lepido placent, sumunda sunt, nisi forte quoi pacem praestare et bellum pati consilium est.

3 "Pro di boni, qui hanc urbem omissa cura[3] adhuc tegitis, M. Aemilius, omnium flagitiosorum postremus, qui peior an ignavior sit deliberari non potest, exercitum opprimundae libertatis habet et se ⟨e⟩[4] contempto metuendum effecit; vos mussantes et retractantes verbis et vatum carminibus pacem optatis magis quam defenditis, neque intellegitis mollitia decretorum vobis dignitatem, illi me

4 tum detrahi. Atque id iure, quoniam ex rapinis consulatum, ob seditionem provinciam cum exercitu adeptus est. Quid ille ob bene facta cepisset, quoius sceleribus tanta praemia tribuistis ?

[3] cura ⟨nostra⟩ *Wirtz*
[4] *Asulanus*

---

[2] The concept that a wicked scheme is most ruinous for the contriver goes back to Hesiod (*Op.* 266) and became proverbial (Otto p. 90). The words here recall fr. 65.

[3] Viz., the proconsul M. Lepidus.

[4] For the senate's reliance on words in lieu of action, cf. §17. If the "prophecies of seers" are to be connected with the Sibylline Oracles, the reference here must be to those circulating in private hands, since the official collection had perished in the fire that destroyed the Capitoline Temple of Jupiter in July 83 and was not replaced until 76 at the earliest (Fenestella, *FRHist* 70F19 = fr. 18P).

takings to prove the ruin of their proponents.[2] But on the   [fr. 67]
contrary, everything has been thrown into turmoil by civil
dissensions and by men who ought rather to have prevented upheaval;[3] in short, good and wise men are forced
to carry out what has been ordained by most evil and
foolish men. For although war and arms are hateful to you,
nevertheless you must take them up because Lepidus
finds them to his liking, unless perhaps anyone intends to
offer him peace and put up with war.

"O you good gods, who still protect this City despite its
negligence, Marcus Aemilius, the lowest of all criminals—
and it is impossible to decide whether he is more vicious
or more cowardly—has an army for the purpose of crush-
ing our freedom and has transformed himself from being contemptible into someone who is to be feared! As
for you senators, mumbling and dragging your feet, with
mere words and the prophecies of seers,[4] you desire peace
rather than defend it, and you do not realize that by the
feebleness of your decrees *you* are losing prestige, *he* his
fear. And rightly so, inasmuch as he acquired a consulship
from his robberies,[5] a province together with an army because of a sedition.[6] What would that man have gained in
return for good conduct, on whose crimes you conferred
such great rewards?

[5] Alleging that cash extorted by Lepidus while governing Sicily in 80 was used to purchase votes in the consular elections of
79.   [6] Lepidus and his consular colleague Q. Catulus were
assigned Etruria as their *provincia* (sphere of command) and sent
with an army to deal with a revolt in the vicinity of Faesulae (see
frr. 57–60), a revolt Lepidus chose to support, rather than to suppress (Gran. Lic. p. 34F).

5   "At scilicet eos qui ad postremum usque legatos, pacem, concordiam, et alia huiuscemodi decreverunt gratiam ab eo peperisse! Immo despecti et indigni re publica[5] habiti praedae loco aestumantur, quippe metu pacem re-
6   petentes quo habitam amiserant. Equidem a principio, quom Etruriam coniurare, proscriptos adcersi,[6] largitionibus rem publicam lacerari videbam, maturandum putabam et Catuli consilia cum paucis secutus sum. Ceterum illi qui gentis Aemiliae bene facta extollebant et ignoscundo populi Romani magnitudinem auxisse, nusquam etiam tum Lepidum progressum aiebant quom privata arma opprimundae libertatis cepisset, sibi quisque opes aut patrocinia quaerundo consilium publicum conruperunt.

7   "At tum erat Lepidus latro cum calonibus et paucis sicariis, quorum nemo diurna mercede vitam mutaverit; nunc est pro consule cum imperio non empto sed dato a vobis, cum legatis adhuc iure parentibus, et ad eum concurrere homines omnium ordinum conruptissumi, flagrantes inopia et cupidinibus, scelerum conscientia exagitati, quibus quies in seditionibus, in pace turbae sunt. Hi tu-

[5] indigni re publica] *Arus. GL 7.480.19 = p. 157DC*
[6] arcessi *Maurenbr.*

---

[7] Doubtless a reference to Lepidus' law to distribute grain to the Roman people (Gran. Lic. p. 34F).

[8] Whereas in the previous year, Lepidus' power *was*, in Philippus' view, "purchased" (see §4n.).

[9] Among them was M. Perperna (pr. 82?), who fled in 77 with the remnant of Lepidus' forces to join Sertorius in Spain, and M. Brutus (the father of Caesar's later assassin), who was put to death

"But it is obvious that those who right up to the very [fr. 67]
end voted for embassies, peace, harmony, and other such
things, won his favor! On the contrary, despised and regarded as unworthy of playing a role in government, they
are valued as the equivalent of plunder, since they are
seeking peace out of the very dread that caused them to
lose the peace they had. For my own part, from the very
outset, when I saw Etruria conspiring, the proscribed being summoned, the nation being torn apart with lavish
handouts,[7] I thought that it was necessary to make haste,
and with a few others I followed the counsels of Catulus.
But the appeasers who kept extolling the fine deeds of the
Aemilian family and kept saying that the greatness of the
Roman people had increased through granting pardon and
that Lepidus had taken no decisive step even at the time
when he had taken up arms on his own responsibility to
crush out liberty—they, by the act of each one seeking
resources for himself or patronage, have sabotaged public
policy.

"But at that time, Lepidus was a mere bandit accompanied by soldier's attendants and a few cutthroats, whose
lives were not even worth a day's wages; now he is a proconsul with military power (not purchased but conferred
by you senators[8]), with deputy commanders[9] who are still
legally obeying him; and the most degenerate men of all
ranks flock to him, inflamed by poverty and desires, driven
on by the consciousness of their crimes, men who find rest
from their troubles in the midst of upheaval, turmoil in
settled times. These men sow rebellion after rebellion,

by Pompey in violation of the terms of surrender at Mutina, in
Cisalpine Gaul.

SALLUST

multum ex tumultu, bellum ex bello serunt, Saturnini
olim, post Sulpici, dein Mari Damasippique, nunc Lepidi
8   satellites. Praeterea Etruria atque omnes reliquiae belli
adrectae, Hispaniae armis sollicitae; Mithridates in latere
vectigalium nostrorum quibus adhuc sustentamur, diem
bello circumspicit; quin praeter idoneum ducem nihil
abest ad subvortundum imperium.
9   "Quod ego vos oro atque obsecro, patres conscripti, ut
animadvortatis neu[7] patiamini licentiam scelerum quasi
rabiem ad integros contactu procedere. Nam ubi malos
praemia secuntur, haud facile quisquam gratuito bonus
10 est. An expectatis dum exercitu rursus admoto ferro atque
flamma urbem invadat? Quod multo propius est ab eo quo
agitat statu, quam ex pace et concordia ad arma civilia,
quae ille advorsum divina et humana omnia cepit, non pro
sua aut quorum simulat iniuria, sed legum ac libertatis
11 subvortundae. Agitur enim ac laceratur animi cupidine
et noxarum metu, expers consili, inquies, haec atque illa
temptans, metuit otium, odit bellum; luxu atque licentia

[7] neu *Carrio*: ne V

---

[10] All four men met violent deaths while promoting revolutionary activity: L. Saturninus and P. Sulpicius as tribunes in 100
and 88, respectively, the younger Marius as consul, and Damas-
sipus (see *Cat.* 51.32n.) as praetor in 82. Less likely did S. have
in mind Marius senior.

[11] The rebel Q. Sertorius, who had been put in command of
Spain by the anti-Sullan government in 83/82, carried on highly
successful guerrilla warfare until his death in 73.

[12] Mithridates, king of Pontus on the Black Sea, posed a threat
to the province of Asia, whose revenues surpassed those of all
other Roman territories (cf. Cic. *De imp. Cn. Pomp. 14*).

64

war after war, these former minions of Saturninus, after- [fr. 67]
ward of Sulpicius, next of Marius and Damasippus,[10] and
now of Lepidus. Moreover, Etruria and all the other smoldering embers of war are aroused; the Spanish provinces
are disturbed by arms;[11] Mithridates, on the flank of our
tribute-paying territories from which we still receive support,[12] is on the lookout for an opportune time for war;
indeed, nothing is lacking for the overthrow of our dominion except a suitable leader.

"Therefore, I beg and implore you, Members of the
Senate, to pay attention to this and not to allow the license
of crime, like a frenzy, to infect those who are as yet sound.
For when rewards attend the wicked, it is not at all easy
for anyone to be gratuitously virtuous. Or are you waiting
until Lepidus brings up his army again[13] and attacks the
City with sword and fire? And it is a much shorter step to
that state of affairs from the position in which he is now
operating than is the gap between harmonious peace and
civil warfare, which Lepidus has undertaken in defiance
of all that is human and divine, not in order to avenge a
wrong done to him personally or to those whom he pre-
tends to represent, but to overthrow our laws and our
liberty. For he is hounded and tormented in mind by ambition and dread of punishment, is devoid of purpose,
restless, trying now this, now that course of action. He
dreads tranquility, hates war; he sees that he must abstain

[13] Late in the previous year, 78, Lepidus had approached
Rome with his army and then withdrawn to the north, after negotiations (Gran. Lic. p. 35F)

carendum videt atque interim abutitur vostra socordia.
12 Neque mihi satis consili est, metum an ignaviam an de-
mentiam eam adpellem, qui videmini tanta mala quasi
fulmen optare se quisque ne adtingat, sed prohibere ne
conari quidem.

13 "Et, quaeso, considerate quam convorsa rerum natura
sit; antea malum publicum occulte, auxilia palam instrue-
bantur, et eo boni malos facile anteibant: nunc pax et concordia disturbantur palam, defenduntur occulte; quibus
14 illa placent in armis sunt, vos in metu. Quid expectatis, nisi
forte pudet aut piget recte facere ? An Lepidi mandata
animos movere? Qui placere ait sua quoique reddi et
aliena tenet, belli iura rescindi quom ipse armis cogat,
civitatem confirmari quibus ademptam negat, concordiae
gratia tribuniciam potestatem restitui, ex qua omnes discordiae adcensae.

15 "Pessume omnium atque inpudentissume, tibine eges-
tas civium et luctus curae sunt, quoi nihil est domi nisi
armis partum aut per iniuriam? Alterum consulatum petis,
quasi primum reddideris, bello concordiam quaeris quo

---

[14] As the next clause reveals, the point is that Lepidus does
not curtail these vices.

[15] Cf. fr. 49.18.

[16] I.e., reversing the consequences that followed from Sulla's
victory (cf. "the rights of peace," fr. 49.16).

[17] Cf. fr. 49.12: Sullan laws aimed at stripping Roman citizenship from some Italian communities had been virtually set aside
by the date of this speech (Cic. Dom. 79).

[18] Cf. S's criticism of the abuse of power by tribunes of the
plebs (Cat. 38.1).

from luxuriousness and lawlessness,[14] and meanwhile he [fr. 67] takes advantage of your lack of resolve. And I cannot adequately decide whether to call it apprehension or cowardice or madness on your part who seem to desire individually that such terrible evils may not touch each of you like a thunderbolt, but seem to make not the slightest effort to prevent them.

"Consider, please, how the natural order of things is inverted; formerly public disorder was prepared secretly, protection against it openly; and by this means, good men easily forestalled the wicked. Nowadays peace and harmony are disturbed openly, defended secretly; men who favor those circumstances are in arms; you are in dread. What are you waiting for, unless perhaps right conduct causes you to feel shame or disgust? Or is it the case that your hearts are moved by the directives of Lepidus? He asserts that he is in favor of having each person receive back his own property, and yet he keeps property belonging to others;[15] is in favor of rescinding the rights of war,[16] while he uses armed compulsion; is in favor of securing the citizenship of those from whom he denies it has been taken,[17] and for the sake of harmony to restore the power of the tribunes, which gave rise to all our discords.[18]

"O vilest and most shameless of all men, do you, who possess nothing in your house except products of arms or injustice, feel concern for the poverty and grief of the citizens? You strive after a second consulship, as if you had ever given up your first one; you seek harmony by means of war which is disturbing the harmony already attained—

parta disturbatur, nostri proditor, istis infidus, hostis omnium bonorum! Ut te neque hominum neque deorum
16 pudet, quos per fidem aut periurio violasti! Qui quando talis es, maneas in sententia et retineas arma te hortor, neu prolatandis seditionibus, inquies ipse, nos in sollicitudine adtineas. Neque te provinciae neque leges neque di penates civem patiuntur; perge qua coeptas⟨ti⟩,[8] ut quam maturrume merita invenias.

17   "Vos autem, patres conscripti, quo usque cunctando rem publicam intutam patiemini et verbis arma temptabitis? Dilectus advorsus vos habiti, pecuniae publice et privatim extortae, praesidia deducta atque inposita; ex lubidine leges imperantur, quom interim vos legatos et decreta paratis. Quanto mehercule avidius pacem petieritis, tanto bellum acrius erit, quom intelleget se metu magis quam
18 aequo et bono sustentatum. Nam qui turbas et caedem civium odisse ait et ob id armato Lepido vos inermos retinet, quae victis toleranda sunt ea, quom facere possitis, patiamini potius censet; ita illi a vobis pacem, vobis ab illo
19 bellum suadet. Haec si placent, si tanta torpedo animos obpressit,[9] ut obliti scelerum Cinnae, quoius in urbem

---

[8] *Steup (cf. Jug. 102.9)*

[9] haec . . . obpressit] *Non. p. 229M = 339L.4 [Chris. GL 1.86.12–13 = p. 109B.1, attests, without quoting, S.'s use of* torpedo]: obrepsit *L[2] Non.*

---

[19] The senate.

[20] The people whose injury Lepidus professed to be avenging by taking up arms (cf. §14).

[21] Lit., *penates,* presumably a reference to the *penates populi Romani,* which were housed in a shrine near the temple of Vesta, at the eastern end of the Roman Forum (Tac. *Ann.* 15.41.1) and

a traitor to us,[19] unfaithful to that constituency of yours,[20]   [fr. 67]
an enemy of all good citizens. How shameless you are
before both men and the gods, whom you have insulted
by your faithlessness or perjury! Since such is your character, I urge you to remain true to your purpose and to
retain your arms, and (granted that you yourself are restless) not to keep us in a state of anxiety by deferring your
rebellious plans. Neither the provinces, nor the laws, nor
the tutelary gods[21] tolerate you as a citizen. Proceed along
the path you have begun, so that you may meet with your
deserts as quickly as possible.

"But you, Members of the Senate, for how long will you
suffer the nation to be defenseless by your hesitation, will
you combat arms with words? Forces have been levied
against you, money extorted from the public coffers and
from individuals, garrisons removed and installed; laws
are being arbitrarily put into force, while you in the meantime are getting ready envoys and decrees. But, so help
me Hercules, the more eagerly you seek peace, the more
fierce the war will be, when he realizes that he has been
sustained more by your dread than the justice and righ-
teousness of his cause. For a person who professes hatred
for turmoil and the slaughter of citizens and on that account keeps you unarmed while Lepidus is in arms, is
proposing instead that you suffer what the conquered
must endure, although you have the ability to take action.
He urges from you peace toward Lepidus, and from him
war toward you. If you are in favor of this outcome—if
such torpor has numbed your spirits that forgetting the
crimes of Cinna, upon whose return to the City the flower

thought to be guardian gods brought to Italy by the Trojan hero
Aeneas (Serv. ad *Aen.* 3.148); cf. fr. 2.86.1.

reditu decus ordinis huius interiit, nihilo minus vos atque
coniuges et liberos Lepido permissuri sitis, quid opus de-
20   cretis, quid auxilio Catuli? Quin is et alii boni rem publicam frustra curant.

"Agite ut lubet, parate vobis Cethegi atque alia prodi-
torum patrocinia, qui rapinas et incendia instaurare cu-
piunt et rursus advorsum deos penatis manus armare. Sin
libertas et vera magis placent, decernite digna nomine et
21   augete ingenium viris fortibus. Adest novos exercitus, ad
hoc coloniae veterum militum, nobilitas omnis, duces op-
tumi; fortuna meliores sequitur; iam illa quae socordia
nostra[10] conlecta sunt, dilabentur.

22   "Quare ita censeo: quoniam ⟨M.⟩[11] Lepidus exercitum
privato consilio paratum cum pessumis et hostibus rei
publicae contra huius ordinis auctoritatem ad urbem ducit, uti Ap. Claudius interrex cum Q. Catulo pro consule
et ceteris, quibus imperium est, urbi praesidio sint ope-
ramque dent ne quid res publica detrimenti capiat."

[10] vostra *Dietsch*   [11] *Orelli*

---

[22] During the bloodletting of late 87, carried out by Cinna
when he regained his consulship by arms in alliance with the
exiled Marius.

[23] P. Cornelius Cethegus (pr. after 87?), a former supporter of
Marius, switched sides and acquired vast political power behind
the scenes under the new Sullan regime (Cic. *Parad.* 5.40). The
implication is that Cethegus, and men like him, will change sides
once more (hence styled "traitors") and serve as powerbrokers
under the tyranny of Lepidus.

[24] Here, as opposed to above in §16, the *deos penates* may be
standing by metonymy for the houses and property of which they
were the guardians, property that would be seized by the victors
from the rightful owners.

of this order perished,[22] you will none the less entrust to   [fr. 67]
Lepidus yourselves, as well as your wives and your children—what need is there of decrees? What need of Catulus' help? Surely it is in vain that he and other good citizens
are showing concern for the nation.

"Do as you please! Make ready for yourselves the patronage of Cethegus[23] and of other traitors, who are eager
to renew looting and arson and to arm their hands once
more against household gods.[24] But if you prefer liberty
and integrity, pass decrees worthy of your renown, and
strengthen the inclination of brave men. We have at our
disposal a fresh army, as well as colonies of veterans,[25] all
the nobles, and superb leaders. Fortune attends the better
cause;[26] soon those hostile forces which have gathered as
a result of our lack of resolve will melt away.

"Therefore this is my recommendation: inasmuch as
Marcus Lepidus, in defiance of the authority of this body
and in concert with the worst elements and the enemies
of the nation, is leading against the City an army raised on
his own authority, I propose that Appius Claudius the interrex,[27] with Quintus Catulus, the proconsul and others
who have military power, provide protection for the City
and see to it that no harm come to the nation."[28]

[25] See fr. 41.

[26] Fortune is proverbially said to favor the brave (Otto p. 144).

[27] Since no consuls had been elected for 77, the procedure
was to appoint one of the patricians (in this case an ex-consul of
79) to exercise supreme power. The office changed hands every
five days and lapsed when new consuls were finally elected.

[28] Cf. *Cat.* 29.2–3.

68 78M, 69Mc, 100D, 103K

numeroque praestans, privos ipse militiae

Arus. *GL* 7.503.4 = p. 240DC: to illustrate *privus* ["devoid" *OLD* 3] + gen.

69 79M, 70Mc, 50D, 52K

apud Mutinam

Prisc. *GL* 3.67.2: to illustrate the use of a prep. with the name of town instead of the locative.

70 80M, 68Mc, 107D, 115K

fugam maturabat

Arus. *GL* 7.492.24 = p. 199DC: to illustrate *maturare* + acc. of thing.

71* 82M, 71Mc, 51D, 54K

COSAS: civitas Tusciae, quae numero dicitur singulari secundum Sallustium.

Serv. ad *Aen.* 10.168.

68 78M, 69Mc, 100D, 103K

In early 77, Lepidus marched on Rome with a vast army to demand a second consulship (Plut. Pomp. 16.4; cf. Gran Lic. p. 35F).

excelling in number, yet devoid himself of military expertise

69 79M, 70Mc, 50D, 52K

Pompey deprived Lepidus of his province of Cisalpine Gaul by bringing about the surrender of Lepidus' legate M. Brutus (father of the future tyrannicide, M. Brutus, pr. 44) at Mutina (Plut. Pomp. 16.4–6).

at Mutina

70 80M, 68Mc, 107D, 115K

After returning from Cisalpine Gaul (see fr. 69), Pompey joined Q. Catulus (cos. 78) in defeating Lepidus in a battle near the Mulvian Bridge, putting him to flight (Flor. 2.11.6; cf. Exsuper. 6 [39Z]; App B Civ. 1.107).

he hastened his flight

71* 82M, 71Mc, 51D, 54K

After his defeat outside Rome (fr. 70), Lepidus withdrew to the north and embarked his forces from Etruria by way of the costal town Cosa (Rut. Namat. 1.297), fleeing to Sardinia (Liv. Per. 90).

COSAS: a Tuscan city whose name is singular [Cosa] *according to Sallust.*

72 81M, 72Mc, 109D, 117K

profectionem festinantes

Arus. *GL* 7.474.31 = p. 138DC: to illustrate *festinare* + acc. of thing.

DOMESTIC AFFAIRS (77 BC), FRR. 73–75

73* 84M, 73Mc, 54D, 56K

M. Lepido cum omnibus copiis Italia pulso, segnior neque minus gravis et multiplex cura patres exercebat.

Mar. Victor. *Rhet.* p. 205H.29: to illustrate a summing up in a narrative by the use of a verb in the third person.

{Sacerd. *GL* 6.458.1 (*Marco . . . segnior*): to illustrate a concessive abl. absol. without *tamen* to introduce the main clause; Serv. & Serv. auct. ad *Aen.* 1.630 (*segnior . . . cura*): to illustrate the carryover of a negative expressed only once but to be understood with a second member.}

74* 85M, 74Mc, inc. D, 68K

Ardebat omnis Hispania citerior.

Adnot. super Luc. 2.534: to illustrate the metaphorical use of *ardeo* to describe a region seething with war or revolt; Mar. Victor. *Rhet.* p. 158H.27 (without attribution to S.).

75 86M, 75Mc, 52D, 55K

Curionem quaesit,[1] uti adulescentior et a populi suffragiis integer aetati concederet Mamerci.

Prisc. *GL* 2.535.16: to illustrate pf. *quaesi,* instead of *quaesivi.*

[1] *G,* quaesivit *rell.*

72 81M, 72Mc, 109D, 117K

Possibly the same context as fr. 71.

hurrying their departure

DOMESTIC AFFAIRS (77 BC), FRR. 73–75

73* 84M, 73Mc, 54D, 56K

In 77, concern in Rome shifted to the war in Spain.

After the expulsion of Marcus Lepidus from Italy with all of his forces, a less immediate, but no less serious or complex concern occupied the senators.

74* 85M, 74Mc, inc. D, 68K

Widespread revolt of Spain under Sertorius.

All of Hither Spain was ablaze.

75 86M, 75Mc, 52D, 55K

Mam. Lepidus, who had suffered an earlier defeat for the consulship (Cic. Off. 2.58), was successful at the consular elections for 77 (postponed from 78 to the early months of 77 because of Lepidus' revolt) in part because C. Curio, the future consul of 76, stepped aside.

He [Catulus, Philippus, or some other senior member of the senate?] asked Curio to yield to the seniority of Mamercus, given the fact that he [Curio] was younger and had as yet suffered no electoral defeat.

SERTORIUS AND THE WAR IN SPAIN, FRR. 76–113

Early Career and Deeds of Sertorius, frr. 76–81

76* 88M, 77Mc, 55D, 57K

1 Magna gloria tribunus militum in Hispania T. Didio impe-
rante, magno usui bello Marsico paratu militum et armorum fuit, multaque tum ductu eius ⟨manu⟩[1]que patrata[2]
primo per ignobilitatem, deinde per invidiam scriptorum
⟨in⟩celebrata[3] sunt, quae vivos facie sua ostentabat ali-
2 quot adversis cicatricibus et effosso oculo. Quin[4] ille
dehonestamento corporis maxume laetabatur neque illis
anxius,[5] quia relicua gloriosius retinebat.

Gellius 2.27.2: cited as an example of a passage modeled on Demosthenes' description of the wounds, including the loss of an
eye, suffered by King Philip of Macedon (*De cor.* 67).

{Donat. ad Ter. *Eun.* 482 (*dehonestamento tamen . . . laetabatur*):
to illustrate scars as marks of prowess.}

[1] *Linker (cf. Plut. Sert. 4.3):* iussu *Hertz*   [2] *Dietsch:*
rapta *codd.:* peracta *Mähly*   [3] *Iac. Gronovius:* celata
Ciacconi   [4] *Dietsch:* quid *codd.*   [5] neque illis anxius]
transp. ante quin *Maurenbr.*

77* 89M, 78Mc, 56D, 58K

et[1] ei voce maxuma v⟨ehementer⟩ g⟨ratula . . . ⟩[2]

Donat. ad Ter. *An.* 939 and 946 (*et ei v. m. v. g.* [sic]): to illustrate
the meaning of *gratulor* in contrast with *gaudeo*.

[1] *om. ad An. 939*   [2] vehementer gratulabantur] *suppl.*
edd.

SERTORIUS AND THE WAR IN SPAIN,
FRR. 76–113

Early Career and Deeds of Sertorius, frr. 76–81

76* 88M, 77Mc, 55D, 57K

S. begins with a sketch of Sertorius' early career: glory won while serving under T. Didius (procos. of Hither Spain 97–93) and in the Social (Marsic) War of 91–87 (cf. Plut. Sert. 4.1–2).

With great distinction, he served as a military tribune in Spain, under the command of Titus Didius, and was of great service in the Marsic War by procuring troops and arms. Many accomplishments at that time both under his leadership and by his own hand(?) are unrecorded, first because of his humble birth, and next through the jealousy of writers; these achievements he displayed while alive by his outward appearance, by a number of frontal battle scars and a gouged-out eye. As a matter of fact, he took tremendous delight in that disfigurement of his body and was not troubled by those losses because with greater glory he preserved the remainder.[1]

[1] Plut. *Sert.* 4.4 attributes this same sentiment to Sertorius.

77* 89M, 78Mc, 56D, 58K

At about the time of his failed candidacy for the tribunate in 89 or 88, Sertorius was greeted by applause and shouts of praise when he entered the theater (Plut. Sert. 4.5).

and heartily congratulated him with a thunderous cry

78* 90M, 79Mc, inc. 76D, inc. 42K

Inter arma civilia aequi bonique famas petit.

Sen. *Ep.* 114.19: the historian L. Arruntius imitated S.'s idiosyn-
cratic use of the pl. *famae.*

79* 91M, 81Mc, 57D, 28K

Quoius advorsa voluntate conloquio militibus permisso,
conruptio facta paucorum, et exercitus Sullae datus est.

Donat. ad Ter. *Eun.* 467: citing fr. inc. 43 and this fragment to
illustrate *"convenire et conloqui"* in Terence, used in the sense
of a parley.

80* 92M, 80Mc, 57D, 28K

 quoi nisi pariter obviam iretur

Donat. ad Ter. *Eun.* 92: to illustrate *pariter = similiter.*

81* 93M, 82Mc, 59D, K

 Hispaniam sibi antiquam patriam esse

Serv. & Serv. auct. ad *Aen.* 1.380 and ad *Aen.* 3.297 (om. *antiquam*): to illustrate that it is not normal to designate a region/
province, as opposed to a state (*civitas*), as a *patria* (homeland).

78* 90M, 79Mc, inc. 76D, inc. 42K

Sertorius took no part in the excesses perpetrated in the turmoil after the victory of Cinna and Marius in 87/86 BC (Plut. Sert. 5.6).

Amid the civil conflict, he seeks the repute of a just and decent man.

79* 91M, 81Mc, 57D, 28K

In 83, Sertorius opposed allowing the soldiers in the armies of the consul Scipio and Sulla to fraternize (vetante Sertorio colloquia, *Exsuper. 7 [45Z]; Plut. Sert. 6.3–4); cf. fr. 31.*

And when, contrary to his desire, the soldiers were given an opportunity for conversation, corruption of a few occurred, and the army was given over to Sulla.

80* 92M, 80Mc, 57D, 28K

After the desertion of the consul Scipio's army to Sulla in 83 (see previous fragment) and the election of Cn. Carbo and the younger Marius (cf. fr. 32) to the consulship of 82, Sertorius expressed the view that "unless decisive resistance was offered to Sulla, all would be lost and the war effort would fail" (cui nisi obviam iretur, actum iam ac debellatum foret, *Exsuper. 8 [50Z]).*

and unless resistance was offered to him in a like manner [equalling Sulla's purposeful valor]

81* 93M, 82Mc, 59D, K

Possibly words uttered by Sertorius in indirect discourse to win the support of the Spaniards, by alluding to his long-standing connection with the region (see fr. 76). Servius, to whom we owe this fragment, states that the words were used metaphorically (ad laudem . . . non ad veritatem).

that Spain was his ancient native land

81 BC: Expulsion of Sertorius from Spain,
frr. 82–90

82 97M, 86Mc, 108D, 116K

paucos saltum insidentis

Arus. *GL* 7.480.16 = p. 156DC: to illustrate *insido* + acc.

83* 95M, 85Mc, deest in D et K

qui forte propter amorem historiarum Sallustii **Calpurnius** *cognomento* **Lanarius** *sit*

Hieron. *Ep.* 70.6.2: an often repeated pseudonym coined by
Jerome for his adversary Rufinus (cf. *Ep.* 102.3.1, *Calpurnius
cognomento Lanarius; adv. Rufin.* 1.30, *Sallustianus Calpurnius*).

84* 96M, 84Mc, deest in D et K

Salinator in agmine occiditur.

Comm. Bern. ad Luc. 1.478: defining the expression *"in agmine
esse"* as meaning one who is making a journey/march.

81 BC: Expulsion of Sertorius from Spain,
frr. 82–90

82 97M, 86Mc, 108D, 116K

When in the spring of 81 Sulla dispatched C. Annius as proconsul to govern one, or probably both Spains (MRR 3.15), with the charge to expel Sertorius, Sertorius sent his legate Livius (called Julius by Plut.) Salinator with six thousand men to block the passes in Pyrenees and so prevent C. Annius from crossing into Spain (Plut. Sert. 7.1).

a few men [a detachment of Salinator's soldiers?] occupying a defile

83* 95M, 85Mc, not included in D and K

Same context as fr. 82. P. Calpurnius Lanarius was an officer on Annius' staff in 81 (MRR 3.46), who found a way to turn the pass occupied by Sertorius' forces. Plut. (Sert. 7.3) mistakenly identifies Lanarius as a traitor among the blockading Sertorian forces.

a man who, perhaps on account of his fondness for *Sallust's* Histories, might be *a* **Calpurnius** *with* **Lanarius** as his cognomen

84* 96M, 84Mc, not in D and K

Same context as frr. 82–83. According to Plut. (Sert. 7.3), Salinator died at the hands of Lanarius.

Salinator is killed while on the march.

85 98M, 87Mc, 60D, K

earum aliae paululum[1] progressae nimio simul et incerto[2] onere, quom pavor corpora agitaverat, deprimebantur

Gell. 10.26.10; Non. p. 453M = 726L.4–6: S. employs *progressus* to describe the motion of vessels, specifically *scaphae* (skiffs) in the passage above.

[1] paulum *Non.*   [2] nimio progressae †inter cum sicco† *Non.*

86* 99M, 88Mc, inc. 35D, inc. 1K

Quom Sertorius[1] neque[2] erumpere, tam[3] levi copia, navibus[4]

Serv. auct. ad *Aen.* 2.564: to illustrate *copia* in the sing. having the meaning *exercitus.*

[1] com Sertorios *codd.*   [2] nequiret *Schoell*   [3] erumpere tam] *Kritz*: rumperet an *codd.*   [4] copia navibus] *Putschius*: copiam avibus *codd.*: <se commisit> *suppl. Schoell.* post navibus

87††† 103M, 89Mc, inc. 94D, inc. 63K

more[1] humanae cupidinis ignara visendi

Gell. 9.12.22 (assigned to S. without specifying title of work); Non. p. 129M = 188L.20 (assigned in error to *Jug.;* Non. otherwise seems to draw upon Gell.): to illustrate *ignarus* in the sense "unknown" (*OLD* 3), as opposed to "ignorant" (*OLD* 1).

[1] *Gell.*: amore *Non.*

85 98M, 87Mc, 60D, K

*After being expelled from Spain by C. Annius and fleeing to Mau-
retania in 81, Sertorius returned later in the year, and in alliance
with Cilician pirates, he briefly occupied one of the Pityussae islands (lying southwest of the Balearics, off the east coast of Spain).
C. Annius arrived with a substantial force to expel him, and Sertorius fought a sea battle despite having only light ships not built
for combat (Plut. Sert. 7.5–7).*

> some of them [the skiffs], after advancing a little,
> began to sink as a result of too much unstable weight
> when panic had caused the passengers to shift about

86* 99M, 88Mc, inc. 35D, inc. 1K

*Same context as fr. 85: in the sea battle, foul weather prevented
Sertorius' light ships from escaping onto the open sea, and hostile
forces prevented a landing (Plut. loc. cit.).*

When Sertorius ‹was able?› neither to sally forth from his
ships, owing to his forces being so light-armed,[1] ‹nor escape onto the high sea owing to a storm?›

[1] Text uncertain; this is the meaning of *levi copia* at Tac. *Ann.*
2.52.4, the only other instance of this expression in classical Latin.
As interpreted, S. related the two difficulties experienced by Sertorius in the reverse order from Plutarch's.

87††† 103M, 89Mc, inc. 94D, inc. 63K

*After fleeing from the battle described in frr. 85–86, Sertorius
sailed to the southwest coast of Spain, just beyond the Strait of
Gibraltar, and met with sailors who brought back tales of far-
away, Atlantic islands called Isles of the Blessed (Plut. Sert. 8.2).*

> with the customary human desire to visit unknown
> places

88† 100M, 90Mc, 61D, K

Quas[1] duas insulas, propinquas inter se et decem ‹milia›[2] stadium procul a Gadibus sitas, constabat suopte ingenio alimenta mortalibus gignere.

Non. p. 495M = 795L.40 (assigned to "lib. XI," corr. "I" edd.): to illustrate *–um* standing for gen. pl. *–orum*.

　　[1] *Roth*: cuius *codd*.　　　[2] *Mercier (cf. Plut. Sert. 8.2, as measured from Africa)*

89* 101M, 91Mc, 62D, K

Secundum philosophos Elysium est **Insulae Fortunatae** *quas ait Sallustius* **inclitas** *esse* **Homeri carminibus**.

Serv. & Serv. auct. ad *Aen.* 5.735.

90 102M, 92Mc, 61D, K

Traditur fugam in Oceani longinqua agitavisse.

Serv. auct. ad *Aen.* 2.640: to illustrate *agito = dispono* or *cogito;* Anon. *brev. expos. Verg. G.* 2.197 (assigned to Book 1): to illustrate *longinquus = porro sita* (situated far off).

{Ps.-Acro ad Hor. *Epod.* 16.41, *Insulae Fortunatae, ad quas Sallustius* [sic] *in historia dicit victum voluisse ire Sertorium.*}

88† 100M, 90Mc, 61D, K

Same context as fr. 87. Location of the Isles of the Blessed. The description of the climate suggests identification with the two largest islands of the Madeira Archipelago (Porto Santo and Madeira), the former being ca. 750 miles (roughly 6,500 stades) from Gades (mod. Cádiz).

And it was held that those two neighboring islands, located 10,000 stades from Gades, produced of their own accord nourishment for mortals.

89* 101M, 91Mc, 62D, K

Same context as fr. 87. Isles of the Blessed identified with Homer's Elysium (Plut. Sert. 8.5).

According to philosophers, Elysium is identical with of the **Isles of the Blessed***, which Sallust states are* **celebrated in Homer's verses** *[Od. 4.563–68]*

90 102M, 92Mc, 61D, K

Kritz, followed by Dietsch, joined fr. 88 to this one as its continuation, retaining the paradosis cuius *in fr. 88, which will have* Oceani *here as its antecedent. Plut., however, first describes separately, in language closely resembling fr. 88, the two islands (Sert. 8.2–3) and somewhat later (9.1) mentions that Sertorius contemplated withdrawal there.*

According to tradition, he contemplated flight to distant regions of the Ocean.

80 BC: Beginning of the Sertorian War, frr. 91–98

91* 94M, 83Mc, inc. 79D, inc. 45K

Modico quoque[1] et eleganti[2] imperio percarus fuit.

Adnot. super Luc. 7.267: to illustrate the meaning of *modicum* = *cum modo viventem* (living with moderation).

[1] modico quoque] *ARV*: modicoque *W*
[2] diligenti *Dietsch*: clementi *Roth*

92 104M, 93Mc, 65D, 64K

Itaque Sertorius, levi praesidio relicto in Mauretania, nanctus obscuram noctem aestu secundo furtim aut celeritate vitare proelium in transgressu conatus est.

Gell. 10.26.2: reporting Asinius Pollio's criticism of S. for using *transgredior* (in preference to the *transfretare,* which is, in fact, post-Augustan) to describe a crossing of a strait by ship.

{Non. p. 453M = 726L.1–3 (*nactus . . . secundo*): drawing on Gellius; *transgressus* of a crossing by ship.}

93 105M, 94Mc, 66D, 65K

80 BC: Beginning of the Sertorian War, frr. 91–98

91* 94M, 83Mc, inc. 79D, inc. 45K

The reputation of Sertorius as a fair-minded and capable com-
mander caused the Lusitanians to summon him to return to Spain
from Mauretania—to which he had withdrawn in 81—to lead
a revolt against the Romans in 80 (Plut. Sert. 10.1–5, 11.1). Mau-
renbr. and McGushin, by contrast, assign this fragment to 82 BC,
when Sertorius first arrived in Spain and won the loyalty of the
Spaniards by his moderate administration (Exsuper. 8 [51Z]:
modeste tuendo atque blandiendo . . . ut et carus esset).

He was very much beloved as a result also of his temperate
and refined manner of command.

92 104M, 93Mc, 65D, 64K

Same context as fr. 91: describing Sertorius' crossing of the Strait
of Gibraltar.

And so Sertorius, having left a light-armed garrison in
Mauretania, took advantage of a dark night with a favorable tide and tried by means of stealth or speed to avoid a
battle in his crossing.

93 105M, 94Mc, 66D, 65K

Gell. and Non. state that this fragment was found slightly later in
the same passage from which they quoted fr. 92. According to Plut.
(Sert. 12.2), Sertorius arrived in Lusitania with 2,600 Romans
and 700 Libyans.

Transgressos omnis recipit mons * * *[1] praeceptus a Lusi-
tanis.

Gell. 10.26.3; Non. p. 453M = 726L.3–4: a further example in the
discussion reported under fr. 92.

{Serv. & Serv. auct. ad *Aen.* 1.518 (*transgressos . . . mons Balleia*):
to illustrate how the modifier *transgressos* limits the otherwise
open-ended meaning of *omnis*.}

   [1] *om. Gell., Non.*: Balleia *Ta Serv.*: belleia *(corr) Pa*: palleia *A*:
tralaeta *N*: talet *PbM*

94   106M, 97Mc, 87D, K

gens[1] raro egressa finis suos

Arus. *GL* 7.469.28 = p. 119DC; Serv. & Serv. auct. ad *Aen.* 2.713:
to illustrate *egredior* + acc.

   [1] *om. Serv. et Serv. auct.*

95   108M, 95Mc, 68D, K

et mox Fufidius adveniens cum legionibus, postquam tam ⟨al⟩tas ripas,[1] unum[2] haud facilem
pugnantibus vadum, cuncta hosti quam suis oppor-
tuniora videt,

Non. p. 231M = 343L.22–24: to illustrate the masc. *vadus,*
instead of neut. *vadum.*

{Charis. *GL* 1.34.9 + corr. 607 = p. 37B.21–22 (*unum . . . vadum*):
to illustrate sing., in contrast with neut. pl. *vada*.}

   [1] tam altas ripas] *Mauren.*: tantas spiras *codd.*: tantas asperi-
tates *Junius*: tantas copias *Dietsch*: cautes asperas *Quicherat*
   [2] *om. Non.*

A mountain * * * ,[1] which had been occupied in advance by the Lusitanians, received [as a place of refuge] all who had crossed.

[1] The name is not found in the quotation by Gellius and Nonius. The probable landing place of Sertorius was B(a)elo (Belon), a town in Spain just west of the Strait of Gibraltar (Strabo 3.1.8, p. 140; Plin. *HN* 5.2). Possibly the corruptions in Servius' version of the fragment arose under the influence of Aemilius Asper, the second-century AD commentator on S.

94 106M, 97Mc, 87D, K

Possibly referring to the seven hundred Libyan followers of Sertorius (Plut. Sert. 12.2).

a people who had seldom left their own territory

95 108M, 95Mc, 68D, K

Shortly after Sertorius crossed over from Mauretania in 80, as reported in frr. 92–93, Fufidius, the governor of Farther Spain (see fr. 49.21n.), was defeated by Sertorius on the banks of the river Baetis (Plut. Sert. 12.4).

Fufidius, soon arriving with his legions, after he saw the terribly steep banks,[1] the one ford by no means easy for combatants, all conditions more advantageous for the enemy than for his own forces,

[1] See textual note. The paradosis *tantas spiras* (such large masses/units of troops) presumes a meaning for *spira* attested elsewhere in Classical Latin only in Ennius (*Ann.* fr. 510V).

96 111M, 96Mc, 69D, 71K

Domitium proconsulem ex citeriore Hispania cum omnibus copiis, quas paraverat, arcessivit.

Prisc. *GL* 2.534.21: to illustrate verbs in *–so* that form the pf. in *–ivi*.

97 107M, 98Mc, 67D, 66K

Ac per omnem provinciam magnae atque atro‹ces fa-mae›[1] ‹erant›,[2] quom ex suo quisque terrore quinquaginta aut amplius hostium milia, novas inmanis f‹ormas fluctibus›[3] Oceani | ac*cit*as,[4] corporibus hominum | vescentis[5] contenderent. | . . . a Domiti‹o› . . . ovi . . | i . ios . . . cog. . . . . |m. . . . . .

Schol. Veron. ad *Aen.* 4.178 (*Ac per . . . contenderent*) "*in primo Historiarum*": to illustrate S.'s use of the pl. of *fama* (cf. fr. 78), in contrast with the sing. in Virgil.

Cod. P. Vindob. L 117 recto column 1, lines 1–5 (ac*cit*as . . . *a Domitio . . . m* . . .). This fragment and fr. 98 are preserved on a part of a bifolium that once belonged to a fourth-century parchment codex written in rustic capitals, having two columns of twenty-six lines each to a page; column 2 of recto and column 1 of verso are missing. The symbol "|" marks the divisions of the lines in the manuscript, while italics signifies that transcription is uncertain.

[1] *Keil*

[2] *Maurenbr.*: ibant *Keil*

[3] *Keil*: f‹ormas e finibus› *Maurenbr.*: *lacuna in* Schol. Veron.

[4] *cod. Vindob.*: . . puls . . . cod. Schol. Veron.: ‹ap›puls‹as› *Maurenbr.*

[5] *cod. Vindob.*: vesci *Schol. Veron.*

96 111M, 96Mc, 69D, 71K

After his defeat, Fufidius summoned help from M. Domitius Calvinus (pr. 81, MRR 3.84), governor of the adjoining province of Hither Spain (Plut. Sert. 12.4).

He summoned the proconsul Domitius from Nearer Spain with all the forces Domitius had raised.

97 107M, 98Mc, 67D, 66K

The reference to Domitius (governor of Hither Spain, see previous fragment) in the portion of this fragment preserved on the recto of the leaf of the Vienna codex permits this text to be placed in the context of the one that precedes. The fearsome enemy is presumably the Libyans, who crossed over with Sertorius from Mauretania (cf. frr. 92–94; Plut. Sert. 12.2).

And throughout the whole province there were tall and grim tales, since each person, according to his own alarm, insisted that were fifty thousand or more of the enemy, beings of huge and strange aspect that had been brought ashore by the waves of the Ocean and who fed upon human flesh. * * * by Domitius * * *

98 136M (Non. et Donat.), 100Mc, 88D (Non.) et inc. 34D (Donat.), 88K (Non. et Donat.)

1 . . . |vere equis armisque minus | aliquanto tamen quam | metu concedebatur, nisi qui|a Domitium a*d*stantem *et* | quos noscitabat or*a*ntem | ‹ne arma›[1] et se duce‹m›[2] . . . ‹h›ostilb‹us›[3] . . ‹da›rent[4] cum pos.m | [±6]*e* interfec*ere* *pars* | [±7] ‹leg›ato[5] . Septi|mio .c.c . . s . . i . . olaec . . no| *ate*. . . . erat *ex* . . . stra per|c*u*‹ss›*it*. [6]

2 *Hic*[7] vero formidine | quasi[8] adtonitus neque ani|mo neque auribus[9] aut lin|gua satis[10] conpetere at . . . | ‹omni mod›o[11] intentus qua vi|‹a›[12] [±7]s erat exsanguis | [±8] iebria et *r* . . . | [±3/4]um se adpella*b*‹at›[13] | [±5] ‹d›iebus qu*at*‹tuor›[14] . . . | [6 lines missing]

Cod. P. Vindob. L 117 verso column 2, lines 1–20. See above on fr. 97. The symbol "|" marks the divisions of the lines in the manuscript, while italics indicates that transcription is uncertain.

{Non. p. 276M = 424L.15 (§2 *sic* [for *hic*] . . . *conpetere*) "*Historiarum lib. I*": to illustrate *conpetere* meaning "to have one's wits about one"; Donat. ad Ter. *Ad.* 310 (§2 *neque animo . . . conpetere*): to illustrate the opposite of *compos animi* and identifying Septimius (septimo *codd.*) as the person being described.}

[1] *conieci*　　　[2–4] *Bloch*　　　[5] *Bischoff*　　　[6] *Bloch*　　　[7] *cod. Vindob.*: sic *Non.*　　　[8] formidine quasi] *cod. Vindob. (cf. Jug. 72.2)*: quasi formidine *Non.*　　　[9] neque auribus *om. Donat.*　　　[10] *om. Non.*: lin‹gua sati›s *cod. Vindob.*　　　[11–14] *Bloch*

98 136M (Non. et Donat.), 100Mc, 88D (Non.) et inc.
34D (Donat.), 88K (Non. et Donat.)

*The text of this fragment, preserved on the verso of the leaf from
the Vienna codex, provides a continuation of the narrative contained in fr. 97 after a gap of more than two columns (= ca. 30±5
lines of OCT text) and reports of the death of M. Domitius Calvinus, the governor of Nearer Spain. He was killed in 80, while
fighting Sertorian forces commanded by Sertorius' quaestor L.
Hirtuleius (Liv. Per. 90. Plut. Sert. 12.4; Flor. 2.10.6). The Septimius referred to in the passage and mentioned by Donatus in
connection with the portion of the text he preserves may have been
Domitius' legate.*

. . . they were on the point of falling back, somewhat less
on account of the horses and arms [of enemy] than out of
fear, except that Domitius standing close by and begging
those whom he recognized ‹not to give their arms› and
himself, their commander, to the enemy . . . they killed . . .
‹It fell?› to his legate Septimius . . . ‹to take charge?›. . . .
. . . [he] pierced.

But he [Septimius], as though dumbstruck, was not
sufficiently in control of his reason or his hearing or speech
. . . with all of his attention on how ‹he could extricate
himself and his army from danger?› . . . he was pale with
fright[1] . . . he called himself ‹wretched?› . . . ‹and died?›
. . . within four days . . .

[1] Or "he had lost a lot of blood," if *percu‹ss›it* is adopted in
the last line of the preceding paragraph and describes Septimius
being wounded.

79–78 BC: Military Operations of Metellus Pius in Farther Spain, frr. 99–113

99 110M, 101Mc, 70D, K

et numeri eorum Metellus per litteras gnarus

Arus. *GL* 7.476.18 = p. 143DC: to illustrate *gnarus* + gen.

100 112M, 102Mc, 86D, K

Illo profectus vicos castellaque incendere et fuga culto-
rum deserta igni vastare, neque late[1] aut †fetustissimus†,[2]
metu gentis ad furta belli peridoneae.

Non. p. 310M = 483–84L.11: to illustrate the noun *furtum* =
insidiae.

{Serv. ad *Aen.* 11.515 (*gens . . . peridonea* [sic]): *furta = insidiae.*}

[1] *Gerlach ed. min.*: elate *codd.*   [2] securus nimis *Müller*:
fretus simul a *Roth*: fretus se nimis *Frassinetti-di Salvo*: festinus
nimis *Garbugino*

101 113M, 106Mc, 75D, 74K

et Diponen, validam urbem, multos dies restantem,
pugnando vicit

Non. p. 526M = 845L.12: to illustrate the acc. of duration of time.

*79–78 BC: Military Operations of Metellus Pius in
Farther Spain, frr. 99–113*

99 110M, 101Mc, 70D, K

*By late 80, after the defeats of Fufidius and Domitius (frr. 95–98),
word of the growing size of Sertorius' forces in Lusitania (Farther
Spain) must have reached Rome.*

and Metellus, ⟨made?⟩ aware of their number
through a dispatch

100 112M, 102Mc, 86D, K

*This fragment, which is identified as coming from Book 1, may
describe Metellus' tactics early in his proconsulship, since Frontinus' description of the facility of light-armed Spaniards at laying
an ambush (Str. 2.5.31, "aptissimos ad furta bellorum") bears a
striking verbal resemblance to S.*

Setting out from there, he burned villages and strongholds, and with fire laid waste to regions deserted owing
to the flight of the cultivators, not far afield or * * * out of
his fear of a people very adept at snares of war.

101 113M, 106Mc, 75D, 74K

*Dipo, a town on the Anas River, ca. thirty-five miles west of Metel-
linum (mod. Medellín), a base of operations utilized by Metellus,
may have been an early target of his strategy aimed at reducing
strongholds in Lusitania (see preceding fragment).*

and he overcame by warfare the strong city of Dipo
despite its holding out for many days

102* 119M, 108Mc, inc. 70D, inc. 36K

Ille Conisturgim apud legiones[1] venit.

Pomp. *GL* 5.273.11: to illustrate the rare use of *apud* with a verb of motion (*OLD* 2). Pomp. states that the second-century AD commentator Asper defended S.'s choice of *apud* on the grounds that the prepositional phrase defines Conisturgis as the place where the legions were stationed.

[1] apud legiones] caput regionis *Pecere*

103* 115M, 103Mc, 71D, 37K

iam repente visus lenire[1] Tagus

Serv. auct. ad *Aen.* 10.103: to illustrate the description of a change in the world of nature.

[1] *Thilo*: lanire *F*: saevire *Daniel*

104* 114M, 107Mc, inc. 68D, inc. 34K

Lusitaniae gravem civitatem

Serv auct. ad *Aen.* 12.458: to illustrate *gravis = fortis.*

105* 120M, 104Mc, inc. 42D, inc. 8K

Consedit in valle virgulta nemorosaque.

Serv. auct. ad *Aen.* 3.516: to illustrate the adj. *virgultus* (covered with brushwood), in place of *virgultosus* (unattested in Classical Latin).

102* 119M, 108Mc, inc. 70D, inc. 36K

The precise location of Conisturgis is unknown, but it was in the territory of the Cunei (Conii), a Lusitanian people living south of the Tagus River in Hispania Ulterior, in a region of modern southwest Portugal (App. Hisp. 57). Hence it may have been mentioned in connection with one of Metellus' campaigns.

He came to Conisturgis, where the legions were.[1]

[1] Asper thus glossed the text, which may already have been corrupt in the second century. The conjecture *caput regionis* produces an appositive: "Conisturgis, the chief city of the region."

103* 115M, 103Mc, 71D, 37K

The reference in this fragment to the Tagus (mod. Tajo), a river in Metellus' province of Farther Spain, one that flowed into the Atlantic at Olisipo (mod. Lisbon), suggests that the text was part of a description of a military operation in the Sertorian War that was affected by a sudden change in the intensity of the river's flow.

now suddenly the Tagus seemed to abate

104* 114M, 107Mc, inc. 68D, inc. 34K

Possibly the same context as fr. 103 and describing fighting near Olisipo (mod. Lisbon).

a mighty (or "important") city of Lusitania

105* 120M, 104Mc, inc. 42D, inc. 8K

During the course of Metellus' campaign against the Langobrigae in the northwest of the Iberian Peninsula (Plut. Sert. 13.7–12), modern Portugal, Sertorius concealed three thousand men in a shady gully to lay an ambush for Metellus' legate Aquinus, who had been sent to forage (ibid. §11).

He took up a position in a wooded and leafy valley.

106 121M, 105Mc, 95D, 97K

neque se recipere aut instruere proelio quivere

Prisc. *GL* 2.539.20: to illustrate the pf. of *queo.*

107 135M, 109Mc, 71D, 69K

Iussu Metelli[1] cornicines occanuere[2] tubis.[3]

Prisc. *GL* 2.529.5 (*"in I historiarum"*); Diom. *GL* 1.374.1 (*"in prima historiarum"*); *Gloss. Vatic.* p. 86M: to illustrate the pf. *occanui* of the compound verb *occano* (of trumpets/trumpeters "to sound a call").

(cf. fr. dub. 12, *cornua occanuerunt.*)

[1] Metelli Celeris *Gloss. Vatic.*   [2] occanere *Diom.*
[3] *om. Prisc., Diom.*

108 116M, 110Mc, 92 et inc. 113D, 94 et inc. 80K

sanctus alias[1] et ingenio validus

Charis. *GL* 1.194.22 = p. 253B.2: an example of *alias = aliter* (see fr. 52)

{Serv. auct. ad *Aen.* 3.594 (*sanctus alia*): to illustrate a Greek acc. [of respect] with adj. *sanctus.*}

[1] alia *(acc. pl.) Serv.*

109 118M, 111Mc, 99D, 101K

neque detrusus aliquotiens terretur[1]

Prisc. *GL* 3.78.25: to illustrate the suffix *–iens.*

[1] deterretur *codd. deteriores*

106 121M, 105Mc, 95D, 97K

*Possibly the same context as fr. 105: Aquinus' troops were thrown
into confusion.*

and they were unable to pull back or marshal themselves for battle

107 135M, 109Mc, 71D, 69K

*Some action in the Sertorian War, as can be surmised from the
reference to Metellus and the assignment to Book 1. The identification of Metellus as "Metellus Celer" in the glossator, a late
source, is not to be trusted.*

At the command of Metellus, the horn-blowers gave a
sudden blast with their trumpets.

108 116M, 110Mc, 92 et inc. 113D, 94 et inc. 80K

*This description could have been applied to Metellus (so Mau-
renbr.) or Sertorius (Büchner; cf. fr. 78). "Alias" indicates that
somewhat before, or after, these words S. criticized some short-
coming.*

a man irreproachable in other respects and of a
sound disposition

109 118M, 111Mc, 99D, 101K

*Possibly a description of Sertorius' resiliency in carrying on gue-
rilla warfare despite setbacks.*

and though driven off a number of times, he is not
frightened off

110* 125M, 2.70Mc, 1.73D, 2.20K

traxit autem hoc de Celtiberorum more, qui, ut in Sallustio legimus, . . . **se regibus** *devovent et post eos vitam refutant*.

Serv. ad *G* 4.218: to illustrate the devotion of bees to their monarch by means of an example taken from the world of man.

111 126M, 112Mc, 74D, 73K

Sertorius, portis[1] turbam morantibus[2] et nullo, ut in terrore solet,[3] generis aut imperi discrimine, per calonum corpora ad medium quasi,[4] deinsuper adstantium[5] manibus in murum adtollitur.

Non. p. 282M = 435L.23: to illustrate the word *discrimen* = *separatio*, from *discerno;* Non. p. 530M = 851L.26: to illustrate the adv. *deinsuper* (a hapax), = *desuper* (from above).

{*Sallustius . . . Sertorium umeris sublatum per muros ascendisse commemorat* (Serv. ad *Aen.* 9.555).}

[1] *Mercier*: fortis *codd. p. 282M*: partis *codd. p. 530M* [2] turbam morantibus] *Mercier*: turba morantibus *codd. p. 282M*: turbam orantibus *codd. p. 530M* [3] semet *codd. p. 530M* [4] evasit *Mercier* [5] deinsuper adstantium] deinsuper stantium *codd. p. 530M*: dein supera stantium *Müller*

112 122M, 113Mc, 72D, K

110* 125M, 2.70Mc, 1.73D, 2.20K

As a preface to his account of a heroic rescue of Sertorius by his companions after the fall of a town, which closely resembles the circumstances in the next fragment, which is assigned to Book 1, Plutarch (Sert. 14.5; cf. Val. Max. 2.6.11) mentions the commitment of the Celtiberians to share the death of their commanders in battle.

He [Virgil] took this from the practice of the Celtiberians, who, as we read in Sallust, **consecrate themselves to their kings and refuse to outlive them**.

111 126M, 112Mc, 74D, 73K

Iberian attendants rescued Sertorius from capture, after the fall of a town (Plut. Sert. 14.6). Servius (ad Aen. 9.555), without giving the context, paraphrases S.'s account: "Sertorius was lifted up on the shoulders of his men and mounted the walls."

While the gates were slowing down the crowd and there was, as usual in a panic, no distinction of class or authority, Sertorius was raised up to about the midpoint of the wall on the shoulders of his attendants, then onto the wall by the hands of those standing close by, from up above.[1]

---

[1] Text uncertain and probably corrupt; see textual notes.

112 122M, 113Mc, 72D, K

In 78 BC, L. Manlius (pr. 79?), the governor of Transalpine Gaul, together with three legions and 1,500 cavalry, suffered defeat at the hands of Sertorius' proquaestor Hirtuleius in Nearer Spain and took refuge in the town of Ilerda (mod. Lérida) with the few survivors (Oros. 5.23.4; cf. Plut. Sert. 12.5). This fragment may describe either a place of temporary refuge occupied by Manlius' defeated troops prior to escaping to Ilerda (cf. Jug. 38.7) or an

occupatusque collis editissumus apud Ilerdam[1] et[2]
eum multa opera[3] circumdata[4]

Arus. *GL* 7.460.6 = p. 85DC: to illustrate a "thing" (*re‹s›*) *circumdata* + accusative, but the text of Arus. may be corrupt.

{Prisc. *GL* 3.66.21 (*apud . . . circumdata*): to illustrate the use of a prep. with the name of a town.}

[1] apud Ilerdam] *om. Arus.*   [2] *om. Prisc.*   [3] multa opera] multo opere *Dietsch*   [4] circumdat *Parrhasius*

113 124M, 114Mc, 77D, 76K

Illum raptis[1] forum in[2] castra nautica Sertorius mutaverat.

Pomp. *GL* 5.163.6 {Non. p. 206M = 304L.18 (*illum . . . forum*)}: to illustrate the masc. noun *forus* having the same meaning as *forum* (neut.).

[1] nautis *Non.*   [2] *Frassinetti:* et *codd.*

COMMENCEMENT OF THE PIRATE WAR IN CILICIA (78–77 BC), FRR. 114–18

114* 127M, 115Mc, 78D, 77K

Itaque Servilius aegrotum Tarenti collegam prior transgressus

Prisc. *GL* 3.64.19: to illustrate the gen. (= loc.) *Tarenti,* to express place where.

outpost or camp established by Hirtuleius in the face of the superior number of Manlius' forces.

a very lofty hill near Ilerda was seized, and many defensive works were placed round about it[1]

[1] Or, reading *multo opere circumdat* (see textual notes): "he enclosed it with great effort."

113 124M, 114Mc, 77D, 76K

In 78/77 BC, Sertorius established a naval base on the east coast of Spain, near the promontory Dianium (Strabo 3.4.6, p. 159; cf. Cic. 2 Verr. 1.87, 5.146).

Sertorius had converted that marketplace for plunder into a naval base.

COMMENCEMENT OF THE PIRATE WAR IN CILICIA (78–77 BC), FRR. 114–18

114* 127M, 115Mc, 78D, 77K

In 78, P. Servilius Vatia (cos. 79) and his consular colleague Ap. Claudius Pulcher left for their provinces in the East. Possibly the verb reliquit *(left behind) formed the predicate (so Maurenbr.).*

And so Servilius crossing over first <left behind?> his ill colleague at Tarentum

115* 130M, 116Mc, 2.32D, K

Lyciae Pisidiaeque agros despectantem

Serv. & Serv. auct. ad *Aen.* 1.420: to illustrate *despectare* (to look down upon), used to describe the view from an elevation.

116 129M, 117Mc, 79D, K

ad Olympum atque Phaselida

Prisc. *GL* 3.66.19: to illustrate a prep. with the name of town to express place to (frr. 116–17), at (frr. 118–19), and from which (fr. 120).

117 131M, 118Mc, deest in D et K

ad Corycum

Prisc. *GL* 3.66.20: see fr. 116.

118 132M, 119Mc, deest in D et K

apud Corycum

Prisc. *GL* 3.66.20: see fr. 116.

WAR IN MACEDONIA AND THRACE (77 BC), FRR. 119–20

119 133M, 120Mc, 81D, 81K

apud Lete oppidum

Prisc. *GL* 3.66.21: see fr. 116.

115* 130M, 116Mc, 2.32D, K

Strabo (14.5.7, p. 671) so describes the prospect as seen from Olympus, the town and mountain stronghold of the pirate chieftain Zenicetes, in eastern Lycia.

looking down upon the fields of Lycia and Pisidia

116 129M, 117Mc, 79D, K

The coastal towns of Olympus and Phaselis in Lycia were subdued by Servilius in his campaign against the pirate chieftain Zenicetes (Cic. 2 Verr. 4.21; Strabo 14.5.7, p. 671).

to Olympus and Phaselis

117 131M, 118Mc, not included in D and K

A coastal town of Lycia near Olympus (Strabo 14.3.8, p. 666), subdued by Servilius (Strabo 14.5.7, p. 671; Ps.-Ascon. p. 237St.24–25).

to Corycus

118 132M, 119Mc, not included in D and K

See previous fragment.

at Corycus

WAR IN MACEDONIA AND THRACE
(77 BC), FRR. 119–20

119 133M, 120Mc, 81D, 81K

Lete was a town in Macedonia, the province of Ap. Claudius Pulcher (cos. 79).

at the town of Lete

120 134M, 121Mc, 32D, 32K

repulsus a Lete oppido

Prisc. *GL* 3.66.21: see fr. 116.

FRAGMENTS OF UNCERTAIN
PLACEMENT IN BOOK 1, FRR. 121–39

121 137M, 122Mc, 111D, 102K

ea paucis, quibus peritia et verum ingenium est,[1] abnuentibus

Serv. auct. ad *Aen.* 12.694: quoting this fragment and fr. 2.89 to illustrate the adj. *verus* = that which is *rectum et bonum* [i.e., "morally upright," *OLD* 9].

[1] erat *Dietsch*: esset *Kritz*

Battles, frr. 122–24

122 139M, 99Mc, 96D, 98K

equi sine rectoribus exterriti aut saucii consternantur

Prisc. 2.436.5: mistakenly identifying the first conj. verb *consternor* as a deponent verb, in contrast with the third conj. verb *sterno*. For one other possible instance of *consternare* in S., cf. fr. dub. 30.

120 134M, 121Mc, 32D, 32K

See fr. 119. Possibly describing the repulse of some Thracian enemy.

driven back from the town of Lete

FRAGMENTS OF UNCERTAIN PLACEMENT IN BOOK 1, FRR. 121–39

121 137M, 122Mc, 111D, 102K

Possibly from the Preface.

a few, who possess expertise and an upright nature, rejecting them [views, statements, practices?]

Battles, frr. 122–24

122 139M, 99Mc, 96D, 98K

Possibly the context is the battle leading up the death of M. Domitius (see fr. 98).

the horses, terror-struck without their riders or wounded, were thrown into confusion

123 41M, 124Mc, 103D, 107K

dubitavit acie pars

Prisc. *GL* 2.366.11, assigned to Book 1; op. cit. 367.6, quoting fr. 127 as well; Serv. ad *G.* 1.208; Prob. *GL* 4.3.17; *Fr. Bob. GL* 5.555.9: to illustrate the spelling of the gen. sing. of a fifth decl. noun in *–e,* rather than in *–ei.*

124 138M, 125Mc, 89D, 91K

obviam ire et conmori hostibus

Arus. *GL* 7.462.6 = p. 92DC: to illustrate *commorior* + dat.

Operations in War, frr. 125–28

125 140M, 126Mc, 98D, 100K

Locum editiorem, quam victoribus decebat, capit.[1]

Arus. *GL* 7.465.2 = p. 102DC; Serv. ad *Aen.* 8.127; Ambr. 3.16 (without attribution to S.): to illustrate *decet* + dat.

[1] *om. Serv. et Ambr.*

126 141M, 127Mc, 83D, K

et stationes sub vineas removebat

Arus. *GL* 7.509.9–10 = p. 262DC: to illustrate *removeo* with *sub* + acc.

127 142M, 128Mc, 97D, 99K

At inde nulla munitionis aut requie mora processit ad oppidum.

Prisc. *GL* 2.367.7, quoting also fr. 123 (see ad loc.).

123 41M, 124Mc, 103D, 107K

Possibly a reference to the defeat of Sulla's left wing in the Battle of Colline Gate in November 82 (App. B Civ. 1.93): so Maurenbr.

part of the battleline wavered

124 138M, 125Mc, 89D, 91K

to go to meet and die with the enemy

Operations in War, frr. 125–28

125 140M, 126Mc, 98D, 100K

Possibly describing the placement of Q. Catulus' camp after his victory over Lepidus at Cosa as described in frr. 71–72 (so de Brosses).

He took up a loftier position than it was becoming for victors to adopt.

126 141M, 127Mc, 83D, K

A maneuver during the siege of a town.

and he pulled the pickets back under the mantlets

127 142M, 128Mc, 97D, 99K

But from there he proceeded to the town with no delay for entrenchment or rest.

128 143M, 129Mc, 102D, 105K

Quom murum hostium successisset, poenas dederat.[1]

Serv. auct. ad *Ecl.* 5.5; Arus. *GL* 7.507.15 = p. 256DC (quoting this fragment as well as fr. 3.106 and fr. 4.3): to illustrate *succedo* + acc. of thing. [cf. *OLD* 2a]

{Serv. ad *Aen.* 8.125 attests S.'s use of *succedo* + acc.}

[1] poenas dederat] *om. Arus.*

War, frr. 129–33

129 145M, 130Mc, 93D, 95K

nisi cum ira belli desenuisset

Prisc. *GL* 2.512.11: noting that *senui,* the pf. of *senesco* (inchoative "to grow old") is formed from the verb *seneo* (to be old).

130 40M, 123Mc, 101D, 104K

vacuam istam urb⟨em homin⟩ibus[1] militari aetate

Arus. *GL* 7.514.10 = p. 280DC: to illustrate *vacuus* + abl.

[1] *Lindemann in nota*

131 146M, 131Mc, 104D, 110K

militiae periti

Arus. *GL* 7.498.13 = p. 222DC: to illustrate *peritus* + gen.

128 143M, 129Mc, 102D, 105K

After he had approached close to the enemy's wall, he had paid the penalty.

War, frr. 129–33

129 145M, 130Mc, 93D, 95K

Possibly describing the collapse of popular support for Lepidus' uprising in 77.

if it had not languished along with war's fury

130 40M, 123Mc, 101D, 104K

If the text as emended is correct, the city may be Rome shortly before being attacked by the Samnites in November 82 (App. B Civ. 1.92)—so Maurenbr.—or by M. Lepidus in January/February 77—so Gerlach.

a city devoid of men of military age

131 146M, 131Mc, 104D, 110K

Possibly a description of Sulla's veterans at the time of Lepidus' revolt in 78/77 (cf. fr. 67.21).

experienced in military service

132 147M, 132Mc,105D, 111K

doctus militiam

Arus. *GL* 7.464.20 = p. 101DC: to illustrate *doctus* + acc.

133 148M, 113Mc, 106D, 112K

egregius militiae

Arus. *GL* 7.470.19 = p. 122DC: to illustrate *egregius* + gen.

Miscellaneous, frr. 134–39

134 149M, 134Mc, 2,77D, 2,102K

diei medio

Arus. *GL* 7.493.17 = p. 202DC: to illustrate *medius* + gen., instead of *medius* used as a modifying adj.

135 117M, 135Mc, 110D, 118K

solis viis

Donat. ad Ter. *Phorm.* 979: to illustrate *solus* meaning "lonely, deserted" (*OLD* 3).

136 150M, 136Mc, 114D, 113K

animi inmodicus

Arus. *GL* 7.484.17 = p. 170DC: to illustrate an adj. + gen. of thing. [See K-S 1.446–47, and for other instances of an adj./partic. + *animi* in the *Historiae*, cf. frr. 2.60; 3.21, 39, 105; 4.45, 51, 67, 73.]

132 147M, 132Mc,105D, 111K

expert in military matters

133 148M, 113Mc, 106D, 112K

outstanding in military matters

Miscellaneous, frr. 134–39

134 149M, 134Mc, 2,77D, 2,102K

at midday

135 117M, 135Mc, 110D, 118K

Maurenbr. speculated that the byways mentioned by S. in Book 1 were those used by Sertorius for making his escape or laying ambushes (cf. Plut. Sert. 13.2). Other candidates are the routes of escape taken either by Marius in 88 (cf. frr. 22–23) or by the supporters of Sulla after Rome fell to Marius and Cinna in late 87 (cf. fr. 28).

by means of deserted roads

136 150M, 136Mc, 114D, 113K

immoderate in spirit

137 151M, 137Mc, 116D, 119K

agreste

Charis. *GL* 1.120.30 = p. 154B.23: to illustrate the abl. sing. of
the third decl. adj. *agrestis* in –*e*.

138 152M, 138Mc, 113D, 108K

quos inter maxume

Charis. *GL* 1.236.21 = p. 308B.2: to illustrate anastrophe of a
prepostion.

139 153M, 139Mc, deest in D et K

quaesere

Eutych. *GL* 5.483.8; Phoc. *GL* 5.436.5: to illustrate a rare instance of the inf. of the defective verb *quaeso* (s.v. *OLD*).

137 151M, 137Mc, 116D, 119K

Charisius cites Book 2 of the Elder Pliny's Sermo dubius *in defense of the abl. sing. in –e when the adj.* agrestis *describes an animal, as opposed to something inanimate. Possibly S. used this word to describe some fauna or tribe in a region of Mauretania or Spain in connection with the Sertorian War.*

wild (uncouth?)

138 152M, 138Mc, 113D, 108K

especially among them

139 153M, 139Mc, not included in D and K

to request[1]

[1] Or "they sought, demanded," if the grammarians mistook a third pl. pf. of *quaero* (cf. fr. 75 *quaesit*) for an inf. of *quaeso*.

BOOK 2

OUTLINE

LIBER II

DEFEAT AND DEATH OF LEPIDUS IN SARDINIA (77 BC), FRR. 1–15

Description of Sardinia and Corsica, frr. 1–13

1* 1M, Mc, D, K

> quom praedixero positum insulae

Donat. ad Ter. *Phorm.* 97: in commenting on Terence's substitution of the participle *situs* for *positus* to describe a corpse laid out for mourning, S. is cited to illustrate the opposite, viz. the substitution of the rare and poetical fourth-decl. noun *positus* for *situs* (used at *Jug.* 17.1), meaning "the layout of a region, its geography."

2 2M, Mc, D, K

Sardinia in Africo mari facie vestigi humani in orientem quam occidentem[1] latior prominet.[2]

Gell. 13.30.5; Non. p. 53M = 74L.1–2: to illustrate *facies* in the sense of "shape" or "form" and applied to things, as well as persons. {*Gloss.* 5, p. 236.21; Isid. *Etym.* 14.7.1 (*in orientem . . . prominet*): to illustrate the verb *promineo* applied to land masses extending into the sea; cf. Isid. *Etym.* 14.6.39 (*in Africo . . . prominet,* without attribution to S.), Plin. *HN* 3.85; Mart. Cap. 6.645 (p. 225W.3): reporting the resemblance of the shape of Sardinia to a human footprint.}

BOOK 2

DEFEAT AND DEATH OF LEPIDUS IN SARDINIA (77 BC), FRR. 1–15

Description of Sardinia and Corsica, frr. 1–13

1* 1M, Mc, D, K

Possibly introducing S.'s remarks on Sardinia, scene of the defeat of M. Lepidus (cos. 78) and his rebel forces after they had been expelled from Italy by Lepidus' consular colleague Q. Catulus. Conceivably, however, this fragment could have introduced S.'s excursus on the island of Crete (3.46–51)—so Keyser—since the restoration of "in II" in the text of Donatus rests on "in H" in one late manuscript.

when I have first mentioned the layout of the island

2 2M, Mc, D, K

Same context as fr. 1.

Sardinia, in the African sea, has the shape of a human footprint and bulges more to the east than the west.

---

1 in occidentem quam in orientem] *Non.*
2 *om. Non.*

3* 3M, 3Mc, 2D, 3K

Sardinia quoque, quam apud Timaeum Sandaliotin legimus, **Ichnusam** *apud Crispum, in quo mari sita sit, quos incolarum auctores habeat, satis celebre est.*

Solinus 4.1.

4 13M, 5Mc, 82D, 80K

Nam procul et divorsis ex regionibus

Charis. *GL* 1.215.5–6 = p. 278B.5–6: informs us that the second-century AD commentator Asper interpreted the adv. *procul* in this context as referring to place of origin, glossing *procul e loco.*

5* 6M, 8Mc, 4–5D, 7–8K

Aristaeum . . . **Apollinis et Cyrenes filium** . . . *hic, ut etiam Sallustius docet, post laniatum a canibus Actaeonem filium* **matris instinctu Thebas reliquit et Ceam insulam tenuit primo,** *adhuc hominibus vacuam; postea, ea relicta,* **cum Daedalo ad Sardiniam transitum fecit.**

Serv. ad *G.* 1.14: background information on Aristaeus.

{Prob. *GL* 4.7.27 (*Apollinis filia* [sic] *et Cyrenes*): to illustrate gen. sing. in –*es* of a f. noun having nom. in –*e; Schol. Bern.* ad *G.* 4.283 (*Aristaeus filius Apollinis et Cyrenes,* without mention of S.); Serv. ad *Aen.* 6.14 states that according to S., Daedalus made his way first to Sardinia and afterward to Cumae; *Gloss.* 5, p. 176.30 states that according to S., Aristaeus first settled on Cea after leaving his native land.}

3* 3M, 3Mc, 2D, 3K

Same context as fr. 1.

*Also as to Sardinia, which we find referred to as Sandaliotis in Timaeus and **Ichnusa**[1] in [Sallustius] Crispus, it is quite widely known in what sea it is located and who were the progenitors of its inhabitants.*

[1] From the Greek ἴχνος, meaning "footprint."

4 13M, 5Mc, 82D, 80K

Possibly the same context as fr. 1, describing places from which settlers came to Sardinia. Maurenbr. instead assigned this fragment to S.'s description of the many outlaws and exiles who flocked to Sertorius in Spain after the collapse of M. Lepidus' uprising in 77 (cf. fr. 15).

For from far off and separate regions

5* 6M, 8Mc, 4–5D, 7–8K

Same context as fr. 1: Aristaeus is said to have been the second settler to arrive in Sardinia, after immigrants were brought from Libya under the leadership of Sardus, from whom the island took its name (Paus. 10.17.3, rejecting, for reasons of chronology, the tradition that Daedalus accompanied Aristaeus).

Aristaeus . . . **the son of Apollo and Cyrene** . . . , *as S. too states,* **left Thebes at the prompting of his mother** *after his son Actaeon had been torn apart by his dogs, and* **at first possessed the island of Cea** *[Ceos], up until then devoid of people; afterward, he left that island behind and* **with Daedalus made the crossing**[1] **to Sardinia**.

[1] Sc. "from Sicily," see fr. 8.

6* 4M, 6Mc, inc. 122D, 2.9K

Geryonis

Serv. ad *Aen.* 7.662: to give an example of the gen. sing. *–is* of the first decl. Greek noun *Geryones, –ae*.

7 5M, 7Mc, 26D, 32K

ut alii tradiderunt,[1] Tartessum Hispaniae civitatem,
quam nunc Tyrii mutato nomine Gaddir[2] habent

Prisc. *GL* 2.154.3–5, 234.12–14: to illustrate S.'s treatment of *Gaddir* as a neut. noun; Donat. ad Ter. *Eun.* 401: to illustrate (mistakenly) the meaning of *habeo* = *dico* (to call), whereas, instead, the meaning in Terence is "have (the facts)" (*OLD* s.v. *habeo* 11), and in this fragment = *colere* (to inhabit), cf. *Cat.* 6.1; *Jug.* 17.7.

{Avien. *Descript.* 610–16, without citing S., traces the evolution of the place-name from Cotinussa to Tartessus (so called by Tyrians), and finally Gades from the Cathaginian "Gaddir," a word meaning a "place enclosed on all sides with a rampart."}

[1] ut alii tradiderunt] *om. Donat.*   [2] Gadirum *Donat.*

8 7M (Prisc.), 9Mc, 3D (Prisc.) , 5K (Prisc.)

6* 4M, 6Mc, inc. 122D, 2.9K

Possibly the same context as fr. 1: settlers were brought from Spain to Sardinia by Norax, the eponymous founder of the town Nora; he was the son of Mercury and Erytheia, the daughter of Geryon (Paus. 10.17.4; cf. Solin. 4.1).

of Geryon

7 5M, 7Mc, 26D, 32K

Norax (see fr. 6) is said to have come from Tartessus (Solin. 4.1), a region of southwest Spain, the name of which was sometimes extended to the Phoenician emporium Gaddir (= Gades; mod. Cádiz).

according to another tradition, the Spanish community of Tartessus, which with a change of name the people of Tyre now occupy as Gaddir

8 7M (Prisc.), 9Mc, 3D (Prisc.) , 5K (Prisc.)

Same context as fr. 1: descendants of Hercules were led by Hercules' nephew Iolaus to Sardinia, where they settled (Strabo 5.2.7, p. 225; cf. Paus. 10.17.4). During a period when Sardinia was largely, but not exclusively, under Carthaginian control, Libyan or Iberian deserters from the Carthaginian army joined settlers from abroad (Corsica?) in the mountains of Sardinia; they were known as "Balari," meaning "fugitives" in the Corsican language (Paus. 10.17.5).

Col. 1 (12 lines)

[. . . ±7 . . .] *a*n Iolao [.. ±5 ..] | [. . . ±7 . . .]m incertum tra|[. . .] *ari*ri [. . .]*is* an testimo|‹ni›um adscitae gentis. Ba|‹lar›os Corsi transfugas | [. . .]llanteos,[1] alii Numi|‹das›, *p*ars Hispanos putant | ‹e Po›enorum[2] exercitu; ge|‹nus› ingenio mobili aut | ‹so›ciorum metu infidum, | ‹fu›sci[3] veste cultu barba. | ‹Be›llo Celtiberico et la|

Col. 2 (2 lines + supplement)

| di[. . .] | Dae‹dalum ex Sicilia pro›[4]|fectu‹m quo Minonis iram›[5] | ‹atque opes fugerat›[6]

Pap. Oxyrh. 68 6B.20/L (10–13)a, fr. b, recto[A] (= col. 1) recto[B] (= col. 2), portions of two columns each originally ca. 20 lines long and ca. 18–22 letters in width, written in rustic capitals in a papyrus roll of the second/third century(?), from which fr. inc. 2 is also preserved. Supplements are by Roberts, unless otherwise indicated; italics indicates that the transcription is uncertain; the symbol "|" marks the division of lines in the papyrus.

{Prisc. GL 2.255.2–3 (*Daedalum . . . fugerat*), assigned to Book 2: to illustrate the gen. sing. *Minonis,* instead of *Minois.*}

[1] ‹Pa›llanteos *Roberts*　　[2] *Funari*　　[3] *Morel*　　[4–6] *suppl. ex Prisc.*

9* 9M, 4Mc, 6D adnot., 10K

*Illo tempore invadendarum terrarum causa fuerat navigatio, uti Sallustius meminit, **facili tum mutatione sedum**.*

Serv. & Serv. auct. ad *Aen.* 1.299: in explaining how it was the fate of the Trojans to be exiles from their homeland and how they came to land on the shores of Carthage.

. . . or to Iolaus . . . uncertain . . . or evidence of foreign stock. The Corsicans suppose the Balari to be fugitives from * * *; others suppose them to be Numidian or Spanish deserters from the Carthaginian army: a treacherous race owing to its fickle disposition or fear of allies; of dark clothing, adornment, and beard. In the Celtiberian War [151–133 BC] and * * *

[ca. 15±10 lines in the papyrus separate this part of the fragment from the one preceding.]

* * * Daedalus, having set out from Sicily, to which he had fled to escape the wrath and might of Minos . . .

9* 9M, 4Mc, 6D note, 10K

Same context as fr. 1 if this fragment formed part of S.'s description of Trojans coming by sea to Sardinia (see next fragment). Alternatively, this fragment might have been part of S.'s excursus on the settlement of Crete (frr. 3.46–51) and the growth of piracy (so Keyser, comparing Thuc. 1.2.1–2 and Diod. Sic. 5.80.1).

At that time [after the fall of Troy, trad. in 1184 BC], *seafaring had been the cause of incurions into foreign lands, as Sallust recalls,* **since a change of abodes was easy then**.

10* 8M, 10Mc, 6D, 11K

cum multi evaserint Troianorum periculum, ut Capys qui
Campaniam tenuit, . . . ut alii qui **Sardiniam**, *secundum*
Sallustium

Serv. & Serv. auct. ad *Aen.* 1.242; id. ad *Aen.* 1.601 (*alii Sardi-*
niam secundum Sallustium)

11 83M, 11Mc, 91D, 92K

   frugum pabulique laetus ager

Arus. *GL* 7.490.4 = p. 190DC ("*Sal. Hist. II*"); Serv. & Serv. auct.
ad *Aen.* 1.441; Serv. auct. ad *Aen.* 11.338: to illustrate *laetus* +
gen.

12* 10M, 12Mc, 2D [adnot. ad 2K]

In Sardinia enim nascitur quaedam **herba**, *ut Sallustius*
dicit, **apiastri similis**. *Haec* **comesa ora hominum ric-**
tus dolore contrahit et quasi ridentis interimit.

Serv. ad *Ecl.* 7.41: to explicate Virgil's *Sardoniis herbis* (Sardinian
herbs).

{Isid. *Etym.* 14.6.40: *herba . . . apiastri similis, quae comesa ora*
hominum rictus dolore contrahit et quasi ridentis interimit; cf.
Sol. 4.4.}

13 11M, 13Mc, 2D, 2K note

10* 8M, 10Mc, 6D, 11K

Same context as fr. 1: according to Pausanias (10.17.4), refugees from Troy mingled with the Greek settlers on Sardiania who had arrived under Iolaus (cf. fr. 8).

since many of the Trojans escaped danger, as for instance Capys, who made for Campania, . . . and others who made for **Sardinia**, according to Sallust

11 83M, 11Mc, 91D, 92K

Possibly the same context as fr. 1: a description of the fertility of Sardinia (so La Penna [1971].61–62, adducing a like description of Sardinia in Claud. De bell. Gild. 509: "farmland rich in crops" (dives ager frugum). Maurenbr. connected, instead, with a region in the vicinity of the Taurus Mountains.

land rich in crops and fodder

12* 10M, 12Mc, 2D [included in note on 2K]

Same context as fr. 1: a poisonous plant native to Sardinia (possibly hemlock water dropwort, which resembles celery and whose root contains a potent neurotoxin that produces a "sardonic" death rictus).

For in Sardinia there grows a certain **plant**, as Sallust states, **resembling bee balm. If eaten, it constricts human faces with a painful grimace and kills them as though they are smiling**.

13 11M, 13Mc, 2D, 2K note

The island Corsica received its name from Corsa, a Ligurian woman who led settlers there after being tempted to explore the island when she noticed that a bull in her herd was swimming out to the island and returning well fed (Isid. Etym. 14.6.41).

> sed ipsi ferunt taurum ex grege, quem prope litora
> regebat Corsa nomine Ligus mulier

Prisc. *GL* 2.264.9–10: to illustrate the adj. *Ligus,* which, like *vetus,* has one form in each case, common to all three genders.

{Isid. *Etym.* 14.6.41 (without naming S.): *Corsa nomine Ligus mulier, cum taurum ex grege, quem prope litora regebat . . .* }

Defeat of Lepidus, frr. 14–15

14* 12M, 14Mc, 7D, 12K

> Tharrhos[1]

Prob. *GL* 4.22.26; Sacerd. fr. line 110: cited as the only instance of a noun (foreign) ending in *–hos,* said to be always pl.

{Prob. *GL* 4.27.32 ("Tarros") and Sacerdos, *GL* 6.478.25 ("Tharros"): remarking, without mention of S., that the "T." is always pl.}

[1] Tarrhos *Keil*: tharros *corr.* tharrhos *B (Prob. 4.22)*

15 14M, 15Mc, 94D, 97K

> orbe terrarum extorres

Arus. *GL* 7.472.7 = p. 127DC: to illustrate *extorris* + abl.

but they themselves [the Corsicans?] relate that a bull belonging to a herd, which a Ligurian woman named Corsa was tending near the shore

Defeat of Lepidus, frr. 14–15

14* 12M, 14Mc, 7D, 12K

It was possibly near Tharros (apparently spelled by S. –hos), a town on the west coast of Sardinia, that the rebel M. Lepidus tried to land with a reduced number of followers in 77 and was defeated by the propraetorian legate C. Valerius Triarius (Ascon. 19C.1; Exsuper. 6 [39–41Z]).

Tharrhos

15 14M, 15Mc, 94D, 97K

Possibly a description of the followers of M. Lepidus' failed uprising in 77, those who made their way from Sardinia under Perperna to Spain, where they fought under Q. Sertorius (Plut. Sert. 15.2–3; App. B Civ. 1.107–8; Exsuper. 7 [42Z]).

men banished from the world [i.e., from all Roman territory]

POMPEY SENT TO SPAIN (77 BC), FRR. 16–21

16 15M, 16Mc, 30D, 36K

Ad hoc rumoribus advorsa in pravitatem, secunda in ca-
sum, fortunam[1] in temeritatem declinando conrumpebant

Non. p. 385M = 614L.2–4: to illustrate *rumor* = *opinio*.

[1] fortuita *Müller*: fortia *Pecere*

Character Sketch of Pompey, frr. 17–21

17* 16M, 17Mc, inc. 75D, inc. 41K

oris probi, animo inverecundo

Suet. *Gram.* 15.1–2: this unfavorable description of Pompey by
S. is credited with causing Pompey's freedman, the grammarian
Lenaeus, to compose a vicious satire attacking S.

{Cf., in descriptions of Pompey, without attribution to S., *probi
oris* (Plin. *HN* 37.14), *os probum* (Plin. *HN* 7.53), and *animi inve-
recundi* (Sacerd. *GL* 6.462.1).}

18 17M, 18Mc, 86D, 85K

modestus ad alia omnia, nisi ad dominationem

Donat. ad Ter. *Phorm.* 170: to illustrate *modeste* = *moderate*.

POMPEY SENT TO SPAIN (77 BC),
FRR. 16–21

16 15M, 16Mc, 30D, 36K

Possibly describing how backers of Pompey in 77 sought to have him put in charge of the war against Sertorius by denigrating Metellus Pius' conduct of that war (so Maurenbr.). De Brosses, on the contrary, thought the criticism was aimed at Sertorius.

In addition, through gossip, by putting down his setbacks to cowardice, his successes to chance, and his good luck to rashness, they kept undermining

Character Sketch of Pompey, frr. 17–21

17* 16M, 17Mc, inc. 75D, inc. 41K

The first of a series of fragments outlining Pompey's character and past military exploits prior to his being sent to Spain in 77: a summation of Pompey's outward appearance and inward essence. Syme (Tacitus, 150) translates "fair of face but dark within."

of honest face but shameless heart

18 17M, 18Mc, 86D, 85K

Possibly the same context as fr. 17: a description of Pompey.

moderate with regard to all else except domination

19 21M, 21Mc, 12D, 62K

Nam Sullam consulem de reditu eius legem ferentem ex conposito tribunus plebis C. Herennius prohibuerat.

Gell. 10.20.10: to illustrate the use of the term *lex* to describe a bill that was more strictly a *privilegium* (a measure affecting just one person, not the whole community).

20* 19M, 20Mc, 11D, 17K

Cum alacribus saltu, cum velocibus cursu, cum validis vecte[1] certabat.

Veg. *Mil.* 1.9.8: commenting on Pompey's physical training, aimed at making him a match for Sertorius.

[1] fasce *Dietsch*

19 21M, 21Mc, 12D, 62K

Possibly the same context as fr. 17, if describing Sulla's thwarted attempt to recall Pompey from his army in Africa in 80 (Plut. Pomp. 13.1–4). The reference to Sulla as consul places the event in 80 (or 88, if the Cn. Pompeius, to whom Gell. refers, was Pompey's father, Cn. Pompeius Strabo [cos. 89]: see MRR 3.101, 161).

For by arrangement,[1] the plebeian tribune Gaius Herennius had blocked the consul Sulla when he was proposing a law concerning his recall.

[1] It is not clear whether the agreement was struck between Sulla and the tribune, or between Pompey and the tribune. If the former, then Sulla may have used Herennius as a strawman to justify a reversal of his decision to recall Pompey when he encountered popular displeasure.

20* 19M, 20Mc, 11D, 17K

The same context as fr. 17: Pompey's physical training immediately preceding the Sertorian War (as attested by Veg.).

He competed at jumping with the agile, at running with the swift, and at the lever[1] with the strong

[1] The meaning of *vecte* is open to various interpretations. S. may be describing (a) a tool, such as was used to shift heavy boulders in a military operation (e.g., Caes. *B Civ.* 2.11.1), or (b) a practice sword (e.g., Veg. *Mil.* 3.4.4), in which case the meaning is "at fencing" (or conceivably "at jousting," after the fashion of Robin Hood and his men). Dietsch's emendation *fasce* makes S. refer to the carrying of a heavy pack (e.g., Verg. *G.* 3.347)

21* 22M, 22Mc, inc. 11D, 2.16K

Narbone per concilium Gallorum

Cledon. *GL* 5.22.12–13: to illustrate locative *Narbone* (abl.) in place of *Narboni* (dat.).

DOMESTIC AFFAIRS (76 BC), FRR. 22–24

22 25M, 23Mc, 35D, 45K

quia[1] corpore et lingua percitum et inquietem no-mine histrionis vix sani Burbuleium adpellabat

Prisc. *GL* 2.243.3–5: to illustrate an oblique case of the third decl. adj. *inquies.*

[1] qui *L*: quem *Dietsch*

23† 26M, 24Mc, 36D, 3.83K

conlegamque eius Octavium mitem et captum pe-dibus

Arus. *GL* 7.489.5 = p. 489DC: (assigned in error to "*Hist. III*") to illustrate *captus* + abl. of thing.

24 27M, 25Mc, 34D, 44K

21* 22M, 22Mc, inc. 11D, 2.16K

Possibly to be connected with Pompey's activities in Transalpine Gaul, which in the winter of 77/76 he pacified while on his way to take up his command against Sertorius in Spain (cf. fr. 86.5; Cic. De imp. Cn. Pomp. 28, 30).

at Narbo, through the Gallic council

DOMESTIC AFFAIRS (76 BC),
FRR. 22–24

22 25M, 23Mc, 35D, 45K

C. Scribonius Curio (cos. 76) was called "Burbuleius," the name of an actor (Val. Max. 9.14.5; cf. Plin. HN 7.55). Curio may have been so called by the tribune Sicinius, who is credited with making witty remarks in public at the expense of Curio (Cic. Brut. 217).

because he used to call him "Burbuleius," the name of a half-crazy actor, since he was an agitated and restless fellow in his movement and speech[1]

[1] This description of Curio's deportment agrees with Cicero's (*Brut.* 216–17; cf. Quint. 11.3.129).

23† 26M, 24Mc, 36D, 3.83K

Cn. Octavius (cos. 76), who suffered from lameness (Cic. Brut. 217; Quint. 11.3.129).

and his colleague, the mild and lame Octavius

24 27M, 25Mc, 34D, 44K

Possibly describing pressure applied to the tribune Sicinius by the consul C. Curio in 76 to dissuade him from agitating for the res-

ut actione desisteret

Arus. *GL* 7.467.3 = p. 107DC: to illustrate *desisto* + abl. of a thing.

SERTORIAN WAR (76 BC), FRR. 25–33

25* 64M, 26Mc, 21D, 27K

Saguntini, fide atque aerumnis incluti per morta-lis,[1] studio maiore quam opibus—quippe ⟨apud⟩[2] quos etiam tum semiruta moenia, domus intectae parietesque templorum ambusti manus Punicas os-tentabant—

Hieron. in *Hab.* 2.9–11 (p. 604A): to illustrate the statement in Habakkuk 2:11 that "the stones of the wall will cry out" (NIV). {Cf. Mela 2.92, *Saguntum illam* (sc. *urbem*) *fide atque aerum-nis inclutam;* Amm. Marc. 15.10.10, *Saguntinis memorabilibus aerumnis et fide.*}

[1] per mortales] *cod. Par. Lat. 1836 (cf. Tac. Hist. 2.2,* inclutum per indigenas*):* prae mortalibus *cod. Reg. 93*   [2] *suppl. edd.*

26* 65M, 27Mc, 22D, 28K

Saguntium

Charis. *GL* 1.143.9 = p. 181B.10: to illustrate the gen. pl. adop-ted by S., as opposed to *Saguntinorum.*

toration of the powers of the tribunate (Ps.-Ascon. p. 189St.7–9; cf. fr. 3.15.10).

so that he might desist from his course of action

SERTORIAN WAR (76 BC), FRR. 25–33

25* 64M, 26Mc, 21D, 27K

The town of Saguntum on the east-central coast of Spain, a few miles north of the likely site of Lauro, may have been mentioned in describing Pompey's march south in the spring of 76, when he sought to relieve the town of Lauro, which was being besieged by Sertorius (Plut. Sert. 18.5).

the people of Saguntum, famous among mortals for their loyalty and sufferings, with greater zeal than resources—seeing that in their midst, even at that time, half-ruined walls, houses without roofs, and the scorched walls of temples displayed the handiwork of their Punic foes[1]—

[1] The fall of Rome's ally Saguntum to Hannibal in 218, after an eight-month siege begun in 219, precipitated the Second Punic War (218–201).

26* 65M, 27Mc, 22D, 28K

Same context as fr. 25.

of the Saguntines

Battle of Lauro (spring 76 BC), frr. 27–30

27* 29M, 28Mc, 15D, 22K

quis a Sertorio triplices insidiae per idoneos saltus
positae erant; prima, quae forte[1] venientis exciperet

Serv. ad *G.* 2.98 (*quis . . . prima*), id. ad *Aen.* 11.896 (*prima . . .
exciperet*) {Charis. *GL* 1.96.8 = p. 123B.6 (*prima*)}: to note in S.
the use of the sing. *prima* with reference to the pl. noun *insidiae*.

[1] fronte *Mascivius*

28* 30M, 29Mc, 64D, 30K

atque eos a tergo incurrunt

[Rufin.], *Schem lex.* p. 57H.10: prep. *in* to be supplied with *eos* (=
in eos) from the compound verb.

29* 31M, 30Mc, 16D, 23K

Laelius . . . **ab Hirtuleianis interfectus est**, *ut ait
Sallustius:* **receptis plerisque signis militaribus
cum Laeli corpore**

Schol. Bob. ad Cic. *Flacc.* 14 (p. 98St.10–11).

Battle of Lauro (spring 76 BC), frr. 27–30

27* 29M, 28Mc, 15D, 22K

Early in 76, Pompey attempted to relieve the town of Lauro from a siege by Sertorius but was outmaneuvered (Plut. Sert. 18.5–10). His foraging party was cut off by a threefold ambush planned by Sertorius (Frontin. Str. 2.5.31).

against them Sertorius had laid a threefold ambush in woodland gorges ideally suited for the purpose: the first which was to intercept those who happened to come along,[1]

[1] McGushin's "the advancing enemy" presumes the emendation *fronte,* as do Frassinetti-di Luca in their translation, although the latter print *forte.*

28* 30M, 29Mc, 64D, 30K

Same context as fr. 27. A legion under the legate D. Laelius, sent by Pompey to relieve the foraging party, was attacked by Sertorius' cavalry from the rear (Frontin. Str. 2.5.31; cf. App. B Civ. 1.109).

and they rush upon them from the rear

29* 31M, 30Mc, 16D, 23K

Same context as fr. 28. Cf. Obseq. 58, placing Laelius' death on the foraging mission under 77 BC.

*Laelius **was killed by the forces under Hirtuleius**, as Sallust states: **after the recovery of the bulk of the military standards along with Laelius' body***

30* 32M, 31Mc, 95D, 99K

et Metello procul agente, longa spes auxiliorum

Serv. ad *Aen.* 11.544: to illustrate the adj. *longus* meaning "far-removed" (*longe positus*).

Activities of Metellus in Farther Spain (76 BC),
frr. 31–33

31* 1.123M, 2.32Mc, inc. 6D, 1.43K

Ucurbis

Prob. *GL* 4.20.2: to illustrate the gen. of the proper noun *Ucurbis,* identified as a community mentioned by S.

32 33M, 33Mc, 95D, 99K

copiis integra

Arus. *GL* 7.480.24 = p. 157DC: to illustrate the adj. *integer* + abl. of thing.

33* 35M, 34Mc, inc. 36D, inc. 2K

At Sertorius vacuos hieme copias augere

Porph. ad Hor. *Epist.* 2.2.81: to illustrate *vacuus* applied to a person in the sense of *otiosus* (at leisure).

30* 32M, 31Mc, 95D, 99K

Possibly the same context as frr. 27–29: Metellus Pius was not in a position to lend aid to Pompey's forces, because he was engaged in his province of Farther Spain.

> and far-removed ‹was› the hope of reinforcements,
> since Metellus was operating far away

*Activities of Metellus in Farther Spain (76 BC),
frr. 31–33*

31* 1.123M, 2.32Mc, inc. 6D, 1.43K

Possibly a town in Farther Spain, if it is identical with Ucubi ([Caes.] B Hisp. 7). It may have been mentioned in connection with the defeat of the Sertorian commander L. Hirtuleius by Metellus outside Italica (Oros. 5.23.10; cf. Frontin. Str. 2.1.2), a town ca. eighty-five miles to the west of Ucubi.

> of Ucurbis

32 33M, 33Mc, 95D, 99K

Possibly describing the condition of Gaul (the winter quarters of Metellus in 76/75, fr. 86.9), or some region of Spain(?), at the time of devastation elsewhere resulting from the Sertorian War.

> with its forces intact

33* 35M, 34Mc, inc. 36D, inc. 2K

Possibly a reference to the period of Metellus' absence in Gaul (see previous fragment).

> But Sertorius, at leisure[1] in the winter to build up
> his forces

[1] Or, "free from distractions in the winter, built up his forces."

WARS IN THE EAST (76 BC),
FRR. 34–37

34 37M, 36Mc, 87D, 86K

vir gravis et nulla arte quoiquam inferior

Arus. *GL* 7.488.5–6 = p. 182DC: to illustrate *inferior* + dat. of person.

35 39M, 37Mc, 81D, 79K

genus armis ferox et serviti insolitum

Arus. *GL* 7.486.19–20 = p. 177DC: to illustrate *insolitus* + gen. of thing.

{Tert. *De anim.* 20.3: S. applied the description *feroces* to the Dalmatae.}

36*** 40M, 38Mc, inc. 12D, 2.42K

primam modo Iapydiam ingressus

Serv. ad *G.* 3.475: identifies Iapydia as a district of Venetia (a region in northern Illyricum), citing S. for a reference to Iapydia.

37 41M, 39Mc, 69D, 84K

eam deditionem senatus per nuntios Orestis cognitam adprobat

Prisc. *GL* 2.246.4–5: to illustrate the third decl. gen. sing. spelling *–is* of *Orestes*.

WARS IN THE EAST (76 BC),
FRR. 34–37

34 37M, 36Mc, 87D, 86K

Maurenbr. speculated that this fragment may have formed part of a character sketch of Ap. Claudius (cos. 79), which was offered at the time of his death, from illness in 76 while serving as governor of Macedonia (MRR 2.94). For his poor health two years earlier, cf. fr. 1.114.

a grave man, taking second place to no one in any accomplishment

35 39M, 37Mc, 81D, 79K

"Fierce" was S.'s description of the Dalmatae (Tert. l. c.), a people in the province of Illyricum, against whom C. Cosconius (pr. 79?), the governor in 78–76, campaigned (Eutr. 6.4).

a race fierce in arms and unaccustomed to servitude

36* 40M, 38Mc, inc. 12D, 2.42K

Activity in a region of Illyricum lying near the top of the east coast of the Adriatic, north of Dalmatia. Same context as fr. 35.

having entered only the nearest part of Iapydia

37 41M, 39Mc, 69D, 84K

A victory of Cn. Aufidius Orestes (pr. 77) while governing the province of Asia (or Transalpine or Cisalpine Gaul?) in 76 (see MRR 2.96 n. 4, 3.29–30).

the senate approved the surrender, of which it was informed through Orestes' messengers

DOMESTIC AFFAIRS (75 BC), FRR. 38–44

38 42M, 40Mc, 38D (Berlin fr. only), deest in K

1 * * * ⟨apud⟩ | q*uem exerc*itus f|luera*t,* | legionem misit
de||specta[1] | vanitate, idque il|l|li in | sapientiam cesse|lrat.

2 Dein | *L.* Octavius et C. Co|l⟨t⟩ta con|sulatum ingres-
s||⟨i⟩, quorum | Octavius langu||⟨i⟩de et | incuriose fuit,
C||⟨ot⟩ta prom|ptius, sed ambiti|| . . . e[2] tum | in*genio*
largit . || . . . [3] cupi|les gratia⟨m⟩ *sin*g||⟨ul⟩orum[4] | * * *

These words occupy the first 11 lines of a column that is 18–23
letter-spaces in width and was originally 21 lines in length. It is
found on the left portion of a single leaf forming one-half of a
partially preserved double leaf that once belonged to the so-
called Fleury manuscript (*Floriacensis*). The upper portion of
this leaf and a small strip of the adjoining leaf are preserved on
the verso of fol. 20 of the Orleans palimpsest, the Aurelianensis
(**A**), combined with the recto of the Berlin fragment (**B**). The
division between **A** (on the left) and **B** (on the right) is marked
with ||; ends of lines in the manuscript are indicated by |; italics
signifies that the transcription is uncertain. Supplements are to
be credited to Hauler, unless otherwise indicated. The conjectural supplement ⟨*apud*⟩ introducing this fragment would have
been written at the end of the last line of the right-hand column
on the verso of the preceding, no longer extant, leaf. For a schematic reconstruction of the partially preserved double leaf, see
Bloch, *Didascaliae* (1961), fig. 1.

[1] dispecta *Perl*

[2] ambiti⟨on⟩e, *Maurenbr.*

[3] ingenio largitor et] *Perl*: ingenti a largitione *Mommsen*: ingenita largitione *Maurenbr.*

[4] *Mommsen*

DOMESTIC AFFAIRS (75 BC),
FRR. 38–44

38 42M, 40Mc, 38D (Berlin fr. only), not included in K

The transition to the year 75 is marked by names of the new consuls and a brief sketch of their characters. This is preceded by a reference to some military operation, the details of which cannot be recovered. Italics in the translation signifies that the text is uncertain because of the need for supplements.

. . . the one *under whose command* the army had been, discharged a legion *out of contempt for* its unreliability,[1] and that act had passed for wisdom in his case.

Next, upon entering the consulship, Lucius Octavius and Gaius Cotta, of whom Octavius was irresolute and negligent, Cotta more energetic but *thanks to his greed for advancement, both a briber by nature and* desirous of the goodwill of individuals . . .

---

[1] Or, reading *dispecta,* "having discerned its unreliability."

39 43M, 41Mc, 39D, 47K

P(ublius)que[1] Lentulus Marcell⟨inus⟩ | eodem auctore[2]
quaest⟨or⟩ | in novam provinci⟨am⟩ | Cyrenas missus est,
q⟨uom⟩[3] | ea, mortui regis Apio⟨nis⟩ | testamento nobis
d⟨ata⟩, | prudentiore quam ⟨adu⟩llescentis[4] et minus
q⟨uam⟩ | ille[5] avidi imperio co⟨nti⟩lnenda fuit. Praetere⟨a
di⟩lvorsorum ordin⟨um certalmina hoc anno exarserunt⟩.[6]

These words occupy the first eleven lines of the right-hand column on the recto of the same leaf that preserves fr. 38 in the
left-hand column. The two fragments are separated by the loss
of ten manuscript lines at the bottom of the left-hand column (=
approx. five lines of printed text). The text is preserved on the
recto of the Berlin fragment (**B**). Ends of lines in the manuscript
are indicated by |, from which it can be plainly seen that the right
margin of most lines in this column of text has suffered the loss
of two or three letters. For a schematic reconstruction of the partially preserved double leaf, see Bloch, *Didascaliae* (1961), fig. 1.

[1] PQ *B*   [2] *Kreyssig:* actore *B*   [3] cum *Perl:* q⟨uod⟩
Pertz   [4] ⟨adu⟩lescentis] *Perl:* ⟨illas⟩ per gentis *Kreys-
sig*   [5] q⟨uam⟩ | ille avidi] *Perl:* g⟨lo⟩lriae avidi *Kreys-
sig*   [6] *Kreyssig*

40 44M, 62Mc, 79D, 76K

inmane quantum animi exarsere

Non. p. 127M = 185L.30–31: to illustrate an adj. used adver-
bially (= *inmaniter*).

41 45M, 42Mc, 40D, 49K

39 43M, 41Mc, 39D, 47K

In 75, a quaestor was sent (possibly with "imperium pro prae-tore") to organize the new province of Cyrene, which the late Ptolemy Apion had willed to the Roman people in 96 (Liv. Per. 70). The important political figure who is said to have orches-trated this arrangement—referred to here as "the same person"—may be the consul C. Cotta, who is mentioned in the preceding fragment. The gap between it and this one is no more than four to five lines of printed text (representing the loss of ten lines in the manuscript). Italics in the translation signifies that the text or a supplement is uncertain.

And Publius Lentulus Marcellinus was sent as quaestor, through the influence of the same person, to the new prov-ince of Cyrene when that territory, which had been be-queathed to us by the will of the late King Apion, ought to have been *maintained* by a more sensible power than *that of a youth* and of one less greedy than Marcellinus. More-over ⟨*there flared up in this year rivalries*⟩ among the different classes [senate, Knights, and plebeians].

40 44M, 62Mc, 79D, 76K

Possibly a description of the hostile populace at the time of the grain shortage in 76 (see fr. 41).

how monstrously tempers flared

41 45M, 42Mc, 40D, 49K

A mob attack on the consuls in 75 was in reaction to a food short-age, if the text is correctly restored. The incident must have oc-curred ca. June, because it preceded the midsummer elections. This fragment is separated from fr. 39 by no more than four to five lines of printed text (representing the loss of ten lines in the

* * * ⟨annonae intolerabil⟩|is[1] saevitia. Qua re fati⟨ga⟩|ta plebes forte consu⟨lles⟩ ambo, Q. Metellum, quoi[2] | ⟨pos⟩tea Cretico cognomen|⟨tu⟩m[3] fuit, candidatum | ⟨pr⟩aetorium sacra via de|⟨du⟩c⟨en⟩tis,[4] cum magno tul⟨m⟩ultu invadit, fugien|⟨tis⟩que[5] secuta ad Octavi do|⟨mu⟩m, quae propior[6] erat, in | ⟨ipsum domicili⟩um perve|⟨nit⟩[7] * * *

These words occupy the first eleven lines of the left-hand column on the verso of the same leaf that preserves frr. 38 and 39, which form the upper half of the two columns on the recto. The supplement ⟨*annonae intolerabil*⟩ introducing this fragment would have come at the end of line 21, at the bottom of the ten lines that have been lost after the last words of fr. 39. The text is preserved on the verso of the Berlin fragment (**B**). Ends of lines in the manuscript are indicated by |, from which it can be plainly seen that the left margin of most lines in this column of text has suffered the loss of two or three letters. Supplements are to be credited to Pertz (*Berl. Abhandl.* 1847, 221ff.), unless otherwise indicated. For a schematic reconstruction of the partially preserved double leaf, see Bloch, *Didascaliae* (1961), fig. 1.

[1] *Roth*   [2] cui *B*   [3] *Heerwagen*   [4] *Dietsch*   [5] *Kreyssig*   [6] *Kreyssig*: propiore *B*   [7] in ⟨ipsum . . . perve⟨nit⟩] *Perl*

42*   46M, 43Mc, inc. 28D, 4.25K

festinantibus in summa inopia patribus

Donat. ad Ter. *Eun.* 650: to illustrate *festino* in the sense of quick and nervous action.

manuscript). Italics in the translation signifies that the text or a supplement is uncertain.

. . . *⟨unbearable⟩* was the harshness *⟨of the high price of grain⟩*. And afflicted by this, the common people attacked with a great uproar both consuls when they happened to be escorting down into the Forum, along the Sacred Way, Quintus Metellus, a candidate for the praetorship, who afterward had the cognomen Creticus; and pursuing them in their flight to Octavius' house, which was rather close by, *⟨they reached that very dwelling⟩* . . .

42* 46M, 43Mc, inc. 28D, 4.25K

Possibly the context is a food shortage that appears to have been referred to in fr. 41.

the senators acting quickly in the midst of the greatest scarcity

43 47M, 44Mc, 41D, 50K[1]

Oratio C. Cottae Consulis Ad Populum Romanum

1a ‹Post›[2] | paul‖cos dies Cotta mutata | veste p‖ermaestus,[3]
quod pro | cupit‖la volu‹n›tate †plevis a‖valia ‖ funera†,[4]
hoc modo | in co‖ntione populi dis‖seru‖‹it›:

1   "Quirites, multa | mihi ‖ pericula domi mili‖tiaeque,‖
multa advorsa fulere, qu‖orum alia tolera‖vi, parti‖m rep-
puli deorum | auxiliil‖s et virtute mea; in | quis omnibus
numquam animus negotio defuit neque decretis labos;

---

[1] The title and text of the speech (§§1–14) are transmitted by
V (Vat. lat. 3864, ff. 122r–23r). The citation from §4, as noted
below, is assigned to Book 2 by *Exc. Bob.* The opening sections,
§§1a–1 (*paucos dies . . . virtute mea; in*), occupy the first eleven
lines of the right-hand column on the verso of the same leaf that
preserves frr. 38 and 39 (the two columns on the recto) and fr. 41
(the left-hand column on the verso). The supplement ‹*Post*› introducing this fragment would have come at the end of line 21,
at the bottom of the ten lines that have been lost after the last
words of fr. 41. The division between the two scraps of this leaf,
the recto of fol. 20 of the Orleans palimpsest, the Aurelianensis
(**A**) on the right and the verso of the Berlin fragment (**B**) on the
left, is marked with ‖; ends of lines in the manuscript are indi-
cated by |. For a schematic reconstruction of the leaf, see Bloch,
Didascaliae (1961), fig. 1.   [2] *Hauler*   [3] veste permaes-
tus] *Wölfflin*: ulter *B*, ermoestus *A*

43 47M, 44Mc, 41D, 50K

The riot described in fr. 41 preceded the opening words of this fragment by no more than four to five lines of printed text (representing the loss of ten lines in the manuscript). Hence the date of this speech must be ca. June 75, as indicated by the reference to the midsummer elections in fr. 41.

The Consul Gaius Cotta's Speech to the Roman People

A few days later, Cotta[1] changed into mourning clothes because in place of the desired goodwill * * *,[2] and he spoke in this fashion at a public meeting of the people:

"I have encountered many dangers, Citizens, at home and on military service, and many adversities, some of which I have endured,[3] some averted with the help of the gods and my own courage; in all these there was never a

---

[1] C. Cotta (cos. 75) was a prominent orator of his generation and is credited by Cicero with having a controlled, no-nonsense style of speaking (*De or.* 3.31; *Brut.* 202). He is one of the interlocutors in two of Cicero's treatises (*De oratore* and *De natura deorum*). Writing in 46, Cicero (*Orat.* 132) states that no speech by Cotta was extant; hence S. had no written model on which to base this speech.

[2] Text uncertain; see textual notes.

[3] E.g., in 90, he went into exile in anticipation of a vote of condemnation in the special court set up by the *lex Varia* to assign blame for the revolt of Rome's Italian allies (App. *B Civ.* 1.37).

---

[4] plebis a̶llienata (*vel* a̶lbalienata) erat *Bücheler*: plebes abalienata fuerat *Maurenbr.*

malae secundaeque res opes, non ingenium mihi muta-
2 bant. At contra in his miseriis cuncta me cum fortuna
deseruere; praeterea senectus, per se gravis, curam dup-
licat, quoi misero acta iam aetate[5] ne mortem quidem
3 honestam sperare licet. Nam, si parricida vostri sum et bis
genitus hic deos penatis meos patriamque et summum
imperium vilia habeo, quis mihi vivo cruciatus satis est aut
quae poena mortuo? Quin omnia memorata apud inferos
supplicia scelere meo vici.
4 "A prima adulescentia in ore vostro privatus et in magistratibus egi; qui lingua, qui consilio meo, qui pecunia
voluere, usi sunt: neque ego callidam facundiam neque
ingenium ad male faciundum exercui; avidissumus priva-
tae gratiae maxumas inimicitias pro re publica suscepi,
quis victus cum illa simul, quom egens alienae opis plura
mala expectarem,[6] vos, Quirites, rursus mihi patriam
5 deosque penatis cum ingenti dignitate dedistis. Pro quibus
beneficiis vix satis gratus videar, si singulis animam quam
nequeo concesserim; nam vita et mors iura naturae sunt;

[5] *Cf. fr. dub. 14,* senecta iam aetate.   [6] cum [sic] . . .
expectarem] *Exc. Bob., GL 1.549.23* (in oratione Cottae)

---

[4] A gross exaggeration for rhetorical effect. Cotta (b. ca. 124
BC) was roughly fifty years of age.

[5] His recall from exile (see §1n.) in 82 by Sulla provided, as it
were, a second birth—a favorite metaphor applied by Cicero to
his recall from exile (see Shackleton Bailey on Cic. *Att.* 3.20.1).

[6] Lit., "tongue." Cotta was a distinguished advocate and emulated the renowned orator M. Antonius (cos. 99).

[7] These words echo Sallust's assessment of Cotta's character
in fr. 38 (*cupiens gratiam singulorum*).

lack of spirit for a task or a lack of effort for carrying out [fr. 43] decisions. Adversity and prosperity used to alter my resources, not my temperament. But in these present woes, on the contrary, along with Fortune everything has failed me. Furthermore, old age, which is burdensome on its own, doubles my anxiety, since I am not permitted in my wretchedness, near the end of my life,[4] to hope for even an honorable death. For, if I am a traitor to you, and, although twice born,[5] hold cheap my household gods and my native land and its highest power, what torture is enough for me while I live, and what punishment after death? To be sure, by wickedness such as this on my part I have outdistanced all reputed punishments among the inhabitants of the Underworld.

"From early youth, as a private citizen and in magistracies, I have lived my life before your eyes; those who wished to do so have availed themselves of my advocacy,[6] my advice, my cash. And I have not employed for evildoing clever eloquence or my talent. Though very eager for the goodwill of individuals,[7] I shouldered bitter enmities for the sake of the nation. When it and I were simultaneously overwhelmed by these enmities,[8] when being in need of another's help I was expecting further calamities, you restored me once more, Citizens, to my native land and household gods together with lofty rank. In return for these favors I would seem scarcely grateful enough, if I gave up my life for each one of you, which is impossible, for life and death are rights belonging to nature; but to live one's life among one's fellow citizens without disgrace,

[8] At the time of Cotta's exile in 90, the state was embroiled in the Social War (91–87).

ut sine dedecore cum civibus fama et fortunis integer agas, id dono datur atque accipitur.

6   "Consules nos fecistis, Quirites, domi bellique inpeditissuma re publica; namque imperatores Hispaniae stipendium, milites, arma, frumentum poscunt—et id res cogit, quoniam defectione sociorum et Sertori per montis fuga

7   neque manu certare possunt neque utilia parare; exercitus in Asia Ciliciaque ob nimias opes Mithridatis aluntur, Macedonia plena hostium est, nec minus Italiae marituma et provinciarum, quom interim vectigalia parva et bellis incerta vix partem sumptuum[7] sustinent; ita classe, quae conmeatus tuebatur, minore quam antea navigamus.

8   "Haec si dolo aut socordia nostra contracta sunt, agite ut monet ira, supplicium sumite; sin fortuna communis asperior est, quare indigna vobis nobisque et re publica

9   incipitis? Atque ego, quoius aetati mors propior est, non deprecor, si quid ea vobis incommodi demitur; neque mox ingenio corporis honestius quam pro vostra salute finem

10   vitae fecerim. Adsum en C. Cotta consul! Facio quod

---

7 *ed. Rom.*: sumptum V

---

9 I.e., it is within one's power to give or to dedicate one's life to blameless living, in exchange for which a person receives a good reputation and advancement (good fortune).   10 Metellus Pius (cos. 80) and Pompey.   11 Spaniards who defected to the charismatic rebel leader Sertorius.   12 A standard tactic of the guerrilla fighter (e.g., Plut. *Pomp.* 19.6–7).   13 On the key importance of the province of Asia and the threat posed by Mithridates, cf. fr. 1.67.8n.   14 Thracians pressed on the northern frontier of Macedonia, against whom the governor C. Curio (cos. 76) campaigned successfully in 75, the year of this speech (cf. fr. 66).

unblemished in reputation and fortune, that is something [fr. 43]
subject to being given and received as a gift.[9]

"You have elected us to the consulship, Citizens, at a
time when the nation is in dire straits at home and in
war; for our commanders in Spain[10] are demanding pay
for their troops, reinforcements, arms, and grain—and
circumstances compel this, since owing to the defection of
our allies[11] and the flight of Sertorius over the mountains,[12] they can neither contend in battle nor provide for
their requirements. Armies are being maintained in Asia
and in Cilicia because of the excessive power of Mithridates;[13] Macedonia is full of foes,[14] and no less so are the
coastal regions of Italy and the provinces,[15] while in the
meantime, our revenues, scanty and uncertain as a result
of the wars, sustain scarcely a part of our expenditures.
Hence we now sail the sea with a smaller fleet than the
one that used to protect our commerce previously.

"If these circumstances have been brought into being
as a result of misconduct or negligence on our part, go
ahead, as anger urges you,[16] and inflict punishment. But if
it is our common lot that is excessively harsh, why do you
embark upon acts unworthy of you, of us, and of the nation? I, to whose time of life death is not far off,[17] do not
ask to be spared, if my death lessens your ills at all; nor,
given the inherent nature of the body, could I soon put an
end to my life more honorably than on behalf of your
preservation. Behold, here I am, Gaius Cotta, your consul!

---

[15] Piracy had become so widespread that in 74 the praetor M.
Antonius was given a special commission to deal with the evil (see
frr. 3.1–7, 46–54).

[16] A reference to the violence of the mob reported in fr. 41.

[17] Cf. §2n.

saepe maiores asperis bellis fecere, voveo dedoque me pro
re publica! Quam deinde quoi mandetis circumspicite;
11   nam talem honorem bonus nemo volet, quom fortunae et
maris et belli ab aliis acti ratio reddunda aut turpiter mo-
12   riundum sit. Tantum modo in animis habetote non me ob
scelus aut avaritiam caesum, sed volentem[8] pro maxumis
13   benificiis animam dono dedisse. Per vos, Quirites, et gloriam maiorum, tolerate advorsa et consulite rei publicae!
14   Multa cura summo imperio inest, multi ingentes labores,
quos nequiquam abnuitis et pacis opulentiam quaeritis,
quom omnes provinciae, regna, maria, terraeque aspera
aut fessa bellis sint."

[8] *Manutius (ed. Ald. 1509)*: volente V

44* 49M, 45Mc, 42D, 51K

*Nam neque apud Sallustium . . . ullius alterius latae ab eo
legis ‹est›[1] mentio, praeter eam quam in consulatu[2] ‹tulit
invita›[3] nobilitate, magno populi studio, ut **eis ‹qui tribuni plebis›[4] fuissent alios quoque magistratus ‹capere› liceret**,[5] quod lex ‹a›[6] dictatore Sulla paucis ‹ante
annis›[7] lata prohibebat.*

Ascon. p. 66C. 22–67C.4.

[1] *Bücheler*   [2] *Madvig*: contione *codd.*   [3] *Manutius*   [4] *Manutius*   [5] ‹capere› liceret] *Manutius*: aliter
et *codd.*   [6] *Manutius*   [7] *Manutius*

I do what our ancestors often did in savage wars; I consecrate and offer myself for the nation![18] Consider to whom you are going to entrust it next; for no virtuous man will want such an honor, when he must be accountable for the vagaries of fortune and of the sea and of a war conducted by others, or else must die a shameful death. Only bear in mind that I was put to death not on account of crime or avarice, but that I willingly gave my life as a gift in return for the greatest benefits.[19] I implore you in your own name, Citizens, and by the glory of your ancestors: endure adversity, and take counsel for the nation. Inherent in the greatest empire is much responsibility, many heavy burdens, which it is futile for you to refuse while you seek the sumptuousness of peace, when all the provinces, kingdoms, seas, and lands are roiled or exhausted by wars."

[18] By the act of *devotio*, Cotta offers to give up his life as a ritual sacrifice in exchange for the preservation of the community as a whole (cf. §12 below), after the fashion of the war heroes P. Decius Mus in 340 and his son in 295 (see Cic. *Tusc.* 1.89).

[19] I.e., as a scapegoat, for the good of the community as a whole.

44* 49M, 45Mc, 42D, 51K

The consular lex Aurelia of 75, which partially reversed Sulla's curtailment of the tribunate in 82 (cf. fr. 3.15.8).

For there is no mention in Sallust . . . of any other law passed by Cotta except for the one that he carried in his consulship, much against the wishes of the nobility but with the great support of the people, that **it be permitted to those who had been plebeian tribunes to hold other magistracies,** *a right that had been taken away by a law passed by Sulla a few years earlier.*

SERTORIAN WAR (SUMMER OF 75 BC), FRR. 45–56

45 54M, 46Mc, 93D, 96K

> inter laeva moenium[1] et dextrum flumen Turiam,[2] quod Valentiam parvo intervallo praeterfluit

Prisc. *GL* 2.201.19–20: to illustrate that *Turia* is not a neut. noun but masc.

{So too Prisc. *GL* 2.143.18–19 (*inter . . . Turiam*); by contrast the following attest the neut. *Turia* in S.: Prob. *GL* 4.3.13 (*et dextrum flumen Turia*); Aug. *Reg., GL* 5.496.20 (*flumen Turia*); cf. Prob. *GL* 4.7.2.; Sacerd. *GL* 6.471.15; Phoc. *GL* 5.412.29.}

   [1] moenia *Dietsch*   [2] *Prisc.*: Turia *Prob., Aug., Sacerd., Phoc.*

46 56M, 48Mc, 83D, 81K

> dubium an insula sit quod Euri atque Austri[1] superiactis fluctibus circumlavitur

Non. p. 503M = 809L.53: to illustrate (*circum*)*lavit* (third conj.) in place of *lavat* (first conj.).

   [1] *ed. Ald. 1513*: Africi *alii*: astrici *codd.*

47* 58M, 49Mc, 53D, 19K

> apud latera certos locaverat.

Serv. & Serv. auct. ad *Aen.* 1.576: to illustrate the adj. *certus* = *firmus* or *fortis.*

HISTORIES, BOOK 2

SERTORIAN WAR (SUMMER OF 75 BC), FRR. 45–56

45 54M, 46Mc, 93D, 96K

Early in 75, at Valentia, a town friendly to Sertorius on the east coast of Hither Spain, south of the mouth of the river Turia, Pompey won a victory over Sertorian forces under the command of Herennius and Perperna (Plut. Pomp. *18.5). Valentia was destroyed, and Herennius perished in the fighting (fr. 86.6).*

between the fortification walls on the left and on the right the river Turia, which flows past Valentia a short distance away

46 56M, 48Mc, 83D, 81K

New Carthage, Carthago Nova (mod. Cartagena), situated in a coastal bay, on a projecting tongue of land surrounded by the sea on the east and the south (Polyb. 10.10.5; Liv. 26.42.7), was besieged by Sertorius (Cic. Balb. *5), most probably in 75, while Pompey was fighting at Valentia against Sertorius' two lieutenants (see preceding fragment).*

it can be mistaken for an island because it is washed round about by the waves thrown up by [lit. of] the East and South winds

47* 58M, 49Mc, 53D, 19K

In the spring of 75, Q. Metellus defeated Sertorius' general L. Hirtuleius at Segovia in Farther Spain by means of a pincers movement from the flanks (Frontin. Str. *2.3.5). Both Hirtuleius and his brother were killed (Oros. 5.23.12).*

he had stationed his reliable troops on the flanks

48 59M, 50Mc, 17D, 21K

occurrere duci et[1] proelium adcendere, adeo uti
Metello in sagum, Hirtuleio in brachium tela ve-
nirent

Non. p. 538M = 863L.23–24: to illustrate the noun *sagum* meaning a "military cloak."

[1] duci et] duces (*vel* ducibus) et *Gerlach ed. mai. in app.*:
duces [et] *Müller*

49 60M, 51Mc, 76D, 98K

vespera

Charis. *GL* 1.223.26 = p. 288B.17: attesting an example in S. of
the first decl. *vespera.*

50 61M, 52Mc, 64D, 73K

neque[1] inermos ex proelio viros quemquam agno-
turum

Serv. auct. ad *Aen.* 4.23; Prisc. *GL* 2.511.11–12, "*in II historiarum*": to give an example of *agnotus,* instead of the more usu.
agnitus, participle of the verb *agnosco.*

[1] nec *Serv.*

51* 62M, 53Mc, inc. 80D, inc. 46K

conmunem habitum transgressus

Prisc. *GL* 3.39.7–8: illustrating the compound *transgressus* meaning *supergressus.*

48 59M, 50Mc, 17D, 21K

Same context as fr. 47, describing eagerness for battle on both sides.

they rushed upon the opposing general and stoked the battle, so much so that weapons pierced Metellus' cloak and Hirtuleius' arm

49 60M, 51Mc, 76D, 98K

Possibly the context is the battle in 75 between Sertorius and Pompey at the river Sucro (south of Valentia), which was begun late in the day, toward evening (Plut. Sert. 19.4, Pomp. 19.2).

(in the?) evening

50 61M, 52Mc, 64D, 73K

Possibly the context is the battle at the river Sucro in 75, in which Sertorius rallied the troops on the left wing of his army who were being routed by Pompey (Plut. Sert. 19.7).

and that no one would recognize as true men those who left the battle unarmed

51* 62M, 53Mc, inc. 80D, inc. 46K

Possibly the context is the battle at the river Sucro in 75, in which a large Spanish warrior wounded Pompey (Plut. Pomp. 19.4).

surpassing the normal build

52* 63M, 54Mc, inc. 85D, inc. 53K

equo atque armis insignibus

Serv. ad *Aen.* 10.539: the second-century AD commentator Aemilius Asper cited this fragment in defense of the reading *insignibus armis* at *Aen.* 10.539 (as opposed to *insignibus albis,* the reading preferred by Probus).

53 66M, 55Mc, 27D, 33K

antequam regressus Sertorius instruere pugnae
suos quiret[1]

Arus. *GL* 7.481.10–11 = p. 159DC: to illustrate *instruitur* + dat. of thing.

[1] *Keil*: suosque rhetor *N1*

54 102M, 56Mc, 55D, 64K

neque subsidiis, uti soluerat, conpositis

Prisc. *GL* 2.489.10: to illustrate the pf. act. of *soleo* (*solui*), in place of the usual deponent *solitus sum.*

55†† 67M, 57Mc, 19D, 25K

avidis itaque[1] promptis ducibus ut Metellus ictu tragulae
sauciaretur

Non. p. 398M = 639L.7 (assigned to "*Hist. lib. II*"): to illustrate *saucius = vulneratus;* p. 553M = 888L.25–26 (assigned to "*Hist. lib. III*"): to illustrate *tragula = hasta.*

[1] *Lindsay (p. 398M)*: avidisque ita *Gerlach ed. mai.*: avidis ita promptisque *Kritz*: avidisque ita *codd. p. 398M*: avidissimis atque *codd. p. 553M*

52* 63M, 54Mc, inc. 85D, inc. 53K

After Pompey was wounded in the battle at the river Sucro in 75, he managed to escape by abandoning his horse, whose rich trappings diverted the attention of the enemy from pursuit when they sought to claim a share of the spoils (Plut. Pomp. *19.5). A verb of the sort* potiti sunt *(they gained possession of) may have formed the predicate (so Maurenbr.).*

his horse and distinctive arms

53 66M, 55Mc, 27D, 33K

Possibly describing the battle of Segontia *(App.* B Civ. *1.110; Plut.* Sert. *21.1–2, giving the locale as Saguntum) near the river Durius (cf. fr. 86.6) in north central Spain, where Sertorius unexpectedly had to contend with the combined armies of Pompey and Metellus.*

before Sertorius, upon his return, was able to draw up his men for battle

54 102M, 56Mc, 55D, 64K

Possibly the same context as fr. 53

and the reinforcements not having been marshaled as had been customary

55†† 67M, 57Mc, 19D, 25K

Same context as fr. 53. Metellus Pius was wounded by a spear, while fighting bravely in the encounter with Sertorius (Plut. Sert. *21.2).*

the generals [Metellus and Sertorius] being so eager and ready that Metellus was wounded with a blow of a spear

56 69M, 58Mc, 70D, 88K

haec postquam Varro in maius more[1] rumorum
audivit

Arus. *GL* 7.488.12–13 = p. 183DC: to illustrate *in maius audire,*
wrongly equating *in maius* with *plusquam.*

[1] *Bondamus*: in ore *N1*

BACKGROUND TO THIRD
MITHRIDATIC WAR, FRR. 57–65

57 71M, 83Mc, 48D, 57K

quos advorsum multi ex Bithynia volentes adcur-
rere, falsum filium arguituri

Prisc. *GL* 2.505.6–7: to illustrate the supine stem in *-uitum,* as
opposed to the more usual *-utum,* of verbs terminating in *-uo.*

58* 72M, 84Mc, deest in D et K

vir cum cura dicendus

Sen. *Ben.* 4.1.1 attributes the expression *cum cura dicendum* to
S., whereas two occurrences of the expression *cum cura dicendus*
modifying *vir,* without assignment to S. (Sen. *Prov.* 5.9; *Tranq.*
14.10), suggest that S. applied the words to a person.

56 69M, 58Mc, 70D, 88K

Since the writer M. Varro is known to have served on Pompey's staff in Spain (Varro, Rust. 3.12.7), Maurenbr. places this fragment in the context of events immediately after the Battle of Segontia in the autumn of 75, on the assumption that Varro may have filled the vacancy resulting from the death of Pompey's proquaestor and brother-in-law C. Memmius, who was killed in that battle (Plut. Sert. 21.2; Oros. 5.23.12).

after Varro had heard these reports, exaggerated as is customary with rumors

BACKGROUND TO THIRD MITHRIDATIC WAR, FRR. 57–65

57 71M, 83Mc, 48D, 57K

The death of King Nicomedes IV of Bithynia in late 75 and his will leaving his kingdom to the Roman people provided the catalyst for Mithridates to invade Bithynia and renew his struggle with Rome for control of Asia Minor. Mithridates did so on the pretext of setting the son of Nysa, wife of King Nicomedes, on the Bithynia throne. This fragment may describe Bithynians who came to Rome to challenge the legitimacy of that child against other Bithynians who sought to have him recognized as king.

against whom many willingly hastened from Bithynia, intending to prove the son an imposter

58* 72M, 84Mc, not included in D and K

Since this expression recalls Vellius Paterculus' characterization of Mithridates, king of Pontus, as "a man not to be passed over in silence or to be spoken of lightly" (2.18.1, "vir neque silendus neque dicendus sine cura"), it may have formed part of S.'s biographical sketch of Mithridates.

a man to be spoken of with due regard

59* 73M, 85Mc, 44D, 53K

Ita Darius regnum optinuit, a quo **Artabazes** *originem ducit, quem* **conditorem regni Mithridatis** *fuisse confirmat Sallustius Crispus.*

Ampel. 30.5

60 74M, 86Mc, 92D, 93K

ipse animi atrox

Arus. *GL* 7.455.24 = p. 69DC: to illustrate *atrox* + gen. of thing. [For comparable instances of *animi* in the *Historiae,* see on fr. 1.136.]

61* 75M, 87Mc, 45D, 54K

sed Mithridates extrema pueritia regnum ingressus, matre sua veneno interfecta

Serv. & Serv. auct. ad *Aen.* 5.295: to illustrate *pueritia,* which Varro distinguished as one of the five periods in the lifetime of a human being, each of those five periods being subdivided, in turn, into three phases: early, middle, and advanced (here *extrema*).

62* 76M, 88Mc, 46D, 55K

Mithridates *. . . auctore Sallustio* **et fratrem et sororem occidit.**

Schol. Gronov. ad Cic. *De imp. Cn. Pomp.* 22 (p. 318St. 30).

59* 73M, 85Mc, 44D, 53K

The founder of Mithridates' Pontic kingdom.

In this way Darius came to power, and from him **Artaba-zes** *traces his ancestry, the man who, according to Sallust, was the* **founder of Mithridates' kingdom**.

60 74M, 86Mc, 92D, 93K

Possibly a description of Mithridates' ruthlessness (App. Mith. 112).

he himself savage in spirit

61* 75M, 87Mc, 45D, 54K

Mithridates committed matricide to gain his throne (App. Mithr. 112).

but late in his boyhood[1] Mithridates ascended the throne after killing his mother with poison

[1] Mithridates' age when he came to power is variously given as eleven (Strabo 10.4.10, p. 477), twelve (Eutr. 6.12.3), or thirteen (Memnon, *FGrH* 434F22.2).

62* 76M, 88Mc, 46D, 55K

Mithridates' murder of his brother and of his sister(s) are also mentioned by App. (Mithr. 112) and Plut. (Luc. 18.2), respectively.

Mithridates killed both his brother and sister *according to Sallust.*

63* 77M, 89Mc, 47D, 56K

Mithridates corpore ingenti, perinde[1] armatus

Quint. 8.3.82: to illustrate an effective conciseness of expression.

[1] *ed. Ald. 1514, Paris lat. 7530*: proinde *AB*

64 78M, 90Mc, 49D, 58K

ibi Fimbriana e[1] seditione qui regi per obsequel-
lam[2] orationis et maxume odium Sullae graves ca-
rique[3] erant

Non. p. 215M.32–216M.2 = 318L: to illustrate the rare fem.
noun *obsequella* (= *obsequium*).

[1] Fimbriana e] *Mercier*: fimbriane se *L B^A*: fimbriana se
F^3   [2] obsequentiam *Müller*   [3] grave scarique *F^3*: grave
om. L B^A

63[*] 77M, 89Mc, 47D, 56K

Armor dedicated by Mithridates at Delphi and Nemea is said to have furnished proof of his great physical size (App. Mithr. 112).

Mithridates of huge stature, armed in similar fashion[1]

[1] I.e., his armor was huge in size as well. Cf. Florus' description of the Gallic Senones as *ipsa corporum mole, perinde armis ingentibus* (2.7.4), "by the very massiveness of their bodies, as well as by their huge arms."

64 78M, 90Mc, 49D, 58K

L. Magius and L. Fannius, Romans who had served in the First Mithridatic War under Gaius Fimbria (86–85) and remained in Asia after the war ended, were sent by Mithridates in ca. 75 to Sertorius in Spain to work out the details of a treaty (Cic. 2 Verr. 1.87; Ps-Ascon. p. 244St.1–5).

there [at the court of Mithridates] men from the Fimbrian mutiny[1] who were influential and dear to the king owing to the obsequiousness of their speech and especially their hatred of Sulla

[1] C. Fimbria, a legate under L. Flaccus (cos. 86), seized control of the army in a mutiny in which Flaccus was killed. He pursued the war against Mithridates on behalf of the Cinnan regime, but after some successes, Fimbria's army deserted to Sulla in 85 and remained in Asia after the war was concluded. Those closest to Fimbria, and hence enemies of Sulla, sought refuge with Mithridates.

65* 79M, 91Mc, 3.12D, 3.9K

Illi tertio mense pervenere in Pontum multo celerius spe
Mithridatis.

Arus. *GL* 7.463.6–7 = p. 95DC: to illustrate *celerius* + abl. of
thing.

WARS IN EAST (75 BC), FRR. 66–74

Campaigns in Macedonia, frr. 66–67

66 80M, 60Mc, 33D, 41K

Eodem anno in Macedonia C. Curio, principio veris cum
omni exercitu profectus in Dardaniam, ⟨a⟩[1] quibus potuit,[2] pecunias Appio[3] dictas coegit.

Non. p. 280M = 432L.25–28: to illustrate *dicere = promittere.*

[1] *Müller*   [2] quibus potuit modis *Carrio ex codice ali-
quo*   [3] *Roth*: appia *L* A^A: *om. B*^A

67 38M, 61Mc, inc. 15D, 3.13K

65* 79M, 91Mc, 3.12D, 3.9K

Return of L. Magius and L. Fannius (cf. fr. 64), the envoys sent by Mithridates to Sertorius in Spain to conclude an alliance (App. Mithr. 68).

Those men reached Pontus in the third month, much more quickly than Mithridates had expected.

WARS IN EAST (75 BC), FRR. 66–74

Campaigns in Macedonia, frr. 66–67

66 80M, 60Mc, 33D, 41K

In 75, C. Curio (cos. 76), the governor of Macedonia, exacted payment from enemies conquered by his predecessor as governor, Ap. Claudius (cos. 79), who had died while on campaign in 76 (fr. 34).

That same year in Macedonia, Gaius Curio set out at the beginning of spring with his whole army for Dardania,[1] and collected from whom he could[2] the money committed to Appius.

[1] A region northwest of Thrace and north of the province of Macedonia.

[2] Or "by whatever means he could," if we adopt Carrio's text.

67 38M, 61Mc, inc. 15D, 3.13K

If this fragment is from Book 2 (as Serv. auct. ad G. 4.144 suggests), it is possibly to be connected with the mutiny that broke out in Curio's army in 75, during his campaign against the Dardani near Dyrrachium, when one of his five legions refused to follow him on a "difficult and hazardous expedition" (expeditionem asperam et insidiosam, Frontin. Str. 4.1.43): so Maurenbr.

serum[1] bellum in angustiis futurum

Serv. & Serv. auct. ad *Aen.* 5.524; Serv. ad *Aen.* 6.569, 12.864; *Schol. Vatic.* ad *G.* 4.144 (in duo *cod.*: in II *edd.*): to illustrate *serus* = *gravis* (5.524, 6.569), = *diuturnum* (12.864), = *vetulus et magnus* (*G.* 4.144).

[1] serum] enim *add. Pa Serv.*, ss. *Ta Serv.*

Campaigns Against Isaurian Pirates, frr. 68–74

68 81M, 63Mc, 1.80D, K

Iter vertit ad Corycum, urbem inclutam portu atque[1] nemore in quo crocum gignitur.

Non. p. 202M = 297.7–8: to illustrate the neut. *crocum.*

{*in qua* (*quo,* Gloss.) *crocum gignitur* (Serv. and *Schol. Bern.* ad *G.* 4.182; *Schol. Stat.* ad *Theb.* 6.195; *Gloss.* 5, p. 186.31: to illustrate the neut. *crocum;* cf. Serv. auct. ad *G.* 1.56 ‹*nam et crocum in Ci›licia apud Corycum nasci Sallustius* ‹*meminit›.*}

[1] portu atque] *Stowasser:* pastusque *codd.*: specu atque *Havercamp*

69* 1.128M, 64Mc, inc. 10D, 2.39K

Fessus in Pamphyliam se receperat.

Serv. ad *Aen.* 8.232; *Gloss.* 5, p. 200.7: to illustrate *fessus* denoting more than mere physical exhaustion (*fatigatus*).

⟨he/they complained?⟩ that warfare in narrow passes would be long drawn out[1]

[1] Or, if *angustiae* does not refer to physical places but is instead metaphorical: "war in straightened circumstances would be too late" (*OLD* s.v. *serus* 4, citing this fragment).

Campaigns Against Isaurian Pirates, frr. 68–74[1]

[1] Placement of the fragments dealing with Servilius' campaign in 75 can be made relative to Pompey's letter (fr. 86) written in the autumn of 75 and found near the end of Book 2, thanks to the remains of the Fleury manuscript (see testimonia for fr. 74).

68 81M, 63Mc, 1.80D, K

S. located the town of Corycus, famed for its production of saffron (Strabo 14.5.5, p. 670), in Cilicia (Serv. auct. ad G. 1.56). If this fragment refers to a visit paid to that city by P. Servilius Vatia (cos. 79, procos. Cilicia 78–74), it attests his presence far to the east of where he is known to have conducted most of his campaigns against the Cilician pirates, in Lycia and Pamphylia (in 77–76) and against the Isauri (in 75) to the north of the Taurus mountain range. Possibly, therefore, S. or his source has confused Corycus in Lycia (cf. frr. 1.117–18), which lay on Servilius' route to the Isauri, with the town of the same name in Cilicia.

He turned his course to Corycus, a city famed for its port and woods in which the crocus [saffron plant] grows.

69* 1.128M, 64Mc, inc. 10D, 2.39K

Possibly describing the return of Servilius (cf. previous fragment) from the northern slopes of the Taurus Mountains, where he conquered the Isaurians in 75 and gained the agnomen "Isauricus" (MRR. 2.99).

Worn out he had returned to Pamphylia.

70 82M, 65Mc, 85D, 83K

omnis qui circum sunt praeminent altitudine milium passuum duorum

Arus. *GL* 7.503.9–10 = p. 241DC: to illustrate *praemineo* + acc.
and abl.

71 84M, 66Mc, 31D, 38K

nisi qua[1] flumen Clurda[2] Tauro monte defluens

Prisc. *GL* 2.202.9–10: to illustrate the name of a river ending
in *-a*.

[1] *Hertz:* quia *codd.*   [2] *Hertz (cf. Plin. HN 5.108* Cludro
flumini*):* clurdia *D:* durda *AH* lurda *Bh*

72 85M, 67Mc, 80D, 78K

genus hominum vagum[1] et rapinis suetum magis
quam agrorum cultibus

Arus. *GL* 7.510.8–9 = p. 266DC, quoting fr. 75 and this fragment:
to illustrate *suetus* + dat. of thing.

[1] *N2 (corr. Parrhasius):* vagi *N1*

73* 86M, 68Mc, inc. 88D, inc. 56K

pocula et alias res aureas, dis sacrata instrumenta,
convivio[1] mercantur[2]

Serv. auct. ad *Aen.* 8.278: to illustrate the inclusion of "drinking
cups" (*pocula*) among objects employed in sacred rites. Assignment to Book 2 rests solely on Schoell's emendation *historiarum
secundo* for the corrupt *his sunt secundum* in Serv.

174

70 82M, 65Mc, 85D, 83K

*Possibly a description of the rugged terrain that faced Servilius
on his campaign against the Isauri in 75.*

by a height of two thousand feet they tower over all
that are round about

71 84M, 66Mc, 31D, 38K

Same context as fr. 70.

except where the river Clurda, flowing down from
the Taurus mountain,

72 85M, 67Mc, 80D, 78K

*Possibly a description of the Isaurians, against whom Servilius (cf.
fr. 68) campaigned in 75.*

a nomadic race of men, more accustomed to plunder than to the tilling of fields

73* 86M, 68Mc, inc. 88D, inc. 56K

*Possibly a reference to plunder taken by pirates from Greek and
Roman temples and sacred shrines (Plut. Pomp. 24.6–7) that was
purchased by Isaurians.*

for use at banquets they purchase drinking cups and
other golden items, equipment consecrated to the
gods

---

1 *Mascivius*: convivo *F*: <ad> convivia *Thilo*
2 *Commelinus*: mereantur *F*

74 87M, 69Mc, deest in D et K

‹Oppidani noctu clam ad impetum omnia para›[**A**] re.[1]
1 De*i*n signo dato prae|cipiti iam se*c*unda vigi|lia sim*u*l
u*t*rimque pugna*m* | occipiunt, magno tumu*l*|tu primo emi-
nus pe‹r› obs|curam noc*te*m tela in in|certum iacien‹te›s,[2]
post, ubi | Romani de industria no*n* | tela neque clamorem
*r*edde|bant, perculsos formidi|ne aut desertam muniti-
o|nem [g]rati[3] avide in *f*ossas | et inde velocissumu*m* ge|nus
2 per vallum ‹p›*r*operat.[4] | At superstantes tum de|nique
saxa, pila, sudes *ia*cere | et multos prope *e*gressos | com-
minus plagis aut um|bonibus deturbare;[5] qua repen|tina
formidine pars val|lo[6] transfixa, alii super te- [**B**] -la sua
*p*raecipitati, ruinaque | multorum fossae sem*i*ple|tae sunt,

A–D = four columns of text, each 21 lines in length and 18–23
letter-spaces in width, inscribed on the recto (AB) and verso
(CD) of a single leaf forming one-half of a partially preserved
double leaf that once belonged to the so-called Fleury manuscript (*Floriacensis*). Approximately three-quarters of this double
leaf is preserved on ff. 15v, 18r, 18v, and 15r of the Orleans pa-
limpsest, the Aurelianensis (**A**). Ends of lines are marked by |;
italics indicates that the transcription is uncertain. The text of
the conjectural supplement ‹*Oppidani noctu clam ad impetum
omnia para*› introducing this fragment would have been written
at the bottom of the right-hand column, on the verso of the preceding leaf. For a schematic reconstruction of the double leaf,
see Bloch, *Didascaliae* (1961), fig. 2.

[1] *suppl. Hauler*   [2] incertum iacientes] *Hauler*: inceptum
iaciens *A*   [3] *Hauler*   [4] *Mommsen*

74 87M, 69Mc, not included in D and K

Military operations of Servilius in 75 against the Isaurians and the fall of a stronghold. (Italics in the translation signifies that the text or a supplement is uncertain.)

⟨*At night the townsmen secretly made everything ready for the attack*⟩ [**A**] Then, when the signal had suddenly been given—it being already the second watch[1]—they simultaneously began fighting on both sides,[2] in a great uproar, first hurling their missiles from a distance, through the darkness of the night, at undefined targets; afterward, when the Romans deliberately did not return fire or the shouting, the enemy thinking them paralyzed with fear or the fortifications abandoned, eagerly hastened into the trenches and from there the swiftest tried to make their way across the palisade. But it was then that those standing above [the Romans] hurled rocks, spears, and stakes, and by means of blows at close quarters and with the bosses of their shields,[3] they dislodged many of the enemy just as they had emerged nearby. And as a result of this sudden fear, some were shot through on the palisade, others were hurled headlong [**B**] on top of their own weapons. The trenches were half filled with the destruction of many; the

---

[1] I.e., an hour or two before midnight.   [2] I.e., the Isaurians attacked the Roman camp from opposite sides.   [3] See texual note. For this means of fighting at close quarters, cf. Livy 5.47.4 (*umbone ictum deturbat*), Tac. *Hist.* 4.29.

---

[5] umbonibus deturbare] *Heraeus*: omnib(us) decubare A^1 (depulsare A^2): omni re deturbare *Hauler*

[6] ⟨in⟩ vallo *Maurenbr.*

ceteris fuga tuta | fuit incerto noctis et me|tu *i*nsidiarum.

3 Dein post | *p*aucos dies *e*gestate aquae co|acta deditio est,
oppidum | incensum et cultores ve|nundat*i* eoque terrore
mo*x* | Isaura Nova *l*egati pacem | [m]orantes venere ob-
sides|que et iussa facturos *p*romit|tebant.

4 Igitur Servilius prudens | ferociae hostium, neque *il*|lis
taedium bel*l*i sed repen|tinam formidinem pacem | sua-
dere, ne de missione mu|tarent *a*nimos, quam pri|mum
moenia eorum cum | om*n*ibus co*pii*s adcessit, mol- [**C**] -lia
interim legatis *o*sten|tans et deditionem cun|c|tis praesen-
5 tibus facilius con|ven*t*uram. Praeterea *mil*|ites a p‹o›pu-
lationibus[7] agro|rum et omni noxa reti|nebat; frumentum
et a|lios conmeatus oppidani | dabant ex eorum volun|tate;
ne ‹se›[8] suspectum habe|rent, cast*r*a in plano loca|verat.

6 Deinde ex imperio | datis centum obsidibus u|bi perfugae,
arma torment|taque omnia poscebantur, | iuniores pri-
mum ex con|silio, deinde uti quisque | acc*i*derat, per totam
ur|bem ma*x*umo clamore tu|multum faciunt, neque se |
arma neque socios, dum [**D**] animae essent, prodi|tu|ros
7 firmabant. At illi qui|bus *a*etas i‹n›bellior et vetus|tat‹e›
vis Romanorum mul|tum cognita *e*rat, cupere | pacem, sed
conscientia no|*x*arum metuere, ne dat*i*s | ar*m*is mox tamen
8 extre|ma victis paterentur. *In*|ter quae trepida cunctis|que

[7] *Mommsen*: appellationibus *A*
[8] *Heerwagen*: suspectum ‹sese› *Hauler*

[4] Possibly those who had lived through the campaign of M.
Antonius against the Cilician pirates in 102.

rest found safety in flight, thanks to the cover of darkness [fr. 74] and the dread of an ambush. Then, after a few days, the lack of water compelled surrender; the town was burned, the inhabitants sold into slavery; and as a result of this terror, soon ambassadors from Isaura Nova came begging for peace; and they promised hostages and to carry out orders.

Therefore, Servilius, conscious of the enemy's ferocity and that not weariness of war but sudden fear was urging them to peace, approached their walls with all his forces as soon as possible to prevent them from changing their minds about the dispatch [of hostages]; [C] meanwhile he held out to the envoys lenient terms and that surrender would be more easily worked out when everyone was present. Moreover, he restrained his soldiers from plundering the fields and from inflicting all harm. The townsmen gave grain and other supplies according to the wishes of the Romans. So that they would not hold him in suspicion, Servilius had situated his camp in the plain. Next, after the delivery of one-hundred hostages in compliance with orders, when all deserters, arms, and catapults were demanded for surrender, the men of military age, at first by prearrangement, then as each happened along, made an uproar with tremendous shouting throughout the whole city and asserted that they would give up neither weapons nor their allies as long as [D] they still had breath in their bodies. By contrast, those who were beyond the age for military service and well acquainted with Roman power from of old,[4] desired peace but owing to their consciousness of wrongdoing feared that after giving up their arms they might nevertheless soon suffer the ultimate penalties imposed upon the conquered. Amid these ap-

in un*um* tumultuos*e* con|su*l*tantibus Servilius fu|tilem deditionem ratus, | ni met⟨u⟩s urgeret, de inpro|viso montem, ex quo in | iuga[9] oppidi teli coniec|tus erat, occupavit sacrum | Matri Magnae; et in eo cre|debatur epulari *die*bus cer|tis dea, quoius[10] erat d*e* no|mine, exaudiri sonores
* * *

[9] *Mommsen*: fugam *A*: forum *vel* tuguria *Hauler*: rugam *vel* infima *Buecheler*: terga *Hirschfeld*: fundam *Hartel*: fanum *Domaszewski*: in superiora *Friedrich*   [10] cuius *A*

SERTORIAN WAR (AUTUMN 75 BC), FRR. 75–86

75 88M, 71 Mc, 67D, 77K

genus militum suetum a pueritia latrociniis

Arus. *GL* 7.510.8–9 = p. 266DC, quoting this fragment and fr. 72: to illustrate *suetus* + dat. of thing.

76 89M, 72Mc, 54D, 63K

noctu diuque stationes et vigilias temptare

Charis. *GL* 1.207.17–18 = p. 268B.24: to illustrate the phrase *noctu diuque.*

prehensions, and while the whole populace was taking counsel for a single purpose in a disorderly fashion, Servilius, since he thought the surrender insubstantial unless fear pressed upon them, suddenly seized a mountain sacred to the Magna Mater from which there was a missile trajectory against the *ridges* of the town. (And it was believed that the goddess, from whose name the mountain was called, feasted there on specific days, that sounds were heard . . .)

SERTORIAN WAR (AUTUMN 75 BC), FRR. 75–86[1]

[1] After Sertorius' defeat at the hands of the combined forces of Pompey and Metellus in the summer of 75 at Segontia (frr. 53–55), he withdrew to Clunia (Liv. *Per.* 92), a town in the mountains, in order to draw off the Roman forces and so permit his Celtiberian allies to regroup. He eventually slipped away and kept up guerilla tactics against Pompey's forces, which remained in the northwest sector of Nearer Spain during the winter of 75/74.

75 88M, 71 Mc, 67D, 77K

This fits the description of Sertorius' Spanish forces (Plut. Sert. 14.1).

soldiers of a kind accustomed to banditry from boyhood

76 89M, 72Mc, 54D, 63K

Possibly a description of Sertorius' tactics in the autumn of 75.

to make trial of their outposts and watches by day and by night

77 90M, 74Mc, 56D, 65K

ad hoc pauca piratica,[1] actuaria navigia

Non. p. 535M = 857L.2: cited under the lemma *actuariae,* which Non. defines as swift, light ships (*naviculae celeres*), so named because they are able to be driven (*agi*) swiftly.

[1] *Junius*: piraticae (–ce) *codd.*: piratica e‹t› *Mähly*

78 91M, 73Mc, 13D, 18K

Neque virgines nuptum a parentibus mittebantur,[1] sed ipsae belli promptissumos deligebant.[2]

Arus. *GL* 7.503.13–14 = p. 241DC: to illustrate *promptus* + gen. of thing.

[1] ‹pro›mittebantur *Ursinus*   [2] diligebant *A*

79 92M, 75Mc, deest in D et K

1 ‹A matribus parentum facino›lra militaria viri‹s memora›lbantur[1] in bellum a‹ut ad la›ltrocinia pergent‹ibus, ubi[2] il›llorum fortia facta ‹ca›lnebant.

2   Eo[3] postqua‹m Pom›lpeius infenso exer‹citu›l adventare conper‹tus›l est, maioribus natu p‹acem›l et iussa uti faceren‹t sua›ldentibus, ubi nihil ab‹nu›lendo[4] profici-

3 unt, se‹para›ltae a viris arma cep‹ere.›[5]l Occupato prope

[1] *suppl. ex Serv. ad Aen. 10.281*

[2] *Maurenbr.*: qui *Hauler*: quae *Jordan in app.*

[3] *Maurenbr.*: ea *A*: eae *Jordan in app.*

[4] admonendo *von Hartel*

[5] *Reynolds*: cep‹ere et› *Maurenbr.*

77 90M, 74Mc, 56D, 65K

In the autumn of 75, Sertorius cut off the supplies of Pompey and Metellus by sea by means of piratical vessels (Plut. Sert. 21.7).

in addition, a few piratical, light galleys[1]

[1] *Actuariae naves* = vessels propelled by both sails and oars (Isid. *Etym.* 19.1.24).

78 91M, 73Mc, 13D, 18K

The content of this fragment appears to harmonize with the description of the martial spirit of the Celtiberian women found in fr. 79, which is preserved in the Orleans palimpsest.

Nor were maidens sent in marriage by their parents, but they themselves used to chose men most inclined to war.

79 92M, 75Mc, not included in D and K

If the name of the town mentioned in §3 of this passage is correctly restored (Meo<riga>), the campaign may have been one conducted by Pompey against the Vaccaei in northwest Hither Spain, where he spent the winter of 75/74 (Plut. Sert. 21.8). (Italics in the translation signifies that the text or a supplement is uncertain.)

Whenever the men set off to war or banditry, <*their mothers*> used to remind them of their <*fathers'*> martial <*deeds*> when they sang of the brave achievements of those heroes.

After it was learned that Pompey was approaching that district with a hostile army, when the women made no headway with opposing the elders who urged peace and compliance with the orders [of the Romans], they withdrew from the men and took up arms. After they had taken

183

Meo⟨rigam⟩[6] | quam tutissumo[7] loc⟨o, e⟩los[8] testabantur
ino⟨pes pa⟩ltriae parientumque ⟨et⟩l libertatis, eoque
uber⟨a⟩,[9]l partus et cetera mul⟨ierum⟩[10]l munia viris ma-
4 ne⟨re⟩. Quis rebus adcensa iu⟨ven⟩ltus decreta senior⟨um
as|pernata⟩ * * *

This fragment forms a column of text 21 lines long and 18–23
letter-spaces wide on the left-hand portion of the recto of a leaf
that once belonged to the so-called Fleury codex (*Floriacensis*).
It is preserved on fol. 16v of the Orleans palimpsest, the Aurelianensis (**A**), and formed part of the same gathering in the *Floriacensis* as the one containing fr. 74, from the last line of which
it was separated by either one or two no longer extant leaves (4–8
columns of text, = 84–168 lines in the manuscript, = approx.
40–80 lines of printed text), depending on whether the gathering
was a quaternio (Bloch, *Didascaliae* [1961], 66) or a quinio (Perl
[1968], 33–35). Slightly less than half of this leaf has survived,
since it is missing two columns of text (the right-hand column of
the recto and the left-hand column of the verso). Ends of lines
in the manuscript are indicated by |, from which it can be plainly
seen that the right margin of most lines in this column of text has
suffered the loss of three to six letters. Italics indicates that the
transcription is uncertain, or that a supplement is highly conjectural or merely hypothetical. Supplements are to be credited to
Hauler, unless otherwise indicated. The text of the conjectural
supplement ⟨A matribus . . . facino⟩ introducing this fragment
would have been written at the bottom of the right-hand column,
on the verso of the preceding, no longer extant, leaf.

{Cf. Serv. ad *Aen.* 10.281: noting that according to S., it was the
custom of Spaniards for mothers to recall the deeds of their fathers to young men setting out for war: *in bella euntibus iuveni-
bus parentum facta memorarentur a matribus.*}

possession of the securest possible place near Meo‹riga›,[1]   [fr. 79]
they solemnly declared that the men were destitute of
homeland, of women to bear their children, and of freedom; and for that reason what remained for the men was
the nursing of children and giving birth and other functions of women. Stirred by this protest, the youth *rejected*
the decisions of their elders . . .

[1] The name of a town in the territory of the Vaccaei as given
by some manuscripts of Ptolemy (*Geog.* 2.6.49), although the
majority read "Lacobriga," a name also attested by Plin. (*HN*
3.26) and the *Itineraria Antonini Augusti* (395, 449, 454).

---

[6] *Hauler (ex Ptolem. Geog. 2.6.49 var. lect.)*

[7] tutissimo *A*

[8] *Hauler*: loc‹o ill›os *Maurenbr.*

[9] *von Hartel*

[10] *Wölfflin*

80 93M, 76Mc, deest in D et K

1 ⟨*oppidani confirmant religione iuris iu*|*randi*⟩[1] interposita, *si* exempl|⟨ti ob⟩sidione forent, fidem |⟨et soci⟩etatem[2] acturos; nam |⟨ant⟩ea inter illum Pom|⟨peiu⟩mque fluxa pace dubil⟨tav⟩erant.

2 Tum Romanus |⟨exe⟩rcitus frumenti gral⟨tia⟩[3] remotus in Vascones |⟨est it⟩emque[4] Sertorius mol⟨vit s⟩e,[5] quoius[6] multum in|⟨terer⟩*at*, ne ei *periret* As*iae* |⟨*spes.* ⟩[7]

3 Aquandi[8] facultate |⟨Pom⟩pe*ius* aliquot dies |⟨cas⟩tra stativa *h*abuit, |⟨mo⟩*di*ca valle disiunctis |⟨ab eo⟩[9] hostibus, ne*que* propin|⟨quae⟩ civitates Mutudurei |⟨et . . . ⟩*e*ores hun*c* aut illum |⟨com⟩meatibus iuvere; fames

4 |⟨am⟩bos fatigavit. Dein tal⟨me⟩n Pompeius quadrato |⟨agmine procedit⟩ * * *

This fragment forms a column of text 21 lines long and 18–23 letter-spaces wide and occupies the partially intact right-hand portion of the verso of the leaf containing fr. 79 on the left-hand portion of the recto. The gap between this fragment and fr. 79 is forty-two lines in the manuscript (the right-hand column of recto and left-hand column of verso, which were inscribed on the missing portion of this leaf), = approx. only twenty lines of printed text. See Bloch, *Didascaliae* (1961), 67. Ends of lines in the manuscript are indicated by |, from which it can be plainly seen that the left margin of most lines in this column of text has suffered the loss of two to four letters. Italics signifies that the transcription is uncertain, or that a supplement is highly conjectural or merely hypothetical. The text of the conjectural supplement ⟨ *oppidani confirmant religione iuris iu*| introducing this fragment would have been written at the bottom of the column that once occupied the missing left-hand portion of this verso.

[1] *Pecere*   [2] ⟨*et soci*⟩*etatem Perl*   [3] *Wölfflin*   [4] *Wölf-flin*   [5] *Hauler*   [6] *cuius A*

80 93M, 76Mc, not included in D and K

A scarcity of supplies forced Pompey and Sertorius to withdraw eastward from the territory of the Vaccaei to the region occupied by the Vascones at the foot of the Pyrenees. (Italics in the translation signifies that the text or a supplement is uncertain.)

‹*The townsmen gave assurances by*› pledging ‹*the sanctity of an oath*› that they would observe a faithful alliance, if they were released from the siege; for previously they had vacillated between Sertorius and Pompey with a wavering peace.

Then the Roman army was withdrawn into the territory of the Vascones for the sake of grain. And Sertorius likewise altered his position; it was greatly in his interest not to lose his *hope* of Asia.[1] For a few days Pompey maintained a stationary camp thanks to a means of fetching water, being separated from the enemy by just a modest valley; and the nearby communities, the Mutudurei and the * * *, did not aid Pompey or Sertorius with supplies. Hunger wore out both sides. Then, however, Pompey ‹*advanced with his line of march*› in a squared formation . . .

[1] I.e., of help from that region thanks to an alliance with Mithridates, king of Pontus (cf. frr. 64–65); but the text is highly uncertain.

---

7 periret Asiae ‹spes›] *Hartel*: perinde Asiae . . . A
8 *Wölfflin*: atque vadi e A
9 *Wölfflin*

81 94M, 77Mc, 28D, 34K

Titurium legatum cum cohortibus quindecim in Celtiberia
hiemem agere iussit praesidentem socios.

Arus. *GL* 7.498.24–25 = p. 223DC: to illustrate *praesideo* + acc.
of thing.

82 95M, 78Mc, 29D, 35K

Hi[1] saltibus occupatis Termestinorum[2] agros invasere, fru-
mentique ex inopia gravi satias facta.

Non. p. 172M = 253L.11–13: to illustrate *satias = satietas.*

[1] *Iunius*: in *codd.*: i *Müller*: his *Mercier*   [2] *Lipsius*: tmex-
trinorum (*an* termextrinorum) *L*: termextrinorum *F*[3]: tamen ex-
ternorum *B*[A]

83 96M, 79Mc, 51D, 48K

multique conmeatus interierant insidiis latronum

Non. p. 449M = 721.26–27: to illustrate the use of such verbs as
interfici and *occidi* with inanimate subjects.

84* 34M, 80Mc, 73D, 37K

quae pecunia ad Hispaniense bellum Metello facta
erat

Donat. ad Ter. *Phorm.* 38; *Schol. Bemb.* in Ter. loc. cit.
(***p>*ecunia ad* | [. . .]*m facta erat* | [. . .]): to illustrate the
simple verb *facere* with the meaning of the compound *conficere*
(to amass).

81 94M, 77Mc, 28D, 34K

The distribution of Pompey's forces in the winter of 75/74.

He [Pompey] ordered his legate Titurius to spend the winter in Celtiberia with fifteen cohorts, watching over their allies.

82 95M, 78Mc, 29D, 35K

Roman forces—possibly those under Titurius, fr. 81—raid enemy territory for grain in the winter of 75/74.

These forces, after occupying the passes, invaded the territory of the Termestini,[1] and in place of a serious shortage, a sufficiency of grain was produced.

[1] The inhabitants of Termes, a town in northern Spain, southwest of Numanita, on good terms with Sertorius (Flor. 2.10.9).

83 96M, 79Mc, 51D, 48K

Interruption of supplies during the winter of 75/74 caused by guerilla tactics (cf. Plut. Sert. 21.7).

and many supply trains had perished as a result of ambushes by bandits

84* 34M, 80Mc, 73D, 37K

A financial strain pressed especially on Pompey, whereas Metellus Pius had been provided for from the treasury.

money which had been appropriated for Metellus to fund the Spanish war

85 97M, 72D, 94K

argentum mutuum arcessivit

Prisc. *GL* 2.534.24: to illustrate that verbs terminating in *–so*
form the pf. in *–ivi*.

86 98M, 82Mc, 96D, 3.1K

Epistula Cn. Pompei Ad Senatum[1]

1 "Si advorsus vos patriamque et deos penatis tot labores et
pericula suscepissem, quotiens a prima adulescentia ductu
meo scelestissumi hostes fusi et vobis salus quaesita est,

A–D = four columns of text, each 21 lines in length and 18–23
letter-spaces in width, inscribed on the recto (AB) and verso
(CD) of a single leaf forming one-half of a partially preserved
double leaf that once belonged to the so-called Fleury manuscript (*Floriacensis*). Somewhat less than three-quarters of this
double leaf is preserved on ff. 16r, 17v, 17r, and 16v of the Orleans palimpsest, the Aurelianensis (**A**). It belonged to the same
gathering as the one containing fr. 80, from the last line of which
this leaf is separated by one, no-longer-extant, double leaf (eight
columns of text, = 168 lines in the manuscript). Since approx. one
and a half of those eight columns would have been occupied by
the opening of Pompey's letter (§§1–3a), the gap between fr. 80
and the opening of the letter is approx. 140 lines in the manuscript, = 75 lines of printed text. See Bloch, *Didascaliae* (1961),
67–68. Ends of lines are marked by | only for the portion that is
preserved solely by **A** (§§11–12); italics indicates that the transcription is uncertain.

[1] The title and text of the speech (§§1–10) are transmitted by
V (Vat. lat. 3864, fol. 125r–v). The citation from §3, as noted below, is assigned by Diomedes to Book 2.

85 97M, 72D, 94K

Possibly a reference to money borrowed by Pompey to pay his troops (cf. fr. 86.9).

he raised borrowed money

86 98M, 82Mc, 96D, 3.1K

At the end of his third campaign season since being appointed to fight Sertorius (§2), in the autumn of 75 (§11), Pompey found himself cut off from supplies (cf. fr. 83) and unable to force the enemy to a decisive battle (fr. 43.6). Having long since exhausted his own means (§§2, 9), Pompey wrote to the senate, requesting reinforcements and money. The device of having a letter serve the function of a speech was employed by Thucydides, and Pompey's dispatch shares much in common with the report sent by the general Nicias to Athens in the autumn of 414, when the Syracusan expedition was in dire straits (Thuc. 7.11–15).

Gnaeus Pompey's Dispatch to the Senate

"If I had undertaken *against* you and my native land and tutelary gods[1] so many dangerous exertions on those many occasions when from my early youth[2] your most wicked foes have been routed and your safety secured through my

---

[1] See 1.67.16n.

[2] In 83, at the age of twenty-two, Pompey had raised an army on his own initiative to fight for Sulla in the civil war.

nihil amplius in absentem me statuissetis quam adhuc agitis, patres conscripti, quem contra aetatem proiectum ad bellum saevissumum cum exercitu optume merito, quantum est in vobis, fame, miserruma omnium morte, confecistis. Hacine spe populus Romanus liberos suos ad bellum misit? Haec sunt praemia pro volneribus et totiens ob rem publicam fuso sanguine? Fessus scribundo mittundoque legatos omnis opes et spes privatas meas consumpsi, quom interim a vobis per triennium vix annuus sumptus datus est. Per deos inmortalis, utrum censetis me vicem aerari praestare[2] an [A] exercitum sine frumento et stipendio habere posse ?

4 "Equidem fateor me ad hoc bellum maiore studio quam consilio profectum, quippe qui nomine modo imperi a vobis accepto, diebus quadraginta exercitum paravi hostisque in cervicibus iam Italiae agentis ab Alpibus in Hispaniam submovi; per eas iter aliud atque Hannibal, nobis opportunius, patefeci. Recepi Galliam, Pyrenaeum,

2

3

5

---

[2] utrum . . . praestare] utrum vicem me aerari praestare credi-tis, *Diom. GL 1.366.12–13*

---

[3] Pompey was only twenty-eight years old when he was sent to Spain in 77 to fight Sertorius.

[4] The years 77, 76, and 75, since his posting in 77, after the suppression of the revolt of Lepidus.

[5] An exaggeration: Pompey already had at his disposal an army that been entrusted to him early in 77 to suppress the rebellion of Lepidus (Plut. *Pomp.* 16.3), one he refused to disband (op. cit. 17.3). Forty days are also said to have been the length of Pompey's African campaign in 81 and the first phase of his campaign against the pirates in 67 (op. cit. 12.8, 26.7).

command of military forces, you would have passed no   [fr. 86]
more severe measures against me in my absence than you
are doing up to now, Members of the Senate. For after
having flung me, in spite of my youth,[3] into a most cruel
war, you have, so far as it is in your power, destroyed me
along with a well-deserving army by starvation, the most
wretched of all deaths. With this expectation did the Roman people send their sons to war? Are these the rewards
for wounds and for so often shedding our blood for the
nation? Wearied from writing and sending envoys, I have
exhausted all my personal resources and hopes, while, in
the meantime, over the course of three years[4] you have
given me the means of meeting barely one year's expenses.
By the immortal gods! Do you suppose I can play the role
of a treasury or [A] maintain an army without food and
pay?

"For my part, I admit that I set out for this war with
more zeal than deliberation, seeing that within forty days
of receiving from you merely the title "commander," I
made ready an army[5] and removed from the Alps into
Spain an enemy that was already active on the neck of
Italy.[6] Over those mountains, I opened a different route
from the one taken by Hannibal, one more convenient for
us.[7] I recovered Gaul, the Pyrenees, Lacetania, and the

6 A reference to the suppression of unrest in Transalpine Gaul
(cf. §5 *recepi Galliam* and fr. 21).

7 Appian (*B Civ.* 1.109) places this new route in the region of
the sources of the Rhone and the Po rivers (which are some 150
miles apart). Pompey's route may have been through the Cottian
Alps, via the Mount Genèvre Pass.

Lacetaniam, Indigetis et primum impetum Sertori victoris novis militibus et multo paucioribus sustinui hiememque castris inter saevissumos hostis, non per oppida [**B**] neque ex ambitione mea egi.

6   "Quid deinde proelia aut expeditiones hibernas, op-pida excisa aut recepta enumerem, quando res plus valet quam verba? Castra hostium apud Sucronem capta et proelium apud flumen Durium[3] et dux hostium C. Heren-nius cum urbe Valentia et exercitu deleti satis clara vobis sunt; pro quis, o grati patres, egestatem et famem redditis.

7   Itaque meo et hostium exercitui par condicio est; namque stipendium neutri datur, victor uterque in Italiam venire

8   potest. Quod ego vos moneo quaesoque ut animadvortatis [**C**] neu cogatis necessitatibus privatim mihi consulere.

9   Hispaniam citeriorem, quae non ab hostibus tenetur, nos aut Sertorius ad internecionem vastavimus praeter mari-

---

[3] *AV (cf. Cic. Balb. 5)*: Turiam *Ciacconius*

---

[8] Lacetania, a region, and the Indigetes, a people, were lo-cated in the extreme northeast of Spain.

[9] As he might have done by quartering his troops in the rela-tive comfort of native towns.

[10] Captured by Pompey's legate L. Afranius (cos. 60) from Sertorius' deputy commander M. Perperna in the most recent campaign season (Plut. *Sert.* 19.9; cf. App. *B Civ.* 1.110, mistak-enly crediting Metellus Pius with this accomplishment).

[11] Perhaps the Battle of Segontia (cf. fr. 53), the last in a se-quence of three major battles in 75, coming after Valentia and Sucro. Recent modern editors who accept Ciacconius' conjecture *"Turiam"* make this clause refer to the Battle of Valentia, which is also alluded to in the next clause (cf. fr. 45).

Indigetes;[8] with unseasoned soldiers, far fewer in number,   [fr. 86]
I withstood the first onslaught of Sertorius fresh from past
victories; and I spent the winter in camp, amid the most
savage foes, not in the towns, [**B**] and not with a view to
ingratiate myself with the troops.[9]

"Why then should I enumerate battles or winter campaigns, the towns destroyed or recaptured, since action
speaks louder than words? The capture of the enemy's
camp at Sucro,[10] the battle at the Durius River,[11] and the
destruction of Gaius Herennius,[12] leader of the enemy,
together with his army and the city of Valentia, are quite
well known to you. And in return for these, O grateful
senators, you give me want and hunger. Thus the condition of the enemy's army and mine is the same; for neither
receives pay, and each can arrive in Italy in victory.[13] I
warn and ask you to pay attention to this situation, [**C**] and
not to compel me as a result of dire straits to look after my
own, personal interests. Hither Spain—the part which is
not in the possession of the enemy—either we or Sertorius
have devastated to the point of utter destruction, except

[12] Tribune of the plebs in 80 (or 88?), his name is linked with
Perperna's (Plut. *Pomp.* 18.5), both having escaped to join Sertorius in Spain after having fought in the collapsed revolt of Lepidus
in 77. The battle of Valentia (cf. fr. 45) took place in 75, somewhat
before the battle at Sucro.

[13] I.e., in view of the equal footing on which the senate has
placed the opposing armies (by failing to provide for Pompey's
army), each has an equally good chance to win the war and return
to Italy (disastrous, of course, if Sertorius' army does so).

tumas civitates, ⟨quae⟩ ultro[4] nobis sumptui onerique;[5]
Gallia superiore anno Metelli exercitum stipendio fru-
mentoque aluit et nunc malis fructibus ipsa vix agitat; ego
non rem familiarem modo, verum etiam fidem consumpsi.
10 Relicui vos estis: qui nisi subvenitis, invito et praedicente
me exercitus hinc et cum eo omne bellum Hispaniae in
Italiam transgredien[**D**]tur."

11   Hae litterae principio sequen|tis anni recitatae in
sena|tu. Sed consules decretas | a patribus provincias in|ter
se paravere:[6] Cotta Gal|liam citeriorem habuit, | Ciliciam
12 Octavius. Dein | proxumi consules, L. Lu|cullus et M.
Cotta, litteris | nuntiisque Pompei gravi|ter perculsi,
quom[7] summ(a)e | rei gratia tum ne exerci|tu in Italiam
deducto neq(ue) | laus sua neque dignitas | esset, omni
modo stipen|dium ⟨e⟩t supplementum pa|ravere, adni-
tente maxu|me[8] nobilitate, quoius[9] pleri|que iam tum lin-
gua ferociam | suam ⟨ostentabant n⟩ec[10] dicta factis
seque|⟨bantur⟩.[11]

4 ⟨quae⟩ ultro] *Manutius (ed. Ald. 1509)*: ulterior *Schöne*

5 *Decembrius*: onorique *V*: aerique sunt *A*

6 partivere *Wölfflin* (cf. *Jug. 43.1, sed vide Cassius Hamina, FRHist 6F14 = fr. 11P*, de regno par⟨ar⟩ent inter se)

7 cum *A*

8 maxime *A*

9 cuius *A*

10 ⟨ostentabant n⟩ec] *Shackleton Bailey*: et *A*

11 *Hauler*: aequabant *Diggle fort. recte*

for the coastal towns, which are an expense and a burden   [fr. 86]
to us on top of everything else.[14] Last year, Gaul supported
the army of Metellus with pay and grain, and now it can
scarcely survive on its own because of a failure of the
crops; I myself have exhausted not only my personal
means but also my credit. You are my one remaining re-
source; unless you come to my rescue, the army, and with
it the whole Spanish war, will, against my wishes—but you
have been forewarned by me—cross over from here into
Italy."

[**D**] This dispatch was read in the senate at the beginning of the following year.[15] But the consuls[16] arranged
between themselves the provinces decreed by the senate:
Cotta had Hither Gaul, Octavius Cilicia. Afterward, the
succeeding consuls, Lucius Lucullus and Marcus Cotta,
having been gravely dismayed by Pompey's letter and envoys, both on account of the seriousness of the matter and
for fear that they would have no renown and standing if
the army returned to Italy, used every means to provide
pay for the troops and reinforcements.[17] And they were
aided especially by the nobles, most of whom were already
even then displaying their customary arrogance in speech
and not following up their words with deeds.[18]

[14] Text uncertain. If the emendation *"ulterior"* is adopted,
place a semicolon after "costal towns" and substitute for the relative clause "Farther Spain is an expense and burden to us."

[15] 74

[16] Those of the previous year, 75, now proconsuls.

[17] Two additional legions were sent to Spain in 74 (App. *B Civ.*
1.111).

[18] The text after "even then" is uncertain.

FRAGMENTS OF UNCERTAIN
PLACEMENT IN BOOK 2, FRR. 87–110

*Assigned to Various Contexts by Maurenbr.,
frr. 87–92*

87 18M, 92Mc, 71D, 91K

belli sane sciens[1]

Arus. *GL* 7.509.25 = p. 265DC (assigned to *"Hist. II"*): to illustrate *sciens* + gen.; *Schol.* Γ ad Hor. *Epist.* 1.15.5: to illustrate *sane = valde.*

[1] bellica nesciens *N1 Arus.*

88 20M, 93Mc, 25D, 31K

quem ex Mauretania rex Leptasta proditionis insimulatum cum custodibus miserat

Prisc. *GL* 2.143.12–14: to illustrate a masc. proper noun ending in *–a.*

89* 55M, 47Mc, inc. 5D, 1.41K

FRAGMENTS OF UNCERTAIN
PLACEMENT IN BOOK 2, FRR. 87–110

*Assigned to Various Contexts by Maurenbr.,
frr. 87–92*

87 18M, 92Mc, 71D, 91K

*Maurenbr. speculated that these words described Pompey, but
they could equally well have described Sertorius since they closely
resemble Appian's characterization of him: "no one else was more
skilled in the art of war" (οὔτε πολεμικώτερος ἄλλος, B Civ.
1.112).*

truly knowledgeable in war

88 20M, 93Mc, 25D, 31K

*Maurenbr. speculated that this incident involving the king of
Mauretania figured in the summary of Pompey's past achievements, including his Numidian campaign in 81, but Leptasta is
otherwise unattested.*

whom king Leptasta had sent from Mauretania, under guard and accused of treason

89* 55M, 47Mc, inc. 5D, 1.41K

*Possibly to be assigned to the context of Pompey's victory in early
75 over Sertorian forces under the command of Perperna and
Herennius (see fr. 45). Since Servius quotes the fragment to illustrate the adj. verus in the sense of "good" or "upright," the
statement presumably concerns something admirable that is being
contrasted with the criticism implicit in tam paucis prospectis.
Consequently, it is best to supply a noun denoting "bravery," such
as fortitudo or virtus (Maurenbr.), rather than culpa (Schulten)
or ratio (Frassinetti).*

Perpernae[1] tam paucis pro‹s›pectis[2] vera est aesti-
manda

Serv. auct. ad *Aen.* 12.694: quoting fr. 1.121 and this fragment:
to illustrate the adj. *verus* = that which is *rectum et bonum* [i.e.,
"morally upright," *OLD* 9].

[1] *Mähly*: Perpenna *F*   [2] *Mascivius*: pro pectus *F*

90 48M, 94Mc, 90D, 89K

quom multa dissereret ludis Apollini circensibus

Arus. *GL* 7.490.25–26 = p. 192DC: to illustrate the dat. of a god
with the noun *ludi* (games).

91 51M, 95Mc, 88D, inc. 83K

et continetur gravis[1]

Non. p. 315M = 492L.5: to illustrate *gravis* = *molestus* (troublesome).

[1] gravius *Mercier*

Perperna's ⟨bravery?⟩[1] must be judged honest, despite his having taken so few precautions

[1] If, instead of a word meaning "bravery," *culpa* is supplied, the translation becomes "proper blame is to be assigned to P., since he took so few precautions"; or if *ratio*, "P. ought to have given more weight to calculation."

90 48M, 94Mc, 90D, 89K

Because the holding of a public meeting during the annual festival in honor of Apollo (July 6–13), especially on the day of the chariot races in the circus (July 13), would have been rare and seems to point to a political crisis, Maurenbr. speculated that the occasion was a struggle over passage of the lex Aurelia *in 75 (see fr. 44). Dietsch, by contrast, assigned this fragment to the clash between the tribune Sicinius and consul C. Curio in 76. Certainty is impossible.*

while he was speaking at length during the circus games in honor of Apollo

91 51M, 95Mc, 88D, inc. 83K

Maurenbr. conjectured that the missing subject of the verb may have been seditio *(strife), or* tumultus *(uprising), or* ira *(rage) and so refer to the popular unrest in 75 that was curbed by the consul Cotta (see frr. 40–43), but certainty is impossible.*

and troublesome _____ is kept under control

92 53M, 96Mc, 93D, 96K

post, ubi fiducia nimius

Arus. *GL* 7.495.16 = p. 209DC: to illustrate *nimius* + abl. of thing.

A Battle Near a River, frr. 93–97: Possibly in Spain, Near Valentia and the River Turia (cf. fr. 45), or the River Sucro (cf. frr. 49–52 and fr. 86.6), or the River Durius (cf. fr. 53 and fr. 86.6)

93 99M, 97Mc, 57D, 66K

Parte[1] legio‹nis›[2] flumen transducta, castra dilatavit.

Arus. *GL* 7.513.22–23 = p. 278DC: to illustrate *transductus* + acc. of thing.

   [1] *Keil dubitanter in app.*: parva *Kritz*: parco *N1*   [2] *Keil dubitanter in app.*: legio‹num› *Maurenbr.*

94 100M, 98Mc, 62D, 71K

Suos equites hortatus vado transmisit.

Arus. *GL* 7.513.27–28 = p. 278DC: to illustrate *transmitto* + abl. of thing [means].

95 101M, 99Mc, 63D, 72K

Ictu eorum qui in flumen ruebant[1] necabantur.

Donat. ad Ter. *Ad.* 319: to illustrate *ruo* as a v.t. ("to hurl head-long"), and yet *ruo* is intransitive in this and the two other examples given by Donat. (Verg. *G.* 3.255 and Hor. *Epist.* 2.2.75)—hence Maurenbr.'s proposed suppl. *se.*

92 53M, 96Mc, 93D, 96K

*Maurenbr. speculated that S. may have been describing one of
Sertorius' lieutenants, Herennius or Perperna, who was instructed
by Sertorius in 76 to use caution in keeping Pompey at bay (Livy
91, fr. 22), but certainty is impossible. Cf. fr. 89.*

afterward, when with excessive confidence

> *A Battle Near a River, frr. 93–97: Possibly in
> Spain, Near Valentia and the River Turia (cf. fr.
> 45), or the River Sucro (cf. frr. 49–52 and fr. 86.6),
> or the River Durius (cf. fr. 53 and fr. 86.6)*

93 99M, 97Mc, 57D, 66K

Having led part of the legion across the river, he enlarged
the camp.

94 100M, 98Mc, 62D, 71K

After encouraging his own cavalry, he sent them across by
means of a ford.

95 101M, 99Mc, 63D, 72K

They were slain by the impact of those who were rushing
into the river.

---

[1] ‹se› ruebant *Maurenbr.*

96 4.67M, 2.100Mc, 2.52D, 2.59K

ruinaque pars magna[1] suismet aut proxumorum telis, ceteri vicem[2] pecorum obtruncabantur

Non. p. 497M = 799L.29–30: to illustrate the use of a nom. or
acc. where an abl. would be more usual (here *vicem* in place of
vice).

[1] magna pars *Müller*   [2] *Passerat*: vece L A^A: vete
C^A: vice B^A

97 107M, 101Mc, 68D, 82K

Murum ab angulo dexteri lateris ad paludem haud procul
remotam duxit.

Serv. auct. ad *Aen.* 1.423: to illustrate the use of *duco* = *aedificare*
(to build) with *murum*.

Miscellaneous, frr. 98–110

98 110M, 102Mc, 65D, 74K

omnia sacrata[1] corpora[2] in rates inposuisse

Arus. *GL* 7.483.28–29 = p. 168DC: to illustrate *impono* with *in*
+ acc. of thing.

[1] sauciata *Dietsch*: s**ciata *V3*   [2] pecora *Wölfflin*

99 103M, 103Mc, 59D, 68K

Ille festinat subsidiis principes augere et densere frontem.

Eutych. *GL* 5.482.22–23: to illustrate the second conj. verb *den-
seo,* in contrast with first conj. *denso.*

96 4.67M, 2.100Mc, 2.52D, 2.59K

Maurenbr. supposed that this fragment (assigned by Non. to Book 2) belonged instead to Book 4 and described the crush at the Battle of Tigranocerta (Plut. Luc. 28.5). It may, however, have complemented the preceding fragment, describing a confused battle in the riverbed, modeled on Thuc. 7.84.3 (so McGushin).

and in the melee a great many were being cut down by their very own weapons or those of their neighbors, the rest after the fashion of cattle

97 107M, 101Mc, 68D, 82K

Possibly a defensive measure taken by Sertorius to protect his camp at the Battle of Sucro, near which was the swamp of Albufera (so La Penna).

He extended the wall from the corner of the right side [of his camp?] up to a swamp not far away.

Miscellaneous, frr. 98–110

98 110M, 102Mc, 65D, 74K

to have placed all the consecrated[1] bodies on rafts

[1] Or "wounded," if the conjecture *sauciata* is adopted. Kritz explicated "sacred bodies" as "bodies of men dedicated to the gods," hence, "priests" (cf. Verg. *Aen.* 11.591, describing Camilla).

99 103M, 103Mc, 59D, 68K

He hastened to augment the foremost troops with reinforcements and to make the front deeper.

100 104M, 104Mc, 60D, 69K

Terror hostibus et fiducia suis incessit.

Arus. *GL* 7.488.1 = p. 182DC: to illustrate *incedo* + dat.

101 105M, 105Mc, 61D, 70K

†Circumventis[1] dextera nuda[2] ferrum erat,[3] saxa aut quid
tale capita[4] adfligebant.[5]†

Arus. *GL* 7.456.6–7 = p. 71DC, citing fr. 3.76 and this fragment:
to illustrate *adflictus* + acc. of thing [complementary, instead of
the customary dat. when *adfligo* = "dash" (*OLD* 1)].

  [1] circumventi *V1*: circumventus *Keil dub. in app.*   [2] unda
V2 A: unde *Mai*   [3] *secl. Dietsch*   [4] (vel caput) *Parrha-
sius*: capit *N1*   [5] ferro, saxo, aliis telis capita adfligebant‹ur›
Dietsch

102 106M, 106Mc, 53D, 60K

E muris †canes†[1] sportis[2] demittebant.

Non. p. 177M = 260L.18: to illustrate the noun *sporta* (woven
basket, hamper).

  [1] panes *de Brosses ap. Quicherat*: cives *Lipsius*   [2] spartis *Kritz*

100 104M, 104Mc, 60D, 69K

The enemy was infused with terror, and his own troops with confidence.

101 105M, 105Mc, 61D, 70K

The text is highly uncertain: hence italics for translation. As transmitted, it does not illustrate the point under discussion (adflictus + acc.), whereas the example that immediately precedes it in Arusianus (fr. 3.76) is apropos. Hence, since Arusianus normally gives only one example per construction, conceivably the second example, which is furnished by this fragment, may have been intended to illustrate adfligo *in the active voice, which could have been treated in a lost portion of Arusianus' text immediately preceding this quotation.*

†*Surrounded, the men were faced with steel [drawn swords] on their exposed right flank; rocks or the like were pelting their heads.*†

102 106M, 106Mc, 53D, 60K

An incident possibly during the siege of Lauro by Sertorius in 76 (see fr. 27) or during the siege of Sertorius in Clunia by Pompey and Metellus in late 75 (Liv. Per. 92).

They lowered *****[1] down from the walls in wicker baskets.

[1] Kritz interpreted the paradosis *canes* (dogs) as a name given to a type of "grappling hook" (quoting Isid. *Etym.* 20.15.4, *canicula*) and altered *sportis* to *spartis* ("ropes" made of broom). Against this is the fact that Nonius' reason for quoting was to illustrate the noun *sporta*. If we read *panes* (loaves of "bread") in place of *canes*, then possibly S. described a tactic designed by the besieged to taunt the besiegers by demonstrating that there was an abundance of food within.

103 108M, 107Mc, 75D, 100K

  moenibus deturbat

Non. p. 101M = 144L.14: to illustrate *deturbare* = *deicere* (to hurl down) or *demovere* (to drive off).

104 109M, 108Mc, 9D, 14K

  ne illa tauro paria sint

Donat. ad Ter. *An.* 706: to illustrate *ne* = *nedum*.

105 111M, 109 Mc, 89D, 87K

Ita fiducia quam argumentis purgatiores dimittuntur.

Non. p. 310M = 484L.19–20; Serv. auct. ad *Aen.* 2.61: to illustrate *fiducia* = *audacia* (boldness, impudence). Donat. ad Ter. *Hec.* 528, 529; *Phorm.* 205: to illustrate self-confidence as an effective means of combating suspicion.

106 112M, 110Mc, 74D, 95K

  obviam fuere

Charis. *GL* 1.209.7 = p. 271B.2: to illustrate the adv. *obviam* = *obvius,* and reporting that the second-century AD commentator Aemilius Asper "archaically" (*vetuste*) preferred the adv. to the adj. (With verbs not denoting motion, *obviam* is found before S. only in early Latin [*OLD* 3].)

107 113M, 111Mc, 78D, 101K

  audaciter

Prisc. *GL* 3.76.27: to illustrate *audaciter,* the less common spelling of the adv. *audacter.* Cf. Quint. 1.6.17.

103 108M, 107Mc, 75D, 100K

he hurls down from the walls

104 109M, 108Mc, 9D, 14K

Probably belonging to the description of some large animal in Spain, Asia Minor, or Sardania (so Maurenbr.).

still less are those [animals] the equal of a bull

105 111M, 109Mc, 89D, 87K

So they are sent away exonerated more by their self-confidence than by arguments.

106 112M, 110Mc, 74D, 95K

they were to hand

107 113M, 111Mc, 78D, 101K

boldly

108 114M, 112Mc, 84D, 90K

Et Poeni[1] fere[2] advorsus a. n. e. m.[3]

Donat. ad Ter. *Phorm.* 171: to illustrate the use of *et* as an inceptive conjunction. Cf. fr. 1.77 and fr. inc. 5 for similar instances of abbreviated text in Donat.

[1] *cod. Hulsii*: poni *RCOD*: potui *V*   [2] ferunt *Kritz*
[3] a. n. c. m. *COV*

109* 36M, 35Mc, inc. 13D, 2.43K

Stobos

Prob. *GL* 4.20.10: illustrating that the place-name Stobi is pl.

110a–b 52a-bM, deest in Mc, D et K

o . . . | rei . . . | nii . . . | pro . . . | ini . . . | om . . . | mi . . . |
piti . . . | ad . . . | ni . . . | m . . .
. . . in | . . . rent | . . . esar | . . . r sed | . . . enol | . . . ndu‹m›
| . . . gna | . . . oru‹m› | . . . ru‹m› | . . . ni | . . . uic

These few letters are all that remains of the first eleven lines of the left-hand column of twenty-one lines on the recto and the corresponding eleven lines of the right-hand column on the verso of a leaf that once formed one-half of a double leaf in the so-called Fleury manuscript (*Floriacensis*). The adjoining leaf contains the text of frr. 38, 39, 41, and 43.1a-1. The tattered remains are preserved on fol. 20 of the Orleans palimpsest, the Aurelianensis (**A**). Ends of lines in the manuscript are indicated by |. For a schematic reconstruction of the partially preserved double leaf, see Bloch, *Didascaliae* (1961), fig. 1.

108 114M, 112Mc, 84D, 90K

Italics in the translation signifies that text is uncertain, and without more context, it is impossible to expand the abbreviation with which this fragment concludes. If Poeni *is the correct reading (*poni *[to be put] is found in the bulk of the manuscripts), S. may have mentioned the Carthaginians in Book 2 in connection with Sardinia (cf. fr. 8) or New Carthage (cf. fr. 46), as Dietsch and Maurenbr. pointed out.*

And the *Carthaginians generally* against * * *

109* 36M, 35Mc, inc. 13D, 2.43K

Stobi, a town in Macedonia, may have been mentioned in Book 2 in connection with the campaigns of the governors Ap. Claudius (cos. 79) in 76 (so Maurenbr. assumes) or C. Scribonius Curio (cos. 76) in 75.

Stobi

110a–b 52a–bM, not included in Mc, D, and K

*These two fragments are preserved in the Orleans palimpsest, the Aurelianensis (**A**). The first line of fr. 110a stood anywhere from four to six leaves after the leaf on which fr. 43.1a-1 (the preface to and opening words of Cotta's speech of ca. June 75) was inscribed on the verso. It is impossible to recover the content.*

BOOK 3

OUTLINE

LIBER III

OPENING PHASE OF PIRATE WAR
WAGED BY M. ANTONIUS
(74–73 BC): FRR. 1–7

1 1M, 1Mc, 53D, 31K

> inter recens domitos Isauros Pisidasque

Arus. *GL* 7.482.6 = p. 162DC: to illustrate *inter* + acc. = *cum illud agitur* (i.e., stating the context).

2* 2M, 2Mc, 55D, 59K

> qui orae maritumae, qua Romanum esset impe-
> rium, curator ‹nocent›ior¹ piratis

Schol. in Iuv. ad 8.105: quoting S.'s description of M. Antonius (pr. 74) to illustrate Juv.'s reference to provincials suffering at the hands of an Antonius.

{Ps.-Ascon. p. 202St.11–12: identifying the Antonius referred to by Cic., without crediting S. as his source: *curator tuendae totius orae maritimae qua Romanum erat imperium, non solum ipse nequam;* cf. id. p. 239St.5–6 (regarding M. Antonius): *totius curator orae maritimae.*}

¹ curator nocentior] *Maurenbr.*: contrarius *codd.*: curator peior *Wessner*

BOOK 3

OPENING PHASE OF PIRATE WAR
WAGED BY M. ANTONIUS
(74–73 BC): FRR. 1–7

1 1M, 1Mc, 53D, 31K

*The conquest of the Cilician pirates by P. Servilius Vatia (cos. 79)
in 78–75 is mentioned as background to the appointment of the
praetor M. Antonius in 74 to a special command.*

during the recent conquest of the Isaurians and Pi-
sidians

2* 2M, 2Mc, 55D, 59K

A description of M. Antonius (pr. 74).

who, as guardian of the seacoast where Roman rule
extended,[1] more harmful than the pirates

[1] Antonius' power over coastal areas was equal to that of the
governor of each Roman province (Vell. 2.31.2–3).

3† 3M, 3Mc, 54D, 65K

> perdundae pecuniae genitus et vacuos[1] a curis nisi
> instantibus

Ps.-Ascon. p. 239St.7–8: identifying the Antonius mentioned by
Cic.

{Arus. *GL* 7.476.7–8 = p. 142DC (*perdendae pecuniae genitus*)
assigned to "*Sal. Hist. II*" (*N1*), emended to "III" by edd.: to illustrate *genitus* + dat. of a gerundive.}

  [1] genitum et vacuum *Ps.-Ascon.*

4* 7M, 4Mc, inc. 50D, inc. 16K

> graviores[1] bello, qui prohibitum[2] venerant socii, se
> gere⟨re⟩[3]

Donat. ad Ter. *Hec.* 759: to illustrate *gravis* = *molestus* (grievous).

  [1] *Maurenbr.*: graviore *C*: graviorem *V*   [2] *Maurenbr.*:
prohibitur *C*: prohibitus *VD*: prohibituri *Stephanus*   [3] *Maurenbr.*: socii segere *C*: sociis egere *V*

5* 4M, 5Mc, inc. 121D, deest in K

Antonius paucis ante diebus erupit ex urbe.

Audax, *GL* 7.353.27; {Prob. *GL* 4.149.4 (*paucis ante diebus*)}: to
illustrate the adv. *ante*.

6 5M, 6Mc, deest in D et K

3† 3M, 3Mc, 54D, 65K

Quoted from S.'s description of M. Antonius' spendthrift nature (cf. Plut. Ant. 1; Cic. Phil. 2.42, 44).

a man born to squander money and devoid of worries except for those immediately pressing upon him

4* 7M, 4Mc, inc. 50D, inc. 16K

Rome's halfhearted and ineffective measures taken against the pirates prior to Pompey's appointment in 67 caused harm to Rome's allies (Dio 36.23.2). Antonius was notorious for his corrupt management of the campaign (Cic. 2 Verr. 3.213).

that the conduct of those who had come as allies to prevent war was more grievous than the war

5* 4M, 5Mc, inc. 121D, not included in K

Setting the scene for some unknown incident that befell Antonius soon after he had departed from Rome or from some city while on campaign.

A few days earlier Antonius sallied forth from the city.

6 5M, 6Mc, not included in D and K

Antonius makes an unsuccessful attack on a Ligurian stronghold on the southeast coast of Transalpine Gaul and afterward sails to Spain. Slightly more than one or two printed pages of text (approx. 40–80 lines) would have occupied the gap between this fragment and the end of fr. 2.86.12 reporting the reaction to Pompey's dispatch in January 74 (see testimonia). (Italics in the translation signifies that the text or a supplement is uncertain.)

1 * * * | ‹co›pias Antonius ha‹ud fa›|cile prohibens a ‹navi-
   bus›,[1] | quia periac*i* telu‹m pote›|rat angusto intr‹oitu.[2]

2 Ne›|que Mamercus *host*‹es›[3] | in de*x*tera commu‹nis› |
   classis aestate *qu*‹ieta›[4] | tutior in aperto *s*‹eque›|batur.

3 Iamque diebus *al*‹iquot› | per dubitationem ‹tritis›, |
   quom[5] Ligurum praes‹idia cessissent›[6] | in Alpis, Teren-
   tun . . . |citu[7] quaest*i*o fac . . . [8] | Sertorium per*v*e‹hi.

4 Quom› | Antonio ceterisque *p*‹lace›|ret navibus in His-
   pa‹niam› | maturare, post qua‹driduom›[9] | in Aresina-
   rios[10] *v*e‹nere om›|ni copia navium l‹onga›|rum, *q*uas
   reparat‹as ha›|beban*t* quaeque no‹n tempes*|tatibus af-
   flictae erant*›[11] * * *

This fragment forms a column of text 21 lines long and 18–23
letter-spaces wide on the left-hand portion of the recto of a leaf
that once belonged to the so-called Fleury codex (*Floriacensis*). It is preserved on fol. 15r of the Orleans palimpsest, the
Aurelianensis (**A**), and is joined to the leaf containing fr. 2.74
A–D, with which it once formed a double leaf of the *Floriacensis*.
Depending on whether the gathering was a quaternio (as Bloch
[1961], 66 concludes) or a quinio (as Perl [1968], 33–35 argues),
the opening word, *‹co›pias,* was separated from the last word of
fr. 2.86 D by either one or two no-longer extant leaves (4–8 columns of text, = 84–168 lines in the manuscript, = approx. 40–80
lines of printed text). Ends of lines in the manuscript are indica-
ted by |, from which it can be plainly seen that the right margin of
all 21 lines in this column of text has suffered the loss of 4–7 letters. Supplements are to be credited to Hauler, unless otherwise
indicated. Italics signifies that the transcription is uncertain, or
that a supplement is highly conjectural or merely hypothetical.
The concluding words of the conjectural supplement (*tatibus
afflictae erant*) would have been written at the top of the right-
hand column that once filled the missing half of this leaf. For a
schematic reconstruction of the double leaf, see Bloch, *Didascaliae* (1961), fig. 2.

. . . Antonius with some difficulty warding off ⟨*enemy*⟩   [fr. 6]
forces from his ships because a missile could be hurled the
whole distance to its mark in the narrow entrance [to the
harbor]. And on the right wing of the fleet under their joint
command, Mamercus[1] was at similar risk in pursuing the
enemy in open water owing to the summer calm. And now
that some days had been wasted through hesitation, after the Lugurian *garrisons* had withdrawn into the Alps,
. . . of the Terentuni[2] . . . an investigation . . . *to travel to*
Sertorius. Since Antonius and the rest were in favor of
making haste to Spain with their ships, they arrived among
the Aresinarii[3] after a period of four days with the full
complement of their war ships, those that had been repaired, as well as those that ⟨*had not been damaged by
storms*⟩ . . .

[1] A legate of Antonius, possibly Mam. Aemilius Lepidus Li-
vianus (cos. 77): *MRR* 2.105, 109 n. 7.   [2] Possibly a people
in Spain, otherwise unattested.   [3] Possibly to be identified
with the Airenosii (Polyb. 3.35.2), whose territory lay in northeast
Spain, between the Ebro River and the Pyrenees.

---

1 *Maurenbr.*: a ⟨portu⟩ *vel* a⟨b impetu⟩ *Hauler*
2 *Wölfflin*
3 *Reynolds*: hostium navis *Hauler*
4 *Wölfflin*
5 cum *A*
6 *Maurenbr.*: praesidia issent *Hauler*
7 Terentun⟨orum ac⟩citu *Hauler*
8 fac⟨ta ad⟩ *Maurenbr.*: fac⟨ta est ad⟩ *Hauler*
9 *Reynolds*: postqua⟨m vero⟩ *Maurenbr.*
10 *Hauler*: -artos *A*
11 *Maurenbr.*: no⟨vae accesserant⟩ *Hauler*

SALLUST

7 6M, 7Mc, deest in D et K

1 ⟨*disiunctus altis|sum*⟩o flumine Di*l*uno[1] | ⟨ab hos⟩tibus, quem trans|⟨gradi⟩ vel paucis prohiben|⟨tibus ne⟩quibat.

2 Simulatis | ⟨*transi*⟩tibus aliis haud[2] longe | ⟨*a loco i*⟩*llo*[3] classe, quam e|⟨*vocara*⟩t,[4] temereque textis[5] ra|⟨tibus

3 ex⟩ercitum transdu|⟨xit. Tum⟩ praemisso cum equi|⟨tibus ** ⟩ranio[6] legato et par|⟨te na⟩vium longarum ad | ⟨paen⟩[7]insulam pervenit, | ⟨ratus⟩ inproviso metu | ⟨posse⟩ *reci*pi civitatem con|⟨meati⟩bus Italicis oppor-

[1] *vel* Diiuno
[2] *Maurenbr.*: aut *A*
[3] *Maurenbr.*
[4] *Maurenbr.*: emiserat *Hauler*
[5] *Hauler*: temere . m . exis *A*
[6] Afranio *vel* Manio *Hauler*
[7] *scripsi*

7 6M, 7Mc, not included in D and K

An operation in Spain: Antonius, after forcing his way across a river, came to a locale that afforded the enemy natural defenses. (Italics in the translation signifies that the text or a supplement is uncertain.)

. . . ⟨*cut off*⟩ from the enemy by the ⟨*extremely deep*⟩ river *Dilunus*,[1] which he could not cross in the face of even a few men putting up opposition. While feigning crossings at other points, he took his army across not far from that place by means of the fleet, which he had summoned, and by means of hastily fashioned rafts. Then after sending forward his legate ****ranius[2] with the cavalry and some of the warships, he reached a *peninsula*,[3] thinking that he could, by means of unexpected alarm [of a surprise attack], recapture a community ideally suited for resupply from Italy. The enemy, relying on their position with the

---

[1] Spelling uncertain; location unknown.

[2] His name may have been "Manius" (*MRR* 2.105) or "Afranius," depending on how the text is restored. Nothing further is known about him either way. He is clearly not L. Afranius (cos. 60), since the future consul was serving as legate under Pompey at that time, 74 BC (*MRR* 3.12–13).

[3] Possibly the naval base of Sertorius, Dianium (so Hauler), which was located on a promontory on the east coast of Hither Spain, north of Carthago Nova (cf. fr. 1.113). Or (as Schulten, *Hermes* 1925.66–73 argues) it may have been the island town of Emporiae (Emporion), which lay on the far northeast coast of Spain, just below the Pyrenees and at the mouth of the river Clodianus (= Dilunus?). Emporiae had been useful to the Romans in Spanish campaigns in the third and second centuries (Livy 21.60.1–2, 34.8–9).

4 tu|<nam>. Aeque[8] *illi* loco freti nil<hil de> sententia mu*ta*vel<re; qu>ippe tumulum latel<ribus i>n mare[9] et tergo editis, |<ad hoc>fron<te> ut angusto |<ita[10] har>enoso ingressu, dul<*plici muro muniverant*>.

This fragment forms a column of text 21 lines long and 18–23 letter-spaces wide and occupies the right-hand portion of the verso of the leaf containing fr. 6. The gap between this fragment and fr. 6 is 42 lines in the manuscript, = approx. only 20 lines of printed text. See Bloch, *Didascaliae* (1961), 69. Slightly less than half of this leaf has survived, since it is missing two columns of text (the right-hand column of the recto and the left-hand column of the verso). Ends of lines in the manuscript are indicated by |, from which it can be plainly seen that the left margin of all 21 lines in this column of text has suffered the loss of 4–7 letters. Supplements are to be credited to Hauler, unless otherwise indicated. Italics signifies that the transcription is uncertain or that a supplement is highly conjectural or merely hypothetical. The opening portion of the conjectural supplement, *disiunctus altis–*, introducing this fragment would have been written at the bottom of the column that once occupied the missing left-hand portion of this verso.

[8] atque *Hauler*　　　[9] *Hauler*: meri A　　　[10] *Maurenbr.*: et *suppl. Wölfflin*

SERTORIAN WAR (74 BC), FRR. 8–12

8* 43M, 30Mc, inc. 37D, inc. 3K

Cales civitas est Campaniae; nam in Flaminia quae est **Cale** *dicitur. Est et in Gall<aec>ia[1] hoc nomine, quam Sallustius* **captam a Perperna** *commemorat.*

Serv. ad *Aen.* 7.728: distinguishing a community mentioned by Virgil from two others of a similar name.

same degree of confidence, did not change their intention at all; in fact ‹*they had fortified with a double wall*› a knoll that had steep sides seaward and in the rear, and an approach as narrow as it was sandy *at its front*.

SERTORIAN WAR (74 BC), FRR. 8–12

8* 43M, 30Mc, inc. 37D, inc. 3K

Perperna's capture of Portus Cale, a coastal town in the far, northwest region of the Iberian Peninsula (mod. Portugal).

Cales is a Campanian town; for on the via Flaminia [in Umbria] is a town called **Cale**. *There is also one of this name in Gallaecia, which Sallust relates was* **captured by Perperna**.

---

1 *Voss*

SALLUST

9* 44M, 31Mc, 1.76D, 1.75K

quoi nomen Oblivionis condiderant[1]

Serv. & Serv. auct. ad *Aen.* 1.267: to illustrate *nomen* + a [defining] gen.

[1] indiderant *Dietsch in app.*

10†† 2.70M, 2.59Mc, 2.23D, 2.29K

1 At[1] Metellus in ulteriorem Hispaniam post annum regressus magna gloria concurrentium[2] undique, virile et mu-
2 liebre secus, per vias et tecta omnium visebatur. Eum quaestor C. Urbinus aliique, cognita voluntate, quom ad cenam invitaverant,[3] ultra Romanum ac mortalium etiam

Macrob. *Sat.* 3.13.7–9: quoted to illustrate the luxury and haughtiness of Metellus.

{Non. p. 222M = 329L.20–23 (*§1 At Metellus . . . visebatur*), assigned to "lib. II," Prob. *GL* 4.21.4 (*§1 virile sc muliebre secus*), and Charis. *GL* 1.80.15 = p. 101B.13 (*§1 virile secus*): cited to give an example of *secus* (neut.) = *sexus* (m.). Non. p. 180M = 265L.20–21 (*§3 transenna . . . inponebat*), assigned to "lib. II": cited to illustrate the claim that *transenna* is not a *transitus* (passage) but a *fenestra* (window); Non. p. 286M = 442L.18–20 (*§3 cum machinis strepitu demissum . . . inponebant* [sic]), assigned to "lib. III": cited to illustrate *demittere* in the sense of "to lower from above"; Serv. & Serv. auct. ad *Aen.* 5.488 (*§3 machinato strepitu transenna corona in caput inponebatur*): claiming that *transennna* means a "taut rope" (*extentus funis*) (cf. Isid. *Etym.* 19.1.24).}

[1] *Non., P Macrob.*: ac *rell. codd. Macrob.*
[2] *Non.*: concurrentibus *Macrob.*
[3] invitassent *P (ante corr.) Macrob.*

9* 44M, 31Mc, 1.76D, 1.75K

The river Limia/Limaea, lying some sixty miles north of Portus Cale (see preceding fragment), was also called Lethe (cf. Strabo 3.3.4, p. 153; App. Iber. 71, 72) or Oblivio (cf. Liv. Per. 55; Plin. HN 4.115) = "Forgetfulness."

for which they had instituted the name Oblivion

10†† 2.70M, 2.59Mc, 2.23D, 2.29K

The context must be the autumn of 74 (so Maurenbr.), where Livy (Per. 93) places Metellus' return to Ulterior, a year after the unsuccessful siege of Sertorius in Clunia, in late 75, which is reported in Per. 92. The reference in §1 below to an absence of one year fits the statement in Plut. (Sert. 21.8) that Metellus spent the winter of 75/74 in Transalpine Gaul, a period covered toward the end of Book 2. Past editors place this fragment in Book 2 on the basis of two citations from Nonius credited to Book 2 (pp. 180M, 222M), however, the only way to find room in Book 2 for an event in the autumn of 74 is to assume that it was treated proleptically, since Book 3 begins S.'s account of the year 74. A third citation in Nonius (p. 286M) is assigned to Book 3, which is in accord with the structure of S.'s annalistic account of events. Cf. fr. 2.55, which Nonius cites twice, giving different book numbers.

But Metellus, returning to Farther Spain after a year, received a glorious reception on the part of everyone, men and women, pouring from everywhere through the streets and buildings. Whenever his quaestor Gaius Urbinus[1] and others, knowing his wishes, invited him to a dinner, they looked after him in a fashion that was not typically Ro-

---

[1] Not otherwise known.

morem curabant, exornatis aedibus per aulaea et insignia,
scenisque ad ostentationem histrionum fabricatis; simul
croco sparsa humus, et alia in modum templi celeberrimi.
3 Praeterea tum sedenti [in][4] transenna demissum Victoriae
simulacrum cum machinato strepitu tonitruum coronam
capiti inponebat, tum venienti ture quasi deo supplicaba-
4 tur. Toga picta plerumque amiculo erat ei accumbenti;
epulae vero quaesitissumae, neque per omnem modo provinciam, sed trans maria ex Mauretania volucrum et fera-
5 rum incognita antea plura genera. Quis rebus aliquantam
partem gloriae dempserat, maxumeque apud veteres et
sanctos viros, superba illa, gravia, indigna Romano imperio aestimantis.

[4] *Kaster*

11* 2.28M, 3.32Mc, 2.43D, 2.52K

Sed Metello Cordubae hiemante cum duabus legionibus

man or even in keeping with mortal standards. Houses were fitted out with tapestries and finery; stages were constructed for the display of actors. At the same time, the ground was sprinkled with saffron, and there were other extravagances after the fashion of a festive temple. Moreover, at that time, while he was seated, a likeness of Victory, which was let down with a network of cords,[2] to the accompaniment of a mechanically produced din of thunder claps, used to place a crown upon his head; at that time, when he made his approach, they used to worship him with incense, as though he were a god. An embroidered toga[3] generally served as his outer garment when he reclined at table. The food was was sought from far and wide, not only throughout the whole of the province but also a great many previously unknown kinds of birds and game from across the sea, from Mauretania. And by such extravagances, he had lessened his distinction to some extent, and especially so in the eyes of older, upright men who regarded those practices as haughty, heavy-handed, and unbecoming a Roman commander.

[2] *Transenna* elsewhere generally means a "snare" of netting (for birds), or something resembling a net: here, possibly = a weblike network of strings to support the statue, after the fashion of a marionette. Both Val. Max. 9.1.5 and Plut. *Sert.* 22.3 attest mechanical devices lowered from above.

[3] The *toga picta* was the garb of a triumphing general.

11* 2.28M, 3.32Mc, 2.43D, 2.52K

An earthquake in Farther Spain during the winter: possibly that of 74/73 (so La Penna).

But when Metellus was wintering with two legions at Cor-

alione casu an, sapientibus ut placet, venti per cava terrae
citatu[1] rupti aliquot montes tumulique sedere.

Adnot. super Luc. 1.552: to illustrate a sudden, shuddering motion of the earth.

{Isid. *Etym.* 14.1.2 (*venti . . . sedere*); Isid. *De natura rerum* 46.2
(*venti . . . sedere*); Serv. and *Schol. Bern.* ad *G.* 2.479 (*venti . . .
citatu*): all noting the belief that subterranean winds cause earthquakes.}

[1] praecipitati *Isid. Nat.*

12 46M, 33Mc, 1D, 90K

Namque his[1] praeter solita vitiosis[2] magistratibus,[3] quom
per omnem provinciam infecunditate bienni proximi
grave pretium fructibus esset,[4]

Non. p. 314M = 491L.26–28: to illustrate *grave* = *multum*
(considerable).

[1] *LB^A*: eis (*praec.* e) *A^A*: is *Mercier*   [2] vitiis *A^A*   [3] mala
aestatibus *Gerlach ed. min.*: magis aestatibus *Havercamp*: magis
tractibus *Mähly*: agri tractibus *Dietsch*   [4] esse *codd.*

WAR AGAINST THE DARDANI
(74–73 BC), FRR. 13–14

13 49M, 91Mc, 8D, 54K

duba, either as a result of some other chance occurrence or, as is the view of philosophers,[1] owing to the impulse of wind blowing through hollows in the earth, several mountains and hills were torn apart and caved in.

[1] The fifth-century philosopher Archelaus (Sen. *Q Nat.* 6.12.1) or his teacher Anaxagoras (Amm. Marc. 17.7.11) is credited with assigning the cause of earthquakes to subterranean winds (cf. Plin. *HN* 2.192).

12 46M, 33Mc, 1D, 90K

The reference to a food shortage that had grown more serious throughout a province as a result of a second poor growing season may point to the province of Transalpine Gaul, where a previous poor harvest is attested by Pompey's letter written in the autumn of 75 (fr. 2.86.9).

For under these unusually corrupt officials, when throughout the whole province the price of produce was substantial owing to a crop failure of the previous two years,

WAR AGAINST THE DARDANI (74–73 BC), FRR. 13–14

13 49M, 91Mc, 8D, 54K

Possibly to be connected with the operations of C. Curio (cos. 76), governor of Macedonia. Amm. Marc. (29.5.22) attests Curio's ruthless measures against the Dardani living to the northwest of his province.

Atque [cum]¹ Curio² laudatum adcensumque praemiorum spe,³ quibuscum⁴ optavisset, ire iubet.

Non. p. 358M = 568L.16–18: to illustrate *optare* = *eligere* (to choose).

¹ *secl. Lindsay*: *om A^A*: eum *ed. Ald. 1513*   ² (*vel* Caepio) *Lipsius*: cupio *codd.*   ³ spes *LB^A*   ⁴ quibus *A^A*

14† 50M, 92Mc, 4.68D, 4.70–71K

Curio Volcanaliorum die ibidem moratus

Non. p. 489M = 786L.28: (assigned to "lib. IIII"): to illustrate the gen. *Volcanaliorum*, instead of *Volcanalium*.

{Pomp. *GL* 5.196.20 (*religione Vulcanaliorum impeditus*); Charis. *GL* 1.62.19 = p. 77B.25 (*Volcanaliorum*); and, without assignment to S., Pomp. *GL* 5.168.18–19 (*Curio ibidem moratus regione Vulcanaliorum*): to illustrate gen. pl. *–iorum,* instead of *–ium.*}

15 48M, 34Mc, 61D, 82K¹

Oratio Macri Trib. Pleb. ad Plebem

1 "Si, Quirites, parum existumaretis,² quid inter ius a maioribus relictum vobis et hoc a Sulla paratum servitium

¹ The title and text of this speech are transmitted by **V** (Vat. lat. 3864, *ff. 123r–24v*). Citations from §§8, 12, 14, 17, and 21, as noted below, are assigned to Book 3 by Arusianus.
² si . . . existimaretis] *Donat. ad Ter. Phorm. 45*

And after praising and spurring him on with the hope of rewards, Curio ordered him to go with men of his own choice.

14† 50M, 92Mc, 4.68D, 4.70–71K

Whenever possible, the Romans avoided military action on the day of the annual festival of the fire god Vulcan, August 23, since that day was made inauspicious by the defeat of Fulvius Nobilior in Spain in 153 BC (App. Hisp. 45).

Curio delayed in the same place on the day of the Vulcanalia

15 48M, 34Mc, 61D, 82K

The Plebeian Tribune Macer's Speech
to the Commons (73 BC)

This speech is put into the mouth of C. Licinius Macer when, as tribune in 73, he kept up the pressure for the full restoration of the powers of the plebeian tribunes. He assails the dominance of powerful political leaders in the senate. Macer wrote an annalistic history of Rome that is no longer extant (FRHist no. 27), and he was the father of the famous orator and poet Calvus, who was a friend of Catullus. Cicero judged him to be a mediocre orator (Brut. 238) and historian (Leg. 1.7).

"If you were underestimating, Citizens, what a difference there is between the rights left you by your forefathers and this slavery imposed by Sulla, I would have to speak at

interesset, multis mihi disserundum fuit docendique, quas
ob iniurias et quotiens a patribus armata plebes secessisset
utique vindices paravisset omnis iuris sui tribunos plebis:
2 nunc hortari modo relicuom est et ire primum via, qua
3 capessundam arbitror libertatem. Neque me praeterit,
quantas opes nobilitatis solus, inpotens inani specie magistratus pellere dominatione incipiam, quantoque tutius
4 factio noxiorum agat quam soli innocentes. Sed praeter
spem bonam ex vobis, quae metum vicit, statui certaminis
advorsa pro libertate potiora esse forti viro quam omnino
non certavisse.

5 "Quamquam omnes alii creati pro iure vostro vim
cunctam et imperia sua gratia aut spe aut praemiis in vos
convortere, meliusque habent mercede delinquere quam
6 gratis recte facere. Itaque omnes concessere iam in paucorum dominationem, qui per militare nomen aerarium,
exercitus, regna, provincias occupavere et arcem habent
ex spoliis vostris, quom interim more pecorum vos, multitudo, singulis habendos fruendosque praebetis, exuti
omnibus quae maiores reliquere, nisi quia vobismet ipsi[3]
per suffragia, ut praesides olim, nunc dominos destinatis.
7 "Itaque concessere illuc omnes, at[4] mox, si vostra rece-

---

3 *Laetus*: ipsis V
4 *Kritz*: et V

---

1 See *Cat.* 33.3n.
2 The tribunate, which Sulla had stripped of legislative and
veto powers.

[fr. 15]

length, and you would have to be taught the injuries on account of which, and how often, the plebeians took up arms and seceded from the patricians;[1] and also how they established the tribunes of the commons as the protectors of all their rights. But now it only remains to offer encouragement and be the first to proceed along the path by which freedom, I think, must be grasped. And it does not escape my notice how great is the power of the nobles, whom I, a solitary, powerless individual, with the empty semblance of a magistracy,[2] am undertaking to drive from their tyranny; and I know how much more securely a coterie of guilty men can function as compared with innocent persons on their own. But in addition to the good hope you inspire, which has overcome my fear, I have decided that for a brave man, setbacks in a struggle for liberty are preferable to never having struggled at all.

"And yet all the others, though elected to defend your rights, as a result of influence or hope or bribery have turned all their power and authority against you; and they consider it better to do wrong for hire than to do right gratuitously. Therefore, all have now submitted to the mastery of a few men, who, under the pretext of a military situation, have seized control of the treasury, armies, kingdoms and provinces. These men possess a stronghold formed from your spoils, while in the meantime you, after the fashion of cattle, offer yourselves, a great throng, to be controlled and exploited by mere individuals, after having been stripped of all that your forefathers left you, except for the fact that by your ballots you now play a direct role in designating masters for yourselves, just as formerly you did protectors.

"Therefore all men have gone over to their side, but

233

peritis, ad vos plerique; raris enim animus est ad ea quae
8 placent defendunda, ceteri validiorum sunt. An dubium
habetis, num officere quid vobis uno animo pergentibus
possit, quos languidos socordesque pertimuere? Nisi forte
C. Cotta, ex factione media consul, aliter quam metu iura
quaedam tribunis plebis restituit; et quamquam L. Sicinius, primus de potestate tribunicia loqui ausus, mussan-
tibus vobis circumventus erat, tamen prius illi invidiam
metuere, quam vos iniuriae pertaesum est.[5] Quod ego
nequeo satis mirari, Quirites, nam spem frustra fuisse in-
9 tellexistis. Sulla mortuo, qui scelestum inposuerat servitium, finem mali credebatis; ortus est longe saevior Ca-
10 tulus. Tumultus intercessit Bruto et Mamerco consulibus,
dein C. Curio ad exitium usque insontis tribuni dominatus
est.

11   "Lucullus superiore anno quantis animis ierit in L.
Quintium vidistis: quantae denique nunc mihi turbae
concitantur! Quae profecto incassum agebantur, si prius
quam vos serviundi finem, illi dominationis facturi erant,
praesertim cum his civilibus armis dicta alia, sed certatum

[5] quam . . . pertaesum est] *Arus. GL 7.500.14 = p. 229DC*

[3] The right to hold further political office (see fr.
2.44).   [4] A tribune in 76. Cic. (*Brut.* 216) gives Gnaeus as
his praenomen.   [5] The revolt of M. Lepidus in 77.
[6] The tribune was Sicinius (cf. §8). The word *exitium* (destruction) need not denote death but may refer instead to an otherwise
unattested, politically motivated prosecution launched by Curio
(cos. 76) after Sicinius ceased to be tribune on December 10,
76.   [7] A tribune in 74, Quin(c)tius demanded the restoration of the powers of that office (cf. fr. 3.100).

[fr. 15]

presently, if you take back what is yours, most of them will
flock to you; for just a few people have the courage to stand
up for their own views; the rest are controlled by the stronger. Do you, whom men feared even in your weakness and
indifference, have any doubt about whether anything can
get in your way when you advance with a single purpose?
Unless, perhaps, for some other motive than fear Gaius
Cotta, a consul right from the core of the oligarchs, restored certain rights to the plebeian tribunes.[3] In fact,
although Lucius Sicinius,[4] who was the first to dare to talk
about the tribunician power, was thwarted while you only
murmured, yet those opponents feared a backlash even
before you had had your fill of the wrong done you. At this,
Citizens, I cannot sufficiently marvel; for you realized that
your hope had been in vain. On the death of Sulla, who
had imposed wicked slavery upon you, you believed there
was an end of evil; up rose Catulus, far more cruel. A rebellion intervened in the consulship of Brutus and Mamercus;[5] then Gaius Curio played the tyrant, even to the
extent of destroying a guiltless tribune.[6]

"You have seen how vehemently Lucullus assailed Lucius Quintius last year.[7] Finally, what turmoil is now being
stirred up against me! But assuredly that activity was in
vain, if those men were intending to make an end of their
mastery before you did likewise to your slavery,[8] especially
since in this armed civil conflict, other motives have been

[8] I.e., surely the powerful few would not have gone to such
great lengths to resist restoration of the powers of the tribunate,
if it was their intention all along voluntarily to surrender their
tyranny over the commons.

12 utrimque de dominatione in vobis sit. Itaque cetera ex licentia aut odio aut avaritia in tempus arsere;[6] permansit una res modo, quae utrimque quaesita est et erepta in posterum: vis tribunicia, telum a maioribus libertati para-

13 tum. Quod ego vos moneo quaesoque ut animadvortatis neu nomina rerum ad ignaviam mutantes otium pro servitio adpelletis. Quo iam ipso frui, si vera et honesta flagitium superaverit, non est condicio; fuisset, si omnino quiessetis. Nunc animum advortere et, nisi viceritis, quoniam omnis iniuria gravitate tutior est, artius habebunt.

14 "'Quid censes igitur?' aliquis vostrum subiecerit. Primum omnium omittundum morem hunc quem agitis[7] inpigrae linguae, animi ignavi, non ultra contionis locum

15 memores libertatis. Deinde—ne vos ad virilia illa vocem, quo tribunos plebei, modo patricium magistratum, libera ab auctoribus patriciis suffragia maiores vostri paravere— quom vis omnis, Quirites, in vobis sit et quae iussa nunc

---

[6] itaque . . . arsere] *Arus. GL 7.486.30 = p. 178DC*
[7] omittendum (amittendum *codd. Arus.*) . . . agitis] *Arus. GL 7.453.10–11 = p. 58DC*

---

[9] Fair-sounding but hollow slogans such as *concordia, pax, otium* (cf. *Cat.* 38.3).   [10] *Otium* (tranquility, freedom from troubles), the term used to mask the people's "slavery."   [11] Cf. *Jug.* 31.14.   [12] Where "liberty" is the rallying cry of the public orators.   [13] The second of Macer's specific recommendations for action is postponed until §17, where *censebo* (shall advise) recalls *cenes* (advise) in §14.   [14] The consulship, at first a preserve almost exclusively of patricians, was opened to plebeians by a bill passed by the tribunes C. Licinius and L. Sextius in 367.

put forward,[9] but the struggle on both sides has been fo- [fr. 15]
cused on mastery over you. Therefore, other disturbances
have flared up for a time out of lack of restraint or hatred
or avarice; only one issue has persisted, which has been
the object of contention on both sides and has been
snatched from you for hereafter: the tribunician power, a
weapon established by your ancestors for the defense of
liberty. I warn you, and I beg you to pay attention to this
and not to change the names of things to suit your own
cowardice, substituting the term "tranquility" for "slavery." And there is no option to enjoy that very thing,[10] if
wickedness triumphs over integrity and decency; there
would have been the option, if you had remained alto-
gether passive. Now they are paying attention, and if you
do not gain the victory, they will hold you in tighter bonds,
since every wrongful act is more shielded from retribution
by its formidableness.[11]

"'What, then, do you advise?' some one of you may
interject. First of all, that you must give up this habit you
maintain of being all talk and no action, forgetful of liberty
outside of the place of our public meetings.[12] Next[13]—
have no fear that I shall urge you to those manly deeds
whereby your ancestors established tribunes of the commons, gained access to a magistracy previously patrician[14]
and voting free of patrician oversight[15]—when all power
is in your hands, Citizens, and you are undoubtedly able

[15] First the *lex Publilia* of 339 required patrician senators to
sanction in advance votes taken on legislation in the centuriate
assembly, thereby freeing voting from patrician oversight. Later,
the *lex Hortensia* of 287/6 gave bills passed in the plebeian assembly the force of law binding on the whole community.

pro aliis toleratis pro vobis agere aut non agere certe possitis, Iovem aut alium quem deum consultorem expecta-

16 tis? Magna illa consulum imperia et patrum decreta vos exequendo rata efficitis, Quirites, ultroque licentiam in

17 vos auctum atque adiutum properatis. Neque ego vos ultum iniurias hortor,[8] magis uti requiem cupiatis, neque discordias, uti illi criminantur, sed earum finem volens iure gentium res repeto; et si pertinaciter retinebunt, non arma neque secessionem, tantum modo ne amplius san-

18 guinem vostrum praebeatis censebo. Gerant habeantque suo modo imperia, quaerant triumphos, Mithridatem, Sertorium et reliquias exsulum persequantur cum imaginibus suis, absit periculum et labos, quibus nulla pars fructus est.

19 "Nisi forte repentina ista frumentaria lege munia vostra pensantur; qua tamen quinis modiis libertatem omnium aestumavere, qui profecto non amplius possunt alimentis carceris. Namque ut illis exiguitate mors prohi-

---

[8] neque (ego *om.*) vos ultum iniurias hortor] *Arus. GL* 7.477.29 = *p. 147DC*

---

[16] The "relief" or "rest" (*quies*), as defined in the next sentence and in §18, turns out to be a form of passive resistance, viz., the refusal to lift a finger to serve or fight for their country in support of the tyranny of the oligarchs.

[17] Here, metaphorical: strictly speaking, the term denotes a demand made to a foreign power (as though the powerful *nobiles* at Rome were such) for restitution of stolen property (here, the tribunician powers rightfully belonging to the people).

[18] I.e., let them rely on their noble lineage (as represented by the wax masks, *imagines,* of their ancestors: see *Jug.* 4.5n.), in lieu of soldiers—and see how far that will take them.

to execute or to refrain from executing for your own bene- [fr. 15]
fit the orders to which you now submit for the benefit of
others, are you waiting for the prompting of Jupiter or
some other god? That lofty power of the consuls and the
decrees of the senate you yourselves ratify, Citizens, by
carrying them out; and you hasten voluntarily to increase
and abet their license over you. Nor am I urging you to
avenge the wrongs done you but instead to desire relief
from them;[16] and I seek, according to the law of nations,[17]
restitution of what is rightfully ours, not out of a desire for
strife, as those men charge, but from a desire for an end
to it. If they hold out stubbornly, I shall advise not arms
and secession, but merely that you no longer shed your
blood for them. Let them administer and hold their official
powers in their own way; let them seek triumphs, let them
pursue Mithridates, Sertorius, and the remnants of the
exiles in the company of their ancestral images;[18] let those
who have no share in the profits be free also from dangers
and toil.

"Unless, perhaps, your public duties have been coun-
terbalanced by that hastily enacted grain law,[19] by which
they have valued the freedom of all as being worth five
pecks per man, which cannot really be much greater than
the rations in a prison.[20] For just as that scanty sup-

[19] Sponsored by the current consuls (of 73), it provided for
the state to purchase grain in order to stabilize prices and assure
an adequate supply. It gave a limited number of citizens a monthly
allowance of five *modii* (pecks) at a fixed price (Cic. 2 *Verr.* 3.163,
173; 5.52).

[20] Cf. fr. 1.49.11, where Lepidus likened the allowance to that
afforded to mere slaves.

betur, senescunt vires, sic neque absolvi‹t›[9] cura familiari
tam parva res et ignavi quoiusque tenuissumas spes frus-
20 tratur.[10] Quae tamen quamvis ampla quoniam serviti pretium ostentaretur, quoius torpedinis erat decipi et vos-
21 trarum rerum ultro iniuriae[11] gratiam debere? Cavendus
dolus est;[12] namque alio modo neque valent in univorsos
neque conabuntur. Itaque simul conparant delenimenta et
differunt vos in adventum Cn. Pompei, quem ipsum ubi
pertimuere, sublatum in cervices suas, mox dempto metu
22 lacerant. Neque eos pudet, vindices uti se ferunt libertatis,
tot viros sine uno aut remittere iniuriam non audere aut
23 ius non posse defendere. Mihi quidem satis spectatum est
Pompeium, tantae gloriae adulescentem, malle principem
volentibus vobis esse quam illis dominationis socium auc-
toremque in primis fore tribuniciae potestatis.
24 "Verum, Quirites, antea singuli cives in pluribus, non
in uno cuncti praesidia habebatis. Neque mortalium quis-
25 quam dare aut eripere talia unus poterat. Itaque verborum
26 satis dictum est; neque enim ignorantia res claudit,[13] ve-

---

[9] *Putschius*   [10] ignavi . . . frustratur] *Gronovius*: ignam
quiusque tenuissimas perfrustratur V: ignaviam quoiusque tenuis-
sima spe frustratur *Orelli*   [11] *Kritz*: iniuria V   [12] cavendus dolus est] *Arus. GL 7.488.23 = p. 184DC: post* namque
. . . conabuntur V: *huc transp. Fabri*   [13] neque . . . claudit]
Donat. ad Ter. Eun. 164

---

[21] Text uncertain; see textual notes.

[22] Like slaves (*lecticarii*) carrying their master in a litter.

[23] After the revolt of Lepidus had been crushed with the help
of Pompey's forces in 77 and he had been sent to fight Sertorius
is Spain, the senate failed to give him the backing he needed to
win the war (see fr. 2.86.2).

[fr. 15]

ply keeps off death in the case of prisoners, while their strength wanes, so this terribly small allowance does not relieve you of financial worry, and it disappoints the slenderest hopes of everyone who is fainthearted.[21] Still, no matter how great the allowance, since it was being offered as the price of your slavery, what mark of passivity was it to be taken in by it and to feel spontaneous gratitude for the misuse of your own property. You must guard against deception; for by no other means do they prevail against the people as a whole, nor will they try to. Hence, they simultaneously devise soothing measures and put you off until the coming of Gnaeus Pompey, the very man whom they raised up upon their necks[22] when they feared him, but presently, their fear dispelled,[23] they tear to pieces. And these men, self-styled defenders of liberty, despite their great number, are not ashamed not to dare to right a wrong without the backing of one man, or not to be able to defend what is right. For my own part, I am fully convinced that Pompey, a young man of such renown, prefers to be a chief figure with your consent rather than a partner in the tyranny of those men, and that he will take the lead in restoring the power of the tribunes.[24]

"But previously, Citizens, you, as individual members of the community, used to find safety in numbers and did not rely as a collective group on just one person. Nor was any one mortal able to give or take away such things.[25] I have, therefore, said enough; for it is not as a result of ignorance that the enterprise falls short, but a kind of pas-

[24] A thing he did as consul with Crassus in 70 (cf. *Cat.* 38.1).
[25] As the restoration of the powers of the tribunate.

rum occupavit nescio quae[14] vos torpedo, qua non gloria movemini neque flagitio, cunctaque praesenti ignavia mutavistis, abunde libertatem rati, ⟨scilicet⟩ quia tergis abstinetur[15] et huc ire licet atque illuc, munera ditium

27 dominorum. Atque haec eadem non sunt agrestibus, sed caeduntur inter potentium inimicitias donoque dantur in provincias magistratibus. Ita pugnatur et vincitur paucis; plebes, quodcumque accidit, pro victis est et in dies magis erit, si quidem maiore cura dominationem illi retinuerint, quam vos repetiveritis libertatem."

[14] *Carrio*: qua V   [15] scilicet . . . abstinetur] *Serv. ad Aen.*
1.211: scilicet *om.* V

THIRD MITHRIDATIC WAR
(73–72 BC), FRR. 16–37

16* 19M, 9Mc , inc. 51D, inc. 17K

exercitum maiorum more vorteret

Serv. auct. ad *Aen.* 5.408 {Serv. ibid. (*exercitum vertere*)}: mistakenly to illustrate *verto* = *considero* (to examine).

sivity has taken possession of you, as a result of which neither glory nor disgrace moves you. You have traded everything for your present slothfulness and regard your freedom as ample, no doubt, because your backs are spared,[26] and you are allowed to go here and there—kindnesses of your rich masters. Yet even these privileges are denied to the populace in the countryside, but they are being slaughtered amid the feuds of their powerful neighbors, and they are being handed over as gifts to magistrates in the provinces.[27] Thus fighting and conquest are for the benefit of a few; whatever happens, the commons are treated as vanquished. And this will be more so every day, if indeed those men put more care into retaining their mastery than you do into regaining your freedom."

[26] Thanks to the Porcian laws (cf. *Cat.* 51.22).

[27] I.e., sent to serve in wars abroad, where they are at the mercy of magistrates.

THIRD MITHRIDATIC WAR (73–72 BC), FRR. 16–37

16* 19M, 9Mc , inc. 51D, inc. 17K

Soon after arriving in Asia in early 73 BC, Lucullus corrected the indiscipline of the Fimbrian troops (cf. Plut. Luc. 7.3).

he was curbing[1] the army in keeping with ancestral custom

[1] Without context, it is impossible to determine the precise meaning of *verto* (lit., "to turn" around or in some direction). Conceivably *verto* here = *ducto* (lead) or *rego* (control).

17 20M, 10Mc, 14D, 11K

equis[1] et armis decoribus cultus[2]

Prisc. *GL* 2.236.1–2, quoting this fragment and fr. 20: to illustrate the third decl. adj. (*de*)*decor*, (*de*)*decoris* = (*de*)*decorus*, –*a*, –*um*.

[1] equus *B*   [2] cultis *R*

18* 21M, 11Mc, inc. 14D, 3.12K

***Curribus falcatis** usos esse maiores et Livius et Sallustius docent.*

Serv. & Serv. auct. ad *Aen.* 1.476

{*Schol. Stat.* ad *Theb.* 10.544: attests that S. described scythe-bearing chariots.}

19† 23M, 12Mc, 2.58D, 2.67K

At illi, quibus vires aderant, cuncti ruere ad portas, inconditi[1] tendere.[2]

Serv. ad *Ecl.* 2.4 (cited from S. "*in libro V*"): to illustrate *inconditus* = *inconscripta* (without order).

[1] incondita *M, Thilo*   [2] *Gerlach ed. mai.*: temnere *P*: tempnere *LHM*: tempr̄ *R*: tenere *Heinse*

20 24M, 13Mc, 74D, 91K

Dedecores[1] inultique[2] terga ab hostibus caedebantur.

Prisc. *GL* 2.236.2–3: see fr. 17.

[1] decores *RK*   [2] multique *RDKH*

17 20M, 10Mc, 14D, 11K

In the war with Lucullus, in contrast with the previous conflict with Sulla, Mithridates abandoned richly appointed weapons in favor of strict discipline of his troops and weapons on the Roman model (Plut. Luc. 7.4–5).

  adorned with showy horses and arms

18* 21M, 11Mc, inc. 14D, 3.12K

Mithridates' army had a complement of scythe-bearing chariots (cf. Plut. Luc. 7.5).

Both Livy [37.41.5] and Sallust indicate that men of an earlier age employed **scythe-bearing chariots**.

19† 23M, 12Mc, 2.58D, 2.67K

The Roman troops under P. Rutilius Nudus, legate of M. Cotta (cos. 74), were put to flight by Mithridates outside the walls of Chalcedon and cut down in the course of a disorderly dash for the gates (cf. App. Mithr. 71).

But those who had the strength rushed en masse to the gates and made their way in disorder.

20 24M, 13Mc, 74D, 91K

Same context as fr. 19: disorderly flight of Roman soldiers.

Shamefully and without avenging themselves, they were struck in their backs by the enemy.

21 26M, 14Mc, 17D, 15K

Ad Cyzicum perrexit firmatus[1] animi.

Arus. *GL* 7.475.10–11 = p. 139DC: to illustrate *firmatus* + gen. of thing. [For comparable instances of *animi* in the *Historiae,* see on fr. 1.136.]

[1] *Ursinus*: firmatum *N1*

22 28M, 15Mc, 18D, 17K

castrisque conlatis, pugna tamen ingenio loci prohibebatur

Non. p. 323M = 506L.4–5: to illustrate *ingenium* = an inherent quality, applied to things (*OLD* 2).

23 30M, 17Mc, 20D, 21K

unde pons in oppidum pertinens explicatur

Arus. *GL* 7.503.11–12 = p. 241DC: to illustrate *pertineo* construed with *in* + acc.

24 31M, 18Mc, 79D, 97K

exaudirique sonus Bacchanaliorum

Non. p. 489 = 786L.27: to illustrate the spelling of the gen. pl. in *–iorum,* instead of *–ium.*

{*Bacchanaliorum*: Macrob. *Sat.* 1.4.6 (*in tertia*); Charis. *GL* 1.162.19 = p. 77B.24.}

21 26M, 14Mc, 17D, 15K

After his victory over M. Cotta's forces at Chalcedon, Mithridates "moved with confidence against Cyzicus to put the town under siege" (Memnon, FGrH 434F28.1; cf. Plut. Luc. 9.1).

With strengthened resolve, he proceeded toward Cyzicus.

22 28M, 15Mc, 18D, 17K

A description of conditions in the vicinity of Cyzicus after the arrival of Mithridates, who was closely pursued by Lucullus (cf. App. Mithr. 72).

although the camps had been placed in close proximity, fighting was nonetheless impeded by the nature of the place

23 30M, 17Mc, 20D, 21K

Two bridges, or one (cf. fr. 25n.1), connected Cyzicus to the mainland (Strabo 12.8.11, p. 575).

from where a bridge stretches out, extending into the town

24 31M, 18Mc, 79D, 97K

Possibly part of S.'s description of the territory lying near Cyzicus, including Mt. Dindymon, where the goddess Cybele was worshipped (Amm. Marc. 22.8.5) with ecstatic rites similar to those of the god Bacchus.

and the sound of Bacchanalian orgies <was able?> to be heard from afar

25 37M, 23Mc, 19D, 20K

Duos[1] quam maxumos utris levi tabulae subiecit, qua[2]
super omni corpore quietus invicem tracto pede[3] quasi
gubernator existeret; ea inter molem[4] atque[5] insulam mari
vitabundus classem hostium[6] ad oppidum pervenit.

Non. p. 186M = 274L.18–21: to illustrate *vitabundus* meaning
vitans (avoiding).

[1] *om. L*
[2] *corr. ed. a. 1480:* quam *codd.*
[3] ed. *Ald. 1513:* pedes *codd.*
[4] *corr. ed. a. 1470:* inolem *codd.*
[5] *Junius:* quae *codd.*
[6] honestium *L*

26 33M, 19Mc, 36D, 41K

quarum[1] unam epistulam[2] forte cum servo nancti
praedatores Valeriani scorpione[3] in castra misere

Non. p. 553M = 888L.22–23: to give an instance of the noun
scorpio (*OLD* 3), a form of catapult, apparently sometimes hand
held (Veg. *Mil.* 4.22.6), capable of discharging arrows, vel. sim.,
at close range and in rapid succession (Caes. *B Gall.* 7.25.2–3).

[1] quorum *Quichert*
[2] *Iunius:* una epistula *codd.*
[3] *Iunius:* scorpionem *codd.*

25 37M, 23Mc, 19D, 20K

By means of a floatation device, a Roman soldier sent by Lucullus managed to slip through enemy lines, covering a distance of some seven miles by sea and entering Cyzicus to encourage the people to hold out against Mithridates on the assurance that Lucullus' army was coming to their aid (Frontin. Str. 3.13.6; Flor. 1.40.16; Oros. 6.2.14).

He placed two [inflated] leather sacks of the largest size possible underneath a light board, on top of which, while remaining still with this whole body, he played the part of a steersman, as it were, by trailing each foot by turns. After this fashion, he came to the town by sea, between the breakwater and island,[1] taking evasive action against the enemy's fleet.

[1] According to Frontin. (*Str.* 3.13.6), the island [*sic*] on which the city lay was connected to the mainland by a single, narrow bridge.

26 33M, 19Mc, 36D, 41K

The Romans taunt Mithridates after intercepting one of his letters that was possibly sent to request reinforcements and supplies (so Dietsch) or to broach the subject of desertion on the part of Lucullus' two Valerian legions (so Maurenbr. citing App. Mithr. 72 and Memnon, FGrH 434F28.2).

pillaging Valerians[1] by chance stumbled upon one of these letters along with the slave [messenger carrying it] and sent it back into the camp by means of a catapult

[1] The Valerians comprised two legions in Lucullus' army. They had been sent to Asia Minor more than a decade earlier under the command of L. Valerius Flaccus (cos. 86) to fight in the First Mithridatic War (App. *Mithr.* 72).

27* 34M, 20Mc, 23D, 24K

et onere turrium incertis navibus

Serv. auct. ad *Aen* 1.576: mistakenly to illustrate *incertus* meaning *tardus* (slow), when, in fact, in S. it means "unsteady" (*OLD* 13).

28 35M, 21Mc, 21D, 22K

manus ferreas et alia adnexu[1] idonea inicere

Arus. *GL* 7.487.8–9 = p. 179DC: to illustrate the adj. *idoneus* + supine.

　[1] *Lindemann*: adnexa *N1*

29 36M, 22Mc, 22D, 23K

Saxaque ingentia et orbes axe[1] iuncti per pronum incitabantur, axibusque eminebant[2] in modum erici[3] militaris veruta binum pedum.

Non. p. 554.30–555M.3 = 890L: to illustrate the noun *verutum,* defined as a short, thin missile (*telum beve et angustum*).

{*in modum ericii militaris* (Serv. ad *Aen.* 9.503, and Isid. *Etym.* 18.12.6): to illustrate the noun *ericius* (hedgehog), a military device named after the animal.}

　[1] *Turnebus*: ingentia turbae saxae *codd.*　　　[2] *A*[A]: minebant *L B*[A]: minabant *(Bamb.) C*[A]　　[3] *Lindsay*: ericii *ed. Ald. 1513*: erigi *L A*[A]: erigo *C*[A]: hirci *B*[A]: iricii *Serv., Isid.*

30† 4.16M, 4.50Mc, 3.26D, K

27* 34M, 20Mc, 23D, 24K

At the siege of Cyzicus, Mithridates attacked the wall of the town by means of a bridge lowered from a tower erected on two quinqueremes lashed together (App. Mithr. 73–74).

and the ships being unsteady owing to the burden
of towers

28 35M, 21Mc, 21D, 22K

The defenders of Cyzicus used various methods to thwart Mithridates' siege engines and battering rams (App. Mithr. 74).

they hurled [against the siege engines?] grappling
irons and other devices suitable for forming an attachment

29 36M, 22Mc, 22D, 23K

From high ground, the besieged people of Cyzicus rolled heavy objects down the slope to smash Mithridates' engines of war (cf. App. Mithr. 74).

Huge boulders and wheels joined with an axle were set
rolling down the slope, and from the axles projected thin
darts, each two feet long, arranged after the fashion of a
military hedgehog.[1]

[1] A wooden beam with projecting spikes used in war to form a barrier. (Caes. *B Civ.* 3.67.5)

30† 4.16M, 4.50Mc, 3.26D, K

Although both Nonius and Priscian assign this fragment to Book 4, the description most closely resembles circumstances that occurred during the siege of Cyzicus in the winter of 73/72, when a

Quasi[1] par in oppido festinatio, et ingens terror erat ne ex latere nova munimenta madore infirmarentur; nam omnia oppidi stagnabant, redundantibus cloacis advorso aestu maris.

Non. p. 138M = 200L.4–6: to illustrate the noun *mador.*

{Prisc. *GL* 2.235.3–4 (*munimenta madore infirmarentur*): to illustrate the noun *mador, -oris; Exc. Bob. GL* 1.552.12: attesting S.'s use of *mador* in the *Historiae.*} Both Non. and Prisc. assign to bk 4.

[1] quas C^A D^A

31* 38M, 24Mc, 27D, 28K

et morbi graves ob inediam insolita[1] vescentibus

Donat. ad Ter. *Hec.* 337: to illustrate the adj. *gravis* with *morbus.*

[1] *Lindenbrog:* insolitam *codd.*

32* 39M, 25Mc, 28D, 27K

Ordinem secutus est (sc. Virgilius in peste descri- benda) quem et Lucretius tenuit et Sallustius: primo **aerem**, inde **aquam**, post **pabula** esse **cor- rupta**.

Serv. ad *G.* 3.481.

violent storm suddenly fell upon and wrecked Mithridates' naval siege engines (Plut. Luc. 10.3). It caused consternation in the city as well, part of whose wall had hastily been repaired shortly before the storm (App. Mithr. 74).

In the town there was nearly equal scurrying and tremendous fear that the new fortifications of brick[1] might be weakened by the damp; for all regions of the town were flooded seeing that the underground drains were overflowing from the incoming swell of the sea.

[1] The phrase *ex latere* can also mean "from the side" (so McGushin and Frassinetti, "di lato"), if *latere* is to be construed as the abl. of *latus* (neut.). However, in this context, *latere* is better interpreted as abl. of *later* (m.), "brick" (so Kritz). Cf. Cato, *Agr.* 14.4, *parietes ex latere* (walls of brick), and S. *Hist.* fr. 4.70, *lateribus*.

31* 38M, 24Mc, 27D, 28K

At the siege of Cyzicus, Mithridates' army was cut off from supplies by Lucullus and suffered starvation and plague during the winter 73/72, causing them even to resort to cannibalism (App. Mithr. 76; Strabo 12.8.11, p. 576; Plut. Luc. 11.1–2).

and serious illnesses ⟨befell?⟩ those eating unaccustomed fare on account of starvation

32* 39M, 25Mc, 28D, 27K

Plague in the camp of Mithridates at the siege of Cyzicus in winter 73/72.

*[In describing the plague, Virgil] follows the order adhered to by Lucretius and Sallust: first the **air**, then the **water**, lastly the **fodder** were **infected**.*

33* 78M, 26Mc, deest in D et K

quia prominens aquilonibus[1] minus gravescit quam
cetera

Adnot. super Luc. 6.104: to explicate Lucan's description of how
the North wind, blowing over the sea, lessened the effect of the
pestilence in Pompey's camp at Dyrrachium in 48.

[1] *G*: aquilo *WV*

34* 1.43M, 3.27Mc, 3.25D, 3.29K

ne simplici quidem morte moriebantur

Serv. ad *G.* 3.482: explicating a line describing torturous death
in a plague

35 40M, 28Mc, 72D, 87K

ut sustinere corpora plerique nequeuntes arma sua
quisque stans[1] incumberet

Arus. *GL* 7.478.26–27 = p. 151DC: to illustrate *incumbere* + acc.
of thing.

{Serv. ad *Aen.* 9.227 (*ut fessi arma sua quisque stantes incumbere*): to illustrate the stance of Roman soldiers after experiencing fatigue from long periods of standing in place.}

[1] *Gerlach ed. mai.*: instans *N1 Arus.*: stantes *Serv.*

33* 78M, 26Mc, not included in D and K

Possibly describing some region of Cyzicus that was less troubled by the outbreak of pestilence owing to the healthy air brought by the North Wind, as in the passage of Lucan on which the scholiast commented (so La Penna). Maurenbr., on the contrary, assigned this fragment to a description of the Tauric Chersonesus.

because, jutting out, it was less burdened than the other regions thanks to the North Wind

34* 1.43M, 3.27Mc, 3.25D, 3.29K

Possibly describing deaths in the plague at the siege of Cyzicus (so Kritz and La Penna). Maurenbr., on the contrary, linked these words to the death of Marius Gratidianus (see fr. 1.36) and other victims of Sulla's bloodletting, comparing Oros. 5.21.6, "and the pathway of death itself was not simple, nor was it the only suffering" (nec ipsius mortis erat via simplex aut una condicio).

they were dying from multifarious deaths

35 40M, 28Mc, 72D, 87K

Either (a) a description of the defenders of Cyzicus, faint with hunger (cf. similar language in Liv. 5.48.7 describing the Gallic siege of Rome in 390/387), or (b) a description of those of Lucullus' soldiers who fell behind, worn out by the cold of winter and fatigue, when in pursuit of Mithridates' forces withdrawing from Cyzicus (Plut. Luc. 11.4).

so that the majority, being unable to support the weight of their bodies, stood each leaning on his own arms

36* 42M, 29Mc, 29D, 30K

Σαλουστίου . . . τότε πρῶτον ὦφθαι Ῥωμαίοις
καμήλους λέγοντος

Plut. *Luc.* 11.6.

{Cf. Amm. Marc. 23.6.56, *cameli a Mithridate exinde perducti et
primitus in obsidione Cyzicena visi Romanis.*}

37* 29M, 16Mc, 16D, K

laudat Sallustius duces, qui[1] **victoriam incruento exercitu** *reportaverunt*

Serv. ad *Aen.* 11.421; Isid. *Etym.* 18.2.1.

[1] *om. Isid.*   [2] *deportasse Isid.*

THE SLAVE UPRISING LED
BY SPARTACUS: YEAR ONE
(73 BC), FRR. 38–45

38 90M, 60Mc, deest in D et K

Spartacus princeps gladiatorum, *de illis quattuor et*

36* 42M, 29Mc, 29D, 30K

The scene, according to Plut., is the siege of Cyzicus, when Lucullus brought back a large number of prisoners and pack animals captured at the battle near the river Rhyndacus. Amm. Marc. (loc. cit.), without referring to S., similarly mentions "camels brought by Mithridates from there [the land of the Bactrians: mod. N. Afghanistan] and seen by the Romans for the first time at the siege of Cyzicus."

Sallust says that **camels were then seen by the Romans for the first time**.[1]

[1] The novelty to which S. drew attention was the Romans' first encounter with camels having two humps (the Bactrian species). The single-humped Arabian dromedary was well known to them.

37* 29M, 16Mc, 16D, K

Lucullus cut off Mithridates' supplies, forcing him to lift the siege of Cyzicus, thus winning a bloodless victory (Oros. 6.2.20; cf. Plut. Luc. 9.3; App. Mithr. 72).

Sallust praises generals who have brought back a **victory without spilling the army's blood**

THE SLAVE UPRISING LED BY SPARTACUS: YEAR ONE (73 BC), FRR. 38–45

38 90M, 60Mc, not included in D and K

The slave uprising began with the escape of Spartacus and seventy-four fellow gladiators from a training school (ludus) in Capua (Liv. Per. 95).

Spartacus, chief of the gladiators, *one of those 74 who*

septuaginta qui **ludo egressi,** *ut Sallustius in tertio historiarum refert, grave proelium cum populo Romano gesserunt.*

Schol. Γ ad Hor. *Epod.* 16.5.

39 91M, 61Mc, 13D, 10K

ingens ipse virium atque animi

Arus. *GL* 7.480.21 = p. 157DC: to illustrate *ingens* + gen. of thing. [For comparable instances of *animi* in the *Historiae,* see on fr. 1.136.]

40* 93M, 62Mc, inc. 21D, 3.67K

Sin vis obsistat, ferro quam fame aequius perituros

Serv. ad *Aen.* 3.265: to illustrate the painful nature of hunger.

41* 94M, 63Mc, 65D, 75K

Cossinius[1] in proxuma villa fonte lavabatur.

Cledon. *GL* 5.59.11: to illustrate the passive of *lavo* meaning "to wash" = "to wash oneself" (*OLD* 2b).

  [1] *Kritz*: Cossutius *cod.*

42 96M, 64Mc, 67D, 77K

escaped from a gladiatorial establishment and *fought a major battle with the Roman people, as Sallust reports in Book 3 of his Histories.*

39 91M, 61Mc, 13D, 10K

Plut. (Crass. 8.3) thus describes Spartacus.

being himself mighty in strength and spirit

40* 93M, 62Mc, inc. 21D, 3.67K

The attempt of the Roman praetor Clodius (C. Claudius Glaber) to trap Spartacus and his followers in their place of refuge on Mt. Vesuvius failed when the runaways escaped by means of ladders constructed of vines and lowered from a sheer cliff (cf. Plut. Crass. 9.2).

But if force blocks the way, ‹Spartacus reminded his followers that?› it would be preferable for them to perish by the sword than by hunger

41* 94M, 63Mc, 65D, 75K

Spartacus surprised and nearly captured L. Cossinius, a praetor commanding forces sent against him, when Cossinius was bathing near Salinae, not far from Pompeii (Plut. Crass. 9.5).

In a nearby villa, Cossinius was washing in a spring.

42 96M, 64Mc, 67D, 77K

Events leading up to the sound defeat of Roman forces under the praetor P. Varinius in 73 at the hands of Spartacus: at one point the fugitive slaves made a strategic, nighttime withdrawal from their camp, dressing up the scene with corpses propped up to look like sentries in order to fool the Romans (cf. Frontin. Str. 1.5.22). (Italics in the translation signifies that the text or a supplement is uncertain.)

1   [A] . . . ‹sudes[1] ig]›|ni torrere, quibus praeter | speciem
bello necessariam | haud multo secus quam | ferro noceri
poterat.

2   At | Varinius, dum haec agun|tur a fugitivis, aegra par|te
militum autumni gra|vitate, neque ex postrema | fuga,
quom[2] severo edicto | iuberentur,[3] ullis ad sig|na redeun-
tibus,[4] et qui reli|cui erant, per summa fla|gitia detractan-
tibus mili|tiam, quaestorem suum | C. Thoranium, ex quo
prae|sente vera facillume[5] nos|cerentu‹r, Roma›m[6] mise-

3   rat;[7] et ta|men interim cum[8] vo|lentibus numero quattuor
[B] ‹milium, iuxta illos castra | poni›t va‹llo, fossa, per-
mag›|nis[9] operibus commun‹ita›. |

4   Deinde fugitivi, con‹sump›|tis iam alimentis, ne
p‹rae›|dantibus ex propin‹quo hos›|tis instaret, soliti
m‹ore mi›|litiae vigilias sta‹tiones›|que et alia munia
ex‹equi; | secunda vigilia, ‹silentio› | cuncti egredi‹untur
re›|licto bucinato‹re in cas›|tris; et ad vigil‹um speciem›

A–D = four columns of text, each originally 21 lines in length
and 18–23 letter-spaces in width, inscribed on the recto (AB) and
verso (CD) of a single leaf forming one-half of a partially preserved double leaf (bifolium) that once belonged to the so-called
Fleury manuscript (*Floriacensis*), which most likely contained a
complete text of S.'s *Historiae*. The two leaves are preserved as
fol. 92r–v (containing this fragment) and fol. 93r–v (containing fr.
44) of the codex *Vaticanus Reginensis 1283B* (**R**). Ends of lines
in the manuscript are indicated by |, from which it can be seen
that there are sizeable gaps at the end of lines in the right-hand
column of the recto (B) and at the beginning of lines of the corresponding left-hand column of the verso (C), owing to the loss
of the outer edge of the leaf. Italics indicates that the transcription is uncertain.

. . . with fire to harden *stakes* by charring them, by which,   [fr. 42]
besides the look required for war, it was possible to inflict
virtually as much injury as with steel.

But while these activities were being performed by the
runaways, since part of the soldiers were ill owing to the
oppressive autumn weather, and since after the most recent flight neither were any of the soldiers returning to
their regiments, although they had been ordered to do so
by a stern edict, and those who were left were shirking
their military duties in a most shameful fashion, Varinius
had sent his quaestor Gaius Thoranius to Rome so that
from him in person a true assessment of the situation
might most easily be made. Meanwhile, nevertheless, with
those who were willing, [B] some 4,000 in number, *he
pitched a camp near the enemy,* one fortified with *a rampart, ditch,* and vast earthworks.

Afterward the runaways, now that their supply of food
had been used up, were accustomed to carry out in military fashion watches and guard duty and other functions
so as to prevent the enemy from pressing upon them while
they were raiding from close by; in the second watch [of
the night] they went out enmasse, in silence, leaving behind in camp a trumpeter; and to give onlookers from a

---

¹ *Kritz*: hastas *Maurenbr.* ex *Serv. ad Aen.* 9.740
² cum *R*   ³ *Dousa*: iuverentur *R*   ⁴ *Dousa*:
deeuntibus *R*   ⁵ facillime *R*   ⁶ noscerentu‹r Roma›m]
Dousa: noscerentum *R*   ⁷ *Dousa*: miserant *R*   ⁸ quom
R (*cf. Ep. 1.6.5, 1.7.4; TLL 4.1339.65–1340.17*)   ⁹ ‹milium
. . . permag›nis] *Maurenbr.*: ‹milium loco tuto castra poni›t va‹llo
aliisque mag›nis *Hauler*

| procul visen‹tibus palis[10] ere›lxerant fulta ‹ante por-
tam›[11] | recentia ca‹davera et cre›lbros igni‹s fecerant
for›lmidine f . . . ‹Va›lrini ‹milites . . . i›lte‹r› . . . |* * * |
5 * * * [C] * * * | . . . oa . . . | . . . inviis convertere. At[12] |
‹Var›inius multa iam luce | ‹desi›derans solita a fugil‹tivis›
convicia et in casl‹tra c›oniectus lapidum, | ‹ad ho›c stre-
pitus tumull‹tusque e›t sonores undique | ‹urgent›ium,[13]
mittit equites ‹in tumul›um circum prol‹minentem›, ut
6 explorarent, | ‹insequente›s[14] propere vestil‹gia. Sed
fugativ›os[15] credens lonl‹ge abesse muni›to[16] tamen
agl‹mine insidia›s pavens se | ‹recepit, ut exercitu›m
duplil‹caret novis militibus. At› Cumas | . . . ga |* * * | *
7 * * [D] * * * | . . . ‹Post› | aliquot[17] dies contra molrem
8 fiducia augeri nosltris coepit et promi lingua. | Qua Vari-
nius contra slpectatam rem incaute[18] | motus novos
incognitoslque et aliorum casibus perlculsos milites ducit
tamen | ad castra fugitivorum | presso gradu, silentis iam |
neque tam magnifice sumenltis proelium quam postulla-
9 verant. Atque illi certalmine consili inter se iuxlta[19] seditionem erant, Crilxo et gentis eiusdem Galllis atque
Germanis obviam | ire et ultro ‹of›ferre[20] pugnam | cu-
pientibus, contra Spartal‹co impetum dissuadente›.

[10] *Maurenbr.*: visent‹tibus ere›xerant *vulgo*   [11] ante
portam] *Maurenbr. ex Frontin. Str. 1.5.22*: palis fixis
Kritz   [12] ad *R*   [13] *Hauler*: ruentium *Kreyssig*: inru-
entium *Jordan*   [14] *Maurenbr.*: fugitivos *Kritz*: insidiato-
res *Hauler*   [15] *Maurenbr.*   [16] munito] *Hauler*
[17] *Dousa*: aliquod *R*   [18] *Dousa*: incautae *R*   [19] *Dousa*:
iusta *R*   [20] *Dousa*: ferre *R*

distance the appearance of watchmen, they had propped   [fr. 42]
up with stakes, *in front of the gate,* fresh corpses and had
kindled numerous fires *so that* Varinius' *soldiers . . . out of
fear . . . a journey . . .* [2 lines are missing] [C] [2 lines are
missing] . . . inaccessible ⟨regions?⟩ . . . to turn back. But
Varinius, now that it was quite light, missing the accustomed jeers from the runaways and the volleys of stones
into his camp, besides the din and uproar and noise of
those bustling all about, sent cavalry up onto a mound
having a prospect in all directions to reconnoiter and
quickly *follow after* their tracks. Yet, although he believed
the runaways were far off, nonetheless *he withdrew* with
a *reinforced line of march,* dreading *an ambush, with the
goal of* doubling the size of *his army with fresh soldiers.*
But to Cumae . . . [3 lines are missing] [D] [2 lines are
missing] . . . ⟨after⟩ some days, contrary to their past be-
havior, the confidence of our troops began to increase and
be expressed in speech. Varinius was incautiously stirred
by this in the face of observed reality, and he led troops,
though raw and untried and demoralized by the mishap of
the others, in the direction of the camp of the runaways at
a steady pace; the men were now remaining silent and
were not so boastful in taking up battle as they had been
in demanding it. And the enemy were close to mutiny in
their own ranks thanks to dissension over strategy: Crixus
and his fellow Gauls and Germans desiring to go on the
offensive and give battle of their own accord, while Spartacus on the contrary ⟨*urged against an attack*⟩ . . .

263

43 97M, 65Mc, 66D, 76K

> incidere in colonos Abellanos praesidentis agros
> suos

Arus. *GL* 7.498.26 = p. 223DC: to illustrate *praesideo* + acc. of
thing.

44 98M, 66Mc, 67D, 77K

1 [A] . . . | . . . ‹ali›|enis¹ et *ei* . . . | ne, qua ‹ratione² vaga-
rentur a›d | id temp‹oris . . . tu›m|que seclu‹derentur
itinere³ ia›m | et extin‹guerentur⁴ . . . simu›l | curam . . .
is|set hau‹d . . . i›*t*aque⁵ | quam *c*‹elerrume abirent.

2 H›*a*ud | aliam *f*‹ugae rationem c›api|undam⁶ ‹sibi esse
pauci› pru|dentes *p*‹robare, liberi ani›mi |nobiles‹que,
ceteri› . . . lau|dantque, *q*‹uod ille iubet fac›ere; | pars
sto‹lide copi›is ad|fluenti‹bus ferocique inge›*ni*o fi|dens,
ali‹i inhonest›e patri|ae inmem‹ores, at plu›rumi⁷ | servil*i*
‹indole nihil› ultra | prae‹dam et crudeli›*t*atem⁸ | ‹appe-

A–D = four columns of text, each originally 21 lines in length and
18–23 letter-spaces in width, inscribed on the recto (AB) and verso (CD) of a single leaf forming one-half of a partially preserved
double leaf (bifolium) that once belonged to the so-called Fleury
manuscript (*Floriacensis*). See fr. 42. Ends of lines in the manus-
cript are indicated by |, from which it can be seen that there are
sizeable gaps in the middle of lines in the left-hand column of
the recto (A) and the corresponding right-hand column on the
verso (D). Italics indicates that the transcription is uncertain.
Supplements are to be credited to Maurenbr. unless otherwise
noted. Non. p. 456M = 731L.14–15 cites a small portion of this
fragment (see §4n.) and assigns it to Book 3.

¹ alieni *Hauler*   ² *Dietsch*   ³ secluderentur
itinere] *Dietsch*   ⁴ *Dietsch*

43 97M, 65Mc, 66D, 76K

After their victory over Varinius (see preceding fragment), Spartacus and his followers overran the whole of Campania (Flor. 2.8.5).

they happened upon farmers of Abella,[1] safeguarding their fields

[1] A town in Campania.

44 98M, 66Mc, 67D, 77K

Several no longer extant leaves must have separated the leaf bearing this fragment from the leaf joined to it and bearing fr. 42 since now Spartacus counsels his followers to flee from Italy, back to their respective native lands, but the slaves prefer plunder. They overrun southern Campania and proceed farther south into Lucania. Brutal atrocities are committed before the praetor Varinius can take the field with a reinvigorated army. Italic type in the translation signifies that the supplements to the lacunose text in sections A and D are highly conjectural.

[A] . . . [2 lines are missing] . . . *other* and . . . ⟨*fearing*⟩ that, *in the fashion in* which *they were wandering up until* that time . . . they might *be cut off on their journey* and *destroyed . . . at the same time* the concern . . . and in this way to get away as quickly as possible. *A few* sensible individuals, those of a *free* and noble *spirit,* approved the need to adopt precisely this *policy of flight, others* . . . and they praised that *which he [Spartacus] ordered them to do.* Some [of the fugitives] *stupidly* relying on the *recruits* pouring in *and on their fierce temperament,* others *dishonorably having no thought* for their native lands, but

---

[5] *Hauler*   [6] c⟩apie|endam *R*   [7] immem⟨ores, at
plu⟩rimi] *Jordan*   [8] praedam et crudelitatem] *Hauler*

tere . . . [B] . . . I. . . . I cons‹ilium . . . op›Itumum[9] vide-
3 batur. Deinlceps monet in ‹l›axioris agros I magisque
pecuarios I ut egrediantur, ubi, priu‹s›Iquam refecto exercitu I adesset Varinius, auger‹e›Itur numerus lectis
vir‹is›; I et propere nanctus idolneum ex captivis ducem I
Picentinis, deinde Eburilnis iugis occultus ad N‹a›Iris
Lucanas, atque inde prilma luce pervenit ad Anlni Forum,
4 ignaris cultolribus. Ac statim fugitivi co‹n›Itra praeceptum ducis I rapere ad stuprum virg‹i›Ines matr‹ona›sque,[10]
et alii . . . [C] . . . I . . . I . . . n›unc resItantes et eludebant
simul I nefandum in modum perIverso volnere, et
interIdum lacerum corpus seImianimum omittentes; I alii
in tecta iaciebant igInis, multique ex loco serIvi, quos ingenium socilos dabat, abdita a domiInis aut ipsos trahebant
I ex occulto; neque sanctum I aut nefandum quicquam I
5 fuit irae barbarorum I et servili ingenio. Quae I Spartacus
nequiens prolhibere, multis precibus[11] quom I oraret, celeritate praelverterent ‹de re›[12] nuntios [D] . . . I . . . I . . .
6 tur neque I e . . . ‹odiu›m in se I c‹onvertere. Quo›s
crudelI‹iter caedibus occ›upatos I a‹c›. . . gravis plelr‹ique
. . . a›t illum dilem ‹atque proximam›[13] noctem I ib‹idem
commoratu›s duplilca‹to iam fugitiv›orum nulme‹ro[14]
castra movet p›rima cum I luc‹e et consedit› in campo I

[9] timum *R*   [10] Ac statim fugitivi . . . matronasque] *Non.*
p. 456M = 731L.14–15   [11] praecibus *R*   [12] *Hauler*
[13] *Kreyssig*   [14] duplicato . . . numero] *Kritz*

---

[1] The precise location of this town, probably in southern Campania, is not known.   [2] Taking their name from the Lucanian
town Eburum ca. twelve miles to the east and slightly north of
Nares Lucanae.

the vast majority owing to their slavish disposition *sought*   [fr. 44]
nothing beyond booty and cruelty . . . [B] . . . [2 lines are
missing] . . . seemed the best plan. Afterward, he advised
them to go out into more open territory, more abounding
in cattle, where their number might be increased with
picked men, before Varinius appeared with a reinvigorated army; and after quickly obtaining a suitable guide
from the captives taken at Picentia,[1] he then in concealment came to Nares Lucanae by way of the Eburian hills[2]
and from there he reached Anni Forum[3] at first light,
without the inhabitants being aware of their approach.
And immediately the runaways, contrary to the order of
their leader, raped the maidens and wives, and others . . .
[C] . . . [2 lines are missing] . . . those now putting up resistance, and at the same time they treated them outra-
geously by inflicting malicious wounds in an unspeakable
manner and at times by leaving in their wake mutilated,
half-alive bodies. Others tossed fire into houses, and many
slaves from the region, whose temperament made them
natural allies, dragged out property hidden by their masters and their masters themselves from their places of
concealment. Nothing was sacred or off limits to the wrath
of the barbarians and to their servile temperament. Spartacus, being unable to prevent these acts, when he begged
them with many prayers quickly to forestall messengers
concerning their deed [D] . . . [2 lines are missing] . . . nor
. . . to *turn hatred* against themselves. Those who were
cruelly *engaged with slaughter and* . . . serious, the majority . . . *but* after *staying in the same place* that day and the
following night, now that the number *of runaways* had

---

[3] Location in Lucania unknown.

sat‹is lato, ubi colo›nos[15] aedifi|c‹i›is e‹gressos videt›; et
tum | mat‹ura in agri›s erant | aut*u*‹mni frume›nta.[16] |

7   Sed in‹colae iam ple›no die gna|ri ex ‹fuga finit›u-
morum | fugi‹tivos ad se a›dventa|re, *p*‹roperant cum
o›mnibus | ‹suis in montes vicinos›.

[15] satis lato *et* colonos *Kritz*   [16] *ex Porphry. ad Hor.
Epist. 2.1.140, nam et* autumni frumenta *Sallustius dixit*

45   99M, 67Mc, 69D, 79K

Vnus constitit[1] in agro Lucano gnarus loci, nomine Publipor.

Prisc. *GL* 2.236.14–15: to illustrate a compound noun having the
element *–por* (= *puer*); cf. Prob. *GL* 4.16.18, the third decl. noun
Publipor in S.

[1] consistit *K*

FINAL PHASE OF PIRATE WAR
WAGED BY M. ANTONIUS
(73–72 BC), FRR. 46–54

*An Account of the Geography and
History of Crete (frr. 46–51)*

46*   10M, 68Mc, 57D, 60K

doubled, *he moved camp* with first light and *took up a position* in *quite a wide* plain, *where he saw that* the farmers *had come out of* their buildings; and the grain of autumn was then ripe *in the fields*.

But *now in the full light of* day, the *inhabitants being aware* from *the flight of their neighbors* that the runaways *were drawing near to them, had hastened with* all *the members of their families* ⟨*into the nearby mountains*⟩.

45 99M, 67Mc, 69D, 79K

Lucania was overrun by Spartacus and his followers.

There existed[1] in the Lucanian district a single man acquainted with the region, Publipor by name.

[1] Or "halted" (sc. from flight)—so Kritz—if *constitit* is perf. of *consisto,* rather than *consto.* It is impossible to tell without more context.

FINAL PHASE OF PIRATE WAR
WAGED BY M. ANTONIUS
(73–72 BC), FRR. 46–54

*An Account of the Geography and
History of Crete (frr. 46–51)*

46* 10M, 68Mc, 57D, 60K

In 73, Marcus Antonius moved with his fleet against the pirates in Crete, which the first-century AD geographer Pomponius Mela (2.112) similarly describes as being situated "mid sea" (in medio mari), a description of Crete's location that may be traced back to Homer (Od. 19.172).

MEDIO PONTO, *potest quidem intellegi secundum Sallustium longe a continenti.*

Serv. & Serv. auct. ad *Aen.* 3.104: to explicate Virgil's description of Crete as lying *medio ponto.*

47* 11M, 69Mc, 58D, 61K

Creta altior est qua parte spectat orientem.

Serv. ad *Aen.* 6.23: to explicate Virgil's description of Crete as *elata mari* (raised up out of the sea).

48* 12M, 70Mc, 30D, 34K

Tota autem insula modica et cultibus variis est.

Mart. Cap. 5.520 (p. 180W.19–20): in a discussion of prose rhythm, to illustrate the need for an anapest (in this instance, *variis*), or cretic, to precede a final monosyllabic word that is short (*est*).

*The expression "**mid sea**" can be understood, according to Sallust, to mean far from the mainland.*[1]

[1] If *medio ponto*—or more likely *medio mari* (cf. Mela 2.112)—is what S. wrote (so Maurenbr.), and *longe a continenti* are not S.'s words (as Kritz and Dietsch assumed), then Servius possibly misunderstood S.'s point, which was to indicate that Crete lies at the intersection of several seas: the Aegean and Cretan on the north, the Libyan on the south (so Strabo 10.4.2, p. 474).

47* 11M, 69Mc, 58D, 61K

Part of S.'s description of Crete. It is not clear whether Servius is quoting or paraphrasing.

Crete is more elevated in the region where it faces east.[1]

[1] In fact, the highest elevations are Mt. Ida in the central region, and the Leuca Mountains in the west (Strabo 10.4.4, p. 475).

48* 12M, 70Mc, 30D, 34K

If, as Maurenbr. speculated, this fragment formed part of S.'s description of Crete (cf. frr. 46–47), modica (moderate) is best interpreted as a reference to Crete's climate—between the extremes of Scythia in the north and Cyrenica in the south—thus complementing the mention of a variety of crops (especially vines and trees: Solin. 11.12; Isid. Etym. 14.6.16). Less apt is "of moderate size" (so McGushin, in agreement with Frassinetti), since Crete ranks fifth in size among islands of the Mediterranean (after Sicily, Sardinia, Cyprus, and Corsica).

Moreover, the whole island is temperate and subject to various forms of cultivation.

49* 13M, 71Mc, 59D, 62K

*est . . . **Otus in Creta**, secundum Sallustium; unde Otii campi*

Serv. & Serv. auct. ad *Aen.* 3.578: in commenting on S.'s placement of Otus in Crete (a giant best known for joining with his brother Ephialtes in assaulting heaven by attempting to pile Mt. Ossa on Olympus and Pelion on Ossa in the region of Thessaly, on the mainland of Greece [Hom. *Od.* 11.305–20]).

50* 14M, 72Mc, 60D, 63–64K

Hanc totam opinionem, quasi a poetis fictam, Sal‹l›ustius respuit, uoluitque ingeniose interpretari, cur altores Iouis dicantur Curetes fuisse; et sic ait:

quia principes intellegendi divini fuerunt, vetustatem, uti cetera, in maius conponentem, altores Iovis celebravisse.

Lactant. *Div. inst.* 1.21.41.

{Cf. Serv. & Serv. auct. ad *Aen.* 3.104, Serv. ad *Aen.* 8.352: S. accounted for the belief that Jupiter was raised in Crete by observing that the Cretans were traditionally viewed as the inventors of religion.}

49* 13M, 71Mc, 59D, 62K

Part of S.'s description of Crete (cf. frr. 46–48).

. . . **Otus** is **in Crete**,[1] *according to Sallust; whence the plains of Otus[2] [take their name]*

[1] The bones of a giant 46 cubits (= ca. 67 feet) tall were said to have been uncovered in Crete when a mountain was split apart by an earthquake; some identified them with Otus, some with the giant hunter Orion (Plin. *HN* 7.73). According to Solinus (1.91) bones of a giant 33 cubits (= ca. 48 feet) tall were discovered on Crete, after a flood, during the conquest of the island by Q. Caecilius Metellus (68–67 BC).   [2] Location unknown.

50* 14M, 72Mc, 60D, 63–64K

Part of S.'s description of Crete (cf. frr. 46–49). The Curetes, semidivine Cretan warriors, were portrayed in mythology as attendants of Jupiter in his infancy.

Sallust rejected this entire view as a poetic fiction [viz. legends assigning a role to the Curetes and Corybantes in concealing the baby Jupiter on Crete]; he was in favor of this clever explanation for why the foster-fathers of Jupiter are said to have been the Curetes, stating that

because they [the Curetes] were the originators of grasping the divine, men in antiquity, in keeping with their habit of exaggerating, glorified them as the foster-fathers of Jupiter.

51* 15M, 73Mc, inc. 8D, 1.78K

Cares*[1] *insulani populi fuerunt, **piratica famosi, victi a Minoe**, ut et Thucydides et Sallustius dicunt.

Serv. ad *Aen.* 8.725: background information concerning the Carians mentioned by Virgil.

[1] *Gerlach ed. mai.*: Carae *Serv.*

52 8M, 74Mc, 56D, 88K

et forte in navigando cohors una, grandi phaselo vecta, a ceteris deerravit, marique placido a duobus praedonum myoparonibus circumventa

Non. p. 534M = 857.18–20: to illustrate the noun *myoparo*, defined as a pirate ship.

{Non. p. 534M = 857.26–27 (*et forte . . . deeravit*): to illustrate the noun *phaselus*, defined as a Campanian vessel.}

53 9M, 75Mc, 4.40D, 4.48K

in quis notissumus quisque ex malo dependens[1] verberabatur, aut inmutilato corpore in prori[2] patibulo eminens adfigebatur.

Non. p. 366M = 582L.13–15: to illustrate *patibulum* = *crux* (a cross).

[1] *ed. Ald. 1513*: et m. deperdens *codd.*   [2] *Carrio*: inprobi *codd.*: inprobe *Lipsius*

51* 15M, 73Mc, inc. 8D, 1.78K

Part of S.'s description of Crete (cf. frr. 46–50).

The Carians were an island people,[1] **notorious for piracy, subdued by Minos,** *as both Thucydides and Sallust state.*

[1] Thuc. (1.4, 1.8.1–2) and Herodotus (1.171) credit Minos, the legendary king of Crete, with expelling the Carians from the Cyclades; later they dwelled in southwest Asia Minor.

52 8M, 74Mc, 56D, 88K

The assignment of this fragment to Book 3 by the testimonia and the reference to a Roman detachment falling foul of pirates points to some action in Antonius' campaign against the pirates.

and by chance, on the voyage, one cohort, which was being transported by a large, light craft, strayed from the rest and in a calm sea was surrounded by two galleys of pirates

53 9M, 75Mc, 4.40D, 4.48K

The Cretans defeated Antonius and made a mockery of their Roman captives (cf. Flor. 1.42).

among whom, all the most eminent were flogged while dangling from a mast or, with their bodies intact, were fastened on the prow to a fork-shaped yoke, projecting from the ship.

54* 16M, 76Mc, inc. 20D, 3.64K

ibi triennio frustra trito

Serv. & Serv. auct. ad *Aen.* 4.271: to illustrate *tero* meaning to "use up carelessly" (*per neglegentiam consumere*).

CONCLUSION OF THE SERTORIAN WAR (73–72 BC), FRR. 55–63

55* 81M, 77Mc, 3D, 64K

Hanc[1] igitur redarguit Tarquitius.[2]

Donat. ad Ter. *Ad.* 312: to illustrate different shades of meaning (quality and quantity) of *hic, haec, hoc. Hanc* is identified in this context as referring to something written by a Celtiberian (*scriptum Celtiberi*), sc., perhaps, *epistulam.*

[1] hunc *C*   [2] *Carrio*: tarquin(i)us *codd.*

56 82M, 78Mc, 2D, K

cavere‹t›[1] imperator a[2] perfuga[3] Celtibero

Arus. *GL* 7.488.26 = p. 184DC: to illustrate *cavere* construed with *ab* + abl.

[1] *Dietsch*: cavete ‹ab› *Lindemann*
[2] *Dietsch*: imperatore *N1*: imperatorem *Maurenbr.*
[3] *Lindemann*: per kaga *N1*: perfido a *Maurenbr.*

54* 16M, 76Mc, inc. 20D, 3.64K

The reference to three wasted years is perhaps to be connected with Antonius' fruitless campaign against the pirates, begun in 74 and ending with his death abroad in 72, or early 71 (Liv. Per. 97), after he was forced to conclude a treaty with the Cretans (Diod. 40.1).

after three years had been wasted there in vain

CONCLUSION OF THE SERTORIAN
WAR (73–72 BC), FRR. 55–63

55* 81M, 77Mc, 3D, 64K

The scholiast identifies the object of the denial ("this") as "something written by a Celtiberian." Hence, the context may be an attempt by Tarquitius Priscus, a staff officer of Sertorius (Frontin. Str. 2.5.31) and one of the conspirators who plotted with Perperna to murder Sertorius (cf. fr. 57), to refute some written message that was designed to thwart the plot. Maurenbr. assigns this and the following fragment to an otherwise unattested "first" conspiracy that was unmasked.

And so Tarquitius refuted this.

56 82M, 78Mc, 2D, K

Same context as fr. 55: a warning to Sertorius.

that the commander be on his guard against the Celtiberian deserter

57 83M, 79Mc, 4D, 3K

Igitur discubuere: Sertorius inferior in medio, super eum
L.[1] Fabius Hispaniensis senator ex proscriptis; in summo
Antonius, et infra scriba Sertori Versius; et alter scriba
Maecenas[2] in imo, medius inter Tarquitium[3] et dominum
Perpernam.

Serv. ad *Aen.* 1.698 (attributed to S. without specifying title of
work): to illustrate Virgil's *mediam locavit* at a banquet.

{Non. p. 281M = 434L.29–30 (*alter scriba . . . Perpernam*: assigned to Book 3): to illustrate *dominus* meaning the "host of a
dinner party."}

[1] *Commelinus*: tucius *BK*: tut . . . us *L*: titus *M*   [2] mac-
censas *Aγ Servii*: accenas *B Servii*: scribam et c(a)enas *codd.
Nonii*   [3] *Kritz*: Tarquinium *NPbM Servii et codd. Nonii*:
arguinium *rell. Servii*

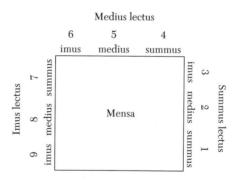

Medius lectus

2. Antonius 3. Versius 4. Fabius 6. Sertorius
7. Perperna 8. Maecenas 9. Tarquitius

57 83M, 79Mc, 4D, 3K

*The banquet given by Perperna at the town of Osca (Vell. 2.30.1),
in the course of which Sertorius was assassinated. Diod. (37.22a)
reports a different placement of the guests, having Sertorius recline between Tarquitius and Antonius, the latter of whom, according to Plut. (Sert. 26.11) struck the first blow.*

And so they reclined at table: Sertorius in the lower position on the middle couch, above him Lucius Fabius Hispaniensis, one of the proscribed senators; on the top couch,
Antonius, and below him Sertorius's scribe Versius; and
the other scribe, Maecenas, in the middle position on
the bottom couch, between Tarquitius and the host Perperna.[1]

[1] Couches were placed along three sides of the table, each
having room for as many as three diners to recline. The diagram
shows the arrangement. Servius, who seems to have mistakenly
concluded that Sertorius was the host, quoted Sallust in support
of the view that Virgil's *"mediamque locavit"* described the usual
position of the host. Sertorius, in fact, was the guest of honor, and
as such he occupied the place reserved for that person, the *locus
consularis,* the lowest (*imus*) position on the middle couch. Fabius, who shared the couch with Sertorius, was a former quaestor
under C. Annius, governor of Spain in 81 (*MRR* 3.86).

58 84M, 80Mc, 68D, 78K

⟨turba?⟩[1] . . . divorsa, uti solet rebus perditis, capessivit;[2] namque alii fiducia gnaritatis locorum occul-
tam fugam sparsi, ⟨pars⟩[3] globis eruptionem temp-
tavere

Non. p. 116 = 167L.25–28: to illustrate the noun *gnaritas*
(knowledge). Cf. *TLL* 6.2.2121.68–75: outside of S., attested only
in Amm. Marc. and Donat.

{Prisc. *GL* 2.535.7 (*diversa . . . capessivit*): to illustrate verbs in
–*so* having the perfect in –*sivi*.}

   [1] *Müller in app., exempli gratia*   [2] lacessivit *GLK Prisc.*:
capessunt *Bentinus (Non. nov. ed. Ald. 1526)*   [3] *Colerus*:
fugam, pars globis *Mercier*

59* 85M, 81Mc, 5D, 5K

Perpernam forte cognoscit mulio redemptoris.

Porph. ad Hor. *Epist.* 2.2.72: to illustrate the noun *redemptor* (a
contractor supplying animals for public couriers).

60* 86M, 82Mc, inc. 62D, inc. 28K

ubi multa nefanda[1] esca[2] super ausi atque passi

Prisc. *GL* 3.46.1–2: to illustrate *super* supposedly employed as an
adv., not a prep.; at the same time, Prisc. offers the more plau-
sible explanation that in this context *super* is a postponed prep.

   [1] *Hertz, vulgo*: nefande *B r*: nefandae *DHGLK*
   [2] *Bernays (cf. Sulpicius Severus, Chron. 2.30.3,* omnia nefanda esca super ausi): casu *codd.*

58 84M, 80Mc, 68D, 78K

Maurenbr. connected this fragment with the flight of Sertorian forces led by Perperna, after their defeat at the hands of Pompey (Plut. Pomp. 20.4–6; Frontin. Str. 2.5.32; App. B Civ. 1.115). Kritz and Dietsch less plausibly assigned this fragment to a description of the runaway Germanic and Gallic slaves under Crixus, who were defeated in 72 by the consul Gellius (cf. frr. 3.68–69).

‹the throng?› . . . had recourse to various expedients, as usual in desperate situations: some, relying on their familiarity with the locale, scattered and attempted undetected flight; others tried a break out in tightly packed bands.

59* 85M, 81Mc, 5D, 5K

Same context as fr. 58. After his defeat, Perperna tried to hide in a thicket but was discovered and dragged before Pompey for execution (App. B Civ. 115; Amm. Marc. 26.9.9).

By chance a contractor's muleteer recognized Perperna.

60* 86M, 82Mc, inc. 62D, inc. 28K

During the lengthy siege of the Sertorian stronghold Calagurris, by Pompey's lieutenant Afranius, the defenders resorted to eating the dead bodies of their women and children when their food failed (Val. Max. 7.6 ext. 3; Oros. 5.23.14).

when, after committing and suffering many abominations respecting their food[1]

[1] Construing *super* as a prep., = "with regard to" (*OLD* 11); or, if the paradosis *casu super* is retained, "over and above what occurs by mere chance," (*OLD* s.v. *super* 12b), cf. K-S 1.572.

61 87M, 83Mc, 6D, 7K

parte consumpta, relicua cadaverum[1] ad diuturnita-
tem usus sallerent[2]

Prisc. *GL* 2.546.12–13: to illustrate the verb *sallo* (*–ere*) in contrast with the verb *sallio* (*–ire*), both meaning "to salt."

{Diom. *GL* 1.375.19–20, assigned to Book 4 (*reliqua . . . sallere*):
to give an example of *sallo.*}

  [1] cadavera *Diom.*   [2] sallere *Diom.*

62 88M, 84Mc, 7D, 6K

Sed Pompeius a prima adulescentia sermone fautorum
similem fore se credens Alexandro regi, facta consultaque
eius quidem aemul[at]us[1] erat.[2]

Non. p. 239M = 357L.4–6: to illustrate *aemulus* meaning *secta-*
tor (a follower) or *imitator.* Non. p. 502M = 805L.2–3: to illustrate an acc. (*facta consultaque*) in place of a gen.

  [1] *Victorius*: aemulator *Dietsch*   [2] facta . . . erat] *om.*
codd., uno versu archetypi praetermisso, Non. p. 502M

63* 89M, 85Mc, 4.29D, 4.53D

de victis[1] Hispanis tropaea in Pyrenaei iugis consti-
tuit

Serv. ad *Aen.* 11.6: to illustrate the practice of placing monu-
ments celebrating a victory on high ground.

  [1] *Dietsch*: devictis *codd.*

61 87M, 83Mc, 6D, 7K

Same context as fr. 60.

> after eating part, they salted the remnants of the
> corpses to extend their usefulness

62 88M, 84Mc, 7D, 6K

*To commemorate his victory in the Sertorian war, Pompey set up
a trophy monument on a summit at Col de Pertus, near the town
of Panissars, in the Pyrenees (Plin. HN 7.96; Exsuper. 8 [56Z];
Dio 41.24.3), slight remains of which have survived in situ to this
day. In a similar fashion, Alexander the Great had marked the
easternmost extent of his conquests in India with a set of twelve
massive altars (Arr. Anab. 5.29.1; Strabo 3.5.5, p. 171).*

But Pompey, believing from his earliest youth, thanks to
the flattery of his supporters, that he would be like King
Alexander, was an emulator of that man's deeds and intentions.

63* 89M, 85Mc, 4.29D, 4.53D

Same context as fr. 62.

> he [Pompey] set up on the slopes of the Pyrenees
> trophies for his conquests of the Spaniards[1]

[1] *De* + abl. of the persons over whom a victory is won (*OLD*
s.v. 6b); or, if the paradosis *devictis* is retained, "after defeating
the Spaniards, he. . . ." Pliny (*HN* 7.96) credits the absence of
Sertorius' name from this monument to Pompey's high-
mindedness (*maiore animo*). Florus 2.10.9 more perceptively
points out that Metellus and Pompey both wanted to present the
war as a foreign one (not a civil war) so that they would be eligible
to be awarded triumphs upon returning to Rome.

THE SLAVE UPRISING LED
BY SPARTACUS: YEAR TWO
(72 BC), FRR. 64–70

64 100M, 86Mc, 64D, 69K

locum nullum, nisi quo armati institissent, ipsis tutum fore

Arus. *GL* 7.481.15 = p. 160DC: to illustrate the verb *insisto* + abl. of place.

65* 101M, 87Mc, inc. 22D, 3.68K

exuant armis equisque

Serv. ad *Aen.* 11.80: to illustrate stripping arms from dead warriors.

66† 102M, 14Mc, 4.1D, 4.22K

Hi locorum pergnari[1] et soliti nectere ex viminibus vasa

Non. p. 554M = 890L.19–22 (assigned to "lib. IV"): to illustrate the noun *parma* = *scutum breve* (a small shield).

{Cf. Serv. ad *Aen.* 7.632, *dicit Sallustius de Lucanis qui de vimine facta scuta coriis tegebant.*}

[1] *Douza*: perignari *codd.*

THE SLAVE UPRISING LED
BY SPARTACUS: YEAR TWO
(72 BC), FRR. 64–70

64 100M, 86Mc, 64D, 69K

These words are perhaps to be connected with the efforts of Spartacus to fashion weapons for his forces and form a cavalry (so Kritz). Florus (2.8.6–7) puts these activities at the end of the first year of marauding, in the winter of 73/72 (cf. App. B Civ. 1.116).

〈Spartacus asserted?〉 . . . that no place would be safe for them except where they had taken a stand equipped with weapons

65* 101M, 87Mc, inc. 22D, 3.68K

Perhaps the same context as fr. 64, Spartacus instructing his men to strip the dead of whatever could be put to use in war.

to take arms and horses 〈from the slain〉

66† 102M, 14Mc, 4.1D, 4.22K

Appian (1.116) and Florus (2.8.6) credit Spartacus' followers with arming themselves by fashioning makeshift weapons during the winter of 73/72 (hence this fragment belongs in Book 3, not 4, as cited), and Florus (l.c.) and Frontinus (Str. 1.7.6) include among those weapons shields made of wickerwork, covered with hides, of the type referred to in this and the following fragment. The men described in this fragment may be Lucanians, shepherds and herdsmen in southern Italy who flocked to join Spartacus (cf. Plut. Crass. 9.4), since according to Servius (ad Aen. 7.632), S. mentioned the manufacture of such hide-covered, wicker shields by Lucanians.

These men being very familiar with the locale and accus-

agrestia, ibi tum, quod inopia scutorum fuerat,[2] ea arte se quisque in formam parmae equestris ⟨clupeo⟩[3] armabat.

[2] H^2: fuere ad *codd. plerique* [3] *Dietsch:* ⟨scuto⟩ *post* armabat *ins. Maurenbr.*

67* 103M, 4.15Mc, 4.2D, 4.23K

Coria recens detracta quasi[1] glutino adolescebant.[2]

Serv. ad *G.* 3.156: to illustrate *recens* meaning *statim.*

{Charis. *GL* 1.88.4 = p. 110B.18 (*quasi glutino adolescebant*), Charis *GL* 1.131.27 = p. 167B.28 (*glutino – inquit – adolescebant*); *Schol. Vatic.* ad Verg. *G.* 4.40 (*hic glutino adolescebat*): to illustrate the second decl. *glutinum,* in contrast with the third decl. *gluten;* cf. Bede, *GL* 7. 274.5–6, attesting S.'s use of the neut. noun *glutinum.*}

[1] *veluti codd. Serv.* [2] adhaerescebant *Funari*

68* 104M, 88Mc, inc. 18D, 3.57K

Germani intectum renonibus corpus tegunt.

Isid. *Etym.* 19.23.4: to give an instance of the word *reno* (an article of clothing made from reindeer hide), which Isid. describes as a native garment of the Germans, one that covered the upper torso, and was water repellent and hairy.

69* 105M, 89Mc, inc. 19D, 3.58K

Vestes de pellibus renones vocantur.

Serv. ad *G.* 3.383: to give an example of primitive clothing made of animal skin.

{Cf. *Schol. Bern.* ad *G.* 3.383, *vestes de pellibus, quae vocantur renones, ut Sallustius dicit.*}

tomed to weave rude containers from wickerwork, there, on that occasion, because they had experienced a shortage of shields, each by means of that art armed himself with a shield after the manner of the small round type carried by cavalry.

67* 103M, 4.15Mc, 4.2D, 4.23K

Same context as fr. 66.

Hides immediately after being removed cure[1] as though applied with glue.

[1] Context appears to require that *adolesco* (lit., to "grow up, become mature") have the meaning "adhere" (so *OLD* 6; *TLL* 1.801.73–74 leaves the matter in doubt). See textual note.

68* 104M, 88Mc, inc. 18D, 3.57K

A large contingent of Germans, under the commander Crixus, a Gaul, parted company with Spartacus and was defeated in a decisive battle in 72 near Mt. Garganus in Apulia (Plut. Crass. 9.9; App. B Civ. 1.117; Liv. Per. 96; Oros. 5.24.4).

The Germans cover their bare bodies with short cloaks of reindeer hide.

69* 105M, 89Mc, inc. 19D, 3.58K

Same context as fr. 68.

Garments made of animal hides are called *"renones."*

70 106M, 90Mc, 70D, 80K

et eodem tempore Lentulus duplici acie locum[1]
editum multo sanguine suorum defensum,[2] postquam ex angustiis[3] paludamenta extare[4] et delectae
cohortes intellegi coepere . . . ‹reliquit et in hostes
impetum fecit›[5]

Non. p. 538M.32–539.3 = 864L: to give an instance of the word
paludamentum (scarlet general's cloak), which Non. states was
in his day referred to by the equivalent Greek term *c(h)lamys*.

[1] *Bentinus*: longum *codd.*   [2] *Kritz*: defensus *codd.*: de-
fensans *Quicherat*: defessus *Bamb.*   [3] *Müller*: sarcinis
codd.   [4] *Dietsch*: ostari $B^A C^A$: astari A^A: adstari L^1: ostentari
Kritz   [5] *suppl. Dietsch in app., exempli gratia*

THRACIAN CAMPAIGN OF
M. LUCULLUS (72 BC), FRR. 71–73

71* 51M, 4.11Mc, inc. 72D, inc. 38K

Aenum et Maroneam viamque militarem

Serv. ad *Aen.* 3.17: to identify places in Thrace associated with
the Aeneas legend.

70 106M, 90Mc, 70D, 80K

After the consul Gellius defeated Crixus and the German gladia-
tors (fr. 68), Spartacus marched north, where he defeated Gellius'
consular colleague Cn. Cornelius Lentulus Clodianus and Gellius
in separate battles in Picenum, and later their combined forces
(App. B Civ. 1.117; cf. Plut. Crass. 9.9). This fragment may refer
to the first or the second battle in which Lentulus suffered a loss
despite, apparently, receiving support from a relief force led ei-
ther by his own legates or by his colleague Gellius. (Italics in the
translation signifies that the text or a supplement is uncertain.)

and at the same time, after the generals' cloaks began to *stand* out from the *defile* and the picked cohorts to be discerned, Lentulus ⟨*abandoned*⟩ the
high ground that *had been defended* with a double
line of battle, at the cost of much blood on the part
of his soldiers, ⟨*and made an attack on the enemy*⟩

THRACIAN CAMPAIGN OF
M. LUCULLUS (72 BC), FRR. 71–73

71* 51M, 4.11Mc, inc. 72D, inc. 38K

Towns on the coast of Thrace, where M. Lucullus (cos. 73, procos.
of Macedonia 72–71) campaigned (cf. Liv. Per. 97).

Aenos and Maronea, and the military road[1]

[1] Doubtless the via Egnatia (built ca. 130 BC), which ran
along the Thracian coast to Byzantium.

72* 4.18M, 4.12Mc, 4.38D, 4.46K

Moesii, *quos Sallustius **a Lucullo** dicit esse **superatos***.

Serv. ad *Aen.* 7.604: identifying the Gaetae, mentioned by Virgil, with the Moesii.

73* 4.19M, 4.13Mc, 4.39D, 4.47K

zo: hac quoque syllaba nullum nomen repperi terminatum nisi unum barbarae civitatis lectum in Sallustio, Vizzo, Vizzonis.[1]   ⟨Bizone⟩

Prob. *GL* 4.11.10–12

[1] Vizo Vizonis ς

THE MITHRIDATIC WAR (72BC),
FRR. 74–81

74 52M, 35Mc, 77D, 94K

Fine inguinum ingrediuntur mare.

Arus. *GL* 7. 475.5 = p. 138DC: to illustrate *fine* + gen. of thing. *Schol. Vatic.* ad Verg. *G.* 3.53: to illustrate *fine* = *tenus* (as far as, up to). [Cf. *OLD* s.v. *finis* 3 quasi-prep. + abl. or gen.]

72* 4.18M, 4.12Mc, 4.38D, 4.46K

The conquests of M. Lucullus in 72–71 extended well into Moesian territory, north of Thrace and south of the Ister (Danube), Eutr. 6.10.

Inhabitants of Moesia, *who, Sallust states, were* **conquered by Lucullus**.

73* 4.19M, 4.13Mc, 4.39D, 4.47K

Kritz surmised that S. may have mentioned among the towns in Thrace and Moesia that were conquered by M. Lucullus during his governorship of Macedonia Bizone *(Mela 2.2.22; Pliny HN 4.44; and Strabo 7.6.1, p. 319), on the basis of which Probus falsely concluded that the nom. was* Vizzo (Vizo = Bizo).

–zo: no noun ending in this syllable is to be found except the one instance of a foreign city mentioned in Sallust: Vizzo, Vizzonis.   ⟨Bizone⟩

THE MITHRIDATIC WAR (72BC), FRR. 74–81

74 52M, 35Mc, 77D, 94K

In the spring of 72, Lucullus landed troops on the island of Lemnos (Plut. Luc. 12.4), or on the nearby island of Chryse (App. Mithr. 77), to attack Mithridates' ships from the rear, when it proved impossible for the Roman fleet to dislodge the enemy's ships from their beached position on the shore.

They [the Romans] waded into the sea up to their groins.

75 53M, 36Mc, 33D, 36K

postquam egressus angustias

Arus. *GL* 7.469.29–30 = p. 119DC: to illustrate *egredior* + acc. of thing.

76 54M, 37Mc, 24D, 25K

Nam qui enare conati fuerant, icti saepe fragmentis[1] navium aut adflicti alveos[2] undarum vi,[3] mulcato foede[4] corpore, postremo[5] intereunt[6] tamen.

Non. p. 406M = 653L.10–12: mistakenly, it seems, to illustrate *tamen* having the meaning *tandem* (cf. [*Ad Caes. sen.*] 2.7.4, *postremo tamen*).

{Arus. *GL* 7.456.5–6 = p. 71DC (*adflicti . . . interibant*), citing this fragment and fr. 2.101: to illustrate *adflictus* + acc. of thing [complementary, instead of the customary dat.].}

[1] *Mercier*: frumentis *codd.*   [2] *N1 Arus.*: alveo *N2 Arus.*: asuis *codd. Non.*: alveis *Mercier*: alvos *Dietsch*   [3] *om. Arus.*   [4] fide *L A^A Non.*: om. *Arus.*   [5] *corr. (ex* postre[mum]*) L B^A Non.*: postremum *rell. Non.*: om. *Arus.*   [6] *Müller*: interibant *N1 Arus.*: intereni *L1 Non.*: i(n)terent *rell. Non.*: interiere *Mercier*

77 56M, 38Mc, 31D, 35K

neque iam sustineri poterat inmensum aucto mari et vento gliscente

Non. p. 22M = 33L.17–18: to illustrate the meaning of the verb *gliscit* (to swell).

75 53M, 36Mc, 33D, 36K

In the spring of 72, Mithridates put to sea from the Bithynian city Nicomedia, lying at the head of the northernmost bay of the Propontis. Owing to the negligence of Lucullus' legate Voconius, Mithridates was able to sail through the Bosporus into the Black Sea (Plut. Luc. 13.1–2).

when, upon emerging from the narrows [the Bosporus?],

76 54M, 37Mc, 24D, 25K

In the spring of 72, soon after Mithridates entered the Black Sea on his retreat to Sinope in Pontus, a massive storm destroyed a large portion of his fleet and left wreckage floating for days (Plut. Luc. 13.2; App. Mithr. 78).

Indeed, those who had tried to swim away, after having been often struck by the debris of the ships, or dashed against the hulls[1] by the violence of the waves, still perished at last with horribly battered bodies.

[1] Or, if the emendation *alvos* (acc. of resp.) is adopted, "injured as to their bellies."

77 56M, 38Mc, 31D, 35K

Same context as fr. 76, possibly describing the swamping of the merchantman in which Mithridates was sailing (Plut. Luc. 13.3; App. Mithr. 78).

nor could it any longer be kept afloat, with the sea enormously swollen and the wind becoming stronger

78* 57M, 39Mc, 50D, 9K

   Amisos[1]

Prob. *GL* 4.28.24–26; Sacerd. *GL* 6.479.16–18: attesting in S. the Greek spelling *Amisos* (= *Amisus* in Latin).

   [1] camisos *codd. Prob., corr. edd. nitentes lectione Sacredotis loci paralleli*

79 58M, 40Mc, 35D, 42K

   castella, custodias[1] thesaurorum, in deditionem acciperent[2]

Charis. *GL* 1.107.12–13 = p. 137B.5–6: to illustrate first decl. gen. sing. in *–as*, instead of *–ae*.

{Serv. & Serv. auct. ad *Aen.* 11.801 (*castella . . . thesaurorum*): reporting that the second-century AD commentator Aemilius Asper regarded *custodias* as a gen. sing. (= *custodiae*), while others construed it as acc.}

   [1] custodiae *F Serv.*   [2] *Gerlach ed. min.*: acciperentur *N fort. recte*

80 59M, 41Mc, 37D, 39K

At Oppius, postquam orans nihil proficiebat, timide veste tectum pugionem expedire conatus a Cotta Vulcioque[1] inpeditur.

Non. p. 553M.31–554M.1 = 889L: to give an example of the noun *pugio* (a dagger), defined as a short sword.

   [1] Vulscioque *B*[A]

   [1] In his speech in defense of Oppius in 69, Cicero argued that it was unclear whether the dagger was drawn by Oppius to commit suicide or to injure Cotta (Quint. 5.10.69).

78* 57M, 39Mc, 50D, 9K

After the storm reported in frr. 76–77, Mithridates traveled on a pirate ship to Sinope in his kingdom of Pontus and from there made his way to Amisos (App. Mithr. 78).

Amisos

79 58M, 40Mc, 35D, 42K

Lucullus' troops were displeased that their commander did not devote more attention to the capture of sources of plunder and enrichment when he invaded Mithridates' kingdom of Pontus in the summer of 72 (Plut. Luc. 14.2)

⟨Lucullus' troops demanded?⟩ that they receive the surrender of fortresses dedicated to the safekeeping of treasures[1]

[1] Even in antiquity, opinion was divided over whether to construe *custodias* as an acc. pl. or an archaic gen. sing., on the model of such expressions as *pater* (*mater*) *familias*. In order for *custodias* to be acc., the text must be emended as printed here (see textual note). Cf. fr. 4.10, where *custodias* is acc., though the grammarians want it to be gen.

80 59M, 41Mc, 37D, 39K

The proquaestor P. Oppius was dismissed by his commander M. Cotta (cos. 74) and charged with bribery and conspiracy when the two were serving in Bithynia (Dio 36.40.3). The incident may have taken place at the siege of Heraclea in 72.

But Oppius, after he accomplished nothing by pleading, was restrained by Cotta and Vulcius when he tried timidly to unsheathe a dagger hidden in his clothing.[1]

81* 60M, 42Mc, 38D, 40K

Dicit se eius opera non usurum, eumque ab armis dimittit.

Serv. ad *Aen.* 12.844: to illustrate the expression *dimittere ab armis* meaning to discharge from military service.

EXCURSUS ON TOPOGRAPHY
OF PONTUS, FRR. 82–99

82* 61M, inc. 22Mc, 3.39D, 33K

DARDANIAE Troiae. Aut a Dardano Iovis et Electrae filio, . . . aut certe, secundum Sallustium, **a rege Dardanorum Mida**, *qui Phrygiam tenuit.*

Serv. & Serv. auct. ad *Aen.* 2.325: to explain how "Dardania" came to be a metonymy for Troy.

83* 62M, 43Mc, 43D, 50K

"Lata" autem ideo, quia **se angustiae Pontici oris illic dilatant**, *ut Sallustius dixit.*

Serv. ad *Aen.* 2.312: commenting on *lata* as a description of the "Sigean strait," so called from the Sigeon promontory on the northwest coast of Asia Minor (where the Hellespont widens in the vicinity of Troy).

84* 63M, 44Mc, 44D, 49K

81* 60M, 42Mc, 38D, 40K

Same context as fr. 80. Servius states that Cotta uttered these words at a public meeting when he dismissed Oppius.

He says that he will not employ his service, and he discharges him from the army.

EXCURSUS ON TOPOGRAPHY
OF PONTUS, FRR. 82–99

82* 61M, inc. 22Mc, 3.39D, 33K

S. mentioned King Midas in describing the mythical history of Troy and the towns in that region.

"DARDANIA" "Troy." [derived] either from Dardanus [founder of the Trojan royal house], the son of Jupiter and Electra . . . or indeed, according to Sallust, **from the king of the Dardanians, Midas**, *who controlled Phrygia.*

83* 62M, 43Mc, 43D, 50K

S.'s description of the Hellespont near the Sigeon promontory (cf. Isid. Etym. 14.7.2).

[Virgil calls the Sigean strait] "broad" because **at that place the narrows of the mouth of the Pontic Sea grows wide**, *as Sallust stated.*

84* 63M, 44Mc, 44D, 49K

S.'s description of the outline of the Black Sea, which ancient writers often likened to the shape of a Scythian bow (Mela 1.102; Pliny HN 4.76; Strabo 2.5.22, p. 125). The Crimea, with bays to the east and the west, produced a northern shoreline resembling the inward-bulging bow handle with its curving horns, while the

Nam[1] speciem efficit Scythici arcus.

Serv. & Serv. auct. ad *Aen.* 3.533: to illustrate Virgil's use of the
expression *in arcum* to describe the curving of a harbor.

[1] *om. Serv.*

85* 65M, 45Mc, 45D, 51K

utque ipsum[1] mare Ponticum dulcius quam cetera,
nebulosumque et brevius[2]

Serv. auct. ad *Aen.* 1.228: to illustrate a comparative adj. standing
for the positive degree. *Exc. Andecav. p. 7DeN:* to illustrate a
comparative denoting less than the positive degree (*dulcior non
magis dulcis, sed paene non dulcis*).

{*mare . . . cetera,* Serv. ad *Aen.* 12.143: to illustrate litotes;
Macrob. *Sat.* 7.12.34: commenting on the fresh water of rivers
flowing into the Black Sea; cf. Donat. *Ars GL* 4.374.29–30; Serv.
Comm. in Don. GL 4.431.10–11; Pomp. *GL* 5.155.28; Diom.
GL 1.325.4; Prisc. *GL* 2.92.15; Prisc. *GL* 3.74.27; Consent. *GL*
5.342.30; Cledon *GL* 5.38.32; *Ars anon. Bern. GL* 8.78.10–11.}

[1] utque ipsum] *om. omnes praeter Serv. auct. et Exc. Andecav.*
(aliqua et ipse)   [2] nebulosumque et brevius] *De Nonno: om.
omnes praeter Exc. Andecav.* (nebulosam †quiete† brevius)

86* 66M, 46Mc, 41D, 53K

qua[1] tempestate vis piscium[2] Ponto[3] erupit

Serv. & Serv. auct. ad *Aen.* 4.132, and *Gloss.* 5, p. 254.7: to illustrate *vis = multitudo,* "a large quantity" (*OLD* s.v. *vis* 8); *Schol.
in Iuv.* ad 4.42: commenting on the fish released by the spring
thaw of the ice.

relatively straight southern shore could be pictured as forming the bow string.

For it produces the appearance of a Scythian bow.

85* 65M, 45Mc, 45D, 51K

S.'s description of the Black Sea.

and as the Pontic Sea itself, less salty than the rest,[1] and subject to fog, and rather shallow

[1] Owing to a great quantity of fresh water from the large number of rivers that flow into it (cf. Amm. Marc. 22.8.46; Isid. *Etym.* 13.16.4).

86* 66M, 46Mc, 41D, 53K

The release of great quantities of fish in the Black Sea when the ice of winter thaws.

the season in which a great quantity of fish bursts from the Pontus

---

[1] *Serv.*: quia *Gloss.*: itaque *Schol. Iuv.*   [2] vis piscium] piscium vis *Schol. Iuv.*   [3] ex Ponto *Serv. & Serv. auct. ante* vis piscium

87* 67M, 47Mc, deest in D et K

Mari nomen inhospitali[a][1] quaesierant.[2]

Adnot. super Luc. 9.960; *Comm. Bern. ad Luc.* ibid.: in commenting on the name *Euxinus* (hospitable) for the Black Sea, the scholiasts remark that it was once the *Axinus* (inhospitable).

[1] *Maurenbr.*: inospitalia *C Adnot.*: inhospitabila *W Adnot.*: inhospitabile *U Adnot.*: inhospitabile *Comm. Bern.*   [2] quaesiverunt *Comm. Bern.*

88 68M, 48Mc, 50D, 4.21K

namque primum Iasonem novo itinere maris Aeetae hospitis domum violasse

Prisc. GL 2.246.5–6: to illustrate the spelling of the gen. sing. of the Greek first decl. masc. noun *Aeetes* in *–ae*.

89* 69M, 49Mc, 40D, 32K

primum Graecorum Achillem

Serv. & *Serv. auct. ad Aen.* 1.96: explaining how Diomedes could be described as "bravest of the Greeks" after the deaths of Achilles and Ajax, who surpassed him.

87* 67M, 47Mc, not included in D and K

The Pontus Euxinus *(Hospitable Sea), the name by which the Black Sea was later known, had previously been called* Axinus *(Inhospitable), because of its roughness (Plin. HN 6.1), or because of the fierce natives dwelling on its shores (Amm. Marc. 22.8.33; Mela 1.102).*

They had selected the name "Inhospitable" for the sea.

88 68M, 48Mc, 50D, 4.21K

The first Greeks to visit the Black Sea region were Jason, on his quest for the golden fleece, and later Achilles, who conducted raids there during the Trojan War (Adnot. super Luc. 9.960; Comm. Bern. ad Luc. ibid.).

for indeed ⟨it is said that?⟩ Jason was the first, by way of a new route over the sea, to violate the house of his host Aeetes

89* 69M, 49Mc, 40D, 32K

Same context as fr. 88. McGushin speculated that S. may have referred to sites in the Black Sea region where Achilles was worshipped, such as the island in the mouth of the Ister (Danube) River (Paus. 3.19.11) or a cape to the east of the mouth of the Borysthenes (Dnieper) River (Strabo 7.3.19, p. 307), or to a temple near Panticapaeum, at the mouth of Lake Maeotis (Strabo 11.2.6, p. 494).

Achilles, foremost of the Greeks

90* 70M, 50Mc, 46D, 43K

Igitur introrsus prima Asiae Bithynia est, multis antea nominibus adpellata. Nam prius Bebrycia dicta, deinde Mygdonia, mox a Bithyno rege Bithynia nuncupata.[1]

Serv. ad *Aen.* 5.373 (*Igitur . . . appellata*): to explain a reference to a person "of the Bebrycian race" as standing for a native of Bithynia. Isid. *Etym.* 14.3.39 (*Prima Asiae minoris Bithynia in Ponti exordio ad partem solis orientis adversa Thraciae iacet, multis antea nominibus appellata. Nam . . . nuncupata*): excerpted and slightly modified, without attribution to S.

{Serv. & Serv. auct. ad *Aen.* 5.203 (*igitur . . . Bithynia est*): to illustrate *interior.*}

    [1] Nam . . . nuncupata] *Isid.*: *om. Dietsch, Kritz*

91* 71M, 51Mc, 47D, 44K

Anacreon, lyricus poeta, ‹T›eius[1] *fuit, ab urbe* **Teio**, *quam in* **Pa[m]flagonia**[2] *esse Sallustius indicat, cum de situ Pontico loquitur.*

Porph. ad Hor. *Carm.* 1.17.18.

    [1] *Holder*: eius *M*: theius *P*
    [2] impamflagonia *M*: in Paplagonia *P*

92 72M, 52Mc, deest in D et K

per hos[1] fluit, qui quondam Lydiae regna disiunxit a Persicis

Adnot. super Luc. 3.272: to identify the river Halys as the boundary between the Lydian kingdom of Croesus and the Persian kingdom of Cyrus.

{Isid. *Etym.* 14.3.37: (without attribution to S.) *Halys amnis per eam fluit, qui quondam Lydiae regna disiunxit a Persis.*}

90* 70M, 50Mc, 46D, 43K

S. described the region of the Black Sea, proceeding from west to east along the south shore. Bithynia also serves as the point of departure for Strabo (12.3.2, p. 541), Solinus (42.1), and Amm. Marc. (22.8.14).

And so, within [after one enters the Black Sea through the Bosporus] the first part of Asia is Bithynia, a region formerly known by many names. For previously it was called Bebrycia, then Mygdonia, and eventually was named Bithynia from King Bithynus.

91* 71M, 51Mc, 47D, 44K

*The lyric poet Anacreon was Teian, from the city **Teios**,[1] which Sallust, when describing the geography of the Pontic region, indicates is in **Paphlagonia**.*

[1] The scholiast on Horace confuses the city of T(e)ios (Tieion), on the shore of the Black Sea, with the Ionian city of Teos (Anacreon's native city), on the Aegean shore, in Lydia. Mela (1.104) identifies the Paphlagonian T(e)ios as a colony of Miletus.

92 72M, 52Mc, not included in D and K

In the eastern region of Paphlagonia, where the Chalybes once dwelled, is found the river Halys ("Salt"), the longest in Asia Minor, which in S.'s day formed the boundary between Nicomedes' kingdom of Bithynia and Mithridates' kingdom of Pontus.

through these [the Chalybes/their lands?] flows ⟨the river Halys⟩, which formerly divided the kingdom of Lydia from that of the Persians,

---

[1] ⟨Halys⟩ *post* hos *adiec. Usener*

93* 73M, 53Mc, 49D, 46K

> dein campi Themiscyrei, quos habuere Amazones,
> a Tanai flumine, incertum quam ob causam, digres-
> sae

Serv. ad *Aen.* 11.659: commenting on the migration of the Amazons from the Tanais River to the region of the Thermodon River
in Pontus, which Serv. mistakenly places in Thrace.

{Isid. *Etym.* 14.3.37 (without attribution to S.): *Themiscyrios
campos, quos habuere Amazones.*}

94* 74M, 54Mc. 52D, 48K

Namque omnium ferocissumi ad hoc tempus Ach⟨a⟩ei[1]
atque Tauri sunt quod, quantum ego conicio, locorum
[a]egestate[2] rapto vivere coacti.

Schol. in Iuv. ad 15.115: explicating the "Maeotid altar," referring
to Lake Maeotis, where the savage Tauri lived.

    1–2 *corr. Wessner*

95* 75M, 55Mc, inc. 17D, 3.19K

93* 73M, 53Mc, 49D, 46K

The plains near the coastal town of Themiscyra, beside the Thermodon River, in Mithridates' kingdom of Pontus, were traditionally inhabited for a time by Amazons (Strabo 11.5.4, p. 505).

next the plains of Themiscyra, which were possessed by the Amazons after they had migrated from the Tanais River,[1] it being uncertain[2] for what reason

[1] The Don, which flows into the Sea of Azov (Lake Maeotis) and was commonly regarded as forming the demarcation between Europe and Asia (Mela 1.15).   [2] Amm. Marc. 22.8.18–19 claims that the Amazons were forced to migrate to a more peaceful abode when their ambitious raids as far west as Athens were unsuccessful and heavy losses weakened their fighting force.

94* 74M, 54Mc. 52D, 48K

A description of savage people living along the north shore of the Black Sea: the Achaei (Ov. Pont. 4.10.27; Mela 1.13) and the Tauri (a Scythian people inhabiting the Tauric Chersonesus, mod. Crimea).

For the fiercest of all people up to this time are the Achaei and Tauri because, so far as I can tell, they have been compelled by the poverty of their territories to live by banditry.

95* 75M, 55Mc, inc. 17D, 3.19K

Possibly a reference to the territory of the Maeotici (Mela 1.14; Plin HN 6.19), a Scythian people who, according to Strabo (11.2.3, pp. 493–94), occupied the north shore of Lake Maeotis (mod. Sea of Azov), which is often described as a marsh (palus or stagnum), because of its shallow waters. In that case, the river will

quem trans stagnum omnis usque ad flumen

Schol. Vatic. ad Verg. *G.* 4.293: to illustrate the adv. *usque* in combination with a prepositional phrase.

96* 76M, 56Mc, 51D, 47K

Scythae nomades tenent, quibus plaustra sedes sunt

Porph. ad Hor. *Carm.* 3.24.9: to illustrate Horace's remark that the Scythians lead a simple life, having wagons for homes.

{Ps.-Acro ad Hor. ibid. (*quibus . . . sunt*): commenting on the nomadic lifestyle of Scythians.}

97* 77M, 57Mc, 48D, 45K

PROXIMUM . . . *ita Sallustius in situ Ponti de* **promunturiis Paphlagonum** *et ‹eo›*[1] *quod* **Criu Metopon** *appellavit, posuit.*

Non. p. 524M = 842L.9–10: to illustrate the use of *proximus* (nearest, closest) to describe objects that are some distance apart but have no object in between.

¹ *Müller*

98 79M, 58Mc, 9D, 55K

Nomenque Danuvium habet, ‹q›uoad[1] Germanorum terras adstringit.

Porph. ad Hor. *Carm.* 4.4.39 {Ps.-Acro ad Hor. *Ars P.* 18 and Arus. *GL* 7.494.19 = p. 206DC (*nomenque . . . habet*)}: to illustrate how the neuter nouns *flumen* and *nomen* cause the name of a river (e.g., Danuvius) to be treated as though it were neuter.

¹ *Christ*: ut ad *codd.* Porph.

be the Tanais (cf. fr. 93), which flows into the eastern end of Lake Maeotis.

and beyond that marsh, all ‹coastal lands?› right up to the river

96* 76M, 56Mc, 51D, 47K

Possibly describing a branch of the Scythian race, the Sarmatians, called Amaxobioi, = "Wagon dwellers" *(Mela 2.2).*

nomadic Scythians, whose abodes are wagons, possess ‹that region?›

97* 77M, 57Mc, 48D, 45K

Criu Metopon (Ramsbrow: Κριοῦ Μέτοπον*), the promontory at the tip of the Tauric Chersonesus (Crimea), lay across the Black Sea from the promontory of Carambis on the coast of Paphlagonia (Strabo 7.4.3, p. 309) and another, on which Sinope stood, ca. eighty miles to the east.*

In his geographical description of the Pontus, S. employed **"proximus"** *[= "next"] concerning the* **promontories of the Paphlagonians** *and the one he called* **Criu Metopon**.

98 79M, 58Mc, 9D, 55K

The river Danuvius (Danube) was identified by S. as the upper course of the river Ister, which empties into the western end of the Black Sea (cf. Mela 2.8).

And it has the name Danuvius so long as it borders the lands of the Germans.

99* 80M, 59Mc, 10D, 56K

Omnium **fluminum**, *quae in maria*, **qua imperium Romanum est, fluunt** . . . *maximum esse Nilum consentitur;* **proxima magnitudine** *esse* **Istrum** *scripsit Sallustius.*

Gell. 10.7.1.

FRAGMENTS OF UNCERTAIN CONTEXT IN BOOK 3, FRR. 100–108

Assigned To Various Contexts by Maurenbr., frr. 100–104

100 17M, 8Mc, 62D, 84K

male iam adsuetum ad omnis vis controvorsiarum

Prisc. *GL* 2.249.14–15: to illustrate the pl. *vis*, of the noun *vis*, in place of *vires.*

101 25M, 93Mc, 71D, 86K

Quod ubi frustra temptatum est, socordius[1] ire miles obcipere,[2] non aptis armis, ut in principio, laxiore[3] agmine.

Non. p. 235M = 350L.14–16: to illustrate the adj. *aptus* meaning "joined or bound together."

  [1] *vulgo*: socerdius *codd.*   [2] *Müller*: obcepere *codd.*
[3] ⟨et⟩ laxiore *Iunius*

99* 80M, 59Mc, 10D, 56K

Relative size of Ister (Danube) in comparison with the Nile (cf. Mela 2.8).

It is agreed that **of all the rivers that flow** into the seas **where the Roman empire exists** the Nile is the largest. Sallust wrote that the **next in size** is **the Ister**.

FRAGMENTS OF UNCERTAIN CONTEXT IN BOOK 3, FRR. 100–108

Assigned To Various Contexts by Maurenbr., frr. 100–104

100 17M, 8Mc, 62D, 84K

A description of a politician who was adept at using intimidation: possibly the plebeian tribune of 74 L. Quinctius (Cic. Clu. 77, 79; cf. fr. 3.15.11), so Maurenbr.; or the political boss P. Cornelius Cethegus (Plut. Luc. 5.4, 6.1–4), so McGushin.

having now become wickedly accustomed to all strongarm tactics in disputes

101 25M, 93Mc, 71D, 86K

Maurenbr. assigned this fragment to the failed attempt of L. Lucullus' soldiers in 73 to persuade their commander to invade and seize control of Mithridates' kingdom of Pontus in his absence, rather than to go to the relief of M. Cotta (cos. 74), who had been defeated by Mithridates and was being besieged in Chalcedon (Plut. Luc. 8.3).

And when this attempt failed, the soldiers began to march more negligently, with arms not properly arrayed, as they had been in the beginning, and with a looser line of march.

102 27M, 94Mc, 15D, 14K

Nam tertia luna[1] erat, et sublima nebula coelum obscurabat.

Non. p. 489M = 785L.9–10: to illustrate the collateral form *sublimus, –a, –um, = sublimis, –e.*

[1] *Mähly*: tunc *codd.*: tunc ⟨luna⟩ *Müller*

103 32M, 95Mc, 80D, 98K

coniuratione claudit

Prisc. *GL* 2.514.16–17: to illustrate *claudo = claudico* (to be deficient).

104 95M, 96Mc, 73D, 89K

Ac tum maxume, uti solet in extremis rebus, sibi quisque carissumum domi recordari,[1] cunctique omnium ordinum ⟨munia⟩[2] extrema sequi.[3]

Non. p. 137M = 199L.8–10: to illustrate *munia = officia* (duties).

[1] *corr. ed. a. 1480*: recordavi *codd.*   [2] *Junius*
[3] exequi *Dietsch (sed cf. fr. 5.8,* sequebantur = exsequebantur*)*

102 27M, 94Mc, 15D, 14K

Maurenbr., adopting the view of Kritz, assigned this fragment to the description of Mithridates' clandestine withdrawal from Chalcedon soon after the evening meal, on a damp night, with the intention of attacking Cyzicus (Plut. Luc. 9.1). However, if the paradosis tunc, *in place of the conjecture* luna, *is allowed to stand, then the text presumably refers to the Roman third hour, hence early morning, 7–9 AM, depending on the season of the year.*

For it was the third moon,[1] and a high haze was darkening the sky.

[1] I.e., the third after the new moon (cf. Hor. *Carm.* 4.2.58; Plin. *HN* 2.219). Text uncertain.

103 32M, 95Mc, 80D, 98K

Maurenbr. detected in this fragment a possible reference to Mithridates' failed attempt to cause the Valerians to defect (cf. fr. 26). Gerlach, on the contrary, assumed a connection with the plot against Sertorius (cf. frr. 55–57).

falters as a result of the conspiracy

104 95M, 96Mc, 73D, 89K

Maurenbr. connected the desperation felt by the troops with the panic experienced by the soldiers under P. Varinius (pr. 73) in the war against Spartacus (cf. fr. 42.2).

And then especially, as usually happens in desperate circumstances, each recalled the one dearest to him at home, and all men of all ranks carried out their final duties.[1]

[1] I.e., put their affairs in order, possibly by drawing up wills—so understood by Kritz and Dietsch—as the soldiers in Caesar's camp did in 58 out of fear of Ariovistus (Caes. *B Gall.* 1.39.5).

Miscellaneous, frr. 105–8

105   107M, 97Mc, 75D, 92K

Perculsis et animi incertis succurritur.

Arus. *GL* 7.487.29–30 = p. 181DC: to illustrate *incertus* + gen. of thing. [For comparable instances of *animi* in the *Historiae,* see on fr. 1.136.]

106   108M, 98Mc, 76D, 93K

   muros successerant

Arus. *GL* 7.507.16 = p. 256DC, quoting fr. 1.128, this fragment, and fr. 4.3: to illustrate *succedo* + acc. of thing. [cf. *OLD* 2a].

107   109M, 99Mc, 78D, 96K

Contra ille calvi ratus quaerit extis num[1] somnio portenderetur thesaurus.

Eutych. *GL* 5.485.7–8: to illustrate the third conj. verb *calvo* = *decipio* (to deceive).

{*contra . . . ratus,* Non. p. 7M = 11L.7, and Pris. *GL* 2.506.10: to illustrate the same as above.}

   [1] quaerit extis num] *Kritz*: quaerit extisne an *Maurenbr.*: ratusq. retextis ne somnio *B*: e querere tectis ne asomno *t*: q. rite textis netui somnio *f*: extis an *P*

108   110M, 100Mc, 81D, 99K

   dubius consilii

Arus. *GL* 7.468.12 = p. 112DC: to illustrate *dubius* + gen. [of resp.: *OLD* 1a].

Miscellaneous, frr. 105–8

105 107M, 97Mc, 75D, 92K

Assistance is offered to the demoralized and faltering in spirit.

106 108M, 98Mc, 76D, 93K

they had approached close to the walls

107 109M, 99Mc, 78D, 96K

"That man" (ille) may possibly be Lucullus, since dreams play a prominent role in Plutarch's account of Lucullus' campaigns against Mithridates—e.g., before the naval battle of Lemnos/ Chryse (Luc. 12.1; cf. fr. 74) and before the capture of Sinope (op. cit. 23.3)—and Lucullus had been advised by Sulla in his Memoirs *to put faith in dreams (op. cit. 23.6).*

That man, on the contrary, thinking that he was being misled, inquired by means of entrails whether a treasure was being foretold in his dream.

108 110M, 100Mc, 81D, 99K

undecided in intention[1]

[1] I.e., regarding what plan to adopt.

BOOK 4

OUTLINE

LIBER IV

URBAN AFFAIRS (72 BC), FRR. 1–2

1 1M, 1Mc, 35D, 50K

At Cn. Lentulus patriciae gentis, collega eius, quoi cognomentum Clodiano fuit, perincertum stolidior an vanior, legem de pecunia, quam Sulla emptoribus bonorum remiserat, exigunda promulgavit.

Gell. 18.4.4: providing the basis for a discussion of the contrast S. draws between two apparent synomyms, *stolidior* and *vanior.*

BOOK 4

URBAN AFFAIRS (72 BC), FRR. 1–2

1 1M, 1Mc, 35D, 50K

The introductory word "At" ("But") and the description of Lentulus as "his colleague" invite the surmise that L. Gellius Publicola (Lentulus' colleague) was mentioned in the preceding sentence. The two shared the consulship in 72 and censorship in 70, but Lentulus' act of proposing legislation establishes 72 as the context, since censors did not have legislative powers (Momm. StR 2.354 n. 1). The law appears not to have been passed, since two years later, in 70, Cicero refers to several decrees of the Senate, rather than a law, as the means by which the treasury sought to recover monies owed from the Sullan proscriptions (Cic. 2 Verr. 3.81).

But his colleague Gnaeus Lentulus, of patrician stock, who had the further name Clodianus—it being entirely unclear whether he was more slow of wit[1] or more devious—sponsored a law to exact the money Sulla had rebated to buyers of property.

---

[1] The second-century AD scholar Sulpicius Apollinaris (ap. Gell.) claims that *stolidus,* in this context, means "disagreeable" (*taeter*) or "churlish" (*molestus*).

2 2M, 2Mc, 11D, 8K

> eum atque Metrophanem senatus magna industria
> perquirebat, quom per tot scaphas, quas ad ostia
> cum paucis fidis percontatum miserant

Non. p. 535M = 858L.8–10: to illustrate the noun *scaphae,* defined as "small ships that accompany larger ones."

MITHRIDATIC WAR (71 BC), FRR. 3–10

3† 4M, 3Mc, 50D, 61K

Turmam equitum castra regis succedere et prope rationem[1] explorare iubet.

Arus. *GL* 7.507.16–17 = p. 256DC, quoting fr. 1.128, fr. 3.106,
and this fragment, which is assigned to *"Hist. II"*): to illustrate
succedo + acc. of thing. [cf. *OLD* 2a]

[1] properationem *codd.*: propere stationem *vel* prope stationem *Bondam*: proeli rationem *Dietsch*: prope munitionem *Keil
in app.*: properatim *vel* prope (= iuxta) rationem *Clausen*

2 2M, 2Mc, 11D, 8K

If the "him," companion of Metrophanes, is L. Fannius—the two being last attested as commanders of Mithridatic forces at the time of the siege of Cyzicus in the winter of 73/72 (Oros. 6.2.16)— the context may be the desertion of Fannius and his fellow ex-Fimbrian L. Magius to the Romans (Ps.-Ascon. p. 244St.4–5). L. Fannius later took part in Lucullus' Armenian campaign (Dio 36.8.2), and Metrophanes served as an envoy of Pompey to Mithridates in 66 (Dio 36.45.2). Cf. fr. dub. 21.

> the Senate was searching for him and Metrophanes with great diligence, both by means of so many skiffs, which they had sent to the outlets [of the river] with a few trusty men to make inquiry, ⟨and . . . ⟩

MITHRIDATIC WAR (71 BC), FRR. 3–10

3† 4M, 3Mc, 50D, 61K

This third of three examples cited by Arusianus from S. to illustrate the same construction is said to have been taken from "Hist. II", but since examples 1 and 2 come from "Hist. I" and "Hist. III", respectively, and since this fragment refers to "the king's camp" (surely, Mithridates), "II" should probably be corrected to "IV." Possibly the text concerns the cavalry engagement that took place in the plain near the city of Cabira in Pontus, where Mithridates had gathered his forces (Plut. Luc. 15.1–2).

He orders a squad of cavalry to draw near the king's camp and investigate the situation from close at hand.[1]

[1] Or, "the nearby lay of the land" (sc. *locorum* with *rationem*: so Keil and Maurenbr.). The text is uncertain at this point (see textual note).

4 5M, 4Mc, 16D, 43K

Igitur legiones pridie in monte positas arcessivit.

Prisc. *GL* 2.535.8–9: to illustrate the formation of the pf. in *–ivi* of verbs ending in *–so*.

5* 7M, 5Mc, inc. 63D, inc. 29K

quo cupidius in ore ducis se quisque bonum et strenuom ostentantes

Serv. auct. ad *Aen.* 10.370 {Isid. *Etym.* 9.3.22 (*quo cupidius . . . bonum*)}: to illustrate that a *rex* is referred to as *dux* when he leads troops in battle.

6† 8M, 6Mc, 3.34D, 3.38K

At Lucullum regis cura machinata fames brevi fatigabat.

Prisc. *GL* 2.382.4 (*"in II historiarum"*): to illustrate the passive of the depon. verb *machinor.*

7* 9M, 7Mc, deest in D et K

Qua nocte ipse fiebat anceps.

Schol. Stat. ad *Theb.* 3.2: to illustrate the adj. *anceps.*

4 5M, 4Mc, 16D, 43K

Possibly the legions were summoned from the mountains to the northwest of Cabira (App. Mithr. 80) to the new location of the Roman camp near Cabira, on high ground, a shift of position that had been made possible thanks to friendly Greek guides, who showed Lucullus how to skirt Mithridates' forces (Plut. Luc. 15.3–4).

And so he summoned the legions stationed the previous day on the mountain.

5* 7M, 5Mc, inc. 63D, inc. 29K

Possibly describing the personal intervention of Lucullus to arrest the flight of a detachment of his men near Cabira (Plut. Luc. 15.6–7).

all the more eagerly each man showing himself to be valiant and energetic before the eyes of his commander

6† 8M, 6Mc, 3.34D, 3.38K

Possibly describing Mithridates' strategy to interdict supplies being transported from Cappadocia to Lucullus' army near Cabira (App. Mithr. 81).

But Lucullus was soon afflicted by famine contrived by the king's effort.

7* 9M, 7Mc, not included in D and K

Panic caused in the camp of Mithridates by news of the failed attack on Lucullus' supply train ultimately led to a disastrous, disorderly evacuation of Mithridates' forces (Plut. Luc. 17.4–5; App. Mithr. 81).

And on that night, he himself became undecided.

8 10M, 8Mc, 45D, 3K

Ita[1] castra sine volnere introitum.

Arus. *GL* 7.488.14–15 = p. 183DC; Serv. ad *Aen.* 10.628 and *Aen.* 11.230: to illustrate the acc. as the object of an impersonal passive verb.

[1] *om. Serv. (bis)*

9 11M, 9Mc, 4D, 26K

et ‹re›vorsi[1] postero die multa, quae properantes deseruerant in castris, nancti, quom se ibi vino ciboque laeti invitarent

Non. p. 321 = 504L.25–27: to illustrate *invitare* meaning *replere* (to give a person his fill): "to regale" (*OLD* 1).

[1] *Dietsch*: et versi *codd.*: reversi *Junius*

10* 12M, 10Mc, 47D, 5K

thesauros[1] custodias regias

Pomp. *GL* 5.180.5–7; *Ars anon. Bern. GL* 8.94.13: mistakenly treating *custodias regias* as an instance of the first decl. Greek gen. sing. in *–as, as if* = τῆς *custodias* τῆς *regias.* [Cf. on fr. 3.79, *castella custodias.*]

[1] thesaurus *Ars anon. Bern., A cod. Pomp.*

8 10M, 8Mc, 45D, 3K

The Romans seized Mithridates' hastily evacuated camp near Cabira (App. Mithr. 81–82).

In this way entry was made into the camp without a wound [being suffered].

9 11M, 9Mc, 4D, 26K

Same context as fr. 8.

> and upon returning the next day, they came upon
> many objects that in their haste the enemy had left
> behind in the camp, and while they were joyfully
> regaling themselves there with food and wine

10* 12M, 10Mc, 47D, 5K

Pomponius supplies the words tenuit Lucullus *(Lucullus had in his power) to provide context. Plut. (Luc. 18.1) states that Mithridates' treasures and fortresses fell under Lucullus' control after he defeated Mithridates' forces at Cabira.*

> ⟨*Lucullus had in his power*⟩ the royal treasuries
> and prisons

CONCLUSION OF THE SLAVE
UPRISING UNDER SPARTACUS
(autumn 72–spring 71 BC), FRR. 11–31

11 20M, 16Mc, 3D, 24K

Rursus iumenta nancti ad oppidum ire contendunt.

Non. p. 258M = 394L.33: to illustrate the verb *contendere* =
intendere (strive).

12 21M, 17Mc, 63D, 64K

   omnis, quibus senecto corpore animus militaris erat

Prisc. *GL* 2.484.5; id. *GL* 2.512.13: treating (incorrectly) the adj.
senectus, –a, um (aged) as a pf. partic. of the intransitive verb
seneo (to be old).

13* 22M, 18Mc, 6D, 27K

Sorte ductos fusti necat.

Serv. & Serv. auct. ad *Aen.* 2.201: to illustrate *sorte* (abl.) with
ductus. Serv. auct. ad *Aen.* 6.22: to provide a counter example to
Virgil's *ductis sortibus* (the lots having been drawn).

CONCLUSION OF THE SLAVE
UPRISING UNDER SPARTACUS
(autumn 72–spring 71 BC), FRR. 11–31

11 20M, 16Mc, 3D, 24K

The context may be a raid carried out by Spartacus' band, which had occupied the mountains in the vicinity of Thurii and the town itself in south Lucania (cf. App. B Civ. 1.117).

Having once more obtained pack animals, they strive to go to the town.

12 21M, 17Mc, 63D, 64K

The raising of new Roman forces after M. Crassus assumed command of the slave war in the autumn of 72. This fragment may refer to the recruitment of seasoned soldiers from among Sulla's veterans who had been discharged a decade earlier, in late 82. They will have had a vested interest in defending their allotments of land against the threat posed by Spartacus' uprising.

all who possessed a martial spirit, despite having an aged body

13* 22M, 18Mc, 6D, 27K

Crassus decimated the troops that had shown the greatest cowardice in the defeat suffered by his legate Mummius at the hands of the fugitive slaves (Plut. Crass. 10.4).

He killed with a cudgel those selected by lot.

*Description of the Geography of Southern
Italy, to which Spartacus Withdrew
(cf. Plut. Crass. 10.6–7), frr. 14–20*

14* 23M, 19Mc, 18D, 33K

Omnis Italia coacta in angustias finditur[1] in duo promun-
turia, Bruttium et Sallentinum.

Serv. & Serv. auct. ad *Aen.* 3.400: to illustrate the location of
the promontory Sallentinum at the tip of the extreme southeast
("heel") of Italy.

[1] funditur *F*

15* 24M, 20Mc, 17D, 32K

Italiae plana ac mollia

Serv. & Serv. auct. ad *Aen.* 3.522: to illustrate Virgil's description
of Italy as "low-lying" (*humilis*) when viewed at a distance by
Aeneas and his Trojan companions approaching Calabria by sea,
from the east.

16 25M, 21Mc, 19D, 34K

*Description of the Geography of Southern
Italy, to which Spartacus Withdrew
(cf. Plut. Crass. 10.6–7), frr. 14–20*

14* 23M, 19Mc, 18D, 33K

*S. refers to the "heel" of Italy (Calabria) by the name of the prom-
ontory at its tip, Sallentinum, whereas he uses the name of the
broader ager Bruttius to refer to the "toe."*

All Italy, which terminates in narrow land masses, is split
into two promontories: Bruttium and Sallentinum.

15* 24M, 20Mc, 17D, 32K

*A description of Calabria, which is relatively low-lying and flat
in contrast with the rugged ager Bruttius, the other of the two
large peninsulas in which Italy terminates.*

the flat, smooth regions of Italy

16 25M, 21Mc, 19D, 34K

*S. reckons the shortest distance from coast to coast in the ager
Bruttius as roughly 35 Roman miles, which is approximately the
distance by air at the latitude of Thurii (ca. 40 English miles). The
neck of land is even narrower (ca. 20 English miles) at the latitude
of Scolacium. Plut. appears to have mistaken this measurement
for the far shorter distance that must have been spanned by the
wall and trench (15 feet wide and 15 feet deep) built by Crassus
to blockade Spartacus and his men in the ager Bruttius (Plut.
Crass. 10.7–8). Plut. claims that the wall stretched 300 stades (ca.
37.5 Roman miles), an impossible length to garrison. More realis-
tically, the wall and ditch were probably intended to cut off the
promontory of Scyllaeum (mod. Scilla), to which Spartacus re-
treated, on the coast of the ager Bruttius, opposite Cape Pelorus
in Sicily (so Ward, Crassus, 89–90).*

ad Siciliam vergens faucibus ipsis non amplius patet
milibus quinque et triginta

Arus. *GL* 7.500.17 = p. 230DC: to illustrate *pateo* + *tot pedibus*
[an abl. of measure of distance].

17* 26M, 22Mc, 20D, 35K

Nam olim[1] Italiae Siciliam coniunctam constat fuisse; sed
medium spatium aut per[2] humilitatem obrutum[3] est, aut
per[3] angustiam scissum. Ut autem[4] curvom sit facit natura
mollioris Italiae, in quam asperitas et altitudo Siciliae aes-
tum relidit.

Serv. & Serv. auct. ad *Aen.* 3.414; *Schol. Stat.* ad *Theb.* 3.597: to
explicate the tradition, found in Virgil and Statius, that Italy and
Sicily were in an earlier age joined together.

{Cf. Isid. *Etym.* 13.18.3, *Sallustius . . . dicens Italiae olim Siciliam
coniunctam fuisse, et dum esset una tellus, medium spatium aut
per humilitatem obrutum est aquis, aut per angustiam scissum;*
14.6.34, *Sallustius autem dicit Italiae coniunctam fuisse Siciliam,
sed medium spatium impetu maris divisum et per angustiam scissum.*}

[1] nam olim] *om. Serv.*   [2] propter *Schol. Stat.*
[3] obruptum *Pa Schol. Stat., NTa Serv.*: abruptum *L Schol. Stat.*
[4] dum *Schol. Stat.*

18* 27M, 23Mc, 21D, 36K

stretching out in the direction of Sicily, it is not wider than 35 miles at its narrowest point

17* 26M, 22Mc, 20D, 35K

Creation of the strait between Italy and Sicily.

For it is agreed that Sicily had once been joined to Italy, but the intervening section had either been submerged as a result of its low-lying nature or severed as a result of its narrowness. Moreover, the rounding of the coast was brought about by the nature of the softer composition of the Italian mainland against which the roughness and height of Sicily casts back the sea's swell.

18* 27M, 23Mc, 21D, 36K

S. describes the region on the coast of the ager Bruttius, to which Spartacus withdrew. The mythical Homeric monster Scylla is connected with a rock formation projecting from the Italian coast, opposite Cape Pelorus in the Strait of Messina, near present-day Scilla.

Scyllam accolae saxum mari inminens adpellant, simile celebratae formae procul visentibus. Et monstruosam speciem fabulae illi dederunt, quasi formam hominis caninis succinctam capitibus, quia conlisi ibi fluctus latratus videntur exprimere.

Isid. *Etym.* 13.18.4: either the exact words of S., or a paraphrase, to judge from the verbal similarities to the report of S.'s account in Serv. & Serv. auct., combined with the fact that Isid. identifies S. as his source for the version of fr. 17 given at 13.18.3.

{Cf. Serv. & Serv. auct. ad *Aen.* 3.420: *SCYLLA . . . Sallustius saxum esse dicit simile formae celebratae procul visentibus. Canes vero et lupi ob hoc ex ea nati esse finguntur, quia ipsa loca plena sunt monstris marinis et saxorum asperitas illic imitatur latratus.*}

19 28M, 24Mc, 22D, 37K

Charybdis, mare vorticosum, quo⟨d⟩¹ forte inlata naufragia sorbens gurgitibus occultis milia XL² Tauromenitana ad litora trahit, ubi se laniata navigia³ fundo⁴ emergunt

Serv. auct. ad *Aen.* 1.117 (*Charybdis mare verticosum*): in explication of the noun *vertex* (whirlpool); Serv. auct. ad *Aen.* 3.425 (*quo⟨d⟩. . . trahit*): to illustrate the verb *traho*; Arus. *GL* 7.472.16 = p. 128DC (*ubi . . . emergunt*): to illustrate *se emergere*.

{Paraphrased Serv. & Serv. auct. ad *Aen.* 3.420; Isid. *Etym.* 13.18.5 (*Charybdis . . . mare verticosum, et inde ibi laniata naufragia profundo emergunt*); cf. Sen. *Q Nat.* 7.8.2, attesting S.'s use of the adj. *vorticosus* of a whirling motion; words and phrases borrowed from this description in Plin. *HN* 3.87; *Pan. Lat.* 2.26.4.}

The inhabitants give the name Scylla to a rock projecting out over the sea, one resembling the well-known shape when people behold it from a distance. And they assigned to it the monstrous appearance of that mythical creature, a human shape, as it were, girded round about by dogs' heads because the waves dashing together there give the impression of producing barking.

19 28M, 24Mc, 22D, 37K

Same context as fr. 18: here describing a whirlpool named after the mythical Homeric Charybdis, situated in the Strait of Messina, near the Sicilian city of Messana (cf. Strabo 6.2.3, p. 268). It supposedly swept wrecks down the east coast to the Sicilian town of Tauromenium.

Charybdis, a whirlpool, which swallows up wrecks carried into it by chance and drags them with underwater currents 40 miles[1] to the shores of Tauromenium, where the wrecked vessels re-emerge from the bottom

[1] The distance given by the manuscript (sixty miles) is nearly two times the actual distance separating Tauromenium from Messana in the Strait.

---

[1] *Daniel* [2] *scripsi*: sexaginta (*i.e.*, LX) *codd.*
[3] naufragia *Pan. Lat., Isid. (cf. Strabo 6.2.3, p. 268)* [4] profundo *Isid.*

20* 29M, 25Mc, 24D, 39K

PELORI: **promontorium Siciliae** *est,*[1] *secundum Sallus-*
tium **dictum a gubernatore Hannibalis illic sepulto**

Serv. & Serv. auct. ad *Aen.* 3.411; Isid. *Etym.* 14.7.4.

[1] est] respiciens Aquilonem *Isid.*

21 30M, 26Mc, 8D, 29K

dolia quae[1] sub trabes locata vitibus aut tergis vinciebant

Arus. *GL* 7.509.14–15 = p. 262DC: to illustrate *sub* + acc. of
thing with *locatus.*

{Serv. ad *Aen.* 9.410 (*tergis vinciebant*): to illustrate *tergum = tergus, –oris* ("hide" from an animal's back used as a material [*OLD*
s.v. *tergum* 7b and *OLD* s.v. *tergus* 3a].}

[1] *Lindemann*: cum *N1*: quoque *Keil*

22 31M, 27Mc, 9D, 30K

Inplicatae[1] rates ministeria prohibebant.

Prisc. *GL* 2.473.8–9: to illustrate *implicatus,* in contrast with
implicitus.

[1] inplicitae *D*: implicitae *GK*: implicite *B*

20* 29M, 25Mc, 24D, 39K

Same context as frr. 18–19. There was a tradition that Hannibal put his pilot Pelorus to death when, on a voyage, the general could not make out in the distance the narrow Strait of Messina (between Cape Pelorus and the "toe" of Italy) and so mistakenly believed that Pelorus had betrayed him by steering him into a trap (Serv. loc. cit.; Mela 2.116; Val. Max. 9.8 ext. 1).

PELORUS: it is a **promontory of Sicily named,** according to Sallust, **after Hannibal's helmsman buried there**

21 30M, 26Mc, 8D, 29K

When the fugitive slaves failed to secure passage to Sicily on pirate vessels belonging to Cilicians, who had struck a bargain with them but then sailed away, leaving them stranded (Plut. Crass. 10.6–7), Spartacus and his men tried to cross the Strait of Messina on makeshift rafts (Flor. 2.8.13; cf. Cic. 2 Verr. 5.5), setting out, no doubt, from their base of operations on Cape Scyllaeum.

large earthenware vessels which they placed underneath planks and secured with vines or strips of leather

22 31M, 27Mc, 9D, 30K

Same context as fr. 21.

The entangled rafts hindered their management.[1]

[1] *Ministerium* in this context must refer to the duties of steering and controlling the craft (so Kritz), a meaning not taken into account by *OLD* or Lewis and Short (but see *TLL* 8.1010.19–53, = *negotium, munus* [i.e., an assigned task]).

23* 32M, 28Mc, 10D, 31K

C. Verres litora Italia[1] propinqua firmavit.

Arus. *GL* 7.500.29 = p. 231DC: to illustrate *propinquus* + abl. of thing.

[1] Italiae *Dietsch* (*cf. Jug. 48.4, 89.5*)

24* 35M, 29Mc, deest in D et K

frigida nocte

Schol. Bern. ad *G.* 4.104: included in a note on the expression *frigida tecta* (beehives that are abandoned and without activity).

25 36M, 30 Mc, 65D, 66K

infrequentem stationem nostram incuriosamque tum[1] ab armis

Arus. *GL* 7.487.19–20 = p. 180DC: to illustrate the adj. *incuriosus* construed with *ab* + abl. of thing.

[1] *Gerlach ed. min.* (*cf. Dict. Cret. 2.42*, tum incuriosique ab armis): tam *N*: iam *Keil in app.*

26* 33M, 31Mc, 7D, 28K

in silva Sila fuerunt[1]

Serv. ad *Aen.* 12.715: quotes S. as part of his discussion of the corruption *silva* for *Sila* in some manuscripts of the *Aen.*

[1] fugerunt *R*: ficerunt *H*: in silvam Silam fugerunt *Dietsch*

23* 32M, 28Mc, 10D, 31K

Same context as fr. 21. Cicero in his prosecution of Verres in 70 scoffed at the claim of the ex-governor that he deserved credit for preventing the war with Spartacus from spreading across the Strait of Messina to Sicily (2 Verr. 5.5). Yet contrary to Cicero's portrayal, it may have been Verres' defensive measures that caused the Cilician pirates to break their agreement to transport Spartacus and his men to the coast of Sicily (Plut. Crass. 10.7).

Gaius Verres fortified the shores near Italy.

24* 35M, 29Mc, not included in D and K

Maurenbr., comparing Plut. Crass. 10.9, detected in these words a reference to the snowy and wintery night on which one-third of Spartacus' forces managed to cross the trench and wall with which Crassus had attempted to seal off Cape Scyllaeum in the vicinity of Rhegium, where the slaves had taken up a position.

on a cold night

25 36M, 30 Mc, 65D, 66K

Same context as fr. 24.

our picket being sparse and inattentive to its arms on that occasion

26* 33M, 31Mc, 7D, 28K

Servius states that the quotation from S. concerns fugitives. Since Sila is a vast, forested mountain in northeast Bruttius ager (Dion. Hal. Ant. Rom. 20.15 [fr. 20.5 Ambr.]), ca. eighty miles in length (Strabo 6.1.9, p. 261), it made a logical hiding place for Spartacus and his band after their escape from Crassus' entrenchment to the south (cf. frr. 24–25).

they were in the forest of Sila

27 37M, 32Mc, 12D, 40K

Dissidere inter se coepere, neque in medium consultare.

Arus. *GL* 7.482.27–28 = p. 165DC: to illustrate *in medium = in commune.*

28 38M, 33Mc, 13D, 41K

sapor iuxta fontis dulcissumos[1]

Arus. *GL* 7.510.12 = p. 266DC: to illustrate *sapor* construed with *iuxta* + acc of thing.

[1] dulcissimus *Keil in app.*

29 40M, 34Mc, 15D, 42K

27 37M, 32Mc, 12D, 40K

Possibly a reference to a division of the fugitives into two rival factions that came into being shortly after their escape from Crassus' blockade (Plut. Crass. 11.1): one of Gauls and Germans under the leadership of Castus and Cannic(i)us (Frontin. Str. 2.4.7, 2.5.34; Plut. Crass. 11.4; named Castus and Gannicus in Liv. Per. 97); the rest remaining loyal to Spartacus. Alternatively, this fragment may describe dissension between Pompey and Crassus during their joint consulship in 70 (Syme, Sallust, 212 n. 149).

They began to disagree among themselves and not to take counsel for a common purpose.

28 38M, 33Mc, 13D, 41K

The German and Gallic contingent of fugitives is said to have encamped in Lucania, near a lake whose water by turns changed from sweet to bitter and back to sweet (Plut. Crass. 11.1).

a taste on a par with the most pleasant springs

29 40M, 34Mc, 15D, 42K

Soldiers who had been sent surreptitiously by Crassus to take up a strategic position prior to an attack on the Gallic-Germanic band of rebels were spotted by two women of the enemy (Plut. Crass. 11.5). According to Plut., those women were engaged in offering sacrifices on behalf of the group. Possibly Plut., or his source, misunderstood S.'s menstrua *as referring to "monthly sacrifices" (*menstrua <sacra>, *the meaning assigned to* menstrua *in this passage by Lewis and Short). The parallel in Lucretius (6.796,* quo menstrua solvit; *cf. Tac. Hist. 5.6) makes it clear that the women were going off to attend to their menstrual cycles in seclusion.*

Quom interim, lumine etiamtum incerto, duae Galliae mulieres[1] conventum vitantes[1] ad menstrua sol-
venda[2] montem ascendunt

Non. p. 492M = 790L.27–29: to illustrate *Galliae* in place of the
adj. *Gallicae*.

[1] *ed. princ. (a. 1470)*: mulieris . . . vitantis *codd.*
[2] ad struem movendam *Dietsch in app.*

30 39M, 35Mc, 14D, 44K

avidior modo properandi factus

Arus. *GL* 7.450.11 = p. 46DC: to illustrate *avidus* + gen. of thing.

31* 41M, 36Mc, inc. 29D, 4.45K

haud[1] inpigre[2] neque inultus occiditur

Donat. ad Ter. *An.* 205: interpreting (incorrectly) *neque . . . haud
. . . non* in Ter. as equivalent to a simple negative, and apparently
regarding *haud . . . neque inultus* in S. as comparable.

[1] *secl. Vogel (cf. Flor. 1.38.18,* Rex . . . dimicans inpigre nec
inultus occiditur*)*   [2] impune V *(man. 2 in rasura)*: inpigro
A: inpigre ⟨pugnans⟩ *Dietsch*

When, meanwhile, in the first uncertain light of daybreak, two Gallic women went up a mountain to attend to their monthly discharge in isolation from the general throng

30 39M, 35Mc, 14D, 44K

In the last phase of the war, after Crassus had defeated the Gallic-Germanic detachment (referred to in frr. 27–29), he made great haste to crush the remaining force under Spartacus in order to forestall Pompey from robbing him of the credit for ending the war (Plut. Crass. 11.8; Nic.-Crass. 3(36).2)—haste characterized as reckless (Plut. Pomp. 21.2).

having become more eager just now for hurrying

31* 41M, 36Mc, inc. 29D, 4.45K

This description of a warrior who is killed in battle after a great struggle, taking many of the enemy with him, fits the narrative of Spartacus' death (Flor. 2.8.14; Plut. Crass. 11.9–10; cf. App. B Civ. 1.120: Spartacus' body not found).

he is cut down by no means with dispatch[1] and not without inflicting vengeance [on his foes]

[1] Text is uncertain (see textual note); a similar problem is posed by *haud impigre* at Liv. 32.16.11 (see Briscoe ad loc.). If *haud* is deleted, trans. "he is cut down fiercely but not without. . . ." For *inpigre* (meaning *agiliter* or *acriter*) with *occidor,* cf. *Jug.* 101.6, *satis inpigre occiso pedite.*

URBAN AFFAIRS (71 BC), FRR. 32–41

32* 42M, 37Mc, 31D, 56K

multisque suspicionibus volentia plebi facturus habebatur

Non. p. 186M = 274L.23: to illustrate *volentia* meaning "what people want" (*quae vellent*).

33 43M, 38Mc, 25D, 57K

M. Lollius[1] Palicanus, humili loco Picens, loquax magis quam facundus

Quint. 4.2.2: (without attribution to S.) as an example of a character sketch.

{Gell. 1.15.13 (*loquax . . . facundus*): S.'s rendering of a pithy descriptive phrase coined by the fifth-century Greek comic playwright Eupolis (fr. 95 Kock).}

[1] *Pighius*: m. ollius *A*: macilius *B*

34 44M, 39Mc, 70D, 73K

magnam exorsus orationem

Arus. *GL* 7. 472.18 = p. 128DC: to illustrate the expression *exorsus orationem*.

URBAN AFFAIRS (71 BC), FRR. 32–41

32* 42M, 37Mc, 31D, 56K

Upon his return to Italy from the Sertorian War in Spain in the spring of 71, Pompey was regarded by some as being too inclined to promote measures popular with the masses (Plut. Pomp. 21.7).

and as a result of many presentiments, it was thought that he was going to do things desired by[1] the commons

[1] For this use of *volentia* (= *optata*) + dat., cf. Tac. *Ann.* 15.36; *Hist.* 3.52.

33 43M, 38Mc, 25D, 57K

After Pompey's election to the consulship of 70, M. Palicanus (tribune of the plebs 71) summoned a contio, at which Pompey delivered a speech in which he promised to restore the powers of the tribunes. (Ps.-Ascon. p. 220St.18–20; Cic. Verr. 45).

M. Lollius Palicanus, from Picenum, of lowly stock, loquacious rather than eloquent,[1]

[1] Cic. (*Brut.* 223) characterizes Palicanus as a speaker well suited for unruly public meetings, where there was no appreciation for true eloquence (*aptior . . . auribus imperitorum*).

34 44M, 39Mc, 70D, 73K

Same context as fr. 33. The speaker is Pompey.

commencing a lengthy speech

35 45M, 40Mc, 30D, 55K

si nihil ante adventum suum inter plebem et patres
convenisset, coram se daturum operam

Prisc. *GL* 3.52.10–12: to illustrate the adv. *coram* meaning "out in
the open," the opposite of *clam.*

36 46M, 41Mc, 26D, 59K

qui quidem mos[1] ut tabes in urbem coiectus[2]

Festus p. 359M = 490L.34: to illustrate *tabes* used metaphorically, meaning "that which produces decay."

   [1] *Ant. Augustinus (ed. Venetiis, 1559):* nos *codd.*   [2] con-
iectus *VWXZ:* coiecit *U:* coierit *Müller*

37 47M, 42Mc, 32D, 58K

multitudini ostendens quam colere plurumum, ut
mox cupitis ministrum[1] haberet,[2] decreverat,

Arus. *GL* 7. 494.7–8 = p. 205DC: to illustrate *minister + dat.*

   [1] ministram *Hoeven*   [2] *Hoeven:* habere *codd.*

38 49M, 43Mc, 28D, 52K

35 45M, 40Mc, 30D, 55K

Same context as frr. 33–34. Commitment made by Pompey, looking ahead to his consulship in 70.

> that if no understanding had been achieved between the commons and the senate before his arrival, he would in person devote his effort ⟨to achieving it?⟩ . . .

36 46M, 41Mc, 26D, 59K

Possibly the same context as frr. 33–35. The "plague" may be the notorious corruption of provincial administration and the failure of the criminal courts under senatorial juries in the 70s to punish malefactors, serious concerns addressed by Pompey in his contio *speech (Cic. Verr. 45).*

> which habit, in truth, foisted upon the City, like a plague,

37 47M, 42Mc, 32D, 58K

Pompey promoted populist measures in order to strengthen and expand his political base (Plut. Pomp. 22.3).

> showing to the throng, which he had resolved to cultivate very assiduously so as to have it soon as an agent for furthering his wishes, that

38 49M, 43Mc, 28D, 52K

The return of Metellus Pius from the Sertorian War in the latter half of 71, sometime after the election of Pompey to the consulship (App. B Civ. 1.121). In contrast with Pompey, who retained his army upon returning to Italy in order to deal with the uprising of Spartacus, as he had been authorized to do by the senate, Metellus dismissed his army.

Exercitum dimisit, ut primum Alpis degressus[1] est.

Arus. *GL* 7.464.26–27 = p. 102DC: to illustrate *digredior* [sic] + acc. of place.

[1] *Keil in app.*: digressus *N1, edd. Sall.*

39 50M, 44Mc, 69D, 72K

quod in praesens modo satis cautum fuerat

Arus. *GL* 7.487.5–6 = p. 179DC: to illustrate *in praesens = ad praesens.*

40 48M, 45Mc, 33D, 54K

collegam minorem et sui cultorem exspectans

Arus. *GL* 7.461.10–11 = p. 88DC: to illustrate *cultor + sui.*

41 51M, 56Mc, 34D, 62K

Crassus, obtrectans potius collegae quam boni aut mali publici gravis[1] exactor,[2]

Arus. *GL* 7.496.30–497.1 = p. 215DC: to illustrate *obtrectans +* dat.

[1] *G P*: gravus *N1 N2*: gnavus *Keil*
[2] *codd.*: aestumator *vel* existumator *Dietsch*: auctor *Kritz*

---

[1] *Exactor* is to be understood in two different senses: = *custos* (guardian) with "public good" and = *expulsor* (remover) with "disorder" (*TLL* 5.2.1136.56ff. and 1135.27ff., resp.). Twice elsewhere (*Cat.* 37.8 and *Hist.* 1.77M.13), S. uses *malum publicum* (modeled on *bonum publicum*); see Briscoe on Sisenna, *FRHist* 26F92 = fr. 111P, now with the corrigendum, per litteras, that Livy has *malum publicum* at 4.44.9.

He disbanded his army as soon as he had descended[1] the Alps.

[1] Since just ahead of this fragment Arus. cites *Jug.* 50.1 as *colli digredi,* for which the manuscripts of S. give *colle degredi,* there is good reason to accept here the emendation *degressus* (descended) for the paradosis *digressus* (departed). For a comparable error in the text tradition of Arusianus, cf. fr.4.72, *demissus* (*dimissus* N1).

39 50M, 44Mc, 69D, 72K

Possibly a reference to the brief political alliance made by Pompey and Crassus before their election to the consulship in 71, a reconciliation of their differences that soon dissolved into rivalry during their year in office (Plut. Pomp. 22.2–3; Crass. 12.1–3).

for which adequate precaution had been taken for the time being only

40 48M, 45Mc, 33D, 54K

Pompey supported Crassus' candidacy for the consulship in 71 so as to put him under obligation to him (Plut. Crass. 12.2).

hoping for a junior colleague, one devoted to him

41 51M, 56Mc, 34D, 62K

Text is uncertain; see textual notes. Possibly the same context as frr. 39–40, describing how the reconciliation between Pompey and Crassus was short-lived.

Crassus, more a disparager of his colleague than a stern overseer[1] of public good or disorder,

MITHRIDATIC WAR (70 BC), FRR. 42–46

42 13M, 46Mc, 42D, 1K

Amisumque adsideri sine proeliis audiebat

Prisc. *GL* 2.435.14–15: to illustrate the passive of *adsideo*.

43 14M, 47Mc, 55D, 14K

scalas pares moenium altitudine

Arus. *GL* 7.500.2–3 = p. 228DC: to illustrate *par* + abl. of thing. [Abl. of measure: cf. K-S 1.391.10.]

44 15M, 48Mc, 43D, 69K

quia[1] praedatores[2] facibus sibi praelucentes ambustas in tectis[3] sine cura reliquerant

Arus. *GL* 7.503.15–16 = p. 242DC: to illustrate *praeluceo* + dat. of person and *lumine* [abl.].

[1] quae *Keil*   [2] *Linker*: praetores *codd.*   [3] ambustas in tectis] *codd.* (ambustum *P1*): ambustis tectis *Keil*

MITHRIDATIC WAR (70 BC),
FRR. 42–46

42 13M, 46Mc, 42D, 1K

The logical person to receive this news is Lucullus, on his journey back to Pontus from Lesser Armenia, after his victory over Mithridates near Cabira in the summer of 71 (Plut. Luc. 19.1). The city of Amisus held out for two years after it was put under siege in 72.

and he heard that Amisus was being besieged without any pitched battles

43 14M, 47Mc, 55D, 14K

Lucullus captured the Pontic city Eupatoria and soon afterward Amisus, by having his soldiers employ ladders to mount a part of the ramparts that were temporarily left unattended (Memnon, FGrH 434F30.4; cf. Plut. Luc. 19.3). Ladders were likewise employed in Lucullus' capture of Sinope (Memnon, FGrH 434F37.8).

ladders equal to the height of the ramparts

44 15M, 48Mc, 43D, 69K

Roman soldiers added to the destruction of Amisus, which had already been set ablaze by the fleeing garrison, by ransacking the houses with flaming torches (Plut. Luc. 19.5).

because pillagers, lighting their way with torches, had carelessly left them smoldering in the buildings

45 56M, 57Mc, 49D, 7K

Tetrarchas regesque territos[1] animi firmavit.

Arus. *GL* 7.470.23–24 = p. 122DC: to illustrate *exterritus* + gen. of thing. [For comparable instances of *animi* in the *Historiae,* see on fr. 1.136.]

  [1] ‹ex›territos *Dietsch*

46* 57M, 58Mc, 48D, 6K

  insolens vera accipiundi

Donat. ad Ter. *An.* 907: to illustrate *insolens* meaning "unaccustomed" (*insuetus, insolitus*).

URBAN AFFAIRS (70 BC), FRR. 47–51

47 17M, 51Mc, 37D, 51K

  atque hiavit humus multa vasta et profunda

Non. p. 318M = 498L.31: to give an instance of the verb *hiare* meaning *aperiri* (to be opened up).

45 56M, 57Mc, 49D, 7K

After Mithridates' flight from Cabira (summer 71), Lucullus' brother-in-law Ap. Claudius (cos. 54) was sent to Tigranes, king of Armenia and Mithridates' son-in-law, to demand his coopera-tion in bringing about the capture of Mithridates. While Claudius waited at Antioch for Tigranes to return from settling affairs in Phoenicia, he tampered with the loyalty of many rulers who were vassals of Tigranes (Plut. Luc. 21.2).

He strengthened the resolve of tetrarchs and kings cowed in spirit.

**46* 57M, 58Mc, 48D, 6K

Same context as fr. 45. The bold and threatening words spoken to king Tigranes by Ap. Claudius were unlike any he had heard for decades, in as much as the king was used to being surrounded by flatterers and subservient courtiers (Plut. Luc. 21.6; cf. 25.1–2, Mithrobarzanes the first to tell Tigranes the truth).

unaccustomed to hearing the truth

URBAN AFFAIRS (70 BC), FRR. 47–51

47 17M, 51Mc, 37D, 51K

Phlegon of Tralles (FGrH 257F12.4) reports an earthquake that did considerable damage at Rome, placing it after Lucullus win-tered at Cabira (71/70) and before the census of 70. S. may be referring to that event or to an earthquake in Phrygia mentioned by Nicolaus of Damascus (FGrH 90F74) as having occurred at the time of the Mithridatic War, without any precise indication of the exact year.

and the ground gaped in an extensive fissure, vast and deep

48† 3.47M, 4.52Mc, 3.63D, 3.85K

post reditum eorum quibus senatus belli Lepidani gratiam fecerat

Arus. *GL* 7.476.10–11 = p. 142DC (assigned to Book 3: *"Sal. Hist. III"*): to illustrate *gratiam* + dat. of person and gen. of offense.

49* 52M, 53Mc, inc. 114D, inc. 85K

fenoribus copertus[1] est[2]

Gell. 2.17.7: to illustrate that the prefix *con–* is lengthened not just before words beginning with *s* and *f;* Gell. 4.17.6: the prefix *con–* is lengthened when the *n* is dropped.

[1] coopertus (compertus *P 4.17.6*) *codd.*
[2] *om. Gell. 4.17.6*

50 53M, 54Mc, 11D, 63K

48† 3.47M, 4.52Mc, 3.63D, 3.85K

Those who had participated in the rebellion of Lepidus in 78–77 were not restored until 70 BC, when the tribune Plautius passed a bill granting pardon (MRR 2.128), a bill that appears from this fragment to have been sanctioned by a decree of the senate. Clearly, therefore, the book number given for this fr. (III) needs to be emended to "IV," since Book 3 leaves off in the year 72, while Book 4 covers the remainder of 72, ending with events in 68.

after the return of those to whom the senate had granted a pardon for [their participation in] the Lepidan war

49* 52M, 53Mc, inc. 114D, inc. 85K

The censors of 70 deprived sixty-four senators of their seats, and one of the grounds for stripping senators of their rank was indebtedness. These words may describe such a person as Cicero's future consular colleague in 63 C. Antonius Hybrida, who was removed from the senate in part for the great magnitude of his debts (Ascon. p. 84C).

he was buried deep in debt[1]

[1] Lit., "overwhelmed by interest on loans."

50 53M, 54Mc, 11D, 63K

Possibly from S.'s account of the trial of Gaius Verres in 70, but the text is uncertain and heavily emended. Verres was accused by Cicero of having taken bribes from robbers to release them from custody, or to allow them a free hand to operate, when Verres was the governor of Sicily from 73 to 71 (2 Verr. 1.9 and 12).

suspectusque fuit, incertum vere[1] an[2] per[3] neglegentiam, societatem praedarum cum latronibus
conposuisse[t][4]

Non. p. 257M = 392L.44–46 (lib. III *A*[A]: lib. IIII *LB*[A]): to illustrate the verb *componere* = *coniungere* (to join together).

[1] *Dietsch*: vero *codd.*   [2] *Iunius*: ac *codd.*   [3] propter *Dietsch*   [4] *Iunius*

51 55M, 55Mc, 27D, 60K

L. Hostilius[1] Dasianus, inquies animi

Arus. *GL* 7.488.3–4 = p. 182DC: to illustrate *inquies* + gen. [For
comparable instances of *animi* in the *Historiae*, see on fr. 1.136.]

[1] *Ruhnken*: hostibus *codd.*

LUCULLUS' INVASION OF ARMENIA
(69 BC), FRR. 52–59

52 58M, 59Mc, 6D, 3.85K

Dein lenita iam ira, postero die liberalibus verbis per-
mulcti sunt.

Prisc. GL 2.487.5–6: to illustrate *mulctum* (as well as *mulsum*) as
the pf. partic. of *mulceo*.

and he was under the suspicion of having formed—
it being doubtful whether in actual fact or through
neglect of his duties—a compact with robbers for
sharing booty[1]

[1] What S. appears to be saying is that it is doubtful whether it
was through negligence or an alliance with robbers that some
dereliction of duty occurred on the part of a Roman official (perhaps Verres).

51 55M, 55Mc, 27D, 60K

*Same context as fr. 50. The Gronovian Scholiast (p. 331St.8, on
Cic. Verr. 6) states that either Piso or Dasianus was said to be the
name of the "Achaicus inquisitor," who allegedly colluded with
Verres in 70 to cause a postponement of Verres' case, by setting in
motion a rival prosecution for extortion in Achaea. Possibly the
L. Hostilius mentioned here is to be identified with L. Hostilius
tribune of the plebs in 68 (so MRR 2.138).*

L. Hostilius Dasianus, restless of spirit,

LUCULLUS' INVASION OF ARMENIA
(69 BC), FRR. 52–59

52 58M, 59Mc, 6D, 3.85K

*Lucullus' soldiers grumbled when they were made to embark
upon a campaign against Tigranes of Armenia in the spring of 69
(Plut. Luc. 24.1).*

Then, after their anger had been calmed, they were as-
suaged on the following day with generous words.

53 59M, 60Mc, 51D, 10K

Quam maxumis itineribus per regnum Ariobarzanis contendit ad flumen Euphraten, qua in parte Cappadocia ab Armenia disiungitur; et quamquam ad ⟨D⟩[1] naves caudicariae occulte per hiemem fabricatae aderant . . .

Non. p. 535M = 858L.13–16: to illustrate a kind of river boat or barge called *codicaria* (sc. *navis*).

[1] *Müller*

54* 60M, 61Mc, inc. 97D, inc. 66K

ut tanta repente[1] mutatio non sine deo videretur

Donat. ad Ter. *Eun.* 875; Serv. auct. ad *Aen.* 2.632; *Schol. Veron.* ad ibid.: to illustrate how a sudden and unexpected turn of events is often credited to the will of a god.

[1] *om. Serv. auct.*

55 61M, 62Mc, 54D, 13K

naphthas,[1] *genus olei cedro simile*

Prob. *GL* 4.29.8; Sacerd. *GL* 2.480.8: treat this Greek first decl. noun as an anomaly, mistakenly classifying it as neut., or possibly as indecl.

{Prob. *GL* 4.22.22 (*naphthas*), Sacerd. fr. line 98 (*napthas*): indecl. noun.}

[1] *Prob. 4.22*: naptha *Prob. 4.29*: naptas *Sacerd. 2.480*

*Sallustius scribit in historiis quod **napta** genus sit fomitis apud Persas quo vel maxume nutriantur incendia*

53 59M, 60Mc, 51D, 10K

Lucullus' march to the Euphrates and crossing in the spring of 69.

By forced marches he hastened through the kingdom of Ariobarzanes to the Euphrates River, in the place where Cappadocia is separated from Armenia; and although there were on hand about 500(?) river barges, which had secretly been constructed during the winter, . . .

54* 60M, 61Mc, inc. 97D, inc. 66K

Same context as fr. 53. The sudden lessening of the winter spate of the Euphrates seemed heaven sent (Plut. Luc. 24.2–3). As further evidence of divine favor toward Lucullus, a sacrificial heifer made a seemingly miraculous appearance after the army had crossed to the other side (Plut. Luc 24.4).

so that such a sudden change of circumstances seem to be not without the will of a god

55 61M, 62Mc, 54D, 13K

Siege of Tigranocerta. Naphtha, a flammable mineral oil found in Mesopotamia (Plin. HN 2.235), was employed by the defenders of Tigranocerta to set fire to Lucullus' siege engines (Dio 36.1b.1–2). Beyond the fact that S. mentioned naphtha, it is impossible to say to what extent, if any, the words used to describe it are quoted directly.

naphtha, *a kind of oil, like cedar oil*

Sallust writes in the Histories that **nap(h)t(h)a** *is a kind of fire-starter among the Persians by which fires are very greatly fed*

Hieron. in *Dan.* 3:46; *Gloss.* 5, p. 225.7 (cf. pp. 312.59, 621.44, without mention of S.): to give a description of *napta* [sic], according to S.

56 63M, 63Mc, 56D, 15K

Pluteos rescindit ac munitiones demolitur, locoque summo potitur.

Non. p. 95M = 135L.22–23: to illustrate *demoliri* = *diruere* (destroy).

57* 64M, 64Mc, 58D, 17K note

  et sequebantur equites[1] catafracti

Serv. ad *Aen.* 11.770: to give an example of the expression *equites catafracti*.

  [1] *edd.*: equi *codd.*

58 65M, 65Mc, 59D, 17K

Equis paria operimenta erant, ⟨nam⟩que[1] linteo[2] ferreas laminas[3] in modum plumae adnexuerant.

Serv. ad *Aen.* 11.770: same context as fr. 57.

  [1] *Thilo dubitanter in app.*: quae (q. *R*) *codd.*
  [2] *ASMF*: lina *R*: linco *H*
  [3] *Thilo dubitanter in app.*: ferreis laminis *codd.*

56 63M, 63Mc, 56D, 15K

Possibly the same context as fr. 55. Lucullus breached the wall of Tigranocerta. Dietsch and Maurenbr., by contrast, (followed by McGushin) interpret as a sally by the defenders against the Roman position, it being possible to understand pluteos *as referring to "defensive screens" erected by the besiegers (OLD 1) as opposed to "parapets" (OLD 2), as translated.*

He tore down the parapets and destroyed the fortifications, and gained control of the high ground.

57* 64M, 64Mc, 58D, 17K note

The battle near Tigranocerta and defeat of Tigranes.

One of the most formidable elements of Tigranes' vast army was his troop of seventeen thousand cataphracts (Plut. Luc. 26.7), men and horses covered with chain mail (Tac. Hist. 1.79; Amm. Marc. 16.10).

and mail-clad cavalrymen followed

58 65M, 65Mc, 59D, 17K

Same context as fr. 57.

The horses had equal coverings, for they fastened iron plates to canvas after the fashion of plumage.

59 66M, 66Mc, 57D, 16K

qui[1] praegrediebantur equites catafracti ferrea omni[2] specie

Non. p. 556M = 893L.14–15: to illustrate the adj. *catafractus*.

[1] cui (quoi) *Müller*   [2] omnes Coler: omnis *Müller*

60 69M, 67Mc, 61D, 19K

Epistula Mithridatis[1]

1   "Rex Mithridates regi Arsaci salutem. Omnes qui secundis rebus suis ad belli societatem orantur considerare debent liceatne tum pacem agere, dein quod quaesitur satisne
2   pium, tutum, gloriosum an indecorum sit. Tibi si perpetua

[1] The title and text of this letter are transmitted by **V** *(Vat. lat. 3864, ff. 126r–27r). Citations from §§15, 16, and 19, as noted below, are assigned to Book 4 by Charisius and Arusianus.*

59 66M, 66Mc, 57D, 16K

In the battle between Lucullus and Tigranes, the cataphracts were posted in front of the right wing of the Armenian army (Plut. Luc. 27.7).

mail-clad cavalrymen who went in the vanguard, having a uniform appearance of iron

60 69M, 67Mc, 61D, 19K

Letter of Mithridates

In the winter of 69/68, after Lucullus crushed the vast forces of King Tigranes of Armenia in the battle near Tigranocerta (cf. §15), Mithridates writes to Phraates III, king of Parthia (whose dynastic name was Arsaces [XII]). His aim is to convince Arsaces that it is in the Parthians' self interest to join in the fight to drive the Romans out of Asia, since the Parthians are bound to be the next victim of Roman aggression. The picture that Mithridates paints grossly distorts the ultimate aims of Rome's foreign policy in that region. Like Pompey's dispatch (fr. 2.86), this letter serves as a substitute for a speech to provide variation, and once again, Thucydides may have provided a model: viz., the letter of appeal for succor written by the ostracized Athenian hero Themistocles to King Artaxerxes of Persia (Thuc. 1.137.4).

"King Mithridates sends greeting to King Arsaces. All persons who in time of prosperity are entreated to enter into an alliance for making war ought to consider whether they are in a position to maintain peace at that time; next, whether what is being asked of them is sufficiently righteous, safe, and honorable or, on the contrary, disgraceful.

359

pace frui licet,[2] nisi hostes opportuni et scelestissumi, egregia[3] fama, si Romanos oppresseris, futura est, neque petere audeam societatem et frustra mala mea cum bonis tuis misceri sperem. Atque ea quae te morari posse videntur, ira in Tigranem recentis belli et meae res parum[4] prosperae, si vera existumare voles, maxume hortabuntur. Ille enim obnoxius qualem tu voles societatem accipiet, mihi fortuna multis rebus ereptis usum dedit bene suadendi et, quod florentibus optabile est, ego non validissumus praebeo exemplum, quo rectius tua conponas.

"Namque Romanis cum nationibus, populis, regibus cunctis una et ea vetus causa bellandi est, cupido profunda imperi et divitiarum; qua primo cum rege Macedonum Philippo bellum sumpsere, dum a Carthaginiensibus premebantur amicitiam simulantes. Ei subvenientem Antiochum concessione Asiae per dolum avortere, ac mox fracto Philippo Antiochus omni cis Taurum agro et decem milibus talentorum spoliatus est. Persen deinde, Philippi filium, post multa et varia certamina apud Samothracas

---

---

1 Tigranes had been placed on the Armenian throne by the Parthians shortly after 100 but subsequently grew strong and invaded Parthian territory, inflicting serious losses (Plut. *Luc.* 21.4).

2 A euphemism for the loss of Mithridates' kingdom.

3 The Second Macedonian War (200–196), against Philip V.

4 Protracted diplomatic exchanges postponed an open clash between the Romans and Antiochus III, the Great, king of the Seleucid Empire in the Middle East, until after the conclusion of the war again Philip. By the Peace of Apamea in 188, Antiochus gave up claim to territories in Asia Minor north of the Taurus Mountains.

If you are in a position to enjoy uninterrupted peace, if [fr. 60]
you are not threatened by strategically placed and utterly
treacherous foes, not destined to have outstanding renown
if you crush the Romans, I would not venture to seek an
alliance with you, and I would hope in vain to unite my
own unfavorable circumstances with your favorable ones.
But those considerations which seem able to give you
pause, such as your anger against Tigranes in connection
with the recent war,[1] and my not very favorable circumstances[2]—if you are willing to make a true appraisal—
will be major incentives. For Tigranes, since he is at your
mercy, will accept an alliance on any terms you desire,
while so far as I am concerned, although Fortune has deprived me of much, she has bestowed upon me the means
of giving good advice; and being no longer at the height of
my power, I furnish a model for you to arrange your own
affairs more correctly, something that those enjoying prosperity should welcome.

"In fact, the Romans have one inveterate motive for
making war upon all peoples, nations, and kings: namely,
a deep-seated desire for dominion and for riches. For this
reason, they first undertook war with Philip, king of the
Macedonians,[3] though they put up a pretense of friendship as long as they were being hard pressed by the Carthaginians. When Antiochus came to Philip's aid, they
craftily diverted him from his purpose by the surrender of
Asia, and then, after Philip's power had been broken, Antiochus was robbed of all territory this side of the Taurus,
and of ten thousand talents.[4] Next Perseus, the son of
Philip, after many contests of varying results—after he

deos acceptum in fidem, callidi et repertores perfidiae,
8   quia pacto vitam dederant, insomniis occidere. Eumenen,
quoius amicitiam gloriose ostentant, initio prodidere Antiocho, pacis mercedem: post, habitum custodiae agri cap-
tivi, sumptibus et contumeliis ex rege miserrumum servorum effecere, simulatoque impio testamento filium eius
Aristonicum, quia patrium regnum petiverat, hostium
9   more per triumphum duxere. Asia ab ipsis obsessa est,
postremo Bithyniam Nicomede mortuo diripuere, quom
filius Nysa, quam reginam adpellaverat, genitus haud du-
bie esset.

10   "Nam quid ego me adpellem? Quem diiunctum undique regnis et tetrarchiis ab imperio eorum, quia fama
erat divitem neque serviturum esse, per Nicomedem bello
lacessiverunt, sceleris eorum haud ignarum et ea quae
accidere testatum antea Cretensis, solos omnium liberos
11   ea tempestate, et regem Ptolemaeum. Atque ego ultus

---

5 The island to which Perseus had fled after his defeat at Py-
dna in 168.

6 In 162, Perseus died in captivity at Alba Fucens in Italy,
after having been exhibited in the triumph of Aemilius Paulus.
His death is said to have resulted either from self-starvation or at
the hands of jailors who prevented him from sleeping (Plut. *Aem.*
37.2–3).

7 Eumenes II of Pergamum was given a share of Seleucid
territory taken from Antiochus in 188 (see n. above).

8 So called because in it Attalus III (d. 133), son of Eumenes
II (d. 158), bequeathed his kingdom to the Romans. Aristonicus,
an illegitimate(?) son of Eumenes II, led an unsuccessful revolt
aimed at preventing the Romans from taking control of the kingdom of Pergamum under the terms of Attalus' will and turning it
into the Roman province of Asia.

had surrendered on good faith, as witnessed by the gods [fr. 60]
of Samothrace[5]—was killed by those crafty inventors of
faithlessness from want of sleep, since they had granted
him his life according to a compact.[6] Eumenes, whose
friendship they boastfully exhibit, they at first betrayed to
Antiochus as the price of peace; later, having treated him
as serving the function of a custodian of captured territory,[7] they transformed him by means of imposts and in-
sults from a king into the most wretched of slaves. Then,
having concocted an unholy will,[8] they led his son Aristonicus in triumph like an enemy, because he had tried to
recover his father's kingdom. Asia was taken possession of
by them; lastly, on the death of Nicomedes,[9] they snatched
away Bithynia, although a son had unquestionably been
born of Nysa, whom Nicomedes had addressed as queen.

"Why should I name myself as an example? Although
I was separated from their dominion on every side by
kingdoms and petty monarchies, yet because word had
spread that I was rich and would not be a slave, they pro-
voked me to war through Nicomedes,[10] though I was by
no means unaware of their wickedness and had previously
called, as my witnesses to what happened, the Cretans—
the only ones truly free at that time—and king Ptolemy.[11]
But I took vengeance for the wrongs inflicted upon me;

9 In 75 (see fr. 2.57); like Attalus, Nicomedes IV left his kingdom by will to the Roman people.

10 In 89, Nicomedes IV was pressured by Rome's legate M.'
Aquillius (cos. 101), who had restored him to the Bithynian
throne, to raid Mithridates' neighboring kingdom, and this invasion precipitated the First Mithridatic War (89–85).

11 Ptolemy IX, ruler of Egypt from 88 until his death, in 80.

iniurias Nicomedem Bithynia expuli Asiamque spolium
regis Antiochi recepi et Graeciae dempsi grave servitium.
12 Incepta mea postremus servorum Archelaus exercitu pro-
dito inpedivit, illique, quos ignavia aut prava calliditas, ut
meis laboribus tuti essent, armis abstinuit, acerbissumas
poenas solvunt, Ptolemaeus pretio in dies bellum prola-
tans, Cretenses impugnati semel iam neque finem nisi
13 excidio habituri.[5] Equidem quom mihi ob ipsorum interna
mala dilata proelia magis quam pacem datam intellege-
rem, abnuente Tigrane, qui mea dicta sero probat, te remoto procul, omnibus aliis obnoxiis, rursus tamen bellum
coepi Marcumque Cottam, Romanum ducem, apud Cal-
14 chedona terra fudi, mari exui classe pulcherruma. Apud
Cyzicum magno cum exercitu in obsidio moranti frumentum defuit, nullo circum adnitente; simul hiems mari prohibebat. Ita, sine vi hostium regredi conatus in patrium

---

[5] *Manutius (ed. Ald. 1509)*: habitur V

---

[12] In 88, Mithridates overran the province of Asia and ordered
a general massacre of all Romans and Italians living in the territory.

[13] Cf. §6.

[14] In 88–87, Mithridates' army under the Greek general
Archelaus (see next n.) overran most of central Greece.

[15] In 86, Archelaus was defeated by Sulla in two separate
battles in Greece and was authorized by Mithridates to work out
the peace agreement ending the First Mithridatic War in 85.
Later, in 83, Archelaus went over to the Roman side when he fell
out with Mithridates.

[16] Ptolemy XII Auletes, who came to power in 80 and relied
heavily on support from the Romans, which he purchased with
bribes, to maintain his position.

I drove Nicomedes from Bithynia, recovered Asia,[12] the [fr. 60]
spoil taken from king Antiochus,[13] and lifted oppressive
servitude from Greece.[14] My undertakings were frustrated by Archelaus, basest of slaves, who betrayed my
army;[15] and those whom cowardice or perverse cunning
kept from taking up arms in order to remain safe while I
did all the work, are paying most grievous penalties: Ptolemy is averting hostilities from day to day by the payment
of money,[16] while the Cretans, now that they have already
been attacked once, will have no end of war except by their
annihilation.[17] As for myself, when I realized that it was
more a postponement of the struggle than a genuine peace
that had been offered to me on account of the Romans'
own domestic troubles[18]—though Tigranes refused to join
with me (he belatedly endorses what I said at the time),
though you were far removed from me, and all the rest
had submitted—I nevertheless commenced war anew[19]
and routed Marcus Cotta, the Roman general, on land at
Chalcedon; on the sea, I stripped him of a fine fleet. While
at Cyzicus with a large army, mired in a siege, I ran short
of grain; no one in the neighborhood gave support; at the
same time, winter cut me off the sea. When I, therefore,

[17] First attacked by M. Antonius (pr. 74) in his campaign
against the pirates, Crete was reduced to a Roman province in 66
and attached to Cyrene at the conclusion of further campaigns
against the pirates carried out by Q. Metellus (cos. 69) in 68–67.

[18] The Peace of Dardanus, which ended the First Mithridatic
War in 85, was negotiated at a time when Sulla was preparing to
invade Italy and drive out his political enemies, who, led by L.
Cinna (cos., 87, 86, 85, 84), had seized power in his absence and
declared him an outlaw.

[19] In 74.

regnum, naufragiis apud Parium et Heracleam militum
15 optumos cum classibus amisi. Restituto deinde apud Ca-
beram[6] exercitu et variis inter me atque Lucullum proeliis,
inopia rursus ambos incessit;[7] illi suberat regnum Ariobarzanis bello intactum, ego vastis circum omnibus locis, in
Armeniam concessi; secutique Romani non me, sed morem suum omnia regna subvortundi, quia multitudinem
artis locis pugna prohibuere, inprudentiam Tigranis pro
victoria ostentant.

16 "Nunc, quaeso, considera nobis oppressis utrum fir-
miorem te ad resistundum, an finem belli futurum putes.
Scio equidem tibi magnas opes virorum armorum et auri
esse; et ea re a nobis ad societatem, ab illis ad praedam
peteris. Ceterum consilium est, Tigranis regno integro,
meis militibus ‹belli prudentibus›,[8] procul ab domo, parvo
labore[9] per nostra corpora bellum conficere,[10] quom[11]

---

[6] Cabera *Cortius*: Cabira *ed. Ven. 1560* [τὰ Κάβειρα]
[7] inter . . . incessit] *Charis. GL 1.119.11 = p. 152B.27–28*
[8] *Charis.: om. V*   [9] parvo labore] *om. Charis.*   [10] scio
equidem . . . conficere] *Charis. GL 1.196.18–22 = p. 255B.21–25*
[11] quō V: quo[m] *Gerlach ed. min.*: quoniam *Reynolds (sed alibi
in V, semper* quoniam, *numquam abbrev.* quoniā: *Hauler 1895,
p. 141)*

---

[20] Actually, M. Cotta's consular colleague L. Lucullus forced
Mithridates to lift the siege of Cyzicus in the winter of 73/72.
[21] Towns on the south shore of the Propontis (Sea of Mar-
mora) and Black Sea, respectively.
[22] Near Cabira, an inland stronghold in Pontus, Lucullus defeated Mithridates in late 71, causing him to flee for safety to
Armenia.

without compulsion from the enemy,[20] attempted to re- [fr. 60]
turn into my ancestral kingdom, I lost, by shipwrecks at
Parium and at Heraclea, my best soldiers together with
the fleets.[21] Then when I had reconstituted my army at
Cabira and done battle with Lucullus with varying success,
scarcity once more befell us both.[22] He had at his disposal
the kingdom of Ariobarzanes,[23] unravaged by war, while I,
since all the country round about had been devastated,
withdrew into Armenia. And the Romans, pursuing not
me but rather their custom of overthrowing all monarchies, hold up Tigranes' lack of judgment as if it were a
victory because they kept Tigranes' massive forces out of
the fight by means of the narrowness of the terrain.[24]

"Do consider now, please, whether you think that when
we have been crushed you will be in a stronger position to
put up resistance, or that there will be an end of war. Indeed I know that you have great stocks of men, of arms
and of gold; and it is for that reason that you are being
targeted by us with a view to an alliance, by the Romans
with a view to spoils. Yet my advice is, while the kingdom
of Tigranes is intact, and while I still have soldiers skilled
in war, to finish the war far from your homes and with
little labor, using our bodies, since we cannot conquer or

[23] Cappadocia, a client kingdom, where Sulla, when governor
of Cilicia in the mid 90's, had reinstated Ariobarzanes to the
throne.

[24] In 69, near the major city of Tigranocerta. Despite a warning from Mithridates (App. *Mith.* 85), Tigranes, relying upon his
vast hordes, risked a battle with Lucullus on unfavorable terrain.

17 neque vincere neque vinci sine tuo periculo possumus. An
ignoras Romanos, postquam ad occidentem pergentibus
finem Oceanus fecit, arma huc convortisse? Neque quicquam a principio nisi raptum[12] habere, domum, coniuges,
agros, imperium? Convenas olim sine patria, parentibus,
pesti[13] conditos orbis terrarum,[14] quibus non humana ulla
neque divina obstant quin socios amicos, procul iuxta si-
tos, inopes potentisque trahant excindant, omniaque non
serva et maxume regna hostilia ducant.

18   "Namque pauci libertatem, pars magna iustos dominos
volunt, nos suspecti sumus aemuli et in tempore vindices
19 adfuturi. Tu vero, quoi Seleucea, maxuma urbium, reg-
numque Persidis inclutis divitiis est, quid ab illis nisi do-
20 lum in praesens et postea bellum expectas?[15] Romani
arma in omnis habent, acerruma in eos, quibus victis spolia maxuma; audendo et fallundo et bella ex bellis serundo
21 magni facti. Per hunc morem extinguent omnia, aut occi-
dent—quod haud difficile est—si tu Mesopotamia, nos

---

[12] *Ciacconius*: partum V   [13] *Douza*: peste V
[14] pesti (pestem *codd. AS Serv.*: perte *rell.*) . . . terrarum] *Serv.
ad Aen.* 7.303   [15] quid . . . exspectas (exspectans *codd.
Arus.*)] *Arus. GL* 7.487.6 = *p. 179DC*

---

[25] In the former case, the Parthians will have to risk making
the Romans their enemies by supporting Mithridates in order to
insure his victory; in the later case (if they do nothing and Mithridates succumbs to the Romans), the Parthians will be the next
victim of Roman aggression.

[26] The text is uncertain. If *peste,* the reading of V is retained;
the meaning is "they have been formed from the scum of the
earth."

be conquered without danger to you.[25] Or are you not   [fr. 60]
aware that the Romans turned their arms in this direction
only after Ocean put an end to their westward progress?
That from the beginning they have possessed nothing except what they have stolen: their homes, wives, lands, and
dominion? That having been once upon a time refugees
without a native land or parents, they have been established to serve as a plague upon the whole world,[26] being
men who are prevented by nothing human or divine from
plundering and destroying allies and friends—those situated far away or nearby, weak and powerful too—and from
considering as their enemies all powers not subservient to
them and especially monarchies,.

"For in fact, while few men want freedom, a great many
want fair-minded masters; we have fallen under suspicion as rivals to the Romans and as, in due course, aveng-
ers to be. But you, who possess the magnificent city of
Seleucea[27] and the kingdom of Persia with its renowned
riches, what do you expect from them other than guile for
the present and war in the future?[28] The Romans have
weapons against all men, the sharpest against those from
whom conquest yields the greatest spoils; they have grown
mighty by audacity and deceit and by sowing wars from
wars. In keeping with this custom, they will destroy everything, or they will perish in the attempt—a thing that is by
no means difficult to bring about—if you from Mesopota-

---

[27] On the west bank of the Tigris, wrested from the Seleucid
Empire by the Parthians in 141.

[28] In 54, M. Crassus embarked on a war of aggression against
the Parthians, which ended in the disastrous defeat of the Romans at Carrhae in 53.

Armenia circumgredimur exercitum sine frumento, sine
22 auxiliis, fortuna aut nostris vitiis adhuc incolumem. Teque
illa fama sequetur, auxilio profectum magnis regibus la-
23 trones gentium oppressisse. Quod uti facias moneo hortorque, neu malis pernicie nostra tuam prolatare quam
societate victor fieri."

LUCULLUS' MARCH INTO ARMENIA
(mid 69–68), FRR. 61–70

61* 71M, 68Mc, 5.9D, 5.11K

Lucullus pecuniam Quintio dedit ne sibi[1] succederetur.

Schol. Gronov. ad Cic. *De imp. Cn. Pomp.* 28 (p. 320St.17–18):
quoting S. to explicate Cicero's comment on political figures who
coveted (*concupiverunt*) provincial assignments.

[1] *scripsi*: illi *cod.*

62††† 70M, 69Mc, 5.6D, 4.8K

imperi prolatandi percupidus habebatur, cetera
egregius

Arus. GL 7.470.19–20 = p. 122DC (mistakenly assigned to *Jug.*):
to illustrate *egregius* + acc. [of respect].

63* 5.10M, 4.70Mc, 5.5D, 5.10K

Σαλούστιος μὲν οὖν φησι χαλιπῶς διστεθῆναι τοὺς
στρατιώτας πρὸς αὐτὸν εὐθὺς ἐν ἀρχῇ τοῦ πολέμου

mia and we from Armenia surround their army, which is without grain, without reinforcements, and intact up until now only thanks to good luck or our own shortcomings. In the course of having set out to aid great kings, you will attain the fame of having crushed the robbers of nations. I warn and urge you to do this and not to prefer merely to postpone your own ruin at the expense of ours rather than to be the victor by means of an alliance."

LUCULLUS' MARCH INTO ARMENIA
(mid 69–68), FRR. 61–70

61* 71M, 68Mc, 5.9D, 5.11K

L. Quinctius (tribune of the plebs 74, cf. fr. 3.15.11) as praetor in 68 played a leading role in having Lucullus' province of Cilicia reassigned to Q. Marcius Rex (cos. 68): Plut. Luc. 33.6. The bribery reported by S., if it took place, presumably occurred in 69, before Quinctius entered office.

Lucullus gave Quin(c)tius money so as not to be replaced by a successor.

62††† 70M, 69Mc, 5.6D, 4.8K

Possibly the same context as fr. 61 and included in S.'s character sketch of Lucullus.

he was regarded as very desirous of prolonging his command, but outstanding in other respects

63* 5.10M, 4.70Mc, 5.5D, 5.10K

Possibly the same context as frr. 61–62.

*Sallust states that **Lucullus' soldiers were ill-disposed toward him right from the beginning of the war, when***

371

πρὸς Κυζίκῳ καὶ πάλιν πρὸς Ἀμίσῳ, δύο χιεμῶνας
ἐξῆς ἐν χάρακι διαγαγεῖν ἀναγκασθέντας.

Plut. *Luc.* 33.3.

64* 72M, 71Mc, 60D, 18K

Apud Gorduenos amomum et alii leves odores gignuntur.

Schol. Vatic. ad Verg. G. 4.49: to give an example of a contrasting
expression to *odor gravis* (a pungent/strong scent).

65 74M, 72Mc, 62D, 20K

> Tum vero[1] Bithynii propinquantes iam amnem Ar-
> saniam[2]

Arus. *GL* 7.500.27–28 = p. 231DC: to illustrate *propinquare* +
acc. of place.

[1] *Dietsch*: utro *codd.*   [2] *Diestch*: Tartanium *codd.*

66 76M, 73Mc, 44D, 2K

Simul eos et cunctos iam inclinatos laxitate[1] loci plures
cohortes atque omnes, ut in secunda re, pariter acres[2]
invadunt.

Non. p. 132M = 192.21–23: to illustrate *laxitas.*

[1] *Mercier*: laxitas et *codd.*   [2] *Mercier*: acre *codd.*

*stationed before Cyzicus and again before Amisus,
since they were compelled to spend two consecutive
winters in camp.*

64* 72M, 71Mc, 60D, 18K

*In the winter of 69/68 Lucullus visited Gordyene, a region of Armenia (present-day Kurdistan) south of Tigranocerta (Plut. Luc.
29.9; Dio 36.2.3–5).*

In the land of the Gordyenes, amonum and other pleasant-
scented plants grow.

65 74M, 72Mc, 62D, 20K

*Lucullus defeated Tigranes in a series of battles fought in 68,
and then moved against Tigranes' capital, Artaxata, crossing the
Arsanias/mod. Murat (Plut. Luc. 31.5–6), a river in western Armenia that rises near Mt. Ararat and is a principal source of the
Euphrates.*

Then indeed the Bithynians,[1] now approaching the
river Arsanias

[1] Possibly a contingent of native troops reinforcing Lucullus'
army.

66 76M, 73Mc, 44D, 2K

*Possibly the same context as fr. 65, since the spaciousness of the
battlefield does not suit the locales of the other two chief scenes of
Lucullus' victories in Book 4 (over Mithridates at Cabira or over
Tigranes near Trigranocerta).*

More cohorts and all equally ferocious, as to be expected
in favorable circumstances, attack both those troops [the
first ones to be routed?] and the whole throng now that
they wavered as a result of the spaciousness of the locale.

67 73M, 77Mc, 71D, 74K

Inpotens et nimius animi est.

Arus. *GL* 7.495.17 = p. 209DC: to illustrate *nimius* + gen. [For comparable instances of *animi* in the *Historiae,* see fr. 1.136.]

68* 77M, 74Mc, 52D, 11K

*Sallustius autem, auctor certissimus, asserit **Tigrim et Euphratem** uno **fonte manare in Armenia**, qui per diversa euntes longius dividuntur spatio medio relicto multorum milium; sed terra quae ab ipsis ambitur Mesopotamia dicitur.*

Isid. *Etym.* 13.21.10.

{Hieron. *Sit. et nom.* p. 150.12–13 (*Sallustius . . . asserit tam Tigris quam Eufratis in Armenia fontes demonstrari*).}

69* 78M, 75Mc, 53D, 12K

Mesopotameni homines effrenatae libidinis *sunt in **utroque sexu**; Sallustius meminit.*

Schol. in Iuv. ad 1.104.

70 79M, 76Mc, 64D, 65K

67 73M, 77Mc, 71D, 74K

After his victory over Tigranes, early winter weather and a mu-
tiny of Lucullus' troops compelled him to abandon his goal of
capturing Artaxata; he turned back and returned to Mesopotamia
(Plut. Luc. 32.4). The following description may come from the
criticism of Lucullus by his discontented soldiers.

He is headstrong and too high-spirited.

68* 77M, 74Mc, 52D, 11K

Lucullus' return to Mesopotamia (see previous fragment) may
have provided the context for S. to give a description of the region.

Moreover, Sallust, a most reliable authority, claims that
the Tigris and Euphrates flow from a *single* **source in**
Armenia;[1] *those rivers flowing through separate regions*
are quite widely parted by a space of many miles left in the
middle; the land that is encircled by them is called Meso-
potamia.

[1] So the text of Isidore, whereas the version of Jerome states
"that the source of the Tigiris, as well as that of the Euphrates, is
pointed out in Armenia."

69* 78M, 75Mc, 53D, 12K

Same context as fr. 68.

The **people of Mesopotamia** *are of* **unbridled lust in the**
case of both sexes. *Sallust relates this.*

70 79M, 76Mc, 64D, 65K

After his return to Mesopotamia (see fr. 67), Lucullus moved in
the late summer of 68 against the city of Nisibis, which was being

clausi lateribus altis pedem

Arus. *GL* 7.456.10 = p. 71DC: to illustrate *altus* + *tot pedes*.

URBAN AFFAIRS (68 BC), FR 71

71 81M, 78Mc, 36D, 61K

Sestertium tricies pepigit a C. Pisone.

Arus. *GL* 7.498.10–11 = p. 221DC: to illustrate *paciscor* (to strike a bargain) over something (acc.) with someone (*a* + abl.).

FRAGMENTS OF UNCERTAIN CONTEXT IN BOOK 4, FRR. 72–77

Assigned to Various Contexts by Maurenbr., frr. 72–73

72 3M, 49Mc, 41D, 49K

demissis partem quasi tertiam antemnis

Arus. *GL* 7.499.24 = p. 227DC: to illustrate *partem* + *demissus* (*corr. Lindemann*: dimissus *N1*).

held by Tigranes' brother Guras (Plut. Luc. 32.5; Dio 36.6.1–3).
The phrase below may describe some feature of the city's elaborate
fortifications, whose walls were made of brick and immense in size
(Dio 36.6.3).

enclosed by bricks[1] a foot high

[1] Or "sides" (so McGushin), another possible meaning of *lat-*
eribus, but this gives a less satisfactory sense. Here *lateribus* is
best interpreted as abl. pl. of *later* (m.) "brick" (so Frassinetti; cf.
fr. 3.30, *ex latere*).

URBAN AFFAIRS (68 BC), FR 71

71 81M, 78Mc, 36D, 61K

In 68, the consul-elect C. Piso escaped prosecution for corrupt
electioneering (ambitus) *by paying vast bribes to buy off his*
accuser(s) (Dio 36.38.3).

He settled with Gaius Piso on a sum of 3 million sesterces.

FRAGMENTS OF UNCERTAIN
CONTEXT IN BOOK 4, FRR. 72–77

Assigned to Various Contexts by Maurenbr.,
frr. 72–73

72 3M, 49Mc, 41D, 49K

A naval maneuver carried out prior to entering battle (cf. [Caes.]
B Alex. 45.2–3) or to reduce speed in the face of strengthening
gales (cf. Sen. Ep. 77.2).

with the yardarms lowered about a third of the way

73 68M, 79Mc, 72D, 75K

anxius animi atque incertus

Arus. *GL* 7.456.11 = p. 71DC: to illustrate *anxius* + gen. of thing. [For comparable instances of *animi* in the *Historiae,* see fr. 1.136.]

Miscellaneous, frr. 74–77

74 82M, 80Mc, 66D, 67K

qui proxumi locos[1] hostium errant[2]

Arus. *GL* 7.498.19 = p. 222DC: to illustrate *proximus* + acc.

[1] loca *G, Lindemann*   [2] erant *GP*

75 83M, 81Mc, 67D, 68K

stolide castra subgressus

Arus. *GL* 7.510.6 = p. 266DC: to illustrate *subgredior* + acc. of place.

76 84M, 82Mc, 73D, 76K

consili aeger

Arus. *GL* 7.453.1 = p. 57DC: to illustrate *aeger* + gen.

73 68M, 79Mc, 72D, 75K

Possibly a description of Tigranes, who suffered dejection after his defeat by Lucullus near Tigranocerta in October 69 (Plut. Luc. 29.2); so Maurenbr. It might equally well, however, describe Mithridates after his defeat at Cabira in summer 71 (so McGushin).

uneasy in his mind and unsure

Miscellaneous, frr. 74–77

74 82M, 80Mc, 66D, 67K

(those) who were wandering closest to the enemy's positions

75 83M, 81Mc, 67D, 68K

having foolishly come close up to the camp

76 84M, 82Mc, 73D, 76K

unsound in counsel

77 85M, 83Mc, 74D, 77K

ne inrumpendi[1] p‹ontis›[2] ... [*desunt c. 15 litt.*][3] ...
sublicibus cavata ... [*desunt c. 17 litt.*] ... ‹es›sent[4]

Festus p. 293M = 376L.3–5 (*Sallustius libro qua‹rto›*): part of a
lacunose passage concerning the pons Sublicius in Rome.

[1] *Ursinus*: inrumiendi *codd.*
[2] *Ursinus*
[3] ‹vis flumini esset› *Maurenbr. in app.*
[4] *Ursinus*

77 85M, 83Mc, 74D, 77K

Possibly from a description of a flood of the Tiber (such as the one described by Dio 37.58.3), included in urban affairs of 69 or 68. Text is very poorly preserved. See textual notes.

so that ⟨the river might not have the force[1]⟩ to smash the bridge . . . had been hollowed out with wooden supports

[1] Translating the tentative supplement of Maurenbr.

BOOK 5

OUTLINE

LIBER V

CONCLUSION OF THE WAR WAGED BY LUCULLUS (68 [autumn]–67 BC), FRR. 1–14

1* 1M, 1Mc, inc. 46D, inc.12K

Repente incautos agros invasit.

Schol. Vatic. ad Verg. *G.* 3.469: to illustrate the adj. *incautus* meaning "undefended, vulnerable."

2* 2M, 2Mc, inc. 25D, 3.72K

Simul inmanis hominum vis multis e locis invasere patentis tum et pacis modo effusas ⟨urbis⟩.[1]

Serv. auct. ad *Aen.* 1.298: cited as evidence that at *Aen.* 1.298 *pateant* (= lit., "stand open [to greet]") can mean "peaceful."

[1] *Dietsch*

BOOK 5

CONCLUSION OF THE WAR WAGED BY LUCULLUS (68 [autumn]–67 BC), FRR. 1–14

1* 1M, 1Mc, inc. 46D, inc. 12K

Because of its close resemblance to Dio's description of a surprise attack on the Romans while they wandered the countryside (36.9.1; cf. App. Mith. 88), this fragment may describe Mithridates' sudden incursion into his former kingdom of Pontus in the autumn of 68 by way of Lesser Armenia, while Lucullus was engaged in the siege of Nisibis (so Maurenbr.). Alternatively, since this fragment is not assigned to a specific book, it could conceivably concern a raid by Spartacus in the Servile War (73–71): so Gerlach (3.71), and La Penna (1963), 47.

Suddenly he invaded undefended territory.

2* 2M, 2Mc, inc. 25D, 3.72K

Same context as fr. 1.

A huge force of men from many locales simultaneously attacked ‹cities› that were then standing open and, after the fashion of peacetime, were off guard.

3* 3M, 3Mc, 1D, 1K

Adeo illis ingenita est sanctitas regii nominis.[1]

Serv. ad *G.* 4.211; *Schol. Bern.* and *Schol. Vatic.* ad loc. cit.: quoted to describe the inhabitants of Media.

[1] regi nominis *M Serv.*: regi in omnibus *AH Serv.*: religionis *Schol. Vatic.*

4* 4M, 4Mc, inc. 31D, 5.5K

et in proeliis actu promptus

Donat. ad Ter. *Eun.* 783: commenting on the duty of an *imperator* not to expose himself to danger.

5 5M, 5Mc, 3D, 4K

peractis LXX annis armatus equom insilire

Arus. *GL* 7.488.16–17= p. 183DC: to illustrate *insilire* + acc. of thing.

6* 6M, 6Mc, 2D, 2K

luxo pede

Prob. *GL* 4.31.16; Sacerd. *GL* 6.482.22: mistakenly crediting S. with treating the fourth decl. noun *luxus* (luxury) as if it belonged to the second decl., when, in fact, *luxo* in S. is the adj. *luxus, -a, -um* (dislocated, sprained).

3* 3M, 3Mc, 1D, 1K

Since the three scholiasts who preserve this fragment state that S. was describing the inhabitants of Media (mod. Azerbaijan), it may belong to the same context as fr. 1 and refer to the former subjects of Mithridates who reverted to loyalty to him out of respect for his hereditary title as king (Dio 36.9.2).

To such an extent was the sacrosanctity of the title king ingrained in those people.

4* 4M, 4Mc, inc. 31D, 5.5K

Possibly the same context as fr. 1. The comment made by the scholiast who preserves this fragment suggests that these words may have formed part of S.'s description of the battle in which Mithridates was wounded (Dio 36.9.5).

and quick to action in battles

5 5M, 5Mc, 3D, 4K

Possibly the same context as fr. 1, since Dio (36.9.5) mentions the fact that Mithridates took a direct role in battle, even though he was more than seventy years of age.

though over seventy ⟨he was accustomed/able?⟩ when fully armed to spring up onto his horse

6* 6M, 6Mc, 2D, 2K

Possibly a reference to the wound suffered by Mithridates in a battle with Lucullus' legate Fabius Hadrianus in late 68, although that wound, caused by a stone, is said to have injured Mithridates' knee, not his foot (App. Mith. 88; cf. Dio 36.9.6).

with a dislocated foot

7* 7M, 7Mc, inc. 30D, 5.3K

Prohibebit[1] nocere venenum, quod tibi datur.

Dub. nom. GL 5.593.15–16.: to illustrate that the gender of the noun *venenum* is neuter.

[1] *M*: prohibet *V*

8* 9M, 8Mc, 8D, 8K

ceteri negotia sequebantur[1] familiaria legatorum aut tribunorum, et[2] pars sua commeatibus mercatis

Non. p. 138M = 201L.8–9: to illustrate the pf. particip. *mercatis* standing for the present *mercantibus*.

[1] exequebantur *Dietsch (sed cf. fr. 3.104,* sequi = exsequi*)*
[2] *del. Diestch*

9 11M, 9Mc, 7D, 9K

quod[1] uxori eius frater erat

Arus. *GL* 7.474.10 = p. 135DC: to illustrate *frater* + dat.

[1] qui *(corr. ex et) V1 A, Keil*

10* 12M, 10Mc, inc. 77D, inc. 43K

ex[1] insolentia avidus male faciundi

Serv. ad *Aen.* 9.341: to illustrate the indiscrimate slaughter carried out by Euryalus, an inexperienced soldier, in contrast with his seasoned companion Nisus, who killed chieftains during their night raid.

[1] *F*: et *rell.*

7* 7M, 7Mc, inc. 30D, 5.3K

The wound suffered by Mithridates (fr. 6) was healed by a Scythian physician, who applied the poison of a serpent (App. Mithr. 88). The fragment below may be part of the healer's words to Mithridates.

It [an antidote?] will prevent the poison that is being given to you from doing harm.

8* 9M, 8Mc, 8D, 8K

Possibly describing the breakdown of discipline in Lucullus' army, especially among the Valerians, after the capture of Nisibis and the winter (of 68/67) spent there in luxury (Dio 36.14.3).

the rest were looking after the domestic affairs of the legates or the tribunes, and part their own, selling the army's supplies

9 11M, 9Mc, 7D, 9K

P. Clodius Pulcher, the brother of Lucullus' wife, fomented a mutiny in Lucullus' army during its stay at Nisibis, winter 68/67 (Plut. Luc. 34.1–5; Dio 36.14.4, 17.2).

because he was his wife's brother

10* 12M, 10Mc, inc. 77D, inc. 43K

Same context as fr. 9. Dio (36.14.4) credits Clodius with inborn zeal for stirring up revolution.

eager for misconduct owing to his arrogance

11 13M, 11Mc, 10D, 14K

legiones Valerianae, conperto lege Gabinia Bithyniam et Pontum consuli datam, sese[1] missos esse

Prisc. *GL* 3.225.17–19, quoting fr. 12 and this fragment: to illustrate an inf. (with subj. acc.) depending on a word in the abl.
(absol.).

[1] *Dousa*: esse *codd.*

12 14M, 12Mc, 11D, 12K

At Lucullus, audito[1] Q. Marcium Regem pro consule per
Lycaoniam cum tribus legionibus ad[2] Ciliciam tendere

Prisc. *GL* 3.225.15–17: see fr. 11.

[1] auditoq(ue) *MDSLn*   [2] *R*: in *rell.*

13 15M, 13Mc, 12D, 13K

sed ubi ille militum voluntatem causatus

Arus. *GL* 7.489.16–17 = p. 187DC: to illustrate *causatus* [ppp. of
depon. verb *causor* = "to plead as an excuse"] + acc.

11 13M, 11Mc, 10D, 14K

News of the reassignment of Lucullus' command caused the Valerians to hold Lucullus in contempt (Dio 36.14.4).

the Valerian legions, after it was learned that Bithynia and Pontus had been assigned by Gabinius' law to the consul[1] and that they had been discharged

[1] M'. Acilius Glabrio (cos. 67), by the *lex Gabinia de provinciis consularibus* (or *de bello Mithridatico*), not to be confused with Gabinius' law assigning Pompey the command to clear the seas of pirates.

12 14M, 12Mc, 11D, 12K

News of the reassignment of Lucullus' command caused his army to refuse further fighting against Mithridates and Tigranes. The troops who remained under arms (after the Valerians accepted their discharge: see fr. 11) withdrew to Cappadocia (Dio 36.15.1–3).

But Lucullus, having heard that the proconsul Q. Marcius Rex was making his way with three legions through Lycaonia toward Cilicia

13 15M, 13Mc, 12D, 13K

Q. Marcius Rex (cos. 68), who had replaced Lucullus as governor of Cilicia, made excuses for refusing to come to Lucullus' aid in the neighboring region of Cappadocia (Dio 36.17.2).

but when he, alleging as his reason [for not coming to Lucullus' aid?] the will of his soldiers

14 16M, 14Mc, 4D, 7K

regem avorsabatur

Arus. *GL* 7.456.24 = p. 73DC: to illustrate the depon. verb *aversor* (to turn away from a person in horror or disgust) + acc.

WAR AGAINST THE PIRATES, FRR. 15–20

15* 18M, 15Mc, inc. 74D, inc. 40K

Ostia exitus fluminum in mare neutro genere semper pluraliter dicuntur. Sed si urbem significare voles, singularem potius numerum observabis, quamvis Sallustius frequenter etiam plurali numero urbem significet.

Charis. *GL* 1.98.14–16 = p. 125B.6–10

16 20M, 16Mc, 13D, 16K

14 16M, 14Mc, 4D, 7K

Maurenbr. speculates that this fragment may refer to Menemachus, a courtier of Tigranes who deserted the king and received sanctuary from Q. Marcius Rex in Cilicia (Dio 36.17.2).

he was recoiling from the king

WAR AGAINST THE PIRATES, FRR. 15–20

15* 18M, 15Mc, inc. 74D, inc. 40K

As part of the background information supplied to justify assigning to Pompey an extraordinary command against the pirates, S. may have recounted the shockingly bold raid carried out by pirates on Ostia, the port of Rome (Cic. De imp. Cn. Pomp. *33; Dio 36.22.2).*

The outlets of rivers into the sea, "ostia," are always expressed in the neuter plural. But if you want to indicate the city, you will be careful to use rather the singular, although S. frequently indicates the city even with the plural.[1]

[1] The more common form is the first decl. *Ostia, –ae* (f.).

16 20M, 16Mc, 13D, 16K

Conceivably Pompey was credited with making this remark in the context of the debate over Gabinius' proposal to authorize an extraordinary command against the pirates (so Maurenbr.). The reflexive sibi *reveals that these words, which take the form of an indirect statement, are to be attributed to Pompey.*

quibus de causis Sullam [in victoria][1] dictatorem
uni sibi descendere equo,[2] adsurgere sella,[3] caput
aperire solitum

Non. p. 236M = 352–53L.18–19: to illustrate *apertum* meaning
nudatum (bare).

{Arus. *GL* 7.454.29–30 = p. 65DC (*Sullam . . . solitum*): to illustrate the dat. (of person honored) with *adsurgo*. Non. p. 397M
= 638L.15–16 (*sella surgere, caput aperire solitum*): to illustrate
surgere meaning "to get up." Serv. & Serv. auct. ad *Aen.* 1.107
and 3.206 (*caput aperire solitus* [sic]), "to bare one's head."}

Both citations in Non. are assigned to Book 5.

[1] *del. Kritz ut dittographiam vocis* dictatorem: *om. Arus.*: victorem ac dictatorem *Madvig*   [2] descendere equo] *Arus.*:
equo descendere *Non. p. 236M*   [3] adsurgere sella] *Arus.*
(*cf. Val. Max. 5.2.9,* sella adsurrexit): surgere de sella *Non.
p. 236M*: sella surgere *Non. p. 397M*

17 21M, 17Mc, 14D, 17K

spe⟨ciem et⟩ celebritate⟨m⟩[1] nominis intellego ti-
mentem

Prisc. *GL* 3.225.20–226.1, quoting this fragment and fr. 18: to
illustrate the substitution of a participle in the acc., in place of an
inf., after a verb introducing indirect discourse.

[1] *Maurenbr.*: spe celebritate *codd.*: super celebritate *Hertz
dubitanter in app.*

18 22M, 18Mc, 15D, 18K

for which reasons, for him alone [Pompey] the dictator Sulla was accustomed to dismount from his horse, rise from his official chair, and bare his head

17 21M, 17Mc, 14D, 17K

The speaker may be Gabinius (cf. his speech in Dio 36.27–29), and the person referred to as experiencing fear may be Pompey, who feigns reluctance to assume the burden of such a great command.

I understand his fearing the splendor and renown attached to the title [of commander in chief of such a mighty force?]

18 22M, 18Mc, 15D, 18K

Same context, possibly, as fr. 17, a speech of Gabinius in support of his piracy bill. The person accused of seeking bribes will be an opponent, such as the tribune of the plebs Trebellius, who tried to block the measure with his veto (Ascon. p. 72C).

Video ingentia[1] dona quaesitum[2] properantem.

Prisc. *GL* 3.226.1–2: see fr. 17.

[1] *DOSL (N corr.)*: ingentem *R*: indigentia *M*: indigentem *Hertz* [2] *Krehl*: quaesiturum *S*: –uram *L*: –ura *NRMOD*

19* 23M, 19Mc, inc. 33D, 5.19K

sane bonus ea tempestate contra pericula et ambi-
tionem

Serv. auct. ad *Aen.* 1.195: to illustrate *bonus = fortis.*

20 24M, 20Mc, 16D, 20K

Nam si in Pompeio quid humani evenisset,

Arus. *GL* 7.470.25–26 = p. 123DC: to illustrate *evenire* with *in*
+ abl.

I see him scurrying to seek huge[1] bribes.

[1] Or, reading *indigentem:* "I see the <u>needy</u> fellow scurrying to seek bribes."

19* 23M, 19Mc, inc. 33D, 5.19K

Possibly describing one of the leading senatorial opponents of Gabinius' bill, Q. Catulus (cos. 78): cf. Dio 36.30.4–36.

at that time, truly stalwart in standing up to the dangers [resulting from incurring the wrath of the people in opposing the bill?] and the ambition [of Pompey?]

20 24M, 20Mc, 16D, 20K

In opposing the bill, Q. Catulus (cf. fr. 19) pointed out that it was risky to rely so heavily upon a single man, Pompey, since, if he were to be killed on the mission, the Roman people would be hard-pressed to replace him with another (Cic. De imp. Cn. Pomp. 59; Vell. 2.31.1; Val. Max. 8.15.9; Dio 36.36a).

For if anything such as can befall mortals[1] should happen in the case of Pompey,

[1] A common euphemism for death (cf. Enn. *Ann.* 125V; Cic. *Phil.* 1.10).

FRAGMENTA INCERTAE
SEDIS

WAR AND MILITARY AFFAIRS,
FRR. 1–25

1* 1.27M, inc. 5Mc, inc. 67D, inc. 33K

exercitum argento fecit

Sen. *Ep.* 114.17: inspired by this expression in S., where *facere* = *parare,* the historian L. Arruntius overused *facere* in various contexts.

2* 1.83M (Serv. auct.), inc. 12Mc, 2.10D (Serv. auct.), 2.15K (Serv. auct.)

1 . . . . | [. . . .] *guber*[. . . .] | [. . . . ..]*e*[. . . . . . .] | [
 . . ±6 . .] ar . . [. . . . ⟨re|f⟩ertus ir⟨a⟩e et doloris in| talibus
2 sociis amissis. Ar|mati navibus e[i]volant[1] | ⟨s⟩caphis aut

Pap Ryl III 473, recto[A] (*r⟨ef⟩ertus . . . in Hispaniam*) = lines 4–18 of a column ca. 20 lines long and ca. 18–22 letters in width, written in rustic capitals in a papyrus roll of the second/third century(?), from which 2.7M/8R is also preserved. Supplements are by Roberts, unless otherwise indicated; italics indicates that the transcription is uncertain; ends of lines in the papyrus are marked by |.

{Serv. auct. ad *Aen.* 1.329 (§3 *perrexere . . . Sardiniam*): to illustrate the use of *an* as a disjunctive conj., = "or rather" (*OLD* s.v. 9).}

FRAGMENTS NOT ASSIGNED
TO BOOKS

WAR AND MILITARY AFFAIRS,
FRR. 1–25

1* 1.27M, inc. 5Mc, inc. 67D, inc. 33K

S. may have been describing various persons, either L. Cinna in 87, when he was expelled from Rome by his consular colleague Octavius (so Maurenbr. adducing Schol. Gronov. p. 286St.8, pretio collegit exercitum, *"he assembled an army by means of money"), or Pompey, when he raised troops for Sulla (so Dietsch) or for the Sertorian War (cf. fr. 2.86.9), or Lepidus (so de Brosses), or M. Crassus, to repress the Spartacan revolt (cf. Crassus' well-known definition of true wealth as that which is enough to maintain an army,* Cic. Parad. 45, Off. 1.25*).*

he created an army with cash

2* 1.83M (Serv. auct.), inc. 12Mc, 2.10D (Serv. auct.), 2.15K (Serv. auct.)

Sundry contexts have been proposed, but certainty is impossible: the revolt of Lepidus (Kritz, Dietsch, Maurenbr., and Rylands), the wandering of Sertorius (Last), or the campaign of M. Antonius (pr. 74) against the pirates (Lepori).

. . . ⟨he was?⟩ filled with rage and grief at the loss of such

nando, pars | <p>uppibus in litus algosum | <i>npulsis; ne-
que eos diuti|<u>s hostes mansere genus | <tre>pidissu-
3   mum[2] Graeco|<r>um et Afrorum semermi|<u>m. Dein
sociis pro fortu|<n>a humatis et omnibus | <qu>ae usui
erant ex propin|<quo> conreptis, ubi nulla | <spe>s esset[3]
patrandi incepti, | <pe>rrexere in Hispaniam | <an Sardi-
niam>[4] [. . . . 2 lines. . . .]

[1] *corr. Ed. Fraenkel*   [2] –ssimum *pap.*   [3] *Roberts:*
est *pap.*   [4] *suppl. ex Serv.*

3* 5.8M, inc. 31Mc, inc. 66D, inc.32K

pressi undique multitudine

Donat. ad Ter. *Ad.* 302: to describe the press of enemy forces.

4* 2.57M, inc. 16Mc, inc. 16D, 3.18K

atque edita[1] undique, tribus tamen cum[2] muris et
magnis turribus

Donat. ad Ter. *An.* 94: to illustrate *tamen* in the absence of a
preceding concessive clause.

[1] edicta *A:* dicta *TC*   [2] tum *vel* circum *Pecere*

---

[1] With this translation, if *cum* + abl. is retained; if, instead, the
abls *muris* and *turribus* were governed by a word such as *munita*
(fortified), then possibly *tum* or *circum* is the correct reading in
place of *cum*.

confederates. Armed they flew forth from the ships by means of skiffs or by swimming, some did so after the sterns of the ships had been driven aground on the sea-weed–strewn shore; and the enemy, a very timorous sort composed of poorly armed Greeks and Africans, did not stand up to them for very long. Next, after burying their comrades as best they could and after seizing everything in the vicinity that was useful, when there was no hope of accomplishing their undertaking, they made their way to Spain or Sardinia . . .

3* 5.8M, inc. 31Mc, inc. 66D, inc.32K

Maurenbr. assigned this fragment to the Battle of Zela in the summer of 67, near Gazioura in Pontus, where the Roman forces under Lucullus' legate Triarius were surrounded and overwhelmed by the numerically superior troops of Mithridates (Dio 36.12.4). But this could be a description of any number of other battles.

hemmed in on all sides by a throng [of hostile forces?]

4* 2.57M, inc. 16Mc, inc. 16D, 3.18K

The description of a well-fortified city; among possible candidates are Carthago Nova (Maurenbr. citing Strabo 3.4.6, p. 158) or Nisibis (de Brosses) or Tigranocerta (Gerlach), or Carthage (cf. App. Pun. 95). Less probably it describes Lucullus' camp at Cyzicus (Kritz).

and elevated on all sides, with[1] nevertheless [despite its natural defenses] three walls and great towers

5* inc. 10M, inc. 46Mc, inc. 60D, inc. 26K

non repugnantibus modo, sed ne deditis quidem a.
b. e. m.[1]

Donat. ad Ter. *Phorm.* 98: to illustrate the figure *auxesis,* whereby a succeeding phrase or clause amplifies the preceding one.
Cf. fr. 1.77 and fr. 2.108 for similar instances of abbreviated text
in Donat.

[1] a⟨rmis⟩ b⟨ellum⟩ e⟨xcitare⟩ m⟨etuentibus⟩ *Maurenbr.*:
a⟨trocis⟩ b⟨elli⟩ c⟨lades⟩ m⟨etuentibus⟩ *de Brosses*

6* inc. 5M, inc. 41Mc, inc. 84D, inc. 51K

pactione amisso Publio legato

Donat. ad Ter. *Phorm.* 141: to illustrate *amittere = dimittere*
(send away), a meaning common in comedy (*OLD* s.v. *amitto* 1).

7* 4.62M, inc. 28Mc, 59D, inc. 25K

in nuda, intecta[1] corpora

Diom. *GL* 1.447.9: to illustrate homoeoteleuton.

[1] intecta corpora] *Gerlach ed. min.*: intectato pora *cod.*: in
tecta corpora *Maurenbr.*: iniecta corpora *Carrio*

5* inc. 10M, inc. 46Mc, inc. 60D, inc. 26K

The text is too abrupt and abbreviated to permit any firm interpretation. Since it is cited as an example of the figure auxesis, *the second half should somehow amplify what precedes. Perhaps these words are datives dependent on a predicate of the sort* non pepercerunt *(they did not spare), and the reference is to the slaughter of the inhabitants of a captured city (so Kritz).*

not only those putting up resistance but not even those who had surrendered * * * *[1]

[1] Or, if we adopt Maurenbr.'s expansion of the abbreviated text "*a. b. e. m.*": "not only putting up resistance, but not even after the surrender ⟨of their arms, being afraid to awaken war⟩."

6* inc. 5M, inc. 41Mc, inc. 84D, inc. 51K

Since the person is referred to only by the common praenomen Publius, it is impossible to be certain that the reference is P. Clodius and his dismissal from the staff of his brother-in-law L. Lucullus in the winter of 68/67 (so de Brosses and Kritz), after which Clodius served under his other brother-in-law, Marcius Rex (cos. 68), the governor of Cilicia (MRR 2.148).

the legate Publius having been dismissed by agreement

7* 4.62M, inc. 28Mc, 59D, inc. 25K

Possibly referring to the Germans in Spartacus' army (cf. fr. 3.68).

against bare, uncovered bodies

8* 3.41M, inc. 19Mc, inc. 41D, inc. 7K

paululum requietis militibus

Serv. ad *Ecl.* 8.4: to illustrate the verb *requiesco* meaning to "cause to rest, stay" (*OLD* 5).

9* 4.34M, inc. 26Mc, deest in D et K

diu noctuque laborare, festinare

Serv. ad *G.* 1.287 {*Schol. Bern.* ad ibid. (*diu . . . laborare*)}: to illustrate the adv. *noctu*.

10* 1.14M, inc. 4Mc, inc. 26D, 3.74K

apertae[1] portae,[2] repleta arva cultoribus

Serv. & Serv. auct. ad *Aen.* 2.27: to illustrate open gates as a sign of peace.

   [1] aparte *C*: aperte *corr. C*[5]   [2] portae *om. C*

11* inc. 8M, inc. 44Mc, inc. 49D, 15K

neu quis miles neve pro milite

Serv. & Serv. auct. ad *Aen.* 2.157: claiming that *pro milite* can designate a veteran called back to active duty, soldiers commonly referred to as *evocati*.

FRAGMENTS NOT ASSIGNED TO BOOKS

8* 3.41M, inc. 19Mc, inc. 41D, inc. 7K

Maurenbr. speculated that this fragment formed part of the description of the hardships that befell Lucullus' army when it went in pursuit of Mithridates on his withdrawal from the siege of Cyzicus in the winter of 73/72 (Plut. Luc. 11.4).

the soldiers having been given a brief rest

9* 4.34M, inc. 26Mc, not included in D and K

Maurenbr. saw a reference to the toil and speed with which Crassus' army blockaded Spartacus and his followers on the peninsula near Rhegium (Plut. Crass. 10.8), but the context could be any number of other military operations.

to toil and hurry day and night

10* 1.14M, inc. 4Mc, inc. 26D, 3.74K

Possibly a description of conditions in Campania and Lucania at the time of the uprising by Spartacus (so de Brosses and Kritz). Maurenbr., on the contrary, detects a reference to the prosperity enjoyed by Italy after the destruction of Carthage and the conquest of Greece.

the gates open, the plowed fields filled with farmers

11* inc. 8M, inc. 44Mc, inc. 49D, 15K

If the meaning Servius assigns to pro milite *is correct, then this fragment may possibly describe the army assembled by Crassus (cf. fr. 4.12) to meet the emergency posed by Spartacus' uprising (so McGushin).*

and so that no soldier or recalled veteran

12* 4.80M, inc. 30Mc, inc. 104D, inc. 73K

⟨nubes⟩ ... foedavere lumen

Serv. & Serv. auct. ad *Aen.* 2.286: commenting on the metaphorical use of *foedare* (to sully), giving as an example S.'s use of this verb in speaking of clouds (*de nubibus*).

13* inc. 37M, inc. 73Mc, inc. 89K

VICES *pugnas, quia per vicissitudinem pugnabatur, ut Sallustius docet.*

Serv. & Serv. auct. ad *Aen.* 2.433.

14* 1.30M, inc. 6Mc, inc. 38D, inc. 4K

speciem captae urbis efficere

Serv. ad *Aen.* 8.557: to illustrate *species* = *imago* (a likeness).

15* inc. 4M, inc. 40Mc, inc. 56D, inc. 22K

12* 4.80M, inc. 30Mc, inc. 104D, inc. 73K

Maurenbr. speculated that the context may have been the moon-less and stormy night on which L. Lucullus breached the walls of Nisibis in the winter of 68/67 (Dio 36.7.1); cf. fr. 4.70. Here, however, Servius indicates that S. was referring to clouds, not the darkness of night.

⟨clouds⟩ marred the daylight

13* inc. 37M, inc. 73Mc, inc. 89K

S. appears to have used the noun vices *to describe the alternating fortunes of fighting.*

"HAZARDS" *[meaning] "battles," because fighting was in the habit of occurring with vicissitudes, as Sallust points out.*

14* 1.30M, inc. 6Mc, inc. 38D, inc. 4K

Possibly, according to Maurenbr., describing the bloodshed and looting carried out by Cinna and Marius after their entry into Rome in the autumn of 87 (Dio fr. 102.9; Liv. Per. 80, velut captam eam caedibus et rapinis vastaverunt, *"they [Marius and Cinna] laid it waste with looting and slaughter, as if it were a captured city"). Alternatively, the scene described could be a city looted by Spartacus (so Kritz), or the looting of Sinope by the fleeing garrison installed by Mithridates (Memnon, FGrH 434F37.7): so Gerlach.*

to produce the appearance of a captured city

15* inc. 4M, inc. 40Mc, inc. 56D, inc. 22K

A maneuver to improve the striking of blows, which Servius characterizes as "Gallic." Possibly, according to Maurenbr., the con-

regressi ad faciliores ictus loco cedebant[1]

Serv. ad *Aen.* 9.746: to illustrate a type of blow styled "Gallic" by Servius.

[1] loco cedebant] locos quaerebant *Guelferbyt. I*

16* 4.75M, inc. 29Mc, inc. 55D, inc. 21K

more equestris proeli sumptis tergis atque redditis

Serv. ad *Aen.* 11.619: to illustrate the tactic of controlled retreat as a stock maneuver in a cavalry battle.

17* 1.87M, 1.76Mc, Inc 65D, Inc 31K

togam[1] paludamento mutavit

Serv. auct. ad *G.* 1.8 (without attribution to S.): to illustrate *mutare* + acc. and abl.

Schol. in Iuv. ad 6.400 and Isidor. *Etym.* 19.24.9 both credit this expression to S. without specifying the work, the former as part of a note on Juv.'s *paludatis ducibus* (generals in military cloaks), and the latter to provide an instance of *paludamentum,* after defining the meaning of the word.

[1] coiam *L (Serv.)*: cogam *S (Schol. in Iuv.)*

18* 1.109M, inc. 13Mc, inc. 61D, inc. 27K

text was fighting by Pompey in Gaul on his way to Spain in 77 or the fighting against the Gauls and Germans under Crixus in 72 (fr. 3.42.9).

having pulled back for easier striking, they gave ground[1]

[1] Or, "sought positions (from which) to inflict . . . ," if the reading *locos quaerebant* is adopted (see textual note).

16* 4.75M, inc. 29Mc, inc. 55D, inc. 21K

The description of an infantry battle fought more in the style of a cavalry engagement, possibly in the war with Mithridates or Tigranes. Maurenbr. assigned this fragment to the battle at the river Arsanias in the summer of 68 (Plut. Luc. 31.5–8). Cf. fr. 4.65.

after the fashion of a cavalry battle, attacking the rear of the fleeing enemy and then themselves retreating

17* 1.87M, 1.76Mc, inc. 65D, inc. 31K

Possibly describing Sertorius in a sketch of his military career (so Dietsch and Maurenbr.) or M. Lepidus (cos. 78) when he embarked upon armed rebellion in 77 (so de Brosses and Gerlach). Cf. fr. dub. 52.

he exchanged his toga for a military cloak

18* 1.109M, inc. 13Mc, inc. 61D, inc. 27K

Possibly describing the success of Sertorius in Spain as foreshadowed by his initial battles in 80 against Cotta and Fufidius, the governor of Further Spain (Plut. Sert. 12.3–4): so Maurenbr. Alternatively, the reference could be to a victory of some other foreign or Roman commander.

Ita sperat pugnam illam pro omine[1] bello[2] futuram.

Serv. auct. ad *Aen.* 1.456: to illustrate *pugna* = *proelium.*

{Serv. ad *Aen.* 10.311 (*pugnam . . . futuram*): to illustrate Virgil's *omen pugnae.*}

[1] omni *Serv. auct. ad Aen. 1.456: SRHM (Serv. ad Aen. 10.311)*: omine ‹omni› *Dietsch dubit. in app.*   [2] belli *Stephanus*

19* inc. 2M, inc. 38Mc, inc. 44D, inc. 10K

in secunda cohortis festinas conposuerat

Serv. auct. ad *Aen.* 9.486: to illustrate the adj. *festinus* = *festinans.*

20* inc. 1M, inc. 37Mc, inc. 43D, inc. 9K

ex[1] parte cohortium praepropere[2] instructa [et][3] stationes locatae pro castris

Serv. auct. ad *Aen.* 12.661: to illustrate *pro* + abl. = *ante* + acc.

[1] *F*: et *rell.*   [2] *Maurenbr.*: praecipere *F*: pro opere *Thilo in app.*: pro tempore *Dietsch*: praesi‹dia pro›pere *Frassinetti-Di Salvo in app.*   [3] *Putschius*

21* 1.70M, inc. 9Mc, inc. 23D, 3.70K

quae cis paucos dies iuncta[1] in armis foret[2]

Cledon. *GL* 5.76.23–24: to illustrate the prep. *cis.*

[1] cuncta *Kritz dubit. in app.*   [2] sunt *Gelach*

Thus he hopes that that battle will serve as an omen for the war.[1]

[1] Or, "for the war as a whole," if Diestch's supplement *omni* is adopted.

19* inc. 2M, inc. 38Mc, inc. 44D, inc. 10K

he had drawn up the fast-moving[1] cohorts in the second line of battle

[1] Presumably those lightly armed (*expeditae,* or *leves*), hence maneuverable.

20* inc. 1M, inc. 37Mc, inc. 43D, inc. 9K

pickets stationed in front of the camp from a hastily marshaled portion of the cohorts

21* 1.70M, inc. 9Mc, inc. 23D, 3.70K

Possibly describing the uniting of Etruria in support of M. Lepidus' uprising in 77 (so Maurenbr.); cf. fr. 1.59. Alternatively, the context may be the war with Sertorius or Spartacus. Kritz, reading sunt *in place of* foret, *supposed the subject to be* servitia, *viz. the slaves who flocked to Spartacus.*

which [some region?] would be united in arms within a few days

22* inc. 3M, inc. 39Mc, inc. 54D, inc. 20K

profectus quidam Ligus ad requisita naturae

Pomp. *GL* 5.293.23: to illustrate a periphrasis for describing a bodily function.

{Quint. 8.6.59 (*ad requisita naturae*) as an example of a periphrasis.}

23* 3.92M, inc. 24Mc, inc. 40D, inc. 6K

radicem montis accessit

Schol. Stat. ad *Theb.* 3.116: to illustrate the omission of a prep. with a verb that normally requires one.

24* inc. 9M, inc. 45Mc, inc. 39D, 5K

Vt res magis quam verba agerentur, liberos parentisque in muris locaverant.

Schol. Stat. ad *Theb.* 10.573: quoted to illustrate the principle that the sight of one's children can rouse soldiers to fight fiercely.

25* inc. 6M, inc. 42Mc, inc. 52D, 18K

hostes aut oppressi aut dilapsi forent

Isid. *Etym.* 18.2.7: to illustrate the two ways of eliminating an enemy force: by destruction or by dispersal.

22* inc. 3M, inc. 39Mc, inc. 54D, inc. 20K

This description of an auxiliary soldier briefly leaving the Roman camp is reminiscent of Jug. 93.2 (foret quidam Ligus) *and also of fr. 4.29 describing the departure of two Gallic women from the camp of Spartacus' followers.*

a Ligurian having departed to attend to the demands of nature

23* 3.92M, inc. 24Mc, inc. 40D, inc. 6K

Maurenbr. advocated connecting this fragment with the attempt of the praetor Clodius (C. Claudius Glaber) to trap Spartacus' band of escaped gladiators on Mt. Vesuvius (Plut. Crass. 9.2), but the reference is too general to permit identification of the context.

he [or, "the army"] approached the foot of the mountain

24* inc. 9M, inc. 45Mc, inc. 39D, 5K

Part of a narrative marking a transition from talk of a settlement to fighting, the aim being to prevent the capture of a native city besieged by the Romans (possibly Nisibis).

To produce deeds rather than words, they had placed their children and parents on the walls.

25* inc. 6M, inc. 42Mc, inc. 52D, 18K

the enemy would either have been crushed or have dispersed

SHIPS AND SAILING, FRR. 26–31

26* 3.64M, inc. 23Mc, 3.42M, 3.52K

crebritate fluctuum, ut aquilone solet

Serv. & Serv. auct. ad *Aen.* 1.116: to illustrate Servius' remark that Aquilo (the North Wind) produces constant waves.

27* inc. 13M, inc. 49Mc, inc. 57D, inc. 23K

inpediebant iussa nautarum

Serv. & Serv. auct. ad *Aen.* 3.129: to illustrate *celeuma* (= the boatswain's call giving the time to the rowers), a Greek term glossed as *praeceptum* (a command).

28* 3.55M, inc. 21Mc, 4.23D, 4.38K

triplici fluctu

Serv. auct. ad *Aen.* 1.116: cited as a Latin expression modeled on the Greek τρικυμία (= a huge wave).

SHIPS AND SAILING, FRR. 26–31

26* 3.64M, inc. 23Mc, 3.42M, 3.52K

Most previous editors place this fragment in the context of S.'s excursus on the region of the Black Sea in Book 3, but it could equally well have been part of S.'s description of the storm that wrecked Mithridates' fleet on his voyage from Nicomedia to Sinope in spring 72 (see fr. 3.76).

owing to the frequency of the waves, as is common with the North wind

27* inc. 13M, inc. 49Mc, inc. 57D, inc. 23K

The close resemblance of this fragment to Ov. Met. 11.484 (impediunt adversae iussa procellae, "hostile gales hamper the orders") suggests that the subject may have been foul weather (so Funari). Possibly it belongs to the same context as frr. 26 and 28.

[stormy gales?] were interfering with the orders given to the sailors

28* 3.55M, inc. 21Mc, 4.23D, 4.38K

Maurenbr. assigns this fragment to S.'s account of the storm that wrecked Mithridates' fleet on his voyage from Nicomedia to Sinope in spring 72 (cf. fr. 3.76). On the contrary, Kritz and Dietsch, rejecting Servius' interpretation of the expression, assumed that it formed part of S.'s description of the mythical whirlpool Charybdis (treated in fr. 4.19), which was said to undergo each day three cycles of absorption and regurgitation (Hom. Od. 12.104–6; Isid. Etym. 13.18.5).

with a huge (lit., triple) wave

29* 1.56M, inc. 8Mc, inc. 45K, inc. 11K

Sed ubi tempore anni mare classibus patefactum est,

Serv. auct. ad *Aen.* 1.146: to illustrate the verb *aperio* (to open) with reference to making the sea accessible to navigation.

30* inc. 12M, inc. 48Mc, deest in D et K

et parvis modo velorum alis remissis[1]

Serv. auct. ad *Aen.* 3.520: to illustrate the metaphor *velorum . . . alas.*

[1] demissis *Maurenbr. (cf. fr. 4.72)*

31* inc. 11M, inc. 47Mc, deest in D et K

dorso fluctus trieris adaequata[1]

Gloss. 5, p. 251.3 (attributed to S.; title of work not specified): to illustrate the adj. *trieris* (sc. *navis*).

[1] *Schmitz*: adaequatum *cod.*

POLITICS AND CIVIL AFFAIRS, FRR. 32–37

32* 5.19M, inc. 33Mc, inc. 32D, 5.15K

29* 1.56M, inc. 8Mc, inc. 45K, inc. 11K

Possibly describing the dispatch of P. Servilius (cos. 79) in 78 to combat the pirates in Cilicia (so Maurenbr.), or the naval expedition against the pirates under either M. Antonius in 74 or Pompey in 67. But it could equally well describe the departure of any governor for his posting abroad.

But when the season of the year had opened up the
sea to ships,

30* inc. 12M, inc. 48Mc, not included in D and K

Although Serv. cites this fragment to illustrate the common poetic metaphor of sails resembling wings, alas velorum *(wings of the sails) at Aen. 3.520 (the example also singled out by Isid. Etym. 19.3.1), here in S.,* alis, *described as "small" (*parvis*), most probably = the ends or corners of the sails, the "reefs" (so OLD 3).*

and with only small reefs of the sails slackened

31* inc. 11M, inc. 47Mc, not included in D and K

A storm at sea.

a trireme made level with the ridge of the wave[1]

[1] I.e., was lifted up to the crest of the wave.

POLITICS AND CIVIL AFFAIRS,
FRR. 32–37

32* 5.19M, inc. 33Mc, inc. 32D, 5.15K

Possibly describing the eagerness of Pompey (Kritz, Maurenbr., citing Dio 36.24.5), or of the Roman people (Dietsch), for the passage of Gabinius' bill that in 67 assigned the pirate war to Pompey. The law referred to, however, could equally well be, for

cupientissumus legis

Diom. *GL* 1.311.28–29; Dosith. *GL* 7.426.10: to illustrate a partic. (in the superl.) + (obj.) gen.

33* 4.54M, inc. 27Mc, 2.37D, 2.46K

Canina, ut ait Appius, facundia exercebatur.

Non. p. 60M = 84L.17: to amplify his discussion of *rabula* (a ranting speaker).

{Lactant. *Div. inst.* 6.18.26 (*sed quia ipse [Cicero] caninam illam facundia, sicut Sallustius ab Appio dictum refert, exercuit.* Cf. Hier. *Ep.* 119.1, 134.1, attributing the expression *canina facundia* to Appius, without mentioning S.)

34* inc. 16M, inc. 52Mc, inc. 92D, inc. 60K

genua patrum advolvuntur

Serv. auct. ad *Aen.* 1.307: to illustrate the omission of a prep. with a verb that normally requires one.

{Arus. *GL* 7.514.23 = p. 282DC (*genua advolvebantur*), a brief notation of the sort *"Sal. Hist."* identifying S. as the author appears to have dropped out of the text immediately ahead of the quotation.}

instance, the one sponsored by C. Cotta in 75 to lift one of the restrictions imposed upon the tribunate by Sulla (cf. frr. 2.44 and 3.15.8), or the legislation of Pompey and Crassus in 70 that restored the powers of the plebeian tribunate, or the law of L. Cotta in the same year that reformed the jury courts.

most eager for the law

33* 4.54M, inc. 27Mc, 2.37D, 2.46K

Possibly belonging to the same context as fr. 2.22 and describing the sharp wit of the tribune Sicinius, who in 76 verbally attacked leading senatorial politicians who opposed the popular demand for the restoration of the plebeian tribunate (Plut. Crass. 7.8): so Kritz and Dietsch. Maurenbr., on the contrary—chiefly, it seems, because Lactantius applied this pejorative to Cicero's eloquence —speculated that S. was describing Cicero in the context of his prosecution of Verres in 70 (cf. fr. 4.23). La Penna (1973) proposed placing it in the preface to Book 1, where S. commented on the state of contemporary rhetoric.

He cultivated a snarling[1] eloquence, as Appius[2] called it.

[1] Lit., "canine."
[2] This Appius may be Ap. Claudius Caecus (cens. 312) or a much later Appius, perhaps either the consul of 79, who was the father of Cicero's enemy P. Clodius (Cic. De or. 2.246), or the father of the consul of 79 (Cic. De or. 2.284).

34* inc. 16M, inc. 52Mc, inc. 92D, inc. 60K

Presumably a description of foreign ambassadors who appeared as suppliants before the senate to beg for redress of wrongs committed by some Roman official.

they prostrate themselves at the knees of the senators

35* 1.76M, inc. 10Mc, 2.41D, 2.50K

in hunc modum disseruit

Prisc. *GL* 3.305.16–17: to illustrate the phrase *in hunc modum,* in place of *hoc modo.*

36* 5.27M, inc. 36Mc, deest in D et K

manum in os intendens

Placid. *Gloss.* p. 27.2: to illustrate *intendere = minari* (to threaten).

37* 5.26M, inc. 35Mc, inc. 99D, inc. 68K

eo redeunte domum, salutatum[1] apud aedem Bellonae

Schol. Veron. ad *Aen.* 5.80: to illustrate *salve* in the sense of "hail and farewell."

{*Schol. Stat.* ad *Theb.* 4.31 (*cum ab eo domum rediens salutaretur*): to illustrate *salutare* meaning "to bid farewell" (*vale*).}

[1] *Maurenbr.*: salutaret *Schol. Veron.*

---

[1] Impersonal pass. accepting Maurenbr.'s emendation; text uncertain. The *Schol. Veron.* is very lacunose immediately preceding this fragment, and the fragment is quoted differently by *Schol. Stat.* Both scholiasts quote S. in the mistaken belief that *salutare* in this fragment has the same meaning as *salve* in Virgil = "farewell" (s.v. *OLD* 3) and *salutare* in Statius (s.v. *OLD* 3).

35* 1.76M, inc. 10Mc, 2.41D, 2.50K

Possibly introducing the speech of Philippus (fr. 1.67), so Maurenbr. The verb dissero *is similarly used to introduce speeches at* Jug. *30.4, 84.5 and* Hist. *2.43.1a.*

he spoke in this fashion

36* 5.27M, inc. 36Mc, not included in D and K

A threatening gesture: possibly that made against the consul C. Piso in 67 when he tried to prevent the tribune C. Cornelius from reading the text of his bill despite the veto of a tribunician colleague (so Maurenbr. citing Ascon. p. 58C, cum ille eos qui sibi intentabant manus prendi a lictore iussisset, *"when Piso had ordered his lictor to seize those who were threatening him with their fists").*

extending his hand to his [opponent's] face

37* 5.26M, inc. 35Mc, inc. 99D, inc. 68K

The occasion is apparently the return of some general to Rome, since the temple of Bellona lay in the Campus Martius, near the Circus Flaminius, outside the pomerium, and for that reason was a frequent meeting place of the senate when it was desirable for a commander possessing military imperium to attend. Possibly the person returning was Pompey, after the completion of the first phase of his campaign in 67 to eradicate piracy (so Maurenbr. citing Plut. Pomp. *27.1–2). If so, this fragment provides the sole piece of evidence that S. gave a reasonably full account of Pompey's eradication of the pirates.*

upon his return home, he was greeted[1] in the temple of Bellona

MISCELLANEOUS, FRR. 38–56

38* inc. 1Mc, deest in M, D, et K,

Multi murmurantium voculis in luco[1] eloquentiae oblectantur.

Fronto p. 148.9: to illustrate the gradual development of eloquence.

   [1] *manus 2*: loco *manus 1*

39* inc. 15M, inc. 51Mc, inc. 81D, inc. 47K

   atque ipse cultu[1] rei

Porph. ad Hor. *Sat.* 2.2.66: to demonstrate that *cultus* (= "mode of life," *OLD* 8) is neither positive nor negative in connotation, requiring a modifier or context to give it color.

   [1] cultus *Kritz*

40* inc. 26M, inc. 62Mc, inc. 106D, inc. 75K

   ad Iovis mane veni[1]

Donat. ad Ter. *Ad.* 582: to illustrate that the noun *templum* can be omitted with *ad* + gen. of the name of a diety.

   [1] mane veni] *Langraf*: mandeuani *C*: manaeuam *cod. Cuiacii*: mande iram *V et dett.*

41* inc. 23M, inc. 59Mc, inc. 107D, inc. 76K

   nihil socordia claudicabat[1]

Donat. ad Ter. *Eun.* 164: to illustrate the verb *claudicare,* which Donat. wrongly equates with *claudier* in Ter.

   [1] claudicabat *C*: claudiebat *T*: claudebat *rell.*

MISCELLANEOUS, FRR. 38–56

38* inc. 1Mc, not included in M, D, and K

Possibly from S.'s description of the style of early historians.

Many are delighted by the thin voices of mutterers in the grove[1] of eloquence.

[1] Or, "in lieu of eloquence," if *loco* is what S. wrote (see textual note).

39* inc. 15M, inc. 51Mc, inc. 81D, inc. 47K

If rei *is the gen. of* reus *(so Kritz), then a plaintiff or prosecutor may have sought to score points off the defendant by making reference to his style of living. Frassinetti, by contrast, ignoring the meaning the scholiast assigns to* cultus *in this fragment, interprets* rei *as the gen. of* res *(sc.* familiaris*) and translates "by cultivation of his assests."*

and he himself [the prosecutor, or plaintiff, argued?] from the accused's style of living

40* inc. 26M, inc. 62Mc, inc. 106D, inc. 75K

I came in the morning[1] to the temple of Jupiter

[1] Italics signifies that the text is uncertain.

41* inc. 23M, inc. 59Mc, inc. 107D, inc. 76K

Possibly a comment on someone's talent (ingenium) *or on an orator's eloquence.*

was not at all deficient as a result of sloth

42* 2.23M, 2.19Mc, inc. 83D, inc. 50K

multos tamen[1] ab adulescentia[2] bonos insultaverat

Donat. ad Ter. *Eun.* 285; Serv. ad *Aen.* 9.631, id. ad *Aen.* 10.643: to illustrate *insulto* + acc. [instead of dat. or *in* + acc. ; cf. *OLD* 3b].

[1] *om. Serv. (bis)*   [2] pueritia *Serv. ad 9.631*

43* inc. 24M, inc. 60Mc, inc. 58D, 24K

quae pacta in conventione non praestitissent

Donat. ad Ter. *Eun.* 467, see fr. 1.79.

44* inc. 25M, inc. 61Mc, inc. 95D, inc. 64K

atque ea cogentis non coactos, scelestos magis quam miseros, obstringi[1]

Donat. ad Ter. *Hec.* 536: to illustrate the principle that the word *miser* is only applicable to one who is not *scelestus* (wicked).

[1] distringi *B*: dici dignum *Dietsch*

42* 2.23M, 2.19Mc, inc. 83D, inc. 50K

Possibly a description of Pompey (so Kritz and McGushin), or Licinius Macer, tribune in 73 and historian (so Dietsch), or the political power broker Cethegus (so de Brosses), or Marcius Philippus (so Gerlach), or Sicinius, tribune in 76 (so Maurenbr.).

nevertheless, from early manhood he had behaved insultingly toward many conservatives [defenders of the status quo]

43* inc. 24M, inc. 60Mc, inc. 58D, 24K

Possibly to be connected with the money that C. Curio exacted in 75 from the Dardanians, under terms imposed by his predecessor (see fr. 2.66).

which [communities?] would not have fulfilled the terms negotiated in the compact

44* inc. 25M, inc. 61Mc, inc. 95D, inc. 64K

These words may have been reported in indirect discourse and represent the claim by someone (possibly a senator or a prosecutor in a court) who denies that persons involved in some enterprise such as, perhaps, the uprising of M. Lepidus in 78–77 (so La Penna) were forced to join in because of their wretched circumstances, but rather they were bad men to begin with.

[he asserted . . .?] and that not those who had been pressured to do so but instigators of the deeds, men who were wicked rather than wretched, *were implicated*[1] [in the enterprise?]

[1] Italics signifies that the text is uncertain. If we adopt Dietsch's *dici dignum*, translate "the instigators of the deeds had not been compelled; it was fitting for them to be called wicked rather than wretched."

45* 1.9M, inc. 3Mc, inc. 102D, inc. 71K

maxumis ducibus, fortibus strenuisque ministris

Diom. *GL* 1.447.14–15: to illustrate homoeoptoton (the repetition of inflections at the ends of phrases).

46* 5.17M, inc. 32Mc, inc. 27D, 3.73K

qui nullo certo exilio vagabantur

Serv. & Serv. auct. ad *Aen.* 1.2: to illustrate *exul* (exile, = wanderer), in contrast with *profugus* (fugitive, = one with a fixed place of abode).

47* 5.25M, inc. 34Mc, inc. 101D, inc. 70K

rebus supra vota fluentibus

Serv. & Serv. auct. ad *Aen.* 2.169: to illustrate that the metaphorical sense of *fluo* (= [of events, plans, etc.] to proceed, develop [in a given manner], *OLD* 9b) varies with context, having in Virgil the meaning of *delabor* (to ebb), whereas in S. it signifies the opposite.

48* inc. 19M, inc. 55Mc, inc. 100D, inc. 69K

45* 1.9M, inc. 3Mc, inc. 102D, inc. 71K

Possibly identifying the causes of Rome's greatness (so de Brosses, Maurenbr.), but certainty is impossible. Cf. Cat. 53.4, paucorum civium egregiam virtutem cuncta patravisse *(all [the great deeds of the Roman people] had been accomplished by the eminent merit of a few citizens).*

the greatest commanders, brave and energetic subordinates

46* 5.17M, inc. 32Mc, inc. 27D, 3.73K

S. may refer to those who threw in their lot with pirates (so Dietsch and Maurenbr.), or with Spartacus' band (Kritz), or with Lepidus' uprising in 77 (de Brosses and Gerlach).

who were wandering with no fixed place of exile[1]

[1] I.e., people who were rootless either by choice (because they felt no attachment to any one place) or from an inability to find a secure place of refuge.

47* 5.25M, inc. 34Mc, inc. 101D, inc. 70K

One among any number of possible instances in which a successful result exceeded expectation may be Pompey's rapid progress in clearing the seas of pirates (so Maurenbr., citing Pomp. Plut. 27.2).

events proceeding beyond their prayers

48* inc. 19M, inc. 55Mc, inc. 100D, inc. 69K

Possibly S. gave the date of an event by linking it to the time of the heliacal rising of Orion, which occurs annually soon after the summer solstice (Plin. HN 18.268; cf. Ov. Fast. 6.717–19).

(**Orion**) qui **oritur** *ut Sallustius dixit* **iuxta solis aestivi pulsum**

Serv. & Serv. auct. ad *Aen.* 5.626: explicating a reference to the rising of Orion at *Aen.* 1.535.

49* 1.5M, inc. 2Mc, inc. 78D, inc. 44K

in quis longissumo aevo plura¹ de bonis falsa² in deterius conposuit

Serv. auct. ad *Ecl.* 8.27: to illustrate that *aevum* can stand for *tempus.*

¹ multa *Dietsch*   ² falso *Kritz*

50* 3.18M, inc. 17Mc, 4.46D, 4.4K

cultu corporis ornata egregio

Serv. auct. ad *G.* 1.3, also quoting *Jug.* 33.1: to illustrate *cultus* meaning "attire" or "adornment," as opposed to physical attributes.

(**Orion**) which **rises**, *as Sallust stated*, **immediately after the repulse**(?)[1] **of the summer sun**

[1] If *pulsum* is what S. wrote (doubted by Kritz and Dietsch, but defended by Hauler, *Arch. f. lat. Lexik.* 5.1888, p. 143), it may stand for *repulsum* and refer to the thrusting back of the sun from its apparent northerly course at the summer solstice (June 20–22).

49* 1.5M, inc. 2Mc, inc. 78D, inc. 44K

Possibly the same context as fr. 38 above. The criticism may be of the Elder Cato (so Kritz, Maurenbr.) or of the scholar and Pompeian partisan M. Terentius Varro (so Dietsch), both of whom were octogenarians.

in which [books, writings?], over the course of a very long (life)time, he perversely wrote a great many falsehoods about decent men

50* 3.18M, inc. 17Mc, 4.46D, 4.4K

Possibly the description of some woman; among candidates suggested are Praecia, the mistress of the political boss Cethegus (so Maurenbr.); Monime, the Milesian wife of Mithridates (so de Brosses, Kritz, Dietsch), whom he won over with the gift of a diadem (Plut. Luc. 18.3); Clodia, the wife of Lucullus and the sister of P. Clodius (La Penna).

decked out with distinctive adornment of her body[1]

[1] Or "endowed with exceptional physical beauty" (McGushin, = Frassenetti), adopting Maurenbr.'s view that *cultu corporis* is a description of physical endowment, not attire. Servius, however, cites this fragment and *Jug.* 33.1 as counterexamples to the meaning *habitudo corporis*. *Pace* Maurenbr., the word *corporis* does not exclude the meaning "attire," since *cultu corporis* at *Cat.* 48.2 undeniably refers to objects of clothing.

51* 2.24M, inc. 14Mc, inc. 91D, inc. 59K

ad mutandum modo in melius servitium

Serv. auct. ad *Aen.* 1.281: to illustrate the phrase *in melius* meaning "for the better."

52* 2.50M, inc. 15Mc, inc. 90D, inc. 58K

quae causa fuerit[1] novandis rebus

Serv. auct. ad *Aen.* 4.290: to provide a parallel (in nearly identical language) for Virgil's use of the dat. with *causa* (*quae rebus sit causa novandis*), in place of the gen.

[1] *T*: fuer *F*: fuerat *Kritz*

51* 2.24M, inc. 14Mc, inc. 91D, inc. 59K

*Maurenbr., building on a suggestion of Kritz that the fragment might concern complaints by a tribune against the Sullan constitution (*servitium *also being the word used by the tribune of the plebs Licinius Macer to describe the reforms imposed by Sulla, 3.15.1), saw a reference to the demand of the tribune Sicinius in 76 for the restoration of the tribunate. Alternatively, the "slavery" could be literal and refer to the aim of Spartacus and the gladiators when they made their escape from Capua in 73 (so de Brosses and Gerlach), or it could describe some oppressed nation suffering at the hands of Mithridates or the Romans.*

so as to alter slavery [i.e., their condition of servitude?] merely for the better

52* 2.50M, inc. 15Mc, inc. 90D, inc. 58K

Maurenbr., noting the past tense of the verb, conjectured that S. was describing the effect of the lex Aurelia of 75, which removed Sulla's ban on further political offices for tribunes of the plebs (see fr. 2.44). Alternatively, it could refer to the activity of the Gracchi (so de Brosses and Gerlach), or to any number of revolutionary designs, or to simply a change in the course of action being pursued (see note below).

which has been [will have been?] a cause for insurrection[1]

[1] Or "for a change of plans," if the passage from *Aen.* 4.290 can be taken as a guide, since the language is nearly identical, and at *Aen.* 4.290 *res novae* does not have its customary political meaning ("revolution") but rather describes Aeneas' altered course of action.

431

53* inc. 14M, inc. 50Mc, inc. 96D, inc. 65K

Quom[1] inferior omni via[2] grassaretur,

Macrob. *Exc. Bob., GL* 5.652.3; Macrob. *Exc. Paris. GL* 5.626.22: to illustrate *grassor,* the frequentative of *gradior.*

[1] dum *ex codice Pithoei (GL 5.626), edd. Sall. praeter Gerlach ed. 1856 et Maurenbr.*   [2] omni vi *Douza*

54* inc. 22M, inc. 58Mc, inc. 103D, inc. 72K

inbecilla est fortitudo dum pendet

Schol. Stat. ad *Theb.* 5.384 (also quoting *Luc.* 3.692–93): to illustrate how the force of blows is lessened when dealt from a position of instability caused by rolling seas.

55* inc. 27M, inc. 63Mc, deest in D et K

⟨datis in⟩[1] | publicum studiis, conrup⟨e⟩|rant [2] | me ver[1]u [2/3] | unum p[2/3]

Schol. Bemb. in Ter. *Haut.* 490: to support the claim that *vera* (lit., "true") in Ter. = *utilia* (useful). The number of letter-spaces indicated within square brackets is approximate for the ends of lines, which are marked with |.

[1] *Maurenbr. in app. crit.*

53* inc. 14M, inc. 50Mc, inc. 96D, inc. 65K

Lack of context makes it impossible to say whether inferior *(lit., "more lowly") refers to a physical situation (e.g., a military force trying to make its way through mountain passes occupied by the enemy: so La Penna) or is applied metaphorically to a person lacking the resources or standing to compete on a level playing field in politics or business and therefore sought his objectives by any means possible.*

Since the man of lower standing was pressing on by every avenue,

54* inc. 22M, inc. 58Mc, inc. 103D, inc. 72K

Lack of context and the brevity of the text make it impossible to say whether S. was referring to strength that was of body or of spirit. The two passages to which the scholiast likens this fragment describe hindrances to physical valor from without.

valor is ineffective while it has no firm footing[1]

[1] *OLD* s.v. *pendeo* 10; or "while it depends on _____" (*OLD* 13, if an abl. with, or without, *ab* or *ex* completed the meaning of *pendet*).

55* inc. 27M, inc. 63Mc, not included in D and K

The text is too lacunose for its meaning to be recovered. It presumably once contained some form of the word verus, *since the scholiast quoted S. to give an example of that word with the meaning "useful." Italics in the translation signifies that the text is uncertain.*

⟨having devoted⟩ zeal ⟨toward⟩ the public good, they had seduced . . . me . . . one * * *

56* inc. 28M, inc. 64Mc, deest in D et K

adcommodatum[1] mandatum credat

Gloss. 5, p. 220.29: glossing *mandet* as *credat* (entrust).

[1] At cum[modatum] *Maurenbr.*

SHORT PHRASES AND SINGLE WORDS, FRR. 57–69

57* inc. 34M, inc. 70Mc, inc. 110D, inc. 93K

duci probare

Quint. 9.3.12: to illustrate the figure *heteroiosis* (a variation of a stock expression) for the sake of novelty, and usually with brevity, citing first *Jug.* 10.1 (the periphrasis *falsum me habuit* for *me fefellit*) and then this fragment and the following two (58 and 59). None is assigned to a specific work by S.

58* inc. 35M, inc. 71Mc, inc. 108D, inc. 77K

non paeniturum

Quint. 9.3.12: see fr. 57; glossed as *non acturum paenitentiam.*

59* inc. 36M, inc. 72Mc, inc. 109D, inc. 92K

visuros

Quint. 9.3.12: see fr. 57; glossed as *ad videndum missos.*

60* inc. 31M, inc. 67Mc, deest in D et K

hic proconsule

Prob. GL 4.126.12: commenting on the seemingly anomalous *hic proconsule* (as opposed to *hic proconsul*).

56* inc. 28M, inc. 64Mc, not included in D and K

let him entrust an appropriate commission[1]

[1] Or, "but when/since he entrusts the commission," if Maurenbr.'s emendation is adopted.

SHORT PHRASES AND SINGLE WORDS, FRR. 57–69

57* inc. 34M, inc. 70Mc, inc. 110D, inc. 93K

to be thought[1] to prove (or "to prove to be led")

[1] *Duci* may be a verb (as translated), or the dat. of *dux*, in which case = "to justify . . . to the leader" (so Frassennetti and McGushin).

58* inc. 35M, inc. 71Mc, inc. 108D, inc. 77K

not about to experience regret

59* inc. 36M, inc. 72Mc, inc. 109D, inc. 92K

men whose mission it was to see

60* inc. 31M, inc. 67Mc, not included in D and K

Possibly a reference to the appointment of Pompey as proconsul to pursue the war in Spain against Sertorius (so La Penna).

he as proconsul

61* inc. 29M, inc. 65Mc, inc. 98D, inc. 67K

⟨confestim⟩

Charis. *GL* 1.196.3–4 = p. 255B.2–3: to illustrate *confestim* = *continuo, sine intervallo* (without delay).

62 inc. 17M, inc. 53Mc, inc. 9D, 1.109K

rumore primo

Charis. *GL* 1.216.25 = p. 280B.7 (book number missing in **N** and its descendants, but transmitted as "I" = Book 1 by the now lost manuscript consulted by Cuyck [pre-1551] and later by Putschen [ed. 1605]): the second-century AD commentator Asper interpreted—incorrectly, it seems—*primo* as an adv., not an adj., comparing it with *primo aspectu* (Verg. *Aen.* 1.613), where *primo* appears to be answered by *deinde* in the next verse and may have an adverbial overtone: "at the first sight of him" = "firstly at the sight of him."

63††† inc. 32M, inc. 68Mc, inc. 118D, inc. 91K

cuncta potiundi

Arus. *GL* 7.498.5 = p. 220DC (assigned to IVG, perhaps a corruption of "IV"): to illustrate *potior* + acc. of thing.

64* inc. 30M, inc. 66Mc, inc. 116D, 88K

luces

Serv. *Comm. in Don. GL* 4.432.20–21: noting that S. employs the anomalous pl. *paces* of *pax* and *luces* of *lux*. Neither word is assigned to a particular work. While *paces* is attested at *Jug.* 31.20, *luces* does not occur in *Cat.* or *Jug.*

61* inc. 29M, inc. 65Mc, inc. 98D, inc. 67K

For a discussion of the textual issues, see fr. dub. 10.

without delay

62 inc. 17M, inc. 53Mc, inc. 9D, 1.109K

Some action taken in response to unsubstantiated information (cf. the same expression at Tac. Ann. 2.77.5). There is very tenuous evidence in the manuscript tradition of the quoting source that this fragment may belong to Book 1.

at the first hearsay

63††† inc. 32M, inc. 68Mc, inc. 118D, inc. 91K

of getting control of everything

64* inc. 30M, inc. 66Mc, inc. 116D, 88K

days(?)[1]

[1] Since S. employs the singular *lux* in the sense of "(light of) day" (e.g., *Jug.* 91.3, 99.1), conceivably the pl. was used as an equivalent of *dies* (pl.). Alternatively, the pl. *luces* may have been introduced under the influence of being included in a series of pl. nouns, after the fashion of *paces* at *Jug.* 31.20.

65* inc. 38M, inc. 74Mc, inc. 112D, inc. 79K

ut primo mense veris **novum** *dicatur* ver, *secundo* **adultum**, *tertio* **praeceps**; *sicut etiam Sallustius dicit ubique.*

Serv. ad *G.* 1.43.

*AESTATE NOVA. Bene "**nova**," quia est aestas*[1] *et* **adulta** *et* **praeceps**, *secundum Sallustium.*

Serv. & Serv. auct. ad *Aen.* 1.430.

[1] *om. Serv.*

66* inc. 20M, inc. 56Mc, inc. 105D, 74K

soleas[1] festinate

Serv. auct. ad *Aen.* 12.425: to give an example from S. in support of the explanation that *properare* + *arma* in Virgil = "give" (*dare*) quickly.

[1] *Masvicius:* solas *F*

67* 1.39M, inc. 7Mc, inc. 120D, deest in K

Samnitium

Fr. Bob. GL 5.561.2: to illustrate an exception to the principle that words of the third decl. such as *Samnis, Samnitis* that end in *–is* in the nom. sing. and are not parisyllabic in the gen. form the gen. pl. in *–um.*

65* inc. 38M, inc. 74Mc, inc. 112D, inc. 79K

As time markers, S. apparently subdivided each season of the year into three parts, corresponding roughly to the three months comprising each of the four seasons.

such that in the first month of spring the season is called "**early**" (***novum***), *in the second* "**full**" (***adultum***), *in the third* "**waning**" (***praeceps***); *this is precisely the way Sallust puts it throughout*

EARLY SUMMER. Rightly "**early**" (***nova***), *because there is also* "**full**" (***adulta***) *and* "**waning**" (***praeceps***) *summer,* according to Sallust.

66* inc. 20M, inc. 56Mc, inc. 105D, 74K

The request to fetch sandals may have been made by guests hurriedly departing from a banquet (so Kritz) or by the praetor L. Cossinius, who had to flee from his bath when attacked by Spartacus in 73 (Plut. Crass. 9.5–6; cf. fr. 3.41): so Maurenbr.

be quick with the sandals

67* 1.39M, inc. 7Mc, inc. 120D, not included in K

Possibly, according to Maurenbr., describing the Samnites who marched against Rome in November 83 in a desperate attempt to draw off the Sullan forces that were blockading the younger Marius in Praeneste.

of the Samnites

68* inc. 18M, inc. 54Mc, deest in D et K

admodum vanus

Serg. *Explan. GL* 4.559.28: to illustrate *admodum* = *valde* (*OLD* s. v. *admodum* 2).

69* inc. 21M, inc. 57Mc, deest in D et K

bene posita urbs

Schol. Bern. ad Verg. *G.* 3.13: to illustrate *pono* = *constituo*.

FRAGMENTS NOT ASSIGNED TO BOOKS

68* inc. 18M, inc. 54Mc, not included in D and K

extremely unreliable (foolish?)

69* inc. 21M, inc. 57Mc, not included in D and K

a well-positioned city

FRAGMENTA DUBIA
ET SPURIA

1* deest in M, Mc, D, K, nuovo 2 Funari

    aquis hiemantibus

Sen. *Ep.* 114.19: inspired by this expression in S., the historian L. Arruntius overused *hiemare* metaphorically in various contexts.

2* dub. 2M, deest in Mc, inc. 111D, inc. 78K

    †volgus†[1] amat fieri[2]

Quint. 9.3.17: to illustrate a Graecism in S.—presumably *amo* + inf. in the sense of Gk. φιλεῖ = "to be accustomed," a usage first attested in S. (*TLL* 1.1956.35–59)—but the text may be corrupt. Recent editors of Quintilian delete *volgus* to produce the equivalent of φιλεῖ γίγνεσθαι = "tends to happen" (cf. Thuc. 3.81.5).

    [1] *del. Radermacher*: *om G¹* (*corr. G²*) *sed vix consulto*: vulgo *Francius*: illud *Wölfflin*   [2] fieri ‹in rebus dubiis› *Winterbottom dubitanter per litt.* (*cf. Amm. Marc. 16.12.40, 17.1.7*)

3* 1.18M (testimonia), 1.16Mc (comm.), 1.33D (testim.), 1.38K (testim.)

    omne ius in validioribus esse

Fronto p. 157.14–15: to illustrate a distinctive Sallustian turn of phrase.

DOUBTFUL AND SPURIOUS
FRAGMENTS

1* not included in M, Mc, D, K, nuovo 2 Funari

This may be a misquotation of Jug. 37.4 (hiemalibus aquis), *but Seneca quotes to illustrate the verb* hiemare, *not the adj.*

    amid the wintry waters

2* dub. 2M, not included in Mc, inc. 111D, inc. 78K

Dietsch speculated that Quintilian misquoted Jug. 34.1 (quae ira fieri amat) *and that* volgus *came to be added under the influence of the context in* Jug. 34.1, *which describes an angry* multitudo *at a public meeting.*

    * * *[1] tends to happen

  [1] In view of the uncertainties, I have obelized *uulgus;* if the paradosis is retained, the meaning is "a mob tends to form" (as pointed out to me by D. H. Berry *per litteras*).

3* 1.18M (testimonia), 1.16Mc (comm.), 1.33D (testim.), 1.38K (testim.)

Possibly a paraphrase, or loose quotation of omne ius in viribus esset *(fr. 1.16).*

    that all right is in the possession of stronger men

4* 2.68M, deest in Mc, 2.20D, 2.26K

sed Metellus in †ulipie h.†[1]

Donat. ad Ter. *An.* 310: to illustrate *sed* as an inceptive conj., virtually equivalent to *atque* (a common usage in S., noted by Serv. ad *Aen.* 10.411, without citing a specific example).

[1] in ulipie h.] *in rasura* V^2: ulipie h. *C*: in ulipie hoc *T*: in ulpie hoc *D*: olimpie h. (h. *om. L*) *P L:* in ulteriorem H(ispaniam) *Wessner*: in volnere *edd. Sall.*

5* 3.45M, inc. 20Mc, 2.24D, 2.30K

sed Metellus in ulteriorem[1] provinciam[2]

Donat. ad Ter. *Phorm.* 192: to illustrate *sed* employed to introduce the conclusion to some previous remark.

[1] in ulteriorem] *om. R C O*   [2] provincia *R O*

6 p. 212M, deest in Mc, 1.41D.5n., inc. 81K

aequor⟨e⟩[1] et terra

Donat. ad Ter. *Phorm.* 243: following upon a quotation of fr. 1.49.4, *nam quid a Pyrrho, Hannibale* (see ad loc.), in commenting on the use of asyndeton side by side with the expression of a conjunction.

[1] *Lindenbrog*

7* p. 212M, deest in Mc, 119D, deest in K

4* 2.68M, not included in Mc, 2.20D, 2.26K

Most editors of S. accept the conjecture volnere *for the obviously corrupt* ulipie h. *and connect this fragment with the wounding of Metellus in the Sertorian War (see fr. 2.55). If, however, we restore with* Wessner *in* ulteriorem H., *the scholiast may have had in mind either a garbled version of fr. 3.10.1 (so McGushin) or fr. dub. 5, if indeed the latter is separate from fr. 3.10.1 (see immediately below).*

moreover Metellus in * * *

5* 3.45M, inc. 20Mc, 2.24D, 2.30K

This fragment so closely resembles the opening words of fr. 3.10.1 (at Metellus in ulteriorem Hispaniam) *that it may simply be a paraphrase, and yet the scholiast presents it specifically to illustrate* sed *meaning "so."*

so Metellus . . . to the farther province

6 p. 212M, not included in Mc, 1.41D.5n., inc. 81K

If Donatus did not misquote fr. 1.49.4 by substituting these words for Philippoque et Antiocho, *it is possible that they were taken from another passage in S.'s* Historiae. *If that is the case, they provide the only example of the poetic* aequor = mare *in S.*

on sea and land

7* p. 212M, not included in Mc, 119D, not included in K

It is by no means certain that Arusianus attributed these words to S. They come after a quotation from Jug. *43.1 and are introduced by* id est, *which Lindemann emended to* idem, *thereby identifying S. as the author. (For Arusianus' use of* idem *to introduce a second quotation from the same author, cf. the next frag-*

advorsus ille[1] nobilitatis

Arus. *GL* 7.451.15 = p. 51DC: following upon a quotation of *advorso populi* (*Jug.* 43.1), to which these words are linked merely by the expression *id est*.

[1] *Lindemann in app*: illi *codd.*

8* inc. 33M, inc. 69Mc. deest in D et K

sciens horum[1]

Arus. *GL* 7.509.25 = p. 265DC (credited to S. without specifying the title of a work; followed by fr. 2.87, which is introduced with the words *idem "Hist. II"*): to illustrate *sciens* + gen. of thing.

[1] locorum *Ruhnken, fort. recte (cf.* Jug. *85.46* locorum sciens*)*

9 dub. 4M, deest in Mc, 3.32D, 3.37K

ment.) Conceivably, however, adversus illi *of the paradosis was not part of the quotation but instead the heading (to introduce an example of* adversus + *dat.), since the preceding heading is* adversus illius.

that well-known opponent of the nobility

8* inc. 33M, inc. 69Mc, not included in D and K

Arusianus, who does not assign this fragment to a specific work by S., is possibly misquoting from memory Jug. 85.46 *(*locorum sciens*).*

knowing these

9 dub. 4M, not included in Mc, 3.32D, 3.37K

The form of citation ("Crispus III"—as opposed to Charisius' practice elsewhere of writing always "Sallustius," frequently accompanied by a title, never with a bare numeral) casts suspicion on this quotation. If the word historiarum *has dropped out in front of "III" and the quotation is from Book 3 of S.'s* Historiae, *the context, as suggested by Kritz, may be shortly after the storm that destroyed Mithridates' fleet on his retreat from Cyzicus in the spring of 72 (cf. frr. 3.76–77). At that time Mithridates sent letters of appeal to Tigranes of Armenia and other neighboring kings (*App. Mithr. 78; Memnon, FGrH 434F29.6*). He conceivably argued that the war being waged by the Romans against him in Pontus was likely to spread to bordering kingdoms after the fashion of a raging fire.*

*Keil (*GL 1.609, Addenda*), on the other hand, adopted the view of Lang, who postulated a lacuna after "Crispus III," speculating that there dropped out of Charisius' text a quotation from S., which was followed by the name of a poet who was the author of the fragment given here. Keil altered the text to produce two trochaic septenarii (*Nonne . . . acriter / haud . . . proxumae*) and assigned them to some unknown comic poet (*Com. Inc. 46–47 Ri.[3]*). But none of this is certain.*

Non[1] tu scis? Si quas[2] aedis ignis cepit acriter, haud facile[3] est[4] defensu quin[5] conburantur proxumae.

Charis. *GL* 1.195.21–23 and Addenda, p. 609 = p. 254B.13–15 (attributed to "Crispus III"): to give an example of the adv. *acriter.*

[1] nonne *Keil*   [2] quando *add. post* quas *Fleckeisen*   [3] faciles *Wagner*   [4] *Keil*: sunt *N*   [5] *Kritz.*: quine *N*: quin ne *C*

10* dub. 5M, deest in Mc, inc. 98D, inc. 67K

†fessit ut†[1] nuntiis confestim lugubribus

Charis. *GL* 1.196.3–4 = p. 255B.2–3: to illustrate *confestim = continuo, sine intervallo* (without delay).

[1] fecit ut *ed. princ. Neap. (1532)*: <funus> faxitur *Della Casa*

11* inc. 7M, inc. 43Mc, inc. 47D, inc. 13K

virtuti[1] satis credebant

Serv. ad *Ecl.* 2.17 and *Gloss.* 5, p. 186.20: to illustrate *credere = confidere* (credited to S. without specifying a work by title).

[1] virtutis *Gloss.*

Do you not know? If a fire has violently seized a house, it is not an easy matter to protect the neighboring houses from being burned up.

10* dub. 5M, not included in Mc, inc. 98D, inc. 67K

The absence of a numeral in the text of Charisius after the words Sallustius libro, *which immediately precede the opening words of this fragment, has led editors of Charisius to postulate a lacuna of indeterminate length between* libro *and* fessit. *Furthermore, since the fragment is directly followed by an annotation credited to the second-century AD commentator Statilius Maximus, Maurenbr. argued that the quotation itself is not from S. but from either Cic. or Cato, since they are the only two authors on whom Statilius is known to have commented. Consequently* confestim *(without delay), the word Charisius is treating in his discussion, is the sole word that can be restored with certainty to the presumed lacuna and credited to S. (fr. inc. 61). On the other hand, nothing precludes the assumption that the only thing missing from Charisius' text is the book number and that the quotation is indeed from S., having been treated by Statilius perhaps in his commentary on Cato, an author S. is known to have imitated.*

* * * speedy, mournful messages

11* inc. 7M, inc. 43Mc, inc. 47D, inc. 13K

Since the two quoting sources merely attribute this fragment to S. without assigning it to a specific work, it may be a loose quotation from Jug. *106.3 (*virtuti suorum satis credere*).*

they had sufficient confidence in valor

12* 1.135M (testimonia), deest in Mc, 1.71D (testimonia), inc. 82K

    cornua occanuerunt

Serv. ad *G.* 2.384 (credited to S. without specifying the title of a work): to illustrate the pf. *occanui* of *occano* (of trumpets/trumpeters "to sound a call").

13* 3.14M testimonia, deest in Mc, 3.60D testimonia, 3.63K

    *licet dicat Sallustius **Cretenses primos invenisse religionem**, unde apud eos natus fingitur Iuppiter*

Serv. ad *Aen.* 8.352: to take note of a rival view contradicting the tradition that the earliest humans were dwellers in Arcadia.

{Serv. & Serv. auct. ad *Aen.* 3.104 (*ut Sallustius dicat . . . quia primos Cretenses constat invenisse religionem*): quoting S. to give the reason for the tradition that baby Zeus was suckled on Crete.}

14* p. 211M, deest in Mc, inc. 115D, inc. 86K

    senecta iam aetate

Serv. ad *Aen.* 11.165: to illustrate *senecta + aetas,* as opposed to *senecta* on its own, with *aetas* to be supplied as is the case in Virgil, loc. cit.

12* 1.135M (testimonia), not included in Mc, 1.71D (testimonia), inc. 82K

Possibly Servius misquotes from memory cornicines occanuere *(fr. 1.107).*

the horns sounded

13* 3.14M testimonia, not included in Mc, 3.60D testimonia, 3.63K

Maurenbr. concluded that Servius was paraphrasing fr. 3.50.

although Sallust states that the **Cretans were the first to invent religion**, whence the invention of the story that Jupiter was born among them

14* p. 211M, not included in Mc, inc. 115D, inc. 86K

Maurenbr. views this as a loose quotation of acta iam aetate *from Cotta's speech (fr. 2.43.2). On the other hand, Serv. quoted specifically to illustrate the adj.* senecta *accompanied by the noun* aetas.

now in old age

15* 4.6M, inc. 25Mc, inc. 24D, 3.71K

SIC OMNES AMOR UNUS HABET "Sic," id est, dum paullatim suis invicem subveniunt, omnes in bellum[1] coacti sunt. Sic Sallustius.

Serv. ad *Aen.* 12.282: to define the sense of *sic* (thus) in Virgil's account of how war flared up again between the Trojans and Latins after the breaking of the truce.

[1] proelium *Dietsch (sed cf. fr. dub. 26)*

16* deest in M, inc. 11Mc, deest in D, K

angustissumo divortio

Schol. in Iuv. ad 10.1: a periphrasis for the Strait of Gibraltar in giving the location of Gades in Spain.

17* 1.66M (testimonia), deest in Mc, D, K, nuovo 3 Funari

maturrumum

Placid. *Gloss.* p. 83.18: to illustrate S.'s preference in the *Hist.* for *maturrimum,* instead of *maturissimum.*

18††† dub. 3M, deest in Mc, 1.63D, K

15* 4.6M, inc. 25Mc, inc. 24D, 3.71K

It is impossible to say which, if any, of these words are being directly attributed to S., as opposed to the concept as a whole.

THUS ALL ARE POSSESSED BY ONE DESIRE [TO SETTLE THE MATTER WITH STEEL]. *"Thus," that is, while little by little they mutually come to each other's aid, all were swept along into war. So Sallust.*

16* not included in M, inc. 11Mc, not included in D, K

Identified by Syme (Eranos 55 [1957]: 171–74) as a possible fragment of S. on the grounds that although this phrase (used to refer to the Strait of Gibraltar) is not credited in the least way to S., the only other instance of the noun divortium *with a superlative adj.* (artissimus) *in the sense of* fretum *(strait) is in Tacitus (Ann. 12.63.1, describing the Bosporus), an author who drew upon S. in dealing with the geography of the Black Sea region.*

   by a very narrow separation

17 * 1.66M (testimonia), not included in Mc, D, K, nuovo 3 Funari

This may be a misquotation of maturrume *(found in frr. 1.58 and 1.67.16) on the part of the glossator.*

   very timely

18††† dub. 3M, not included in Mc, 1.63D, K

The assignment of this fragment to S.'s Jugurtha *by the two quoting sources led Maurenbr. to surmise that it is loosely based on* Jug. *18–19. The fragment may, however, belong to Book 1 of the* Historiae, *where, after mentioning Sertorius' frustrated desire to withdraw to the Isles of the Blessed (frr. 1.88–90), S. recounted*

Maurique, vanum genus, ut alia Africae, contende-
bant antipodas ultra Aethiopiam cultu Persarum
iustos et egregios agere

Prisc. *GL* 3.46.27–47.2 (*in Iugurthino*): to illustrate the prep.
ultra (beyond).

{Non. p. 416M = 672L.29–30 (*Mauri, vanum genus*) *in Iugurtae*
[sic] *bello:* to illustrate *vanum* = *mendax* (untruthful). Tert. *De
anim.* 20.3: S. applied the description *vani* to the Mauri.}

19 dub. 6M, deest in Mc, 1.64D, 1.121K

Ἄζιλις, πόλις Λιβύης, οἱ δὲ περὶ Σαλλούστιον οὐ πόλιν
ἀλλὰ τόπον φασὶ καὶ ποταμὸν εἶναι.

Steph. Byz. p. 32M.

20* M (fasc. 2, p. 60), deest in Mc, 2.2D, 2.4K

Sertorius' sojourn in Mauretania and participation in a successful expedition against the princeling Ascalis in 81 BC (Plut. Sert. 9.2–5): so Kritz and Dietsch.

the Moors, a deceitful race, like others in Africa, claim that fine, upright people adhering to Persian culture are living on the other side of the world, beyond Ethiopia

19 dub. 6M, not included in Mc, 1.64D, 1.121K

Kritz speculated that Azilis may be a corruption of Zelis, a town south of Tingis (mod. Tangier), not far from the Atlantic coast of northwestern Mauretania (Strabo 17.3.6, p. 827), which S. may have treated in connection with Sertorius' activities mentioned in the preceding fragment. Maurenbr. doubted that the Sallust referred to by the sixth-century writer Stephanus of Byzantium was the Roman historian.

Azalis, *a city of Libya, but Sallust and others[1] say that it is not a city but a region and river.*

[1] The Greek says lit., "Sallust and his associates," but the phrase can mean simply "Sallust" (see *LSJ* περί + acc. C I.2), or Stephanus may have chosen a vague expression to imply multiple authorities.

20* M (fasc. 2, p. 60), not included in Mc, 2.2D, 2.4K

Since Isidore is known to have drawn upon S. at Etym. 14.7.1 for information concerning the geography of Sardinia (see fr. 2.2), Isid. may also have relied upon S. for his account of the eponymous hero Sardus. Pausanias (10.17.2) gives the same account, including the detail that Sardus was the son of Makeris (i.e., the Phoenician god Melkart), whom the Egyptians and Phoenicians equated with Herakles.

Sardus Hercule procreatus *cum magna multitudine **a Libya profectus** Sardiniam occupavit et **ex suo vocabulo insulae dedit**.*

Isid. *Etym.* 14.6.39.

21* 3.22M, inc. 18Mc, deest in D et K

Metrophanes promeruit gratiam Mithridatis obsequendo.

Isid. *Etym.* 2.11.1 (repeated at 2.21.14): offered, without indication of author, as one of two examples of a *chria* (Greek, χρεία), which differs from a *sententia* (maxim)—a generalizing statement of the sort "subservience produces friends, the truth enemies"—by making a like observation with reference to a specific case.

22* p. 212M, deest in Mc, 1.34D, 1.38K (testimonia)

qui ⟨plus⟩[1] poterat, plus iuris habere videbatur

Schol. Luc. 1.175 (Guelf. manuscript), p. 33W: to illustrate Lucan's observation that "might (*vis*) became the measure (*mensura*) of right (*ius*)."

[1] *Roth*

23* p. 212M, deest in Mc, inc. 87D, inc. 55K

Staphylus . . . ***primus docuit vinum aqua misceri***, *C. Plinius et Sal⟨l⟩ustius auctor est.*

Ps.-Apul. *De orthogr.* §12 (p. 104).

Sardus, the son of Hercules, upon setting out from Africa with a large throng took possession of Sardinia and *gave his name to the island*.

21* 3.22M, inc. 18Mc, not included in D and K

It is pure speculation that S. is the author, based on the mention of Metrophanes (cf. fr. 4.2), a general of Mithridates who played a role in the fighting around Cyzicus in 73 (Oros. 6.2.16). Maurenbr. assigned this fragment to the first mention of Metrophanes, at the time of Mithridates' invasion of Bithynia in early 74 BC.

Metrophanes gained the favor of Mithridates by being subservient.

22* p. 212M, not included in Mc, 1.34D, 1.38K (testimonia)

Maurenbr., following Kritz, classified this fragment as spurious on the grounds that it is not found in the best sources for scholia on Lucan (one manuscript only preserves it). It looks suspiciously like a dim reflection of ut omne ius in viribus esset *(fr. 1.16). Cf. fr. dub. 3.*

the one who was more powerful seemed to possess more right

23* p. 212M, not included in Mc, inc. 87D, inc. 55K

The work De orthographia, *said to be by one L. Caecilius Minutianus Apuleius, is most probably a forgery of the fifteenth century, although, in that case, it is difficult to imagine where the author drew his information concerning S., since the* Historiae *had long vanished by the fifteenth century. Pliny does mention this detail at HN 7.199.*

Staphylus was the first to teach the mixing of wine with water, according to Pliny and Sallust.

24* p. 212M, deest in Mc, inc. 86D, inc. 54K

Pyrrhus . . . *rex Epiri* . . . **interemptusque** *fuit* . . . **in aede Dianae a quadam muliere**, *Trogo, Sal‹l›u‹stio›que et Luc‹c›eio ‹auctoribus›*

Ps.-Apul. *De orthogr.* §16 (p. 105).

{Serv. ad *Aen.* 2.469: credits S. with deriving the name "Pyrrhus" from the color of his hair.}

PRESERVED IN PEROTTI'S *CORNUCOPIAE,* FRR. 19–49

25* inc. 75Mc

postquam unum in locum omnes convenere

Corn. 406: to illustrate *convenio = congregor* or *coeo.*

26* inc. 76Mc

in eo bello trecenti milites desiderati

Corn. 517: to illustrate *bellum = proelium.*

27* inc. 77Mc

Bona pars militum inde discesserat.

Corn. 518: to illustrate *bonus = magnus.*

24* p. 212M, not included in Mc, inc. 86D, inc. 54K

On the suspect nature of the source preserving this fragment, see fr. 23. If, in fact, the content of fr. 24 goes back to S. (Serv. does attest that S. had occasion to mention Pyrrhus), S. may have alluded to the death of King Pyrrhus in his account of past fighting in southern Italy, where the devastation caused by Spartacus' bands took place (so Gerlach). However, according to Plutarch (Pyrrh. 34.2–3; cf. Justin. 25.5.1), Pyrrhus died after being struck by a roof tile hurled from above by an Argive woman.

Pyrrhus . . . *king of Epirus* . . . *and* **was killed . . . in Diana's temple by some woman,** *according to Trogus, Sallust and Lucceius*

PRESERVED IN PEROTTI'S
CORNUCOPIAE, FRR. 19–49

25* inc. 75Mc

Possibly a loose quotation of postquam in una moenia convenere *(Cat. 6.2).*

after all gathered into a single place

26* inc. 76Mc

in that combat the loss of 300 soldiers

27* inc. 77Mc

A good part of the soldiers had departed from there.

28* inc. 78Mc

his actuariae naves circiter triginta, decem onera-
riae erant

Corn. 568: to illustrate two types of ship: an *oneraria,* so named
from carrying burdens (*onera*), and an *actuaria,* a ship noted for
its speed, so named from the fact that it can be driven (*agi*) easily.

29* inc. 79Mc

prostratisque militibus, fugae se dedit

Corn. 599: to illustrate *prosterno* = *vincere, profligare,* or *exs-
tinguere.*

30* inc. 80Mc

Qua victoria elati hostes, nostri territi atque animis
consternati, discessere.

Corn. 600: to illustrate the first conj. verb *consterno* = *deiicere* (to
cast down); cf. fr. 1.122.

31* inc. 81Mc

in medio campus iacet aquis undique scatens

Corn. 707: to illustrate *iacere* in the metaphorical sense of *esse*
or *exstare.*

32* inc. 82Mc

dummodo putetis vos tutos esse, quoad reliqua
multitudo advenerit

Corn. 713: to illustrate *quoad* = *quousque.*

28* inc. 78Mc

At 2.90M, S. mentioned actuariae *in connection with pirate vessels. Nonius, who preserves that fragment, and Perotti use nearly identical language to explain the nature of* actuariae.

these men had at their disposal roughly thirty light galleys, ten cargo ships

29* inc. 79Mc

and after the soldiers had been annihilated, he gave himself up to flight

30* inc. 80Mc

McGushin saw here a possible reference to the decisive victory of Mithridates over Lucullus' legate Triarius at the Battle of Zela in the summer of 67 (Dio 36.12.4); cf. fr. inc. 3.

And by the victory the enemy was exalted, while our men, frightened and downcast in spirit, scattered.

31* inc. 81Mc

in the middle lies a plain gushing with water everywhere

32* inc. 82Mc

provided that you think yourselves safe until the rest of the throng has arrived

33* inc. 83Mc

pauca timide remisseque locutus abscessit

Corn. 625: to illustrate the adv. *remisse,* derived from *remitto,* = *humiliter.*

34* inc. 84Mc

tum scelerum suorum in primisque conspirationis conscientia sol‹l›iciti, quo se verterent non videbant

Corn. 836: to give an example of *conscientia,* derived from *conscius,* applied to multiple objects of a sense of guilt.

35* inc. 85Mc

priusquam hostis[1] invaderet

[1] hosteis *Corn.*

Corn. 302: to illustrate *invado* = *aggredior.*

36* inc. 86Mc

et piscatoria scapha in altum navigat

Corn. 721: to illustrate *altum* meaning the deep sea, far from land.

37* inc. 87Mc

quo nemo vir melior nec praestantior

Corn. 86: one of several examples of *homo* (or *vir*) expressed with *nemo,* offered to counter Servius' claim (ad *Aen.* 9.6) that *homo* is implicit in *nemo.*

DOUBTFUL AND SPURIOUS FRAGMENTS

33* inc. 83Mc

after uttering a few words apprehensively and sub-
missively, he departed

34* inc. 84Mc

*The language, in part, resembles Philippus' description of those
who joined the revolt led by M. Lepidus (cos. 78): scelerum conscientia exagitati (fr. 1.67.7).*

anxious owing to their sense of guilt over their own
crimes and especially over the conspiracy, they did
not know where to turn

35* inc. 85Mc

before he attacked the enemy

36* inc. 86Mc

*Possibly part of S.'s description of the flight of C. Marius in 88 (so
McGushin); cf. fr. 1.23.*

and he sails out to the deep in a fishing skiff

37* inc. 87Mc

*McGushin suggested that the description may be of Sertorius; cf.
frr. 1.76–77.*

than whom no man [was] better or more outstanding

38* inc. 88Mc

effuso ac profligato peditatu, paulatim retrocedere
coeperunt

Corn. 280: to illustrate the metaphorical use of *effundere* = *pro-sternere* or *profligare.*

39* inc. 89Mc

bis fusos milites

Corn. 278: to illustrate *fundere* = *profligare.*

40* inc. 90Mc

antequam arcem proderet hostibus

Corn. 292: to illustrate *prodo* = *trado.*

41* inc. 91Mc

Verum hostes tandem robore ac viribus praevaluerunt.

Corn. 879: to illustrate *praevaleo* = *antecello, praestantior sum.*

42* inc. 92Mc

quom montem undique circumplexus obsideret

Corn. 276: to illustrate the compound, depon. verb *circumplec-tor,* from *plico.*

43* inc. 93Mc

circumdatos militibus saltus mox occupavit

Corn. 284: to illustrate *circumdo* = *circu(m)eo* (to encircle).

38* inc. 88Mc

after the infantry had been routed and scattered, they began to withdraw gradually

39* inc. 89Mc

twice routed soldiers

40* inc. 90Mc

before he handed over the citadel to the enemy

41* inc. 91Mc

But at last the enemy prevailed through strength and might.

42* inc. 92Mc

McGushin proposed connecting this fragment with the attempt of the praetor Clodius (C. Claudius Glaber) in 73 to trap Spartacus' band of escaped gladiators on Mt. Vesuvius (Plut. Crass. 9.2); cf. fr. 3.40.

when he had completely surrounded the mountain and was besieging it

43* inc. 93Mc

Possibly some operation of Sertorius in Spain (so McGushin).

soon he seized the defiles which had been encircled with soldiers

44* inc. 94Mc

iam omnem exercitum traiecerat

Corn. 8: to illustrate *traiicio* = *transporto* (to convey across).

45* inc. 95Mc

quibus dictis mox proelium commisere

Corn. 626: to illustrate *committo* = *initio, incoho* (to begin).

46* inc. 96Mc

hinc late patescentibus campis exercitum tuto emit-
tit

Corn. 692: to illustrate the verb *patesco* (to be made open) =
pateo (to lie open).

47* inc. 97Mc

armati fores obsidebant

Corn. 151: to illustrate *armo* (to equip with arms), a verb derived
from *arma* (arms).

48* inc. 98Mc

ne forte desperatione adducti vitae mortem prae-
ferrent

Corn. 759: to illustrate the noun *desperatio* (despair).

DOUBTFUL AND SPURIOUS FRAGMENTS

44* inc. 94Mc

Possibly to be connected with Lucullus' crossing of the Euphrates on his Armenian campaign (so McGushin); cf. frr. 4.53–54.

already he had conveyed the whole army across

45* inc. 95Mc

McGushin saw here a possible reference to the haughty words uttered by Tigranes before his disastrous defeat at the hands of Lucullus at the Battle of Tigranocerta in 69 (belittling the Romans as too few to be a fighting force and too many to be ambassadors: Plut. Luc. 27.4; App. Mithr. 85).

and soon after this had been said, they began the battle

46* inc. 96Mc

from here, with the plains lying wide open, he safely dispatches his army

47* inc. 97Mc

Possibly a reference to the angry mob that forced the consuls of 75 to seek refuge in the house of Octavius (see fr. 2.41).

armed men were besieging the door

48* inc. 98Mc

so that they might not happen to be influenced by despair to prefer death to life

49* inc. 99Mc

dum subtendit insidias militi

Corn. 295: to illustrate *subtendo* used metaphorically of devising something for the sake of deception.

50* inc. 100Mc

multi in eo congressu perierunt

Corn. 150: to illustrate *congressus = pugna*.

51* inc. 101Mc

quom forte in eum irruerent, facile repulsi sunt

Corn. 868: to illustrate *irruo = proruo* (to rush violently forward).

52* inc. 102Mc

Quom paludatus incederet, inire quamprimum proelium cogitavit.

Corn. 216: to illustrate the adj. *paludatus* = "wearing a commander's cloak or other insignia of a commander."

53* inc. 103Mc

postquam hi qui signa praeferebant intellecto dis-crimine constitere

Corn. 29: to illustrate the compound verb *praefero*.

49* inc. 99Mc

while he lays an ambush for the soldier

50* inc. 100Mc

many perished in that engagement

51* inc. 101Mc

when they happened to charge against him, they
were easily driven back

52* inc. 102Mc

Cf. fr. inc. 17.

Since he was advancing in a general's cloak, he contemplated beginning battle as soon as possible.

53* inc. 103Mc

after these men who were carrying the standards in
front of them, upon grasping the dangerous situation, halted

54* inc. 104Mc

tum propere consul educit exercitum

Corn. 108: to illustrate the adv. *propere.*

55* inc. 105Mc

consurrexere omnes simulque in eum impetum fe-
cerunt

Corn. 104: to illustrate *consurgo* = *simul* (at the same time) +
surgo.

54* inc. 104Mc

then the consul quickly led out his army

55 * inc. 105Mc

Possibly a description of the assailants who murdered Sertorius at the banquet (Plut. Sert. 26.11): so La Penna.

all rose up together [from their couches?] and made a simultaneous attack on him

LETTERS TO CAESAR

INTRODUCTION

Two essays, cast in the form of open letters of advice addressed to Julius Caesar at the time of the civil war (49–45 BC), have survived thanks to having been copied into a single manuscript written in the late ninth century, **V** = *Vaticanus lat. 3864,* which preserves a collection of the speeches and letters excerpted from the genuine works of Sallust (see vol. 1, pp. lviii, lxi). The letters addressed to Caesar are not directly attributed to S. in the manuscript and appear to have been written as school exercises under the Empire in direct and deliberate imitation of S.'s style (see vol. 1, pp. xxix–xxxi). The first letter discusses problems facing Caesar after his victory in the civil war, chiefly those having to do with debt (5.4–7), but it offers no specific remedies of the sort proposed in the second letter. It is not clear how much time has elapsed since Caesar's victory over Pompey in August 48 (referred to at *Ad Caes. sen.* 1.2.2, cf. 2.7, 4.1), but the absence of any allusion to further fighting or victories in the African campaign of 46 or the Spanish campaign of 45 makes it seem likely that the fictional date is the autumn of 48.

The second essay, by contrast, pictures conditions a year or two earlier, at the outbreak of the civil war. Since there is no explicit reference to fighting, to say nothing of any indication of Caesar's victory over Pompey or other

475

foes, the context is either late 50 or early 49, just shortly
before hostilities commenced in January. This second essay identifies the abuse of wealth as the chief problem
facing Caesar the reformer. To combat that evil, four specific reforms are recommended: (1) New citizens are to be
added to the citizen body, and a mixture of old and new
citizens are to be settled in colonies with the aim of restoring the love of freedom by the infusion of new blood
(5.7–8); (2) the pool from which jurors are selected should
henceforth no longer be restricted to senators and members of the equestrian class but is to be expanded to include citizens of the first census class, and the size of juries
is to be increased (7.10–12); (3) the five census classes in
the Centuriate assembly are no longer to vote, as they always have, with preference being given to the wealthiest
but in an order determined by lot (8.1–2); and finally, (4)
the size of the senate is to be increased and voting in that
body is to be by secret ballot (11.2–7).

SIGLA

V	cod. Vaticanus lat. 3864 (9th c.)
V[1]	the first hand
V[2]	a correcting hand
ed. Rom.	editio princeps Romana (1475)
ed. Mant.	editio Mantuana (1476–1478)
Laet.	editio Pomponii Laeti (1490)
Ald.	editio Aldina (1509)
Faernus	corrections/conjectures reported by Reynolds (1991) from notations marked with "f." (= Gabrielus Faernus, Gabriello Faerno?) found in Bodleian copy of 1521 Aldine edition (Auct. 2R 5.7)

⟨EPISTULAE⟩ AD CAESAREM
SENEM DE RE PUBLICA

⟨I⟩

1. Pro vero antea optinebat regna atque imperia fortunam dono dare, item alia quae per mortaleis avide cupiuntur, quia et apud indignos saepe erant quasi per libidinem data
2. neque quoiquam incorrupta permanserant. Sed res docuit id verum esse, quod in carminibus Appius ait, fabrum esse suae quemque fortunae, atque in te maxume, qui tantum alios praegressus es, ut prius defessi sint homines lau-
3. dando facta tua quam tu laude digna faciundo. Ceterum

---

¹ This is the heading in our sole manuscript **V** (fol. 127r). Since both essays appear to have been cast in the form of an open letter—the second explicitly referred to as such (2.12.1, *perlectis litteris*)—"*Epistulae*" is easily understood. See volume 1, p. xxix n. 34 for a discussion. "Elder" (*senem*) is designed to distinguish Caesar the Dictator (100–44 BC) from his adopted son Octavian Caesar (63 BC–AD 14), the future emperor Augustus. The need for a distinction did not arise until after the spring of 44, when Octavian took the name C. Julius Caesar under the terms of his great-uncle's will (Cic. *Att.* 14.12[366].2).

² The war with Pompey is in the past (§2.2, *bellum tibi fuit*), so the letter postdates the defeat of Pompey at the Battle of

⟨LETTERS⟩ TO THE ELDER
CAESAR CONCERNING THE
AFFAIRS OF STATE[1]

⟨I⟩

[ca. Oct. 48 BC][2]

1. Previously, it used to be taken for granted that Fortune makes a gift of kingdoms and empires, as well as other objects eagerly coveted among mortals, because those possessions were often in the hands of the undeserving, as if given capriciously, and they had not remained intact under anyone's control. But experience has demonstrated that what Appius[3] stated in his verses is true, that "every man is the fashioner of his own fortune," and especially so with regard to you, who have excelled others so much so that men have sooner become weary in praising your deeds than you have in doing deeds worthy of praise. But

Pharsalus (August 9/June 7, 48 Jul.). 46 BC (the date assigned by Vretska 1.1961, 48) seems unlikely in view of the absence of any mention of the African campaign in 46 and Cato's suicide.

[3] Appius Claudius Caecus (cens. 312) composed *Sententiae* in the Saturnian meter, in imitation of the "Golden Verses" of Pythagoras (cf. Cic. *Tusc.* 4.4).

ut fabricata sic virtute parta quam magna industria haberei decet, ne incuria deformentur aut conruant infirmata.

4 Nemo enim alteri imperium volens concedit, et quamvis
bonus atque clemens sit qui plus potest, tamen quia malo

5 esse licet formeidatur. Id eo evenit, quia plerique rerum
potentes pervorse consulunt et eo se munitiores putant,

6 quo illei quibus imperitant nequiores fuere. At contra id
eniti decet, cum ipse bonus atque strenuus sis, uti quam
optimis imperites. Nam pessumus quisque asperrume
rectorem patitur.

7 Sed tibi hoc gravius est, quam ante te omnibus, armis
8 parta componere, quod bellum aliorum pace mollius ges-
sisti. Ad hoc victores praedam petunt, victi cives sunt.
Inter has difficultates evadendum est tibi atque in posterum firmanda res publica non armis modo neque advorsum hostis, sed, quod multo multoque asperius est, pacis

9 bonis artibus. Ergo omnes magna, mediocri[1] sapientia res
10 huc vocat, quae quisque optuma potest, utei dicant. Ac
mihi sic videtur: qualeicumque modo tu victoriam com-
posuereis, ita alia omnia futura. 2. Sed iam, quo melius
faciliusque constituas, paucis quae me animus monet accipe.

---

[1] *Asulanus*: mediocris V

---

[4] It is a topos that tyrants feel kinship with wicked men and
look with suspicion upon the virtuous as a potential threat to their
power (cf. *Cat.* 7.2; Plin. *Pan.* 45.1–2).

[5] Those who fought for Caesar in the civil war.

[6] Cf. *Jug.* 110.6, *paucis accipe de* + abl.

with what great diligence is it fitting for achievements of prowess, as well as material creations, to be maintained so that they may not be spoiled by neglect or be weakened and fall in ruin. For no one willingly yields power to another; and however virtuous and merciful a person may be who has more power, he is nevertheless feared because there is nothing to stop him from being bad. This happens because most people in charge of affairs reason incorrectly and think themselves to be the more secure, the greater the worthlessness of those over whom they exercise authority.[4] But on the contrary, since you yourself are virtuous and valiant, it is fitting for you to aim to exercise authority over the best possible subjects. For the worse a person is, the less inclined he is to put up with control.

But it is a heavier task for you than for all before you to set in order your conquests because you waged war with greater gentleness than others exercise in time of peace. In addition, the victors[5] are demanding booty, while the vanquished are our fellow citizens. Amid these difficulties, you must find your way clear and strengthen the nation for the future, not only by arms and against foreign foes, but also by means of the fine arts of peace, a task far, far thornier. Therefore, the situation calls upon all men, those of great or moderate wisdom, to offer you the best advice each person is capable of giving. And this is my view: in whatever way you solidify your victory, so will all things unfold in the future. 2. But now, so that you may arrange matters better and more easily, hear briefly[6] what my mind prompts me to say.

2   Bellum tibi fuit, imperator, cum homine claro, magnis opibus, avido potentiae, maiore fortuna quam sapientia, quem secuti sunt pauci per suam iniuriam tibi inimici,
3 item quos adfinitas aut alia necessitudo traxit.—Nam particeps dominationis neque fuit quisquam neque, si pati
4 potuisset, orbis terrarum bello concussus foret.—Cetera multitudo volgi more magis quam iudicio, post alius alium
5 quasi prudentiorem secuti. Per idem tempus maledictis ineiquorum occupandae rei publicae in spem adducti homines, quibus omnia probro ac luxuria polluta erant, concurrere in castra tua et aperte quieteis mortem, rapinas, postremo omnia quae corrupto animo lubebat, mini-
6 tari. Ex queis magna pars, ubi neque creditum condonarei[2] neque te civibus sicuti hostibus uti vident, defluxere, pauci restitere, quibus maius otium in castris quam Romae
7 futurum erat: tanta vis creditorum inpendebat. Sed ob easdem causas immane dictust quanti et quam multi mortales postea ad Pompeium discesserint, eoque per omne tempus belli quasi sacro atque inspoliato fano debitores usi.

   [2] *Jordan*: condonari *Cortius*: condonare V

[7] Here and twice in the *Second Epistle* (6.6, 12.1), Caesar is addressed as *imperator,* a title accorded to victorious Roman generals, one that Caesar took as a permanent honor and one that later, from the time of Vespasian, became the official title of the Roman emperor. Cf. *Ep.* 2.12.5.

[8] Pompey: named at 2.7 and 4.1.

[9] I.e., those who had a falling out with Caesar through committing a wrongful act (*iniuria*) against him, wrongful because it was unprovoked.

[10] I.e., those who at the outbreak of the war in 49 falsely, or

You waged war, commander,[7] with a distinguished man[8] endowed with great resources, one greedy for personal power and blessed with greater good fortune than wisdom. He was followed by a few who were your enemies through their own fault,[9] likewise by those who were drawn to his side by a marriage connection or some other tie.—For no one of them had a share in his despotism, and if he had been able to put up with sharing power, the world would not have been convulsed by war.—The rest of the throng followed more in keeping with the habit of the common herd than from deliberate choice, one man lining up behind another, as if the latter were more sensible. At the same time, men whose whole being was stained with infamy and debauchery were influenced by the slanders of unfair critics[10] to hope for an opportunity to seize control of the state; they flocked into your camp and openly threatened peaceable citizens with death, robbery, in short, with everything that appealed to a perverted mind. A considerable number of these, however, when they saw that you were not canceling debts and not treating your fellow citizens as enemies, slipped away; a few remained, who had the prospect of enjoying more peace and quiet in your camp than in Rome, so great was the throng of creditors that threatened them there. But it is shocking to relate how many prominent men went over to Pompey afterward from those same motives; and debtors throughout the whole period of the war employed him like a sacred and inviolable shrine.[11]

mistakenly, predicted that Caesar would not uphold the rights of property owners but pillage and plunder Italy.   [11] I.e., a place of asylum, as a means of shielding themselves from the demands of their creditors.

3. Igitur quoniam tibi victori de bello atque pace agitandum est, hoc uti civiliter deponas, illa ⟨ut⟩[3] quam iustissima et diuturna sit, de te ipso primum, qui ea compo-

2 siturus es, quid optimum factu sit existima. Equidem ego cuncta imperia crudelia magis acerba quam diuturna arbitror, neque quemquam multis metuendum esse, quin ad eum ex multis formido reccidat; eam vitam bellum aeternum et anceps gerere, quoniam neque adversus neque ab tergo aut lateribus tutus sis, semper in periculo aut metu

3 agites. Contra qui benignitate et clementia imperium temperavere iis laeta et candida omnia visa, etiam hostes aequiores[4] quam malis[5] cives.

4 Haud scio an qui me his dictis corruptorem victoriae tuae nimisque in victos bona voluntate praedicent. Scilicet quod ea, quae externis nationibus, natura nobis hostibus, nosque maioresque nostri saepe tribuere, ea civibus danda arbitror, neque barbaro ritu caede caedem et sanguinem sanguine expianda.

4. An illa, quae paulo ante hoc bellum in Cn. Pompeium victoriamque Sullanam increpabantur, oblivio intercepit:[6] Domitium, Carbonem, Brutum alios item, non armatos neque in proelio belli iure, sed postea supplices

---

[3] *Aldus*   [4] *Asulanus:* nequiores V   [5] *Kaster per litteras:* aliis *Asulanus:* alii V   [6] *Faernus (cf. Plin.* Pan. *75.1):* interfecit V

---

[12] Cf. the line directed at Caesar when D. Laberius was compelled by Caesar to perform in one of his mimes in 46 (Sen. *De ira* 2.11.3; Macrob. *Sat.* 2.7.1–5; Suet. *Iul.* 39.2): "inevitably the man whom many fear, fears many" (*necesse est multos timeat quem multi timent*).

3. Therefore, since you must deal as victor with war as well as peace, in order to end this conflict in the spirit of a good citizen, and to make peace as just as possible and long-lasting, first consider what is the best course of action as you embark upon settling affairs. For my own part, I believe that every instance of the cruel exercise of power produces more bitterness than stability, and that no one inspires fear in many without fear recoiling on him from many;[12] such a manner of life wages a never ending, hazardous war inasmuch as you are not safe in front, in the rear, or on the flanks, and you are always living in peril or dread. By contrast, those who have tempered their rule with kindness and mercy experience total joy and cheeriness; even foreign foes are more kindly disposed toward them than fellow citizens are to the wicked.

Possibly some people will describe me, on the basis of the preceding remarks, as a spoiler of your victory and as being too well disposed toward the vanquished. Doubtless because I believe that the same considerations that we and our forefathers have often accorded to foreign peoples, our natural enemies, ought to be granted to our fellow citizens, and that we should not, like barbarians, atone for slaughter by slaughter and for bloodshed by bloodshed.

4. Or has forgetfulness blotted out those complaints that shortly before this war were directed against Gnaeus Pompey and the Sullan victory: namely, that Domitius, Carbo, Brutus and others as well were slain, not in arms nor in battle according to the right of war but afterward, through the utmost wickedness, while they were suppli-

per summum scelus interfectos, plebem Romanam in villa
2 publica pecoris modo conscissam? Eheu quam illa occulta
civium funera et repentinae caedes, in parentum aut libe-
rorum sinum fuga mulierum et puerorum, vastatio do-
muum ante partam a te victoriam saeva atque crudelia
3 erant! Ad quae te idem illi hortantur; [et][7] scilicet id certatum esse, utrius vestrum arbitrio iniuriae fierent, neque
receptam sed captam a te rem publicam, et ea causa [ex-
ercitus][8] stipendiis confectis optimos et veterrimos omnium advorsum fratres parentisque [alii liberos][9] armis
contendere, ut ex alienis malis deterrumi mortales ventri
atque profundae lubidini sumptus quaererent atque essent opprobria victoriae, quorum flagitiis commacularetur
4 bonorum laus. Neque enim te praeterire puto, quali quis-

---

[7] *Burnouf*   [8] *Kaster per litteras*   [9] *Jordan*

---

13 All died at the hands of Pompey: Cn. Papirius Carbo (cos.
85, 84, 82) in 82 in Sicily (see *Hist.* 1.45), and Cn. Domitius Ahenobarbus (son-in-law of Cinna, cos. 87–84) in 81 at Utica, in the
African campaign (see ibid. 1.46)—both in the Sullan civil war;
M. Iunius Brutus (father of Caesar's famous assassin) after the
surrender of Mutina in Cisalpine Gaul in 77 (see ibid. 1.69), at
the time of the Lepidan revolt against Sulla's regime. Among
those designated here by "others as well" is M. Perperna (pr. 82),
whom Val. Max. 6.2.8 adds to the three named victims. Perperna
was put to death in 72 while fighting in the Sertorian revolt in
Spain (see ibid. 3.58–59).

14 Not strictly the "Roman commons" (*plebs Romana*) but
soldiers, chiefly from Samnium, who surrendered after the battle
at the Colline Gate outside Rome on November 1, 82. Thousands
of these unarmed prisoners were executed by Sulla (the figure
ranges from 4,000 [Flor. 2.9.24] to as high as 8,000 [Liv. *Per.* 88]

ants;[13] that the Roman commons were cut to pieces in the Villa Publica just like cattle?[14] Alas! How savage and cruel were those covert deaths and sudden murders of citizens, the flight of women and children to the bosom of their parents or offspring, and the ransacking of houses before your victory was achieved![15] It is to such atrocities that those same men[16] are urging you; doubtless it was the object of the contest to determine which of you two would have the authority to commit outrages, and the nation was not rescued by you but seized; and doubtless the reason why the best and most senior of all soldiers, after finishing their term of service, contended in battle against their brothers and parents was so that the most degenerate mortals might derive from the woes of others the resources to gratify their boundless gluttony and lust, and sully your victory by staining the renown of upright men with their shameful deeds. For I do not think that you failed to ob-

or 9,000 [*De vir. ill.* 75.10]). They were confined in the Villa Publica, a largely open space, equipped with porticoes, in the Campus Martius. It served as the headquarters of state officials when taking the census or levying troops.

[15] The dating of the savagery relative to the achievement of Caesar's victory (in 48) produces the impression that the acts of terror just mentioned in this and the preceding sentence had occurred in the 50s, and yet all of the victims explicitly named in 4.1 belong to 82–77. Presumably the author means that the ever-present fear that Pompey and his supporters might renew those grim acts of revenge was finally put to rest both by the removal of Pompey, the perpetrator of the killings enumerated in 4.1, and by Caesar's enlightened policy of pardoning his defeated enemies.

[16] I.e., political figures who switched allegiance after Caesar's victory over Pompey.

que eorum more aut modestia, etiam tum dubia victoria, sese gesserit quoque modo in belli administratione scorta aut convivia exercuerint non nulli, quorum aetas ne per otium quidem talis voluptatis sine dedecore attingerit.

5. De bello satis dictum. De pace firmanda quoniam tuque et omnes tui agitatis, primum id quaeso, considera quale sit de quo consultas; ita bonis malisque dimotis pa-
2 tenti via ad verum perges. Ego sic existimo: quoniam orta omnia intereunt, qua tempestate urbi Romanae fatum excidii adventarit, civis cum civibus manus conserturos, ita defessos et exsanguis regi aut nationi praedae futuros. Aliter non orbis terrarum neque cunctae gentes conglobatae
3 movere aut contundere queunt hoc imperium. Firmanda igitur sunt vel concordiae bona et discordiae mala ex-
4 pellenda. Id ita eveniet, si sumptuum et rapinarum licentiam dempseris, non ad vetera instituta revocans, quae iam pridem corruptis moribus ludibrio sunt, sed si suam quoi-
5 que rem familiarem finem sumptuum statueris; quoniam is incessit mos, ut homines adulescentuli sua atque aliena consumere, nihil libidinei atque aliis rogantibus denegare pulcherrimum putent, eam virtutem et magnitudinem animi, pudorem atque modestiam pro socordia aestiment.
6 Ergo animus ferox prava via ingressus, ubi consueta non suppetunt, fertur accensus in socios modo, modo in civis,

---

17 An allusion to the comforts in Pompey's camp, as compared with the Spartan conditions in Caesar's (Caes. *B Civ.* 3.96.1; Plut. *Pomp.* 72.5–6), and to the grandiose plans for revenge and rewards that were made by Pompey's followers (Caes. *B Civ.* 3.83).

serve with what conduct and self-control each one of them behaved, even at the time when the victory was uncertain; and how some of them, in the course of managing the war, indulged in prostitutes or feasts;[17] even in peace time, it would have been disgraceful for men of such an age to have any contact with pleasures of those sorts.

5. Concerning the war enough has been said. Concerning the establishment of peace, since both you and all your followers are making plans about this, first, I implore you, consider what sort of thing it is about which you are deliberating; in that way, after separating the good from the bad, you will proceed to the truth along an open highway. My own opinion is this: since everything that has come into being eventually passes away, at the time when Rome's fated destruction approaches, citizens will do battle with their fellow citizens; thus worn out and enfeebled, they will fall prey to some king or nation. Otherwise, not the whole world, nor all the nations banded together, can move or crush this dominion. You must establish, therefore, the blessings of harmony, and cast out the evils of discord. This will come about if you remove unrestrained extravagance and looting, not by calling men back to the old customs, which have long since become a farce thanks to the corruption of our morals, but if you fix each man's material assets as the limit of his expenditures. For it has become the custom for mere youths to think it a very fine thing to waste their own substance as well as that of others, to refuse nothing to their lust and to the requests of others, to regard such conduct as manliness and high mindedness, while regarding modesty and self-control as faintheartedness. Therefore, once a person of savage spirit has embarked on a crooked path, when his usual resources do not

movet composita et res novas veteribus abiectis[10] conqui-
7 rit. Quare tollendus est fenerator in posterum, uti suas
8 quisque res curemus. Ea vera atque simplex via est magistratum populo, non creditori gerere et magnitudinem
animi in addendo non demendo rei publicae ostendere.

6. Atque ego scio quam aspera haec res in principio
futura sit, praesertim is qui se in victoria licentius liberius-
que quam artius futuros credebant. Quorum si saluti potius quam lubidini consules, illosque nosque et socios in
pace firma constitues; sin eadem studia artesque iuventuti
erunt, ne ista egregia tua fama simul cum urbe Roma brevi
concidet.

2 Postremo sapientes pacis causa bellum gerunt, laborem
spe otii sustentant; nisi illam firmam efficis, vinci an vicisse
3 quid retulit? Quare capesse, per deos, rem publicam et
4 omnia aspera, uti soles, pervade. Namque aut tu mederi
potes aut omittenda est cura omnibus. Neque quisquam
te ad crudelis poenas aut acerba iudicia invocat, quibus
civitas vastatur magis quam corrigitur, sed ut pravas artis
5 malasque libidines ab iuventute prohibeas. Ea vera clementia erit, consuluisse ne merito cives patria expelleren-
tur, retinuisse ab stultitia et falsis voluptatibus, pacem et

---

10 *Kroll*: aec V: neclectis *Kurfess*

---

18 The text is corrupt and the meaning consequently uncertain.
19 Of the sorts that were introduced by Pompey's judicial reforms in 52 (see *Ep.* 2.3.3n.).

suffice, he furiously assaults now our allies, now his fellow citizens, he disturbs the established order of things and quests after revolution, rejecting the status quo.[18] Therefore, the moneylender must be eliminated for the future so that each one of us may look after his own property. This is the true and straightforward path, namely that a magistrate govern for the benefit of the people, not a creditor; that he show high mindedness by adding to, not subtracting from our nation's resources.

6. And I know how offensive this policy is going to be in the beginning, especially to those who believed that they would experience in victory more license and freedom than restraint. And if you consult the interests of their welfare rather than their desires, you will establish both them and us, as well as our allies, upon a solid foundation of peace. But if our youths continue to have the same inclinations and practices as at present, truly that eminent renown of yours will shortly come to an end, along with the city of Rome.

Finally, wise men wage war for the sake of peace, they endure toil in the hope of repose; unless you bring about a lasting peace, what difference does it make whether you are defeated or have been victorious? Therefore, by the gods!—take the nation in hand, and surmount all difficulties, as you customarily do. For either you can provide a cure, or everyone must despair of a solution. And no one calls upon you for cruel punishments or harsh sentences[19]—by which our country is ravaged more than it is corrected—but to bar our youths from depraved practices and evil passions. True mercy will consist in these acts, in having taken counsel so that citizens may not deserve to be banished from their native land, in having kept them from folly and deceptive pleasures, in having put peace

491

concordiam stabilivisse, non si flagitis opsecutus, delicta perpessus praesens gaudium quom[11] mox futuro malo concesseris.

7. Ac mihi animus, quibus rebus alii timent, maxume fretus est: negotii magnitudine et quia tibi terrae et maria simul omnia componenda sunt. Quippe res parvas[12] tantum ingenium attingere nequeiret, magnae curae magna
2   merces est. Igitur provideas oportet uti pleps, largitionibus et publico frumento corrupta, habeat negotia sua quibus ab malo publico detineatur; iuventus probitati et in-
3   dustriae, non sumptibus neque divitiis studeat. Id ita eveniet, si pecuniae, quae maxuma omnium pernicies est,
4   usum atque decus[13] dempseris. Nam saepe ego quom[14] animo meo reputans quibus quisque rebus clari viri magnitudinem invenissent quaeque res populos nationesve magnis auctibus[15] auxissent, ac deinde quibus causis amplissima regna et imperia conruissent, eadem semper bona atque mala reperiebam, omnesque victores divitias
5   contempsisse et victos cupivisse. Neque aliter quisquam extollere sese et divina mortalis attingere potest, nisi omissis pecuniae et corporis gaudiis, animo indulgens non adsentando neque concupita praebendo, pervorsam gratiam gratificans, sed in labore, patientia, bonisque praeceptis et factis fortibus exercitando.

---

[11] sic V (cf. 7.4, infra et fr. 3.42.3n.)   [12] parvas ed. Rom.: pravas V   [13] Asulanus: dedecus V   [14] sic V (cf. 6.5n. supra)   [15] Ciacconius: auctoribus V

---

[20] In 58, the tribune P. Clodius passed a law abolishing the price charged for the monthly allotment of grain given to the people of Rome. In 46, Caesar reduced the number of recipients from 320,000 to 150,000 (Suet. Iul. 41.3).

and harmony on a firm footing—not if you grant them momentary pleasure, along with future ruin, by being indulgent to shameful acts and putting up with offenses.

7. And for my own part, my spirit derives tremendous confidence from the circumstances that inspire fear in others; namely, the greatness of the task and because you must set in order simultaneously all lands and seas. Naturally such a great talent as yours could not engage in small matters; great is the reward for great responsibility. Therefore, you ought to see to it that the commons, which has been demoralized by bounties and the public grain dole,[20] have their own jobs to keep them from public mischief; likewise that our youths cultivate honesty and industry, not extravagance and the pursuit of wealth. This will come about, if you remove from money, which is the greatest of all sources of destruction, its advantage and luster. For when I often turned over in my mind how it is that various eminent men had acquired greatness, and what qualities had increased peoples and nations with great growth, and then what causes had brought about the downfall of grand kingdoms and empires, I always discovered the same virtues and vices, and that riches had been scorned by all victors and coveted by the vanquished. In fact, in no other way can any mortal exalt himself and touch upon the divine unless he casts off the delights of wealth and bodily pleasures and devotes himself to his soul, not by giving in to and indulging its cravings, thereby allowing it a perverse gratification, but by exercising it in labor, in patience, and in virtuous precepts and brave deeds.

8. Nam domum aut villam exstruere, eam signis, au-
laeis, alieisque operibus exornare et omnia potius quam
semet visendum efficere, id est non divitias decori habere,
2 sed ipsum illis flagitio esse. Porro ei,[16] quibus bis die ven-
trem onerare, nullam noctem sine scorto quiescere mos
est, ubi animum quem dominari decebat, servitio oppres-
sere, nequeiquam eo postea hebeti atque claudo pro exer-
3 cito uti volunt. Nam inprudentia pleraque et se prae-
cipitat. Verum haec et omnia mala pariter cum honore
pecuniae desinent, si neque magistratus neque alia volgo
cupienda venalia erunt.
4   Ad hoc providendum est tibi, quonam modo Italia atque provinciae tutiores sint, id quod factu haud asperum[17]
5 est. Nam idem omnia vastant suas deserendo domos et per
6 iniuriam alienas occupando. Item ne, uti adhuc, militia
iniusta aut inaequalis sit, cum alii triginta, pars nullum
stipendium faciant.[18] Et frumentum id quod antea prae-
mium ignaviae fuit per municipia et colonias illis dare
conveniet qui stipendiis emeritis domos reverterint.
7   Quae rei publicae necessaria tibique gloriosa ratus
8 sum, quam paucissimis apsolvi. Non peius videtur pauca
9 nunc de facto meo disserere. Plerique mortales ad iudi-
candum satis ingenii habent aut simulant; verum enim ad

[16] *Aldus*: eis V   [17] *Reynolds (cf. Ep. 2.1.1)*: obscurum V
[18] *Ernout*: facient V: faciunt *Jordan*

---

[21] Meaning uncertain: possibly the author refers to those described at *Ep. 2.5.4* who were forced by debt to abandon their
homes and turn to a life of idleness and crime.   [22] Cf.
7.2n.   [23] I.e., his act of going on record and addressing advice to Caesar.

8. For, to erect a town house or country house, to adorn it with statues, tapestries, and other works of art, and to make everything in it more worth seeing than its owner, that is not to possess riches in a way that produces distinction but rather to be an object of disgrace oneself to those very riches. Moreover, as for people whose habit it is to overload their stomachs twice a day, to pass no night in rest without a prostitute: when they have enslaved their mind, which was properly the master, in vain do they later on desire to find it ready for action after it has been dulled and crippled. For folly ruins most things, including itself. But these and all other evils will cease when money is no longer held in honor, if neither magistracies nor other things commonly craved are put up for sale.

Besides this, you must provide a way for Italy and the provinces to be safer, a thing that it is by no means hard to do. For the same men are spreading universal devastation by abandoning their own homes and wrongfully appropriating those belonging to others.[21] Likewise, let military service not be unjust and unfair, as it has been up to now, when some serve thirty campaigns, some none at all. And it will be fitting for the grain that previously was a reward of idleness[22] to be given throughout the free towns and colonies to those soldiers who have returned to their homes after having served their time in the army.

I have set forth in the fewest possible words policies I regarded as necessary for our nation and destined to bring glory to you. Now it seems equally worthwhile to speak briefly about my act of having done so.[23] Most mortals have, or pretend to have, sufficient ability to sit in judg-

reprehendunda aliena facta aut dicta ardet omnibus animus, vix satis apertum os aut lingua prompta videtur quae
meditata[19] pectore evolvat.[20] Quibus me subiectum haud
10 paenitet, magis reticuisse pigeret. Nam sive hac seu me-
liore alia via perges, a me quidem pro virili parte dictum
et adiutum fuerit. Relicuum est optare uti quae tibi pla-
cuerint ea di immortales adprobent beneque evenire si-
nant.

⟨ II ⟩

1. Scio ego quam difficile atque asperum factu sit consilium dare regi aut imperatori, postremo quoiquam mor-
tali, quoius opes in excelso sunt; quippe cum et illis con-
sultorum copiae adsint neque de futuro quisquam satis
2 callidus satisque prudens sit. Quin etiam saepe prava magis quam bona consilia prospere eveniunt, quia plerasque
res fortuna ex libidine sua agitat.
3   Sed mihi studium fuit adulescentulo rem publicam
capessere, atque in ea cognoscenda multam magnamque
curam habui; non ita ut magistratum modo caperem,
quem multi malis artibus adepti erant, sed etiam ut rem
publicam domi militiaeque quantumque armis, viris, opu-

---

19 *Faernus*: medita V   20 *Aldus*: evolat V

---

24 There is no heading in **V** (fol. 129v) but merely a space of
approximately two lines to separate the text of *Ep.* 2 from
Ep. 1.   25 The fictional date presumes that fighting is im-
minent but has not yet broken out. Hence, presumably, before
Caesar's crossing of the Rubicon, on the night of January 11/12,
49 (= November 24/25, 50 Jul.).   26 *Cf. Cat.* 3.3.

ment; but indeed, all burn with passion to censure the deeds or words of others, while their mouth seems scarcely wide enough, or their tongue facile enough, to give utterance to the thoughts in their hearts. I do not at all repent at having subjected myself to the criticism of such men; I would feel more regret at having kept silent. For whether you proceed along this path or another better one, I shall have spoken and given aid in a manly fashion. It only remains to pray that the immortal gods may approve your decision and allow it a successful outcome.

⟨ II ⟩[24]

[late 50/early 49 BC][25]

1. I know how difficult and rough a task it is to give advice to a king or a commander, in short, to any mortal whose power is lofty—all the more so since such men have an abundance of counselors, and no one is sufficiently clever and sufficiently farsighted with regard to the future. For indeed bad advice often turns out better than good because Fortune commonly directs the course of events according to her own whim.

I had from early youth a desire to embark upon a political career,[26] and in acquainting myself with political affairs, I invested a great deal of care not just with the aim of gaining political office, which many had attained through dishonorable means, but also to make myself familiar with the administration of public business at home and in war and with the resources of our country in arms,

4 lentia posset cognitum habuerim. Itaque mihi multa cum animo agitanti consilium fuit famam modestiamque meam post tuam dignitatem haberei et quoius rei lubet periculum facere, dum quid tibi ex eo gloriae acciderit. Idque non temere neque ex fortuna tua decrevi, sed quia in te praeter ceteras artem unam egregie mirabilem comperi, semper tibi maiorem in adversis quam in secundis rebus animum esse. Sed per ceteros mortalis illa res clarior est, quod prius defessi sunt homines laudando atque admirando munificentiam tuam quam tu [in]²¹ faciundo quae gloria digna essent.

2. Equidem mihi decretum est nihil tam ex alto reperiri posse quod non cogitanti tibi in promptu sit. Neque eo quae visa sunt de re publica tibi scripsi, quia mihi consilium atque ingenium meum amplius aequo probaretur, sed inter labores militiae interque proelia, victorias, imperium statui admonendum te de negotiis urbanis. Namque tibi si id modo in pectore consilii est, ut te ab inimicorum impetu vindices, quoque modo contra adversum consulem beneficia populi retineas, indigna virtute tua cogitas. Sin in te ille animus est qui iam a principio nobilitatis factionem disturbavit,²² plebem Romanam ex gravi servi-

---

²¹ *ed. Rom.* ²² *ed. Mant.*: disturbabit V

---

²⁷ The same observation, in nearly the same language, is found at *Ep.* 1.1.2. ²⁸ In particular, the privilege of standing for the consulship in his absence from Rome, a dispensation granted by a law sponsored by all ten plebeian tribunes in 52. ²⁹ Lucius Cornelius Lentulus Crus as consul in 49 took a leading role in pressing for harsh measures against Caesar, which ultimately precipitated the civil war (Caes. *B Civ.* 1.1.2).

men, and money. Consequently, I have reached the decision, after much soul searching, to put your distinction ahead of my own repute and modesty and to venture upon anything whatever, provided only that it will contribute something to your glory. And I have come to this decision not rashly nor as a consequence of your good fortune, but because in you I have found, in addition to other qualities, an unusually admirable one, namely that your spirit is always greater in adversity than in prosperity. But throughout the rest of humanity that fact is quite evident given that men sooner grew weary from praising and admiring your munificence than you did in doing deeds worthy of glory.[27]

2. For my own part, I have reached the verdict that nothing can be discovered that is so deep that it is not within your power when you put your mind to it. And I have written you my views upon public affairs, not because I esteemed my own counsel and talent more highly than is proper, but because it seemed to me that during the toils of war, amid battles, victories and military command, you ought to be reminded of civilian tasks. For if only this is the aim in your heart, to defend yourself from the assault of your enemies and how to retain the benefits conferred by the people[28] in opposition to a hostile consul,[29] your thoughts are unworthy of your prowess. But if you have in you the spirit that has from the very beginning unsettled the clique of nobles,[30] restored the Roman com-

[30] E.g., by means of his support, early in his political career in the 70s, for the restoration of the powers of the tribunate (Suet. *Iul.* 5), referred to in the next clause as the restoration of freedom to the commons.

tute in libertatem restituit, in praetura inimicorum arma
inermis disiecit, domi militiaeque tanta et tam praeclara
facinora fecit, ut ne inimici quidem queri quicquam au-
deant nisi de magnitudine tua: quin tu accipe ea quae dicam de summa re publica. Quae profecto aut vera invenies
aut certe haud procul a vero.

3. Sed quoniam Cn. Pompeius, aut animi pravitate aut
quia nihil eo maluit quod tibi obesset, ita lapsus est ut hostibus tela in manus iaceret, quibus ille rebus rem publi-
2 cam conturbavit, eisdem tibi restituendum est. Primum
omnium summam potestatem moderandi de vectigalibus,
sumptibus, iudiciis senatoribus paucis tradidit, plebem
Romanam, quoius antea summa potestas erat, ne aequeis
3 quidem legibus in servitute reliquit. Iudicia tametsi, sicut
antea, tribus ordinibus tradita sunt, tamen idem illi factiosi
regunt, dant, adimunt quae lubet,[23] innocentis circum-
4 veniunt, suos ad honorem extollunt. Non facinus, non
probrum aut flagitium obstat, quo minus magistratus ca-
piant. Quos commodum est trahunt, rapiunt; postremo
tamquam urbe capta libidine ac licentia sua pro legibus
5 utuntur. Ac me quidem mediocris dolor angeret, si virtute

---

[23] *ed. Mant.*: luget V

---

[31] In 62, Caesar was reinstated to his praetorship after armed
violence had led the senate to suspend him from his magistracy
(Suet. *Iul.* 16).   [32] Not strictly foreign foes (*hostibus*) but
allied and client states, especially in the eastern Mediterranean,
who took up arms to fight in support of Pompey (Caes. *B Civ.*
3.3).   [33] Senators, knights, and *tribuni aerarii* (hardly dis-
tinguishable from the knights), from which jurors had been
drawn since passage of the lex Aurelia in 70. Under Pompey's

mons to freedom in place of grievous slavery, dispersed in your praetorship the arms of personal foes without resort to arms,[31] and has produced such great and such glorious deeds at home and on campaign that not even your personal foes dare to make any complaint except concerning your greatness—now then, hear what I shall say about our country's welfare. You will assuredly find my observations either true or certainly by no means far from the truth.

3. Now, since Gnaeus Pompey, either from perversity of spirit, or because he wanted above all that which was to your disadvantage, has fallen so low as to fling arms into the hands of our enemies,[32] you must restore the nation by the same means by which he has thrown it into disorder. First of all, he has given a few senators supreme power to regulate the revenues, expenditures and courts; by means of biased laws, he has left the commons of Rome, whose power was previously supreme, in slavery. For even though the courts, as before, have been entrusted to the three orders,[33] nevertheless those same political insiders exercise control, giving and taking away whatever they please, defrauding the innocent, elevating their followers to political office. Not crime, not shameful conduct or disgrace bars them from gaining magistracies. They rob and pillage whom it suits them; finally, just as if the city had been taken captive, they indulge their passion and lack of restraint as substitutes for the laws. And I would for my part be feeling only moderate indignation, if, according to

legislation in 52 (Ascon. p. 36C), however, there were new, tighter procedural rules in trials for violence (*vis*) and electoral corruption (*ambitus*).

6 partam victoriam more suo per servitium exercerent. Sed
   homines inertissimi, quorum omnis vis virtusque in lingua
   sita est, forte atque alterius socordia dominationem obla-
7 tam insolentes agitant. Nam quae[24] seditio aut dissensio
   civilis tot tam illustris familias ab stirpe evertit? Aut quorum umquam in victoria animus tam praeceps tamque
   inmoderatus fuit   ?

   4. L. Sulla, quoi omnia in victoria lege belli licuerunt,
   tametsi supplicio hostium partis suas muniri intellegebat,
   tamen paucis interfectis ceteros beneficio quam metu reti-
2 nere maluit. At hercule M. Catoni,[25] L. Domitio, cete-
   risque eiusdem factionis quadraginta senatores, multi
   praeterea cum spe bona adulescentes sicutei hostiae mac-
   tati sunt, quom interea inportunissuma genera hominum
   tot miserorum civium sanguine satiari nequiere;[26] non
   orbi liberi, non parentes exacta aetate, non luctus, gemitus
   virorum mulierum immanem eorum animum inflexit,
   quein acerbius in dies male faciundo ac dicundo dignitate
3 alios, alios civitate eversum irent. Nam quid ego de te

---

[24] ed. Rom.: namque V   [25] hercule M. Catoni]
Orelli: herculem catonem V: hercule a M. Catone Mommsen
[26] nequierunt edd.: nequier V

---

[34] Pompey.   [35] A gross understatement of the number
of victims, which ranges from a purported high of 4,700 (Val. Max.
9.22.1) to a low of 520 (Plut. Sull. 31.5). Among them, there were
said to have been up to 40 senators and approximately 1,600
knights (App. B Civ. 1.95).   [36] The author greatly inflates
the number of casualties resulting from violence in the political
turmoil of the years 54–52, for which the responsibility is unfairly
fastened on the diehard optimates represented by Cato Uticensis

their usual custom, they were employing as their instrument of enslavement a victory produced by valor. But these incredibly lazy men, whose whole might and merit reside in their tongue, are insolently exercising a tyranny presented to them by chance and as a result of the inattentiveness of another person.[34] For what rebellion or civil dissension has utterly destroyed so many illustrious families? Or who ever had in victory a spirit so frenzied and so unbridled.

4. Lucius Sulla, to whom the law of war permitted anything in his victory, realized that by the execution of his foes his party could be strengthened, but he preferred nevertheless, after putting a few to death,[35] to keep the rest under control by kindness instead of intimidation. But, by Hercules!—at the instigation of Marcus Cato, Lucius Domitius, and others of that faction, forty senators and many young men of excellent promise have been butchered like so many sacrificial victims,[36] although meanwhile the blood of so many wretched citizens has not been enough to sate men of the most ruthless sort. Not orphaned children, not aged parents, not the grief of men, the lamentation of women has altered their monstrous purpose, to keep them from proceeding to strip rank from some,[37] citizenship from others[38] through acting and

and his brother-in-law Domitius (cos. 54). The number of senators said to have perished (forty) appears to be a figure drawn from the Sullan proscriptions (see previous note), in which Cato and Domitius played no part.   [37] Those who fell victim to the censors of 50, including Sallust, who was removed from the senate (Dio 40.63.4).   [38] Those who were forced into exile by convictions in capital cases.

dicam, quoius contumeliam homines ignavissimi vita sua commutare volunt, si liceat ? Neque illis tantae voluptati est, tametsi insperantibus accidit, dominatio quanto maerori tua dignitas; quein optatius habent ex tua calamitate periculum libertatis facere, quam per te populi Romani

4 imperium maximum ex magno fieri. Quo magis tibi etiam atque etiam animo prospiciendum est, quonam modo rem

5 stabilias communiasque. Mihi quidem quae mens suppetit eloqui non dubitabo; ceterum tuei erit ingenii probare, quae vera atque utilia factu putes.

5. In duas partes ego civitatem divisam arbitror, sicut a maioribus accepi, in patres et plebem. Antea in patribus

2 summa auctoritas erat, vis multo maxuma in plebe. Itaque saepius in civitate secessio fuit semperque nobilitatis opes

3 deminutae sunt et ius populi amplificatum. Sed plebs eo libere agitabat quia nullius potentia super leges erat neque divitiis aut superbia sed bona fama factisque fortibus nobilis ignobilem anteibat; humillimus quisque in arvis[27] aut in militia nullius honestae rei egens satis sibi satisque patriae erat.

4 Sed ubi eos paulatim expulsos agris inertia atque inopia incertas domos habere subegit, coepere alienas opes pe-

---

[27] *coniec. Dousa*: armis V

---

[39] By recalling Caesar from his Gallic command, thus exposing Italy to the potential of a revolt on the northern frontier.

[40] See *Cat.* 33.3n.

[41] Lit., "in his plowed fields," where the humble yeoman farmer eked out a living when not fighting for his country.

speaking wickedly in a harsher and harsher manner daily. What shall I say concerning you, whose humiliation those utter cowards are willing to purchase at the cost of their own lives, if it were to be permitted? And those men do not derive as much pleasure from their tyranny (although it is more than they had hoped for) as they do grief from your status. In fact, they consider it preferable to endanger liberty as a consequence of your downfall,[39] rather than have you elevate the realm of the Roman people from great to greatest. Consequently, you must all the more consider over and over again by what means you may stabilize and fortify the nation. For myself, I shall not hesitate to utter what my mind prompts, but it will be up to your intellect to determine which of my recommendations you think sound and of practical application.

5. I am of the opinion, as I have learned from our forefathers, that our body of citizens was split into two divisions, patricians and plebeians. Previously, supreme authority resided in the hands of the patricians, while by far the greatest might resided in the commons. Therefore secessions occurred within the community rather frequently,[40] and the power of the nobles was constantly diminished, and the right of the people was increased. But the reason why the commons lived in freedom was because no one's personal power was above the laws, and because the nobleman surpassed the commoner not in riches or haughtiness but in good repute and valiant deeds; the humblest citizen, lacking nothing that was honorable on his farm[41] or on military campaign, satisfied his own needs and satisfied those of his native land.

When, however, idleness and poverty forced the commons, who had gradually been driven from their lands, to

5 tere, libertatem suam cum re publica venalem habere. Ita
paulatim populus, qui dominus erat, cunctis gentibus im-
peritabat, dilapsus est et pro communi imperio privatim
6 sibi quisque servitutem peperit. Haec igitur multitudo
primum malis moribus imbuta, deinde in artis vitasque
varias dispalata, nullo modo inter se congruens, parum
mihi quidem idonea videtur ad capessendam rem publi-
7 cam. Ceterum additis novis civibus magna me spes tenet
fore ut omnes expergiscantur ad libertatem; quippe cum
illis libertatis retinendae, tum his servitutis amittendae
8 cura orietur. Hos ego censeo permixtos cum veteribus
novos in coloniis constituas; ita et res militaris opulentior
erit et plebs bonis negotiis impedita malum publicum facere desinet.

6. Sed non inscius neque inprudens sum, quom ea res
agetur, quae saevitia quaeque tempestates hominum nobi-
lium futurae sint, quom indignabuntur, omnia funditus
misceri, antiquis civibus hanc servitutem inponi, regnum
denique ex libera civitate futurum, ubi unius munere mul-
2 titudo ingens in civitatem pervenerit. Equidem ego sic
apud animum meum statuo: malum facinus in se admit-
tere qui incommodo rei publicae gratiam sibi conciliet; ubi
bonum publicum etiam privatim usui est, id vero dubitare
adgredi, socordiae atque ignaviae duco.

---

42 The reference immediately below to settling these "new
citizens" in veteran colonies suggests that the author may be referring to such persons as those enfranchised as a reward for
performing meritorious military service, e.g., the Romanized
Gauls whom Caesar formed into his Fifth Legion, the Alaudae
(Suet. *Iul.* 24.2).

possess no fixed abodes, they began to go after other persons' property and to regard their own liberty and their nation as objects for sale. Thus gradually the people, which used to be the master and exercise authority over all nations, became degenerate, and in place of a sovereignty shared in common, each man brought into being his own personal slavery. Therefore, this throng first having been tainted with evil habits, next having strayed into varied practices and modes of life—not at all sharing the same views—seems to me quite unfitted to govern. But if new citizens[42] are added to their number, I have high hope that all will be stirred to a sense of freedom; for in the new citizens will arise zeal for retaining their liberty, in the others, zeal for shedding their slavery. I therefore advise you to settle these new citizens, along with the old, in colonies; in this way both our military resources will be the stronger, and the commons, being occupied with worthy tasks, will cease to work public mischief.

6. However, I am not ignorant or unaware of what rage and what tempests will arise among the nobles when this project is carried out. They will be resentful that everything is being utterly muddled, that this amounts to the imposition of slavery upon the original citizens, in short, that a monarchy will come into being in place of a free state, when citizenship is extended to a multitude through the bounty of one man. This is my own personal conviction: that a man who tries to win popular favor at the cost of his country's welfare is guilty of committing a foul crime; yet when the common good is at the same time advantageous to an individual, I consider it a mark of folly and cowardice to hesitate to seize the opportunity.

3   M. Druso semper consilium fuit in tribunatu summa
ope niti pro nobilitate; neque ullam rem in principio agere
4 intendit, nisi illei auctores fuerant. Sed homines factiosi,
quibus dolus atque malitia fide cariora erant, ubi intelle-
xerunt per unum hominem maxumum beneficium multis
mortalibus dari—videlicet sibi quisque conscius malo atque infido animo esse—de M. Druso iuxta ac se existuma-
5 verunt. Itaque metu ne per tantam gratiam solus rerum
poteretur, contra eam nisi, sua et ipseius consilia disturba-
6 verunt. Quo tibi, imperator, maiore[28] cura fideique amici
et multa praesidia paranda sunt.

7. Hostem adversum deprimere strenuo homini haud
difficilest; occulta pericula neque facere neque vitare bo-
2 nis in promptu est. Igitur, ubi eos in civitatem adduxeris,
quoniam quidem renovata plebs erit, in ea re maxume
animum exerceto, ut colantur boni mores, concordia inter
veteres et novos coalescat.

3   Sed multo maxumum bonum patriae, civibus, tibi, liberis, postremo humanae genti pepereris, si studium pecuniae aut sustuleris aut, quoad res feret,[29] minueris. Aliter
neque privata res neque publica neque domi neque mili-
4 tiae regi potest. Nam ubi cupido divitiarum invasit, neque
disciplina neque artes bonae neque ingenium ullum satis

---

[28] *Laetus*: maior V   [29] *Aldus*: referet V

---

[43] When tribune in 91, he attempted to enact reforms that
would have been advantageous both to the nobles and to the
people, and to extend Roman citizenship to Rome's Italian allies.
He fell victim to an unknown assassin.   [44] Namely, citizenship (see the preceding note).   [45] I.e., assumed that his
motives were selfish.   [46] See *Ad Caes.* 1.2.2n.

Marcus Drusus'[43] consistent intention was to exert himself to the utmost during his tribunate for the benefit of the nobles; and at first, he took no step without their sanction. But when partisan politicians, to whom treachery and wickedness were dearer than honesty, perceived that a single individual was conferring an enormous benefit on many mortals[44]—just because each of them was conscious of having an evil and disloyal mind—they held the same opinion of Marcus Drusus as they did of themselves.[45] And out of fear that through such great influence he might gain sole mastery of affairs, they strove against that influence, and thus upset their own planned course of action and Drusus' as well. Hence, commander,[46] you must more carefully provide for yourself both trustworthy friends and many defenses.

7. It is not at all difficult for a resolute man to bring down an open foe; decent men, however, do not find it in their nature to lay hidden snares or avoid them. Since, therefore, when you add new members to the body of citizens the commons will indeed be regenerated, see that you devote particular attention to fostering good morals, to establishing harmony between the old and the new citizens.

But you will confer by far the greatest blessing on your native land, your fellow citizens, yourself, your children, in short, the human race, if you either do away with the pursuit of wealth or reduce it so far as circumstances permit. Otherwise, neither public nor private affairs can be controlled at home or in war. For when an eagerness for riches has made an assault, neither training, nor good practices, nor any mental power is strong enough to pre-

pollet quin animus magis aut minus mature, postremo ta-
5 men succumbat. Saepe iam audivi qui reges, quae civitates
et nationes per opulentiam magna imperia amiserint quae
per virtutem inopes ceperant; id ‹ad›eo[30] haud mirandum
6 est. Nam ubi bonus deteriorem divitiis magis clarum magisque acceptum videt, primo aestuat multaque in pectore
volvit; sed ubi gloria honorem magis in dies, virtutem opu-
7 lentia vincit, animus ad voluptatem a vero deficit. Quippe
gloria industria alitur; ubi eam dempseris ipsa per se virtus
8 amara atque aspera est. Postremo ubi divitiae clarae ha-
bentur, ibi omnia bona vilia sunt: fides, probitas, pudor,
9 pudicitia. Nam ad virtutem una ardua via[31] est; ad pecuniam qua quoique lubet nititur; et malis et bonis rebus ea
creatur.
10 Ergo in primis auctoritatem pecuniae demito. Neque
de capite neque de honore ex copiis quisquam magis aut
minus iudicaverit, sicut neque praetor neque consul ex
11 opulentia verum ex dignitate creetur. Sed de magistratu
facile populi iudicium fit; iudices a paucis probari regnum
est, ex pecunia legi inhonestum. Quare omnes primae
classis iudicare placet, sed numero plures quam iudicant.
12 Neque Rhodios neque alias civitates unquam iudiciorum

---

30 id ‹ad›eo] *Asulanus*: ideo V
31 via *om. V¹, s.s. V²*: una et ardua via *Aldus*: via ardua *Jordan*

---

47 Cf. *Ad Caes.* 1.7.4 for a similar observation.
48 The wealthiest citizens just below the rank of the knights,
the latter supplying the bulk of jurors (see 3.3n.). The minimum
property qualification of the first class (100,000 sesterces) was just
one quarter of that required of knights according to the figure
first securely attested a few decades later.

vent the mind from submitting more or less quickly, but inevitably. Often before now I have heard about kings, about city states and nations which have lost, through opulence, great empires that they had won through valor when poor.[47] Such a loss is not at all surprising. For when a good man beholds a baser person enjoying more renown and popularity as a result of riches, at first he seethes and keeps churning inside; but when more and more each day vainglory prevails over honor, opulence over merit, a good man's mind forsakes the truth in favor of pleasure. In fact, diligence is nourished by glory; when you take that away, virtue itself, on its own, is bitter and harsh. In short, where riches are regarded as a distinction, there all good qualities are of little account: good faith, uprightness, a sense of shame, chastity. For there is but one steep path to virtue; people strive after money by whatever path they please; money is produced by both dishonorable and honorable practices.

Above all, therefore, deprive money of its influence. Let the right to pass judgment concerning capital cases and public office not be greater for some citizens and less for others in proportion to their wealth, just as neither a praetor nor a consul should be chosen because of his riches but because of his worth. Now, on the choice of a magistrate, the judgment of the people is easy. It is tyranny for jurors to be certified by a narrow circle of individuals; for them to be chosen on the basis of money is shameful. Therefore, it seems desirable for all citizens of the first census class[48] to serve as jurors but in greater numbers than at present. Neither the Rhodians[49] nor other states

---

[49] The Rhodians were famous for their system of rotation by which all citizens served as jurors by turns (cf. Cic. *Rep.* 3.48).

suorum paenituit, ubi promiscue dives et pauper, ut quoique fors tulit, de maximis rebus iuxta ac de minimis disceptat. 8. Sed magistratibus creandis haud mihi quidem apsurde placet lex, quam C. Gracchus in tribunatu promulgaverat, ut ex confusis quinque classibus sorte centu-

2 riae vocarentur. Ita coaequantur[32] dignitate pecunia; virtute anteire alius alium properabit.

3   Haec ego magna remedia contra divitias statuo. Nam perinde omnes res laudantur atque adpetuntur ut earum rerum usus est. Malitia praemiis exercetur; ubi ea demp-

4 seris, nemo omnium gratuito malus est. Ceterum avaritia belua fera, immanis, intoleranda est; quo intendit, oppida, agros, fana atque domos vastat, divina cum humanis permiscet, neque exercitus neque moenia obstant, quo minus vi sua penetret; fama, pudicitia, liberis, patria atque pa-

5 rentibus cunctos mortalis spoliat. Verum, si pecuniae decus ademeris, magna illa vis avaritiae facile bonis moribus

6 vincetur. Atque haec ita sese habere tametsi omnes aequi atque iniqui memorant, tamen tibi cum factione nobilitatis haut mediocriter certandum est. Quoius si dolum caveris,

7 alia omnia in proclivi erunt. Nam ii, si virtute satis valerent, magis aemuli bonorum quam invidi essent. Quia desidia et inertia, stupor eos atque torpedo invasit, stre-

---

[32] coaequatur *edd.*

---

[50] In either 123 or 122, a bill otherwise unattested.

[51] Instead of having all the centuries of the first-class cast their votes before calling upon voters in the second-class and so on in succession until a majority was reached, sometimes before all citizens in the lower census classes had cast their ballots.

have felt dissatisfaction with courts in which rich and poor alike, according to the fortune of the lot, decide cases on matters of the greatest as well as the least importance. 8. Now as for the election of magistrates, I for my part find quite to my liking the law proposed by Gaius Gracchus in his tribunate,[50] providing for the centuries to be called upon to vote in a random order of the five census classes determined by lot.[51] In this way voters are put on the same level with respect to their standing and wealth; each person will rush to outdo another in merit.

These are the important correctives I am proposing to counter riches. For in proportion to its usefulness, all things are extolled and sought after. Wickedness is practiced on account of its rewards; if you take them away, no one at all is gratuitously wicked. But greed is a wild beast of prey, monstrous and irresistible; wherever it goes, it devastates towns, the countryside, shrines and homes; it makes no distinction between human and divine; no army and no fortifications stop it from forcing its way through; it robs all mortals of their good repute, their chastity, their children, native land and parents. Yet if you take away from money its luster, the power of greed, great though it is, will easily be vanquished by good morals. But even though all men, fair-minded and prejudiced alike, admit the truth of this, nevertheless you must undertake against the clique of nobles no light struggle. And if you guard against their cunning, all else will be easy. For if those men were deriving sufficient power from merit, they would be emulating the virtuous instead of envying them. Because sloth and indolence, dullness as well as sluggishness have taken possession of them, they resort to abuse and slander,

punt, obtrectant, alienam famam bonam suum dedecus aestumant.

9. Sed quid ego plura quasi de ignotis memorem? M. Bibuli fortitudo atque animi vis in consulatum erupit;

2 hebes lingua, magis malus quam callidus ingenio. Quid ille audeat, quoi[33] consulatus, maximum imperium, maxumo dedecori fuit? An L. Domiti magna vis est, quoius nullum membrum a flagitio aut facinore vacat: lingua vana, manus cruentae, pedes fugaces, quae honeste nominari nequeunt inhonestissima?

3 Unius tamen M. Catonis ingenium versutum, loquax, callidum haud contemno. Parantur haec disciplina Graecorum. Sed virtus, vigilantia, labor apud Graecos nulla sunt. Quippe qui domi libertatem suam per inertiam amiserint, censesne eorum praeceptis imperium haberi posse?

4 Reliqui de factione sunt inertissimi nobiles, in quibus sicut in titulo[34] praeter bonum nomen nihil est. Additamenta[35] L. Postumii M. Favonii mihi videntur quasi

---

[33] *cui* Laetus: qui V   [34] in titulo *Jordan*: instituto V
[35] *Orelli (cf. 11.6)*: addimenti V

---

[52] Bibulus was so far outmatched by his rival Caesar that their joint consulship in 59 was humorously dubbed the consulship of Julius and Caesar (Suet. *Iul.* 20.2).   [53] Cf. 4.2n. Domitius was a sworn political enemy of Caesar and had been designated by the senate to relieve him of his Gallic command in 49.   [54] Lit., "the parts that cannot honorably be named." The language in this section, beginning with "lying tongue," is very close to that in the Pseudo-Sallustian invective against Cicero (3.5).   [55] "Loquacious" (*loquax*), not "eloquent":

they consider the good repute of others a poor reflection on themselves.

9. But why should I say more on this subject, as if it were unknown. Marcus Bibulus' courage and force of intellect came to the fore in his consulship:[52] dull of speech, more wicked than clever by disposition. What would that fellow dare for whom the consulship, the highest power, served as the highest disgrace? Does Lucius Domitius[53] possess great strength, whose every limb is stained with disgrace or crime: his lying tongue, his bloodstained hands, his fleeing feet, his most dishonorable privates?[54]

Marcus Cato, nevertheless, is the one man whose versatile, loquacious,[55] and clever talent I by no means despise. Qualities such as these are the products of Greek training. Yet among the Greeks, valor, vigilance and toil are wholly lacking. Seeing that they lost through inactivity their freedom at home, do you think that power can be maintained by their precepts?

The remaining members of the faction are nobles of utter ineffectiveness, in whom there is nothing except a famous name, as on a commemorative tablet.[56] Men like Lucius Postumius[57] and Marcus Favonius[58] seem to me

Cato was notorious for employing the tactic of a filibuster to thwart his political enemies (e.g., Plut. *Cat. Min.* 31.5, 43.3). [56] As, for example, at the head of a list of titles and public offices affixed as a label to an ancestral mask in the hall of a nobleman (cf. *Jug.* 4.5n.).   [57] Most likely the senator who was instructed by the senate in January 49 to go to Sicily to secure it against Caesar; he refused to go without Cato (Cic. *Att.* 7.15[139].2).   [58] Famous as a devoted follower and slavish imitator of Cato (Plut. *Cat. Min.* 46.1).

magnae navis supervacuanea onera esse; ubi salvi pervenere, usui sunt; siquid adversi coortum est, de illeis potis-
simum iactura fit, quia pretii minimi sunt.

10. Nunc quoniam, sicut mihi videor, de plebe renovanda conrigendaque satis disserui, de senatu quae tibi
2 agenda videntur, dicam. Postquam mihi aetas ingeniumque adolevit, haud ferme armis atque equis corpus exercui, sed animum in litteris agitavi; quod natura firmius
3 erat, id in laboribus habui. Atque ego in ea vita multa legendo atque audiendo ita comperi, omnia regna, item civitates et nationes usque eo prosperum imperium habuisse,
dum apud eos vera consilia valuerunt; ubicumque gratia,
timor, voluptas ea corrupere, post paulo inminutae opes,
deinde ademptum imperium, postremo servitus imposita
est.

4 Equidem ego sic apud animum meum statuo: quoicumque in sua civitate amplior illustriorque locus quam aliis
5 est, ei magnam curam esse rei publicae. Nam ceteris salva
urbe tantum modo libertas tuta est; qui per virtutem sibi
divitias, decus, honorem pepererunt, ubi paulum inclinata
res publica agitari coepit, multipliciter animus curis atque
laboribus fatigatur; aut gloriam aut libertatem aut rem
familiarem defensat, omnibus locis adest, festinat, quanto
in secundis rebus florentior fuit, tanto in adversis asperius
magisque anxie agitat.

---

59 This easy emendation (see textual note) distinguishes Postumius and Favonius from the nobles proper. The precise status of Postumius is unclear, but Favonius is known *not* to have been descended from a consular ancestor and so did not qualify for the title *nobilis*. This supernumerary group is referred to as well at 11.6 (*cum paucis senatoriis*).

mere appendages,[59] like the excess cargo of a large ship. When people arrive safely, it is of use; if any calamity arises, the extra cargo is the first to be jettisoned because it is of least value.

10. Inasmuch as I have now, as it seems to me, said enough about the regeneration and reformation of the commons, let me tell you what I think you ought to do about the senate. Ever since my years and talent reached maturity, I have hardly ever exercised my body with arms and horses, but I have busied my mind with reading; I occupied with toil that part of my being which was by nature the stronger. And in the course of such a life, I have learned by abundant reading and listening that all kingdoms, as well as city states and nations, have maintained their power in a prosperous condition for as long as sound counsels prevailed; whenever favoritism, fear and pleasure have undermined such counsels, shortly thereafter the strength of those nations waned; then their power was wrested from them, and finally slavery was imposed.

Personally, this is the conclusion to which I have come in my own mind: that it is incumbent on whoever has a higher and more distinguished position in his state than others, to feel great concern for the welfare of the nation. For to the rest, the safety of the City merely assures their personal liberty; but those who have won riches, respect and honor through their prowess are filled with manifold anxiety and trouble when the nation has begun to decline and totter ever so little. He stands up for his renown, or his freedom, or his property; he is present everywhere and makes haste; the more prosperous he was in favorable times, the more severely is he troubled and worried in adversity.

6   Igitur ubi plebs senatui sicuti corpus animo oboedit eiusque consulta exsequitur, patres[36] consilio valere decet,

7   populo supervacuanea est calliditas. Itaque maiores nostri, cum bellis asperrumis premerentur, equis, viris, pecunia amissa, numquam defessi sunt armati de imperio certare. Non inopia aerarii, non vis hostium, non adversa res ingentem eorum animum subegit quin quae[37] virtute ce-

8 perant simul cum anima retinerent. Atque ea magis fortibus consiliis quam bonis proeliis patrata sunt. Quippe apud illos una res publica erat, ei omnes consulebant, factio contra hostis parabatur, corpus atque ingenium patriae,

9 non suae quisque potentiae exercitabat. At hoc tempore contra ea homines nobiles, quorum animos socordia atque ignavia invasit, ignarei laboris, hostium, militiae, domi factione instructi per superbiam cunctis gentibus moderantur.

    11. Itaque patres, quorum consilio antea dubia res publica stabiliebatur, oppressi ex aliena libidine huc atque illuc fluctuantes agitantur; interdum alia deinde alia decernunt; uti eorum, qui dominantur, simultas aut gratia fert,[38] ita bonum malumque publicum aestumant.

2   Quodsi aut libertas aequa omnium aut sententia obscurior esset, maioribus opibus res publica et minus potens

3 nobilitas esset. Sed quoniam coaequari gratiam[39] omnium

---

[36] patris V
[37] quin quae *ed. Mant.*: quique V
[38] *ed. Mant.*: fertur V
[39] *Aldus*: gratia V

Therefore, when the commons obey the senate (as the body does the mind) and carry out its decrees, it is proper for the senators to prevail in counsel; cleverness is superfluous for the people. Accordingly, when our forefathers were being hard pressed by the most difficult wars, despite the loss of horses, men and money, they never tired of contending for power by arms. No depleted treasury, no strength of their enemies, no disaster daunted their great courage from maintaining with their last breath what they had won by valor. And their success resulted more from courageous counsels than successful battles. For you see, in their day the nation was united; all citizens had regard for its welfare; a league was formed against foreign foes; each man exerted his body and talent for his native land, not for his own personal power. Today, on the contrary, men belonging to the nobility, whose minds have been seized by indolence and cowardice, though ignorant of toil, of the enemy, and of military service, have organized themselves into a faction on the home front and arrogantly regulate all nations.

11. Thus senators, by whose counsel the wavering state was formerly steadied, are swept along, overpowered and tossed to and fro at the whim of others; they decree sometimes one set of measures, then another; they determine what is in the public interest and its opposite according to the direction dictated by the animosity or influence of those who exercise absolute control.

But if either the independence of all senators were equal, or if their voting were done less openly, the nation would have greater strength and the nobles less political influence. Now, inasmuch as it is difficult for the influence of all senators to be placed on the same footing—for the

difficile est—quippe cum illis maiorum virtus partam reli-
querit gloriam, dignitatem, clientelas, cetera multitudo
pleraque insiticia sit—sententias eorum a metu libera; ita
4   in occulto sibi quisque alterius potentia carior erit. Libertas iuxta bonis et malis, strenuis atque ignavis optabilis est.
Verum eam plerique metu deserunt. Stultissimi mortales,
quod in certamine dubium est quorsum accidat, id per
inertiam in se quasi victi recipiunt.

5   Igitur duabus rebus confirmari posse senatum puto: si
numero auctus per tabellam sententiam feret. Tabella
obtentui erit, quo magis animo libero facere audeat; in
6   multitudine et praesidii plus et usus amplior est. Nam fere
his tempestatibus alii iudiciis publicis, alii privatis suis atque amicorum negotiis inplicati, haud sane rei publicae
consiliis adfuerunt; neque eos magis occupatio quam superba imperia distinuere. Homines nobiles cum paucis
senatoriis, quos additamenta factionis habent, quaecum-
que libuit probare,[40] reprehendere, decernere, ea, uti lu-
7   bido tulit, fecere. Verum ubi numero senatorum aucto per
tabellam sententiae dicentur, ne illi superbiam suam di-
mittent, ubi iis oboediendum erit quibus antea crudelis-
sime imperitabant.

[40] *corr. man. rec.*: probari V^l

---

[60] I.e., he will follow his genuine feelings concerning the best
course of action rather than being cowed by pressure to vote
another way.   [61] Sulla added 300 new members to the senate in 81, increasing its size to the range of 600; Caesar added
approximately 300 more in 45 (Dio 43.47.3).   [62] I.e., pressure exerted by a powerful few over the body as a whole.

prowess of their ancestors has left the nobles a heritage of glory, prestige and patronage, while most of the remaining throng in the senate has been grafted on—free the votes of the latter from fear; thus each man, in a secret ballot, will value himself[60] more highly than the political influence of another. Independence is desirable alike to good men and bad, to the resolute as well as cowards. But most men give up independence out of fear. Through a lack of striving, utterly foolish mortals bring upon themselves, just as though defeated, that which in a contest could have turned out either way.

Therefore, I think that the senate can be strengthened by means of two reforms: if it is increased in size[61] and voting is by ballot. The ballot will serve as a screen so that the body will dare to act with a more independent spirit; the increase in numbers amounts to both more protection and enhanced usefulness. For as a rule, in the present circumstances, some senators being occupied with the criminal courts, others with their own business affairs and those of their friends, do not truly participate in deliberations on matters of public moment; but they are kept from being effective not so much by their engagement in other activities as by arrogant demands.[62] The nobles, together with a few men of senatorial rank whom they treat as an appendage of their clique, do, according to their pleasure, whatever they feel like approving, censuring or decreeing. But when the number of the senators has been increased and the voting is done by ballot, those men will surely lay aside their insolence when they are forced to obey those over whom they formerly exercised merciless control.

12. Forsitan, imperator, perlectis litteris desideres quem numerum senatorum fieri placeat, quoque modo is in multa et varia officia distribuatur; iudicia quoniam omnibus primae classis committenda putem, quae discriptio,

2 quei numerus in quoque genere futurus sit. Ea mihi omnia generatim discribere haud difficile factu fuit; sed prius laborandum visum est de summa consilii, idque tibi probandum verum esse. Si hoc itinere uti decreveris, cetera

3 in promptu erunt. Volo ego consilium meum prudens maxumeque usui esse; nam ubicumque tibi res prospere

4 cedet, ibi mihi bona fama eveniet. Sed me illa magis cupido exercet, ut quocumque modo quam primum res pu-

5 blica adiutetur. Libertatem gloria cariorem habeo, atque ego te oro hortorque ne clarissumus imperator Gallica gente subacta populi Romani summum atque invictum imperium tabescere vetustate ac per summam socordiam

6 dilabi patiaris. Profecto, si id accidat neque tibi nox neque dies curam animi sedaverit, quin insomniis exercitus, furi-

7 bundus atque amens alienata mente feraris. Namque mihi pro vero constat omnium mortalium vitam divino numine invisier; neque bonum neque malum facinus quoiusquam pro nihilo haberi, sed ex natura divorsa[41] praemia bonos

8 malosque sequi. Interea si forte ea tardius procedunt, suus quoique animus ex conscientia spem praebet.

[41] diversa *Aldus*: divisa V

[63] Cf. *Ad Caes.* 1.2.2n.

12. Perhaps, commander,[63] after reading this letter you may want to know what number of senators I recommend to be adopted and in what way they are to be assigned their many varied duties; also, since I think that jury duty should be entrusted to all the members of the first census class, you may wonder what apportionment and what number there should be in each category. It would not have been at all difficult for me to go into all these details, but it has seemed to me that I ought first to work out the general plan and convince you that it is a valid one. If you decide to adopt this course, the rest will be easy. For my own part, I desire my advice to be wise and above all practicable; for wherever your measures result in success, there I shall gain a good name. But I am stirred even more by a desire for our country to be helped somehow or other, as soon as possible. I hold freedom dearer than glory, and I pray and urge you, our most illustrious general thanks to the reduction of the Gallic nation, not to allow the great and unconquered dominion of the Roman people to waste away through decay and to fall apart through an excess of negligence. If that should happen, assuredly neither day nor night would alleviate your mental distress to keep you from being distraught and frantic, carried away by madness, in a state of torment from dreams. As for me, I am firmly convinced that a divine power watches over the life of all mortals; that no one's good or evil action fails to be taken into account, but that by a law of nature different rewards await the good and the wicked. Meanwhile, if by chance those due desserts are rather slow in materializing, the prospect of them is held up to each man's mind as a result of his own conscience.

13. Quodsi tecum patria atque parentes possent loqui, scilicet haec tibi dicerent: "O Caesar, nos te genuimus fortissimi viri, in optima urbe, decus praesidiumque nobis,

2 hostibus terrorem. Quae multis laboribus et periculis ceperamus, ea tibi nascenti cum anima simul tradidimus: patriam maxumam in terris, domum familiamque in patria clarissimam, praeterea bonas artis, honestas divitias, post-

3 remo omnia honestamenta pacis et praemia belli. Pro iis amplissimis beneficiis non flagitium a te neque malum facinus petimus, sed utei libertatem eversam restituas.

4 Qua re patrata profecto per gentes omnes fama virtutis

5 tuae volitabit. Namque hac tempestate tametsi domi militiaeque praeclara facinora egisti, tamen gloria tua cum multis viris fortibus aequalis est. Si vero urbem amplissimo nomine et maxumo imperio prope iam ab occasu restitueris, quis te clarior, quis maior in terris fuerit?

6 Quippe si morbo iam aut fato huic imperio secus accidat, quoi dubium est quin per orbem terrarum vastitas, bella, caedes oriantur? Quodsi tibi bona lubido fuerit patriae parentibusque gratificandi, posteroque tempore re publica restituta super omnis mortalis gloria agita⟨bis⟩[42]

7 tuaque unius mors vita clarior erit. Nam vivos interdum

[42] *suppl. Jordan*: agita (bi, *evanuit*) V

13. But if your native land and your forefathers could speak, they would assuredly say this to you: "We brave men have begotten you, Caesar, in the most excellent of cities, to be our glory and defense, a terror to our enemies. That which we had won at the cost of many dangerous hardships we handed over to you at your birth along with the breath of life: namely, the mightiest native land in the world, the most distinguished house and family in that native land, and in addition, splendid skills, honorable riches, in short, all the ornaments of peace and all the prizes of war. In return for these splendid benefits, we expect from you not disgrace or crime, but that you restore subverted freedom. Once this has been accomplished, the fame of your prowess will surely wing its way throughout all nations. For at present, although you have performed brilliant exploits at home and in war, still, your glory is but on a par with that of many heroes. But if you rescue from almost the brink of ruin the most famous and imperial of cities, who on earth will be more famous than you, who greater? Indeed, if it should turn out otherwise for our dominion as a result of decay[64] or fate, can anyone doubt that all over the world devastation, wars, and bloodshed will spring up? But if you experience a noble passion for showing gratitude to your native land and forefathers, in days to come you will tower above all mortals in glory from having restored the nation, and you will be the one person

---

[64] Lit., "illness" or "disease" (*morbus*), which some have taken as an allusion to Caesar's susceptibility to epilepsy (*morbus comitialis:* Suet. *Iul.* 45.1), but *morbus* is more likely to be a metaphor for a breakdown of the state from internal, as opposed to external, causes.

fortuna, saepe invidia fatigat; ubi anima naturae cessit, demptis obtrectatoribus, ipsa se virtus magis magisque extollit."

8   Quae mihi utilissima factu visa sunt quaeque tibi usui fore credidi, quam paucissimis potui perscripsi. Ceterum deos immortales obtestor uti, quocumque modo ages, ea res tibi reique publicae prospere eveniat.

to be more celebrated in death than in your lifetime. For the living are sometimes hard pressed by fortune, often by envy; but when the breath of life yields to nature, detractors are removed, and merit itself soars higher and higher."

I have written as briefly as I could what I regarded as the most advantageous course of action and what I believed would be to your advantage. For the rest, I implore the immortal gods that in whatever way you act, the result may be propitious to you and the nation.

DIVERGENCES FROM
MAURENBRECHER'S EDITION

The following list excludes the many differences in orthography, such as *quom* for *cum* and *quoius* for *cuius* (see Introduction to this volume, pp. xxiv–xxv). In the three instances where Maurenbrecher has noted corrections to his text, reference is made in column 2 to his "Corrigenda," p. 311.

	This Edition	Maurenbrecher
	BOOK 1	
2	a primordio	a principio
3	disertissumus ⟨multa⟩ paucis	disertissimus paucis
4	recens scrip⟨sit⟩	recens scrip⟨tum⟩
8	in certamine	inter certamina
10.4	alia sibi iura paravit	alia iura sibi paravit
14	omniumque partium	omnium partium
18	fraudi fuit	⟨in⟩grata fuit
43	ut [Sullae] dominatio	ut Sullae dominatio
44	qua offensus	qua fuit offensus
47	obsidium coepit	obsidium cepit
49.7	penes illos	penes illum
49.17	aliena bene parta	aliena bene parata

	This Edition	Maurenbrecher
49.19	Scelerum et contume- liarum	sceleris et contume- liarum
	quorum adeo Sullam	quorum Sullam
49.20	licet et quam audeas	licet et quam audeat
49.21	praeter victoriam	praeter victorem
49.22	honorum omnium de- honestamentum	bonorum omnium de- honestamentum
52	mulierum ‹lubidine›	mulierum . . .
54	fecere ‹M.› Octavius	fecere Octavius
67.6	adcersi	arcessi
67.16	coeptas‹ti›	coeptas
67.19	obpressit	obrepsit
76.1	eius ‹manu›que patrata	eius peracta
76.2	neque illis anxius *post* laetabatur	*transp. Maurenbr. ante* quin
77	voce maxuma	voce magna
	v‹ehementer› g‹ratula . . . ›	vehementer gratula- bantur
88	procul a	= "Corrigenda," p. 311
91	modico quoque et	modicoque et
97	f‹ormas fluctibus› Oceani	‹formas e finibus› Oceani
	ac*citas*	‹ap›puls‹as›
	vescentis contenderent . . . a Domitio	vesci contenderent.
98.1	11+ lines of new text *cod. Vindob.*	
98.2	Hic vero	Sic vero
	formidine quasi	quasi formidine

	This Edition	Maurenbrecher
100	†fetustissimus†	securus nimis
107	Metelli cornicines	Metelli Celeris corni- cines
108	sanctus alias	sanctus alia
113	forum in castra	forum et castra

BOOK 2

2	quam occidentem	quam in occidentem
10	alii qui Sardiniam	alii Sardiniam
25	incluti per mortalis	incliti prae mortalibus
38.2	ambiti . . e	ambiti⟨on⟩e
	ingenio largit . . .	ingenita largitio⟨n⟩e
39	q⟨uom⟩ ea, mortui	q⟨uod⟩ ea mortui
	⟨adu⟩lescentis	⟨illas⟩ per gentis
	q⟨uam⟩ ille avidi	g⟨lo⟩riae avidi
41	in ⟨ipsum domicili⟩um	in⟨de⟩ . . .
	perve⟨nit⟩	⟨pu⟩gnaculum
		perve⟨nit⟩
43.1a	†plevis avalia funera†	plebes a balien⟨ata⟩ fuerat
43.4	facundiam	facundium
43.5	fortunis integer	fortuna integer
46	Euri atque Austri	Euri atque Africi
48	occurrere duci	occurrere duces
55	avidis itaque	avidis ita atque
67	serum bellum	serum enim bellum
74.2	plagis aut umbonibus deturbare	plagis aut omni re de- turbare
	pars vallo transfixa	pars ⟨in⟩ vallo transfixa

	This Edition	Maurenbrecher
79.2	a viris arma cep‹ere›	a viris arma cep‹ere et›
79.3	tutissumo loc‹o e›os	tutissimo loc‹o ill›os
80.1	‹religione iuris iurandi› interposita forent, fidem ‹et soci›etatem	‹mora› interposita forent, fide ‹soci›etatem
80.2	ei periret Asiae ‹spes.› Aquandi facultate	ei perinde Asiae ‹Galli› aeque vad‹eren›t e facultate
82	Hi saltibus	Ii saltibus
86.3	me vicem aerari	vicem me aerari
86.6	apud flumen Durium	apud flumen Turiam
86.9	maritumas civitates, ‹quae› ultro	maritimas civitates, ultro
86.12	ferociam suam ‹ostentabant n›ec dicta	ferociam suam et dicta
93	Parte legio‹nis›	Parte legio‹num›
95	in flumen ruebant	in flumen ‹se› ruebant
96	ruinaque pars magna	Ruinaque magna pars
101	ferrum erat, saxa	ferrum, saxa
102	E muris †canes†	E muris panis
108	Poeni fere	Poeni ferunt

	This Edition	Maurenbrecher

BOOK 3

6.1	Mamercus host‹es›	Mamercus host‹ium navis›
6.3	Terentun . . . citu	Terentun‹orum ac›citu
	quaestio fac . . . Sertorium	questio fac‹ta ad› Sertorium
6.4	post qua‹driduom›	Postqua‹m vero›
7.3	equi‹tibus * * ›ranio	equi‹tibus› Manio
	ad ‹paen›insulam pervenit	ad . . . insulam pervenit
7.4	Aeque illi loco	Atque illi loco
8	*in Gall‹aec›ia hoc nomine quam*	*in Gallaecia quam*
10.1	secus, per vias et tecta omnium	= "Corrigenda," p. 311
10.2	invitaverant	invitassent
10.4	maxumeque apud veteres	maxime apud veteres
13	Atque [cum] Curio	Atque eum Curio
15.15	pro aliis toleratis	pro aliis tolerate
15.25	ignorantia res claudit	ignorantia claudit res
42.1	‹sudes ig›ni torrere	‹hastas ig›ni torrere
44.5	praeverterent ‹de re› nuntios	praeverterent . . . nuntios
51	Cares insulani	Carae insulani
53	quisque ex malo	quisque aut malo

	This Edition	Maurenbrecher
56	cavere‹t› imperator a perfuga	cavere imperatorem perfido a
58	‹turba› . . . divorsa, uti solet	Diversa, uti solet
64	institissent	= "Corrigenda," p. 311
66	locorum pergnari	locorum perignari
	scutorum fuerat	scutorum ferebat
	equestris ‹clupeo› armabat	equestris armabat ‹scuto›
70	ex angustiis	ex sarcinis
76	adflicti alveos undarum	adflicti alvos undarum
	postremo intereunt	postremo interibant
80	Vulcioque	Volscioque
84	Nam speciem	Speciem
85	quam cetera, nebulosumque et brevius	quam cetera
92	per hos fluit	per hos ‹Halys› fluit
107	quaerit extis num somnio	quaerit, extnisne an somnio

BOOK 4

10	thesauros	Tenuit Lucullus thesauros
17	Nam olim Italiae Siciliam	Italiae Siciliam
21	dolia quae sub trabes	dolia cum sub trabes
37	ministrum	ministram
38	degressus	digressus

	This Edition	Maurenbrecher
41	gravis exactor	gnavos aestimator
45	territos	⟨ex⟩territos
50	incertum vere	incertum vero
53	quamquam ad ⟨D⟩ naves	quamquam naves
60.2	pace frui licet	pace frui liceret
	scelestissumi, egregia	scelestissimi, ⟨ni⟩ egregia
60.16	quom neque vincere	quo neque vincere
60.17	pesti conditos	pestem conditos
61	ne sibi succederetur	ne illi succederetur
74	hostium errant	hostium erant

BOOK 5

2	effusas ⟨urbis⟩	effusas
9	quod uxori eius	qui uxori eius

FRAGMENTA INCERTAE SEDIS

7	intecta corpora	in tecta corpora
30	alis remissis	alis demissis
34	advolvuntur	advolvebantur
40	mane veni	mandem †iram
56	adcommodatum mandatum	at cum mandatum

FRAGMENTA DUBIA ET SPURIA

2	†volgus† amat fieri	volgus amat fieri
4	in †ulipie h.†	in volnere

	This Edition	Maurenbrecher
5	in ulteriorem provinciam	in ulteriore provincia
9	Non tu scis?	Nonne tu scis,
	facile est defensu quin	facilest defensu quine
22	qui ⟨plus⟩ poterat	qui poterat
23	primus docuit	primum docuit

CONCORDANCE ONE

Ramsey	Maurenbrecher	McGushin
	BOOK 1	
1	1	1
2	8	2
3	4	3
4	2	4
5	3	5
6	6	7
7	10	6
8	7	8
9	11a	9
10	11b	10
11	15	11
12	12	12
13	16	13
14	13	14
15	17	15
16	18	43
17	19	16
18	20	17
19	21	18
20	22	19
21	23	20

Ramsey	Maurenbrecher	McGushin
22	24	21
23	25	22
24	144	25
25	28	23
26	26	24
27	29	26
28	42	34
29	32	27
30	33	28
31	34	29
32	35	30
33	36	31
34	37	32
35	38	33
36	44	36
37	45	37
38	47	38
39	48	39
40	49	40
41	50	41
42	51	42
43	31	35
44	57	49
45	52	44
46	53	45
47	46	46
48	54	47
49	55	48
50	58	50

CONCORDANCE ONE, BOOK 1

Ramsey	Maurenbrecher	McGushin
51	59	51
52	60	52
53	61	53
54	62	54
55	63	55
56	64	56
57	65	57
58	66	58
59	67	59
60	69	64
61	71	60
62	72	61
63	73	62
64	68	63
65	74	65
66	75	66
67	77	67
68	78	69
69	79	70
70	80	68
71	82	71
72	81	72
73	84	73
74	85	74
75	86	75
76	88	77
77	89	78
78	90	79
79	91	81

Ramsey	Maurenbrecher	McGushin
80	92	80
81	93	82
82	97	86
83	95	85
84	96	84
85	98	87
86	99	88
87	103	89
88	100	90
89	101	91
90	102	92
91	94	83
92	104	93
93	105	94
94	106	97
95	108	95
96	111	96
97	107	98
98	136	100
99	110	101
100	112	102
101	113	106
102	119	108
103	115	103
104	114	107
105	120	104
106	121	105
107	135	109
108	116	110

CONCORDANCE ONE, BOOK 1

Ramsey	Maurenbrecher	McGushin
109	118	111
110	125	2.70
111	126	112
112	122	113
113	124	114
114	127	115
115	130	116
116	129	117
117	131	118
118	132	119
119	133	120
120	134	121
121	137	122
122	139	99
123	41	124
124	138	125
125	140	126
126	141	127
127	142	128
128	143	129
129	145	130
130	40	123
131	146	131
132	147	132
133	148	113
134	149	134
135	117	135
136	150	136
137	151	137

Ramsey	Maurenbrecher	McGushin
138	152	138
139	153	139

BOOK 2

Ramsey	Maurenbrecher	McGushin
1	1	1
2	2	2
3	3	3
4	13	5
5	6	8
6	4	6
7	5	7
8	7	9
9	9	4
10	8	10
11	83	11
12	10	12
13	11	13
14	12	14
15	14	15
16	15	16
17	16	17
18	17	18
19	21	21
20	19	20
21	22	22
22	25	23
23	26	24
24	27	25
25	64	26
26	65	27

CONCORDANCE ONE, BOOKS 1–2

Ramsey	Maurenbrecher	McGushin
27	29	28
28	30	29
29	31	30
30	32	31
31	1.123	32
32	33	33
33	35	34
34	37	36
35	39	37
36	40	38
37	41	39
38	42	40
39	43	41
40	44	62
41	45	42
42	46	43
43	47	44
44	49	45
45	54	46
46	56	48
47	58	49
48	59	50
49	60	51
50	61	52
51	62	53
52	63	54
53	66	55
54	102	56
55	67	57
56	69	70

Ramsey	Maurenbrecher	McGushin
57	71	83
58	72	84
59	73	85
60	74	86
61	75	87
62	76	88
63	77	89
64	78	90
65	79	91
66	80	60
67	38	61
68	81	63
69	1.128	64
70	82	65
71	84	66
72	85	67
73	86	68
74	87	69
75	88	71
76	89	72
77	90	74
78	91	73
79	92	75
80	93	76
81	94	77
82	95	78
83	96	79
84	34	80
85	97	72
86	98	82

Ramsey	Maurenbrecher	McGushin
87	18	92
88	20	93
89	55	47
90	48	94
91	51	95
92	53	96
93	99	97
94	100	98
95	101	99
96	4.67	100
97	107	101
98	110	102
99	103	103
100	104	104
101	105	105
102	106	106
103	108	107
104	109	108
105	111	109
106	112	110
107	113	111
108	114	112
109	36	35
110	52	omitted

BOOK 3

1	1	1
2	2	2
3	3	3
4	7	4

Ramsey	Maurenbrecher	McGushin
5	4	5
6	5	6
7	6	7
8	43	30
9	44	31
10	2.70	2.59
11	2.28	3.32
12	46	33
13	49	91
14	50	92
15	48	34
16	19	9
17	20	10
18	21	11
19	23	12
20	24	13
21	26	14
22	28	15
23	30	17
24	31	18
25	37	23
26	33	19
27	34	20
28	35	21
29	36	22
30	4.16	4.50
31	38	24
32	39	25
33	78	26

Ramsey	Maurenbrecher	McGushin
34	1.43	3.25
35	40	28
36	42	29
37	29	16
38	90	60
39	91	61
40	93	62
41	94	63
42	96	64
43	97	65
44	98	66
45	99	67
46	10	68
47	11	69
48	12	70
49	13	71
50	14	72
51	15	73
52	8	74
53	9	75
54	16	76
55	81	77
56	82	78
57	83	79
58	84	80
59	85	81
60	86	82
61	87	83
62	88	84

Ramsey	Maurenbrecher	McGushin
63	89	85
64	100	86
65	101	87
66	102	14
67	103	4.15
68	104	88
69	105	89
70	106	90
71	51	4.11
72	4.18	4.12
73	4.19	4.13
74	52	35
75	53	36
76	54	37
77	56	38
78	57	39
79	58	40
80	59	41
81	60	42
82	61	inc. 22
83	62	43
84	63	44
85	65	45
86	66	46
87	67	47
88	68	48
89	69	49
90	70	50
91	71	51

Ramsey	Maurenbrecher	McGushin
92	72	52
93	73	53
94	74	54
95	75	55
96	76	56
97	77	57
98	79	58
99	80	59
100	17	8
101	25	93
102	27	94
103	32	95
104	95	96
105	107	97
106	108	98
107	109	99
108	110	100

BOOK 4

Ramsey	Maurenbrecher	McGushin
1	1	1
2	2	2
3	4	3
4	5	4
5	7	5
6	8	6
7	9	7
8	10	8
9	11	9
10	12	10

Ramsey	Maurenbrecher	McGushin
11	20	16
12	21	17
13	22	18
14	23	19
15	24	20
16	25	21
17	26	22
18	27	23
19	28	24
20	29	25
21	30	26
22	31	27
23	32	28
24	35	29
25	36	30
26	33	31
27	37	32
28	38	33
29	40	34
30	39	35
31	41	36
32	42	37
33	43	38
34	44	39
35	45	40
36	46	41
37	47	42
38	49	43
39	50	44

Ramsey	Maurenbrecher	McGushin
40	48	45
41	51	56
42	13	46
43	14	47
44	15	48
45	56	57
46	57	58
47	17	51
48	3.47	4.52
49	52	53
50	53	54
51	55	55
52	58	59
53	59	60
54	60	61
55	61	62
56	63	63
57	64	64
58	65	65
59	66	66
60	69	67
61	71	68
62	70	69
63	5.10	4.70
64	72	71
65	74	72
66	76	73
67	73	77
68	77	74

Ramsey	Maurenbrecher	McGushin
69	78	75
70	79	76
71	81	78
72	3	49
73	68	79
74	82	80
75	83	81
76	84	82
77	85	83

BOOK 5

Ramsey	Maurenbrecher	McGushin
1	1	1
2	2	2
3	3	3
4	4	4
5	5	5
6	6	6
7	7	7
8	9	8
9	11	9
10	12	10
11	13	11
12	14	12
13	15	13
14	16	14
15	18	15
16	20	16
17	21	17
18	22	18

Ramsey	Maurenbrecher	McGushin
19	23	19
20	24	20

FRAGMENTS NOT
ASSIGNED TO BOOKS

Ramsey	Maurenbrecher	McGushin
1	1.27	inc. 5
2	1.83	inc. 12
3	5.8	inc. 31
4	2.57	inc. 16
5	inc. 10	inc. 46
6	inc. 5	inc. 41
7	4.62	inc. 28
8	3.41	inc. 19
9	4.34	inc. 26
10	1.14	inc. 4
11	inc. 8	inc. 44
12	4.80	inc. 30
13	inc. 37	inc. 73
14	1.30	inc. 6
15	inc. 4	inc. 40
16	4.75	inc. 29
17	1.87	1.76
18	1.109	inc. 13
19	inc. 2	inc. 38
20	inc. 1	inc. 37
21	1.70	inc. 9
22	inc. 3	inc. 39
23	3.92	inc. 24
24	inc. 9	inc. 45

Ramsey	Maurenbrecher	McGushin
25	inc. 6	inc. 42
26	3.64	inc. 23
27	inc. 13	inc. 49
28	3.55	inc. 21
29	1.56	inc. 8
30	inc. 12	inc. 48
31	inc. 11	inc. 47
32	5.19	inc. 33
33	4.54	inc. 27
34	inc. 16	inc. 52
35	1.76	inc. 10
36	5.27	inc. 36
37	5.26	inc. 35
38	——	inc. 1
39	inc. 15	inc. 51
40	inc. 26	inc. 62
41	inc. 23	inc. 59
42	2.23	2.19
43	inc. 24	inc. 60
44	inc. 25	inc. 61
45	1.9	inc. 3
46	5.17	inc. 32
47	5.25	inc. 34
48	inc. 19	inc. 55
49	1.5	inc. 2
50	3.18	inc. 17
51	2.24	inc. 14
52	2.50	inc. 15
53	inc. 14	inc. 50
54	inc. 22	inc. 58

Ramsey	Maurenbrecher	McGushin
55	inc. 27	inc. 63
56	inc. 28	inc. 64
57	inc. 34	inc. 70
58	inc. 35	inc. 71
59	inc. 36	inc. 72
60	inc. 31	inc. 67
61	inc. 29	inc. 65
62	inc. 17	inc. 53
63	inc. 32	inc. 68
64	inc. 30	inc. 66
65	inc. 38	inc. 74
66	inc. 20	inc. 56
67	1.39	inc. 7
68	inc.18	inc. 54
69	inc. 21	inc. 57

POSSIBLE AND SPURIOUS FRAGMENTS

1	——	——
2	dub. 2	——
3	1.18 (test.)	1.16 (comm.)
4	2.68	——
5	3.45	inc. 20
6	p. 212	——
7	p. 212	——
8	inc. 33	inc. 69
9	dub. 4	——
10	dub. 5	——
11	inc. 7	inc. 43
12	1.135 (test.)	——

Ramsey	Maurenbrecher	McGushin
13	3.14 (test.)	——
14	p. 211	——
15	4.6M	inc. 25
16	——	inc. 11
17	1.66 (test.)	——
18	dub. 3	——
19	dub. 6	——
20	fasc. 2 p. 60	——
21	3.22	inc. 18
22	p. 212	——
23	p. 212	——
24	p. 212	——
25	——	inc. 75
26	——	inc. 76
27	——	inc. 77
28	——	inc. 78
29	——	inc. 79
30	——	inc. 80
31	——	inc. 81
32	——	inc. 82
33	——	inc. 83
34	——	inc. 84
35	——	inc. 85
36	——	inc. 86
37	——	inc. 87
38	——	inc. 88
39	——	inc. 89
40	——	inc. 90
41	——	inc. 91
42	——	inc. 92

Ramsey	Maurenbrecher	McGushin
43	——	inc. 93
44	——	inc. 94
45	——	inc. 95
46	——	inc. 96
47	——	inc. 97
48	——	inc. 98
49	——	inc. 99
50	——	inc. 100
51	——	inc. 101
52	——	inc. 102
53	——	inc. 103
54	——	inc. 104
55	——	inc. 105

CONCORDANCE TWO

Maurenbrecher	Ramsey
BOOK 1	
1	1
2	4
3	5
4	3
5	inc. 49
6	6
7	8
8	2
9	inc. 45
10	7
11	9 & 10
12	12
13	14
14	inc. 10
15	11
16	13
17	15
18	16
19	17
20	18
21	19

Maurenbrecher	Ramsey
22	20
23	21
24	22
25	23
26	26
27	inc. 1
28	25
29	27
30	inc. 14
31	43
32	29
33	30
34	31
35	32
36	33
37	34
38	35
39	inc. 67
40	130
41	123
42	28
43	3.34
44	36
45	37
46	47
47	38
48	39
49	40
50	41
51	42

Maurenbrecher	Ramsey
52	45
53	46
54	48
55	49
56	inc. 29
57	44
58	50
59	51
60	52
61	53
62	54
63	55
64	56
65	57
66	58
67	59
68	64
69	60
70	inc. 21
71	61
72	62
73	63
74	65
75	66
76	inc. 35
77	67
78	68
79	69
80	70
81	72

Maurenbrecher	Ramsey
82	71
83	inc. 2
84	73
85	74
86	75
87	inc. 17
88	76
89	77
90	78
91	79
92	80
93	81
94	91
95	83
96	84
97	82
98	85
99	86
100	88
101	89
102	90
103	87
104	92
105	93
106	94
107	97
108	95
109	inc. 18
110	99
111	96

CONCORDANCE TWO, BOOK 1

Maurenbrecher	Ramsey
112	100
113	101
114	104
115	103
116	108
117	135
118	109
119	102
120	105
121	106
122	112
123	2.31
124	113
125	110
126	111
127	114
128	2.69
129	116
130	115
131	117
132	118
133	119
134	120
135	107
136	98
137	121
138	124
139	122
140	125
141	126

Maurenbrecher	Ramsey
142	127
143	128
144	24
145	129
146	131
147	132
148	133
149	134
150	136
151	137
152	138
153	139

BOOK 2

Maurenbrecher	Ramsey
1	1
2	2
3	3
4	6
5	7
6	5
7	8
8	10
9	9
10	12
11	13
12	14
13	4
14	15
15	16
16	17

CONCORDANCE TWO, BOOKS 1–2

Maurenbrecher	Ramsey
17	18
18	87
19	20
20	88
21	19
22	21
23	inc. 42
24	inc. 51
25	22
26	23
27	24
28	3.11
29	27
30	28
31	29
32	30
33	32
34	84
35	33
36	109
37	34
38	67
39	35
40	36
41	37
42	38
43	39
44	40
45	41
46	42

Maurenbrecher	Ramsey
47	43
48	90
49	44
50	inc. 52
51	91
52	110
53	92
54	45
55	89
56	46
57	inc. 4
58	47
59	48
60	49
61	50
62	51
63	52
64	25
65	26
66	53
67	55
68	dub. 4
69	56
70	3.10
71	57
72	58
73	59
74	60
75	61
76	62

CONCORDANCE TWO, BOOK 2

Maurenbrecher	Ramsey
77	63
78	64
79	65
80	66
81	68
82	70
83	11
84	71
85	72
86	73
87	74
88	75
89	76
90	77
91	78
92	79
93	80
94	81
95	82
96	83
97	85
98	86
99	93
100	94
101	95
102	54
103	99
104	100
105	101
106	102

Maurenbrecher	Ramsey
107	97
108	103
109	104
110	98
111	105
112	106
113	107
114	108

BOOK 3

Maurenbrecher	Ramsey
1	1
2	2
3	3
4	5
5	6
6	7
7	4
8	52
9	53
10	46
11	47
12	48
13	49
14	50
15	51
16	54
17	100
18	inc. 50
19	16
20	17

CONCORDANCE TWO, BOOKS 2–3

Maurenbrecher	Ramsey
21	18
22	dub. 21
23	19
24	20
25	101
26	21
27	102
28	22
29	37
30	23
31	24
32	103
33	26
34	27
35	28
36	29
37	25
38	31
39	32
40	35
41	inc. 8
42	36
43	8
44	9
45	dub. 5
46	12
47	4.48
48	15
49	13
50	14

Maurenbrecher	Ramsey
51	71
52	74
53	75
54	76
55	inc. 28
56	77
57	78
58	79
59	80
60	81
61	82
62	83
63	84
64	inc. 26
65	85
66	86
67	87
68	88
69	89
70	90
71	91
72	92
73	93
74	94
75	95
76	96
77	97
78	33
79	98

CONCORDANCE TWO, BOOK 3

Maurenbrecher	Ramsey
80	99
81	55
82	56
83	57
84	58
85	59
86	60
87	61
88	62
89	63
90	38
91	39
92	inc. 23
93	40
94	41
95	104
96	42
97	43
98	44
99	45
100	64
101	65
102	66
103	67
104	68
105	69
106	70
107	105
108	106

Maurenbrecher	Ramsey
109	107
110	108

BOOK 4

Maurenbrecher	Ramsey
1	1
2	2
3	72
4	3
5	4
6	dub. 15
7	5
8	6
9	7
10	8
11	9
12	10
13	42
14	43
15	44
16	3.30
17	47
18	3.72
19	3.73
20	11
21	12
22	13
23	14
24	15
25	16

CONCORDANCE TWO, BOOKS 3–4

Maurenbrecher	Ramsey
26	17
27	18
28	19
29	20
30	21
31	22
32	23
33	26
34	inc. 9
35	24
36	25
37	27
38	28
39	30
40	29
41	31
42	32
43	33
44	34
45	35
46	36
47	37
48	40
49	38
50	39
51	41
52	49
53	50
54	inc. 33

Maurenbrecher	Ramsey
55	51
56	45
57	46
58	52
59	53
60	54
61	55
62	inc. 7
63	56
64	57
65	58
66	59
67	2.96
68	73
69	60
70	62
71	61
72	64
73	67
74	65
75	inc. 16
76	66
77	68
78	69
79	70
80	inc. 12
81	71
82	74
83	75

Maurenbrecher	Ramsey
84	76
85	77

BOOK 5

1	1
2	2
3	3
4	4
5	5
6	6
7	7
8	inc. 3
9	8
10	4.63
11	9
12	10
13	11
14	12
15	13
16	14
17	inc. 46
18	15
19	inc. 32
20	16
21	17
22	18
23	19
24	20
25	inc. 47

Maurenbrecher	Ramsey
26	inc. 37
27	inc. 36

FRAGMENTS NOT
ASSIGNED TO BOOKS

Maurenbrecher	Ramsey
1	20
2	19
3	22
4	15
5	6
6	25
7	dub. 11
8	11
9	24
10	5
11	31
12	30
13	27
14	53
15	39
16	34
17	62
18	68
19	48
20	66
21	69
22	54
23	41
24	43
25	44

Maurenbrecher	Ramsey
26	40
27	55
28	56
29	61
30	64
31	60
32	63
33	dub. 8
34	57
35	58
36	59
37	13
38	65

DUBIA VEL FALSA

1	*Jug.* 54.6
2	2
3	18
4	9
5	10
6	19

APP. 1 FALSA, PP. 210–12

5.6K	4.19 test.
fr. inc. 81K	dub. 6
fr. inc. 82K	dub. 12
fr. inc. 84K	*Jug.* 58.5
fr. inc. 87K	dub. 1
fr. inc. 94K	*Cat.* 61.3

Maurenbrecher	Ramsey
fr. inc. 34D	1.98
fr. inc.48D (14K)	4.21
fr. inc. 73D (39K)	2.35
fr. inc. 113D (80K)	1.108
fr. inc. 115D (86K)	dub. 14
fr. inc. 117D (90K)	*Jug.* 37.4
fr. inc. 69D (35K)	——
fr. inc. 119D	dub. 7
1.34D	dub. 22
fr. inc. 86D (54K)	dub. 24
fr. inc. 87D (55K)	dub. 23

I. INDEX FONTIUM
QUOTING SOURCES

Square brackets [ ] enclose sources that do not provide direct quotations or attribution to S. Fragment numbers are set in boldface to distinguish them from page and line numbers of the quoting sources.

Adnot. super Luc.
 1.175: **1.16**
 1.552: **3.11**
 2.134: **1.32**
 2.139: **1.43**
 2.174: **1.36**
 2.534: **1.74**
 2.548: **1.35**
 3.164: **1.7**
 3.272: **3.92**
 3.632: **1.19**
 6.104: **3.33**
 6.347: **1.19**
 7.267: **1.91**
 9.960: **3.87**
Ambr.
 3.16: **1.125**
Amm. Marc.
 [15.10.10: **2.25**]
 [15.12.6: **1.9**]
 [23.6.56: **3.36**]
Ampel.
 19.8: **1.3**
 30.5: **2.59**

Anon. *brev. expos. Verg. G.*
 2.197: **1.90**
Ars anon. Bern. GL 8
 78.10–11: **3.85**
 94.13: **4.10**
Arus. *GL* 7
 450.11 = p. 46DC: **4.30**
 450.16 = p. 47DC: **1.41**
 451.15 = p. 51DC: **dub. 7**
 453.1 = p. 57DC: **4.76**
 453.10–11 = p. 58DC: **3.15.14**
 454.29–30 = p. 65DC: **5.16**
 455.24 = p. 69DC: **2.60**
 456.5–6 = p. 71DC: **3.76**
 456.6–7 = p. 71DC: **2.101**
 456.10 = p. 71DC: **4.70**
 456.11 = p. 71DC: **4.73**
 456.24 = p. 73DC: **5.14**
 459.13–14 = p. 83DC: **1.30**
 460.6 = p. 85DC: **1.112**
 461.10–11 = p. 88DC: **4.40**
 462.2–3 = p. 462DC: **1.12**
 462.6 = p. 92DC: **1.124**
 463.6–7 = p. 95DC: **2.65**

p. 31M = 46L.23: **1.59**
p. 53M = 74L.1–2: **2.2**
p. 60M = 84L.17: **inc. 33**
p. 92M = 131L.6: **1.9**
p. 95M = 135L.22–23: **4.56**
p. 101M = 144L.14: **2.103**
p. 116M = 167L.25–28: **3.58**
p. 127M = 185L.30–31: **2.40**
p. 129M = 188L.20: **1.87**
p. 132M = 192.21–23: **4.66**
p. 137M = 199L.8–10: **3.104**
p. 138M = 200L.4–6: **3.30**
p. 138M = 201L.8–9: **5.8**
p. 140M = 205L.30: **1.46**
p. 172M = 253L.11–13: **2.82**
p. 177M = 260L.18: **2.102**
p. 180M = 265L.20–21: **3.10.3**
p. 186M = 274L.18–21: **3.25**
p. 186M = 274L.23: **4.32**
p. 202M = 297.7–8: **2.68**
p. 206M = 304L.18: **1.113**
p. 215M.32–216M.2 = 318L: **2.64**
p. 222M = 329L.20–23: **3.10.1**
p. 229M = 339L.4: **1.67.19**
p. 231M = 343L.22–24: **1.95**
p. 235M = 350L.14–16: **3.101**
p. 236M = 352–53L.18–19: **5.16**
p. 239M = 357L.4–6: **3.62**
p. 257M = 392L.44–46: **4.50**
p. 257M = 392L.47–48: **1.55**
p. 258M = 394L.33: **4.11**
p. 276M = 424L.15: **1.98**
p. 280M = 432L.25–28: **2.66**
p. 281M = 434L.29–30: **3.57**
p. 282M = 435L.23: **1.111**

p. 286M = 442L.18–20: **3.10.3**
p. 310M = 483–84L.11: **1.100**
p. 310M = 484L.19–20: **2.105**
p. 314M = 491L.26–28: **3.12**
p. 315M = 492L.5: **2.91**
p. 318M = 498L.31: **4.47**
p. 321M = 504L.25–27: **4.9**
p. 323M = 506L.4–5: **3.22**
p. 358M = 568L.16–18: **3.13**
p. 366M = 582L.13–15: **3.53**
p. 385M = 614L.2–4: **2.16**
p. 397M = 638L.15–16: **5.16**
p. 398M = 639L.7: **2.55**
p. 406M = 653L.10–12: **3.76**
p. 416M = 672L.29–30: **dub. 18**
p. 449M = 721.26–27: **2.83**
p. 453M = 726L.1–3: **1.92**
p. 453M = 726L.3–4: **1.93**
p. 453M = 726L.4–6: **1.85**
p. 456M = 731L.14–15: **3.44.4**
p. 489M = 785L.9–10: **3.102**
p. 489M = 786L.27: **3.24**
p. 489M = 786L.28: **3.14**
p. 492M = 790L.27–29: **4.29**
p. 495M = 795L.40: **1.88**
p. 497M = 799L.29–30: **2.96**
p. 502M = 805L.2–3: **3.62**
p. 503M = 809L.53: **2.46**
p. 524M = 842L.9–10: **3.97**
p. 526M = 845L.12: **1.101**
p. 530M = 851L.26: **1.111**
p. 534M = 857L.30: **1.23**
p. 534M = 857.18–20: **3.52**
p. 534M = 857.26–27: **3.52**
p. 535M = 857L.2: **2.77**
p. 535M = 858L.8–10: **4.2**
p. 535M = 858L.13–16: **4.53**

II. INDEX NOMINUM
PERSONS, DEITIES, AND PLACES

The abbreviation *H.* precedes references to the *Historiae; E.* to the *Epistulae ad Caesarem.* Proper names are given according to the spelling attested in the text of S., with alternative spellings noted in parentheses: e.g., Cabera (Cabira or Kabeira); Quin⟨c⟩tius. Names of Romans are arranged alphabetically by *nomina gentilicia,* with cross-references provided for common *cognomina.* After each person's name is given the relevant *RE* number (Pauly-Wissowa) and an indication of political office(s) held and role(s) relevant to the two works contained in this volume. All dates are BC unless otherwise stated. Parentheses enclose persons or places not explicitly found in the fragments but likely to have been included in the text of S. if more context for the fragment had survived. Place-names marked with an asterisk (*) are included on the maps. A query ("?") placed after a reference to a fragment signifies that the text may concern instead some other person or place.

The following abbreviations and symbol are employed: NSEW for the compass points; cens. = censor; cos. = consul; leg. = legate; mod. = modern place-name; mt. = mountain; nr. = near; pr. = praetor; procos. = proconsul; proqu. = proquaestor; qu. = quaestor; s.v. = consult entry for this item elsewhere in this index; tr. pl. = tribune of the plebs; † = death.

Abellani (citizens of the town Abella* in Campania*): *H.* 3.43

Ach⟨a⟩ei (savage people living on N shore of Black Sea): *H.* 3.94

Achilles (Greek hero of Trojan War): *H.* 3.89

pr. 74; father of the Triumvir]: *H.* (3.1–4); 3.5; 3.6.1, 4; (3.7; 3.46; 3.52–54; inc. 2[?]; inc. 29[?])

(Antonius Hybrida, C. [*RE* 19; cos. 63]: 4.49[?])

Apion. *See* Ptolemaeus (Apion)

Apollo (god of prophecy, the arts, and the bow): *H.* 2.5; 2.90

Appius. *See* Claudius Caecus; Claudius Pulcher

Appuleius Saturninus, L. (*RE* 29; tr. pl. 103, 100): *H.* (1.54); 1.67.7

(Aquinus [not in *RE*; leg. of Metellus Pius in Hispania Ulterior* in 79–78]: *H.* 1.105–6)

Archelaus (*RE* 12; a general of Mithridates): *H.* 4.60.12

Aresinarii (possibly a people living in NE Hispania Citerior*): *H.* 3.6.4

Ariobarzanes (*RE* 5; king of Cappadocia*): *H.* 4.53; 4.60.15

Aristaeus (*RE* Aristaios 1; mythical Greek hero): *H.* 2.5

Aristonicus (*RE* 14; illegitimate? son of Eumenes II of Pergamum): *H.* 4.60.8

Armenia*: *H.* 4.53; 4.60.15, 21; 4.68

Armenia Minor. *See* Lesser Armenia*

Arsaces (Phraates III, s.v.; king of the Parthians): *H.* 4.60.1

Arsanias* (mod. Murat; river in

W Armenia*): *H.* 4.65; (inc. 16[?])

Artabazes (not in *RE;* putative founder of Pontic royal dynasty): *H.* 2.59

(Artaxata* [capital city of Tigranes in E Armenia]: *H.* 4.65)

(Ascalis [princeling of Mauretania* in 81]: *H.* dub. 18[?])

Asia: *H.* 2.43.7; 2.80; 4.60.6, 9, 11

Aufidius Orestes, Cn. (*RE* 32; cos. 71): *H.* 2.37

(lex Aurelia [iudiciaria, of 70]: *H.* inc. 32[?])

(lex Aurelia [de tribunicia potestate, of 75]: *H.* 2.44; 2.90[?]; inc. 32[?]; inc. 52[?])

Aurelius Cotta, C. (*RE* 96; cos. 75): *H.* 2.38.2 (x2); (2.39); 2.43 (his speech); 2.43.1a, 10; 2.86.11; 3.15.8; (dub. 47[?])

Aurelius Cotta, M. (*RE* 107; cos. 74): *H.* 2.86.12; 3.80; 4.60.13

Auster (south wind): *H.* 2.46

Aventinus (1 of 7 hills of Rome): *H.* 1.10.4

Azilis (town or region of Africa?): *H.* dub. 19

Bacchanalia (celebration in honor of wine god Bacchus): *H.* 3.24

(B[a]elo* or Belon [coastal town in Hispania Ulterior* W of

(3.48); 3.49; (3.50–51; 3.53–54)

Cretenses: *H.* 4.60.10, 12; dub. 13

Creticus. *See* Caecilius Metellus Creticus

Criu Metopon* (Kriou Metopon; promontory at tip of Crimea*): *H.* 3.97

Crixus (*RE* 2; Gallic commander in Spartacan uprising; † 72): *H.* 3.42.9; (3.58[?]; 3.68)

Cumae* (mod. Cuma; Campanian town on Bay of Naples): *H.* (2.5); 3.42.6

(Curetes [ancient worshippers of Jupiter on Crete*]: *H.* 3.50)

Curio. *See* Scribonius Curio

Cybele. *See* Mater Magna

Cyrenae (Roman province on N coast of Africa, W of Egypt): *H.* 2.39

Cyrene (nymph; mother of mythical hero Aristaeus): *H.* 2.5

Cyzicus* (Mysian town, on S shore of Propontis): *H.* 3.21; (3.22–25; 3.27–37; 3.102[?]; 4.2); 4.60.14; 4.63; (inc. 4[?]; inc. 8[?])

Daedalus (mythical hero who fled from wrath of Minos): *H.* 2.5; 2.8

(Dalmatae [people living in Illyricum, on the Adriatic coast]: *H.* 2.35)

Damasippus. *See* Iunius Brutus Damasippus

Danuvius* (Ister*) (river Danube): *H.* 3.98

Dardani (an Illyrian people): *H.* (2.67[?]; 3.13[?]); (inc. 43[?]); (people of NW Asia Minor): *H* 3.82

Dardania* (region of lower Illyricum, NW of Macedonia*): *H.* 2.66

Dasianus. *See* Hostilius Dasianus

Diana (goddess of the hunt): *H.* dub. 24

(Dianium* [promontory on E coast of Hispania Citerior*]: *H.* 1.113; 3.7.3[?])

Didius, T. (*RE* 5; cos. 98; procos. of Hispania Citerior, 97–93 BC): *H.* 1.76

Dilunus (river in Hispania Citerior*, S of Pyrenees and N of Iberus*): *H.* 3.7.1

(Dindymon* [mt. N of Cyzicus*]: *H.* 3.24)

Dipo* (town on Anas River*): *H.* 1.101

Domitius Ahenobarbus, Cn. (*RE* 22; son-in-law of Cinna): (*H.* 1.46); *E.* 1.4.1

Domitius Ahenobarbus, L. (*RE* 27; cos. 54): *E.* 2.4.2; 2.9.2.

Domitius Calvinus, M. (*RE* 44; pr. 81; procos. Hispania Citerior* 80 BC): *H.* 1.96; 1.97; 1.98.1; (1.122[?])

Drusus. *See* Livius Drusus

possessing Latin rights):
H. 1.20
(Lauro* [town on E coast of
Hispania Citerior*]:
H. 2.27–30; 2.102[?])
(Lemnos* [island in N Aegean]:
H. 3.74)
Lentulus. *See* Cornelius Lentu-
lus
Lepidanum (bellum): *H.* 4.48
Lepidus. *See* Aemilius Lepidus
Leptasta (*RE;* Mauretanian
ruler or chieftain): *H.* 2.88
(Lesser Armenia*: *H.* 4.42[?];
5.1[?])
Lete* (town in Macedonia*):
H. 1.119; 1.120
(Lethe. *See* Oblivio*)
lex Licinia (et Mucia de civibus
redigundis, of 95): *H.* 1.18
Libya (Africa): *H.* dub. 19–20
(Libyans [followers of Sertorius
recruited in Mauretania]:
H 1.93–94; 1.97)
Licinius Crassus, M. (*RE* 68;
cos. 70, 55; millionaire;
suppressor of Spartacan
Revolt): *H.* (4.12–13; 4.16;
4.24; 4.26–27; 4.29–30;
4.39–40); 4.41; (inc. 1[?];
inc. 9[?]; inc. 11)
Licinius Lucullus, L. (*RE* 104;
cos. 74): *H.* 2.86.12;
3.15.11; (3.16; 3.22; 3.25–
26; 3.31; 3.35–37; 3.74–75;
3.79; 3.101; 3.107; 4.4–5);
4.6; (4.7; 4.10; 4.42–43;
4.45; 4.47; 4.52–59);

4.60.15; 4.61; (4.62–68;
4.70; 4.73; 5.1[?]; 5.8–9;
5.11); 5.12; (5.13; inc. 6[?];
inc. 8; inc. 12[?]; dub.
44[?])
Licinius Macer, C. (*RE* 112; tr.
pl. 73; Roman historian):
H. (1.4[?]); 3.15 (his
speech); (inc. 42[?])
Ligures (people living in Ligu-
ria*; region situated on SW
coast of Cisalpine Gaul):
H. 3.6.3; Ligus (mulier):
H. 2.13; (vir): inc. 22
(Limia*/Limaea. *See* Oblivio*)
Livius Drusus, M. (*RE* 18; tr. pl.
91): *E.* 2.6.3; 2.6.4
Livius (Iulius?) Salinator, L.
(Iulius *RE* 453; leg. of Ser-
torius in 81): *H.* (1.82);
1.84
Lollius Palicanus, M. (*RE* 21; tr.
pl. 71): *H.* 4.33
Lucanus (ager) (Lucania*; dis-
trict of S Italy): *H.* 3.45
(Lucretius Afella [Ofella], Q.
[*RE* 25; commander under
Sulla in 82]: *H.* 1.34)
Lucullus. *See* Licinius Lucullus;
Terentius Lucullus
Lusitania* (region of south-
central Hispania Ulterior*;
mod. Portugal): *H.* (1.99;
1.101–2); 1.104
  Lusitani (people of that re-
  gion): *H.* 1.93
Lutatii: *H.* 1.49.3. *See also* Lu-
tatius Catulus, Q.

601

(<Pa>llantei [stock from whom Ba<lar>i, s.v., were descended]: *H.* 2.8, *varia lectio*)

Pamphylia* (coastal region of southern Asia Minor): *H.* (2.68); 2.69

Paphlagones (inhabitants of Paphlagonia*): *H.* 3.97

Paphlagonia* (coastal region of northern Asia Minor, between Bithynia* and Pontus*): *H.* 3.91; (3.92)

Papirius Carbo, Cn. (*RE* 38; III cos. 82): *H.* 1.35; (1.45; 1.49.5; 1.80); *E.* 1.4.1

Parium* (mod. Kemer; town in Asia Minor, at N end of Hellespont, nr. entrance to Propontis): *H.* 4.60.14.

Pelorus* (Sicilian cape on the Strait of Messina): *H.* (4.16; 4.18); 4.20

Perperna (or Perpenna) Veiento, M. (*RE* 6; pr. 82?): *H.* (1.67.7n.; 2.15[?]; 2.45); 2.89; (2.92[?]); 3.8; 3.57; (3.58[?]); 3.59

Persae (the people of Persia): *H.* (4.55); dub. 18

Perses (*RE* Perseus 5; last king of Macedonia*): *H.* 1.2; 4.60.7

Persica (regna) (kingdom of Persia): *H.* 3.92

Persis (Persian Empire): *H.* 4.60.19

Phaselis* (coastal town in Lycia*): *H.* 1.116

Philippus. *See* Marcius Philippus

Philippus (V) (*RE* 10; king of Macedonia*): *H.* 1.49.4; 4.60.5, 6, 7

(Phoenicia*: *H.* 4.45)

(Phraates III [*RE* vol. 18.2.1984–85; ruler of Parthia from 70 to 57 BC, addressee of Mithridates' letter]: *H.* 4.60)

Phrygia (region of west-central Asia Minor): *H.* 3.82; (4.47[?])

Picens (from the coastal district of Picenum* in east-central Italy): *H.* 1.49.17; 4.33

Picentinus (inhabitant of the town Picentia; prob. in southern Campania*): *H.* 3.44.3

Pisidae (inhabitants of Pisidia*): *H.* 3.1

Pisidia* (region of southern Asia Minor, N of Lycia* and Pamphylia*): *H.* 1.115

Piso. See Calpurnius Piso

(Pityussae* [islands off the E coast of Hispania Citerior*]: *H.* 1.85–86)

(lex Plautia de reditu Lepidanorum, of 70?: *H.* 4.48)

Poeni (Carthaginians): *H.* 2.8; 2.108

(lex Pompeia et Licinia de tribunicia potestate of 70: *H.* inc. 32[?])

(Pompeii* [town in Campania*]: *H.* 3.41)

2.43.1, 4, 6, 13; 3.15.1, 8, 15, 16, 24

(Rhegium* [mod. Reggio; town on the "toe" of Italy]: H. 4.24[?]; inc. 9[?])

Rhenus (Rhine River): H. 1.9.1

Rhodii (people of the island of Rhodes*): E. 2.7.12

(Rhyndacus* [river in Bithynia*, E of Cyzicus*]: H. 3.36)

Roma*: H. 3.42.2; E. 1.2.6; 1.6.1

Romani: H. 2.74.1, 7; 3.36; (3.74); 4.60.2, 5, 15, 17, 20; E. 2.4.3; Romanus: H. 1.1; 1.3; 1.9.1; 1.26; 1.49 title, 11, 19, 24; 1.67.6; 2.43 title; 2.80.2; 2.86.2; 3.2; 3.10.2, 5; 3.38; 3.99; 4.60.13; E. 1.4.1; 1.5.2; 2.2.4; 2.3.2; 2.4.3; 2.12.5

Romulus (derisive appellation for the dictator L. Sulla): H. 1.49.5

(Rutilius Nudus, P. [RE 30; leg. of M. Cotta in Bithynia]: H. 3.19–20)

Sacer, mons (ca. 3 mi. NE of Rome): H. 1.10.4

(Sacriportus [locale near Prae-neste* in Latium]: H. 1.33–34)

Saguntini (inhabitants of Sagun-tum*, mod. Sagunto, town on E coast of Hispania Ci-

terior*): H. 2.25; Sagun-tium (= Saguntinorum): H. 2.26

(Salinae [town in Campania*, nr. Pompeii*]: H. 3.41)

Salinator. See Livius (Iulius?) Salinator

Sallentinum* (promunturium) (on the "heel" of Italy): H. 4.14

(Sallustius Crispus., C. [RE 10; pr. 46; the historian]: H. 1.5–6; inc. 55[?])

Samnites (inhabitants of Sam-nium* in southern Apen-nines): H. (1.25; 1.130[?]); inc. 67

Samothraces (dei) (gods of the N Aegean island Samo-thrace): H. 4.60.7

Sardinia*: H. (1.71; 2.1); 2.2; 2.3; (2.4); 2.5; (2.6–9); 2.10; (2.11–15; 2.108[?]); inc. 2.3; (dub. 20)

Sardus (son of Hercules; epony-mous settler in Sardinia*): H. dub. 20

(Sarmatae [people living in W Scythia*]: H. 3.96[?])

Saturninus. See Appuleius Saturninus

Scirtus (not in RE; follower of Sulla): H. 1.49.21

Scribonius Curio, C. (RE 10; cos. 76): H. 1.75; (2.22; 2.24); 2.66; (2.67; 2.90; 2.109); 3.13; 3.14; 3.15.10; (inc. 43[?])

Scylla (rock formation on the

(3.43); 3.44.5; (3.45; 3.64–
66; 3.70; 3.104[?]; 4.11–12;
4.16; 4.18; 4.21; 4.23–24;
4.26–27; 4.31; 5.1[?]; inc.
14[?]; inc. 21[?]; inc. 23[?];
inc. 46[?]; inc. 51[?]; inc.
66[?]; dub. 42[?])

Staphylus (son of the god Dionysus): H. dub. 23

Stobi* (Macedonian town):
H. 2.109

Strait. See Gibraltar, Messina,
Sicilian, Sige(i)on

Sucro* (mod. Júcar; river in
Hispania Citerior*, mod.
SE Spain): H. (2.49–52[?]);
2.86.6; (2.93–97[?])

Sulla. See Cornelius Sulla

Sullanus (adj.): H. 1.28; E. 1.4.1

Sulpicius Rufus, P. (RE 92; tr.pl.
88): H. 1.67.7

Sulpicius Rufus, Ser. (RE 95;
cos. 51): H. 1.9

Tagus* (mod. Tajo, river in Hispania Ulterior*, mod. SW
Portugal): H. 1.103

Tanais (mod. Don River):
H. 3.93; (3.95[?])

Tarentum* (mod. Taranto; town
on S Italian coast):
H. 1.114

Tarquinius Superbus, L. (RE 7;
7th and last king of Rome):
H. 1.10.2

Tarquitius Priscus, C. (RE 8;
officer under Sertorius):
H. 3.55; 3.57

Tartessus (earlier name for re

gion and town of Gades*
in Hispania Ulterior*):
H. 2.7

Tarula (not in RE; follower of
Sulla): H. 1.49.21

Tauri (Scythian people): H. 3.94

Tauromenitanus (of or belonging to Tauromenium*,
mod. Taormina, town on E
coast of Sicily): H. 4.19

Taurus* (mts. in S Asia Minor):
H. (2.11; 2.68–70); 2.71;
4.60.6

T(e)ios (Tieion; town in Paphlagonia* on Black Sea):
H. 3.91

Terentius Lucullus, M. (RE Licinius 109; cos. 73):
H. (3.71); 3.72; (3.73)

Terentius Varro, M. (RE 84 and
suppl. 6; pr. ca. 75):
H. 2.56; (inc. 49[?])

Terentuni (poss. people on
coast of Hispania Citerior*): H. 3.6.3

Termestini (inhabitants of town
Termes* in N Hispania Citerior*): H. 2.82

Tharros* (Tharrhos; town on
west-central coast of Sardinia*): H. 2.14

Themiscyrei (campi) (plains on
S shore of the Black Sea,
nr. Pontic town Themiskyra*): H. 3.93

(Thermodon [river in Pontus]:
H. 3.93)

Thoranius, C. (RE Toranius 4;
qu. 73): H. 3.42.2

Versius (*RE;* scribe of Sertorius): *H.* 3.57

(Vesuvius* (mt. and volcano on
Bay of Naples): *H.* 3.40;
inc. 23[?]; dub. 42[?])

Vettius, L. (*RE* 6; knight who
profited under Sulla's regime; later informed
against Catilinarians in 62
and revealed an alleged
plot vs. Pompey in 59):
H. 1.49.17

Victoria, (goddess): *H.* 3.10.3

Vizzo (poss. a corruption of
the name Bizone, s.v.):
H. 3.73

(Voconius [*RE* 1; naval com-

mander under Lucullus in
73–72]: *H.* 3.75)

Volcanalia (annual festival to
god Vulcan on Aug. 23):
H. 3.14

Vulcius (Volscius? [*MRR* 3.223],
not in *RE;* leg., envoy under M. Cotta in Bithynia*):
H. 3.80

(Zela* [town in Pontus*]:
H. inc. 3[?]; dub. 30[?])

(Zelis [town in Mauretania]:
H. dub. 19[?])

(Zenicetes (*RE;* pirate chieftain
in Lycia*]: *H.* 1.115–18)

MAPS

DARDANIA

ILLYRICUM

MOESIA

ISTER (DANUVIUS) R.

MACEDONIA

BOSPORUS

Dyrrachium

Stobi

THRACIA

Chalcedon

Lete

Maroneia

DINDYMON M.

PROPONTIS

SIGE(I)ON PR.

Parium

Cyzicus

OLYMPUS M.

RHYNDACUS R.

OSSA M.

LEMNOS

Troia

PELION M.

AEGEAN

SEA

ASIA

LYDIA

IONIAN

SEA

ACHAEA

CYCLADES

LYCIA

RHODES

CRETE

MEDITERRANEAN SEA

0   100   200   300 miles

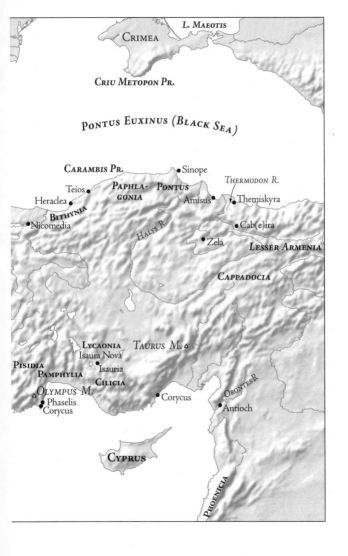

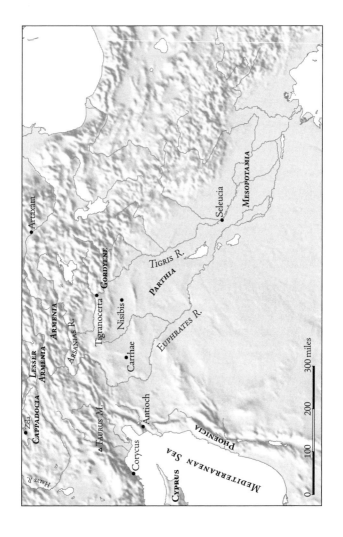